Gigabit Networks
Standards and Schemes for Next-Generation Networking

Paul Izzo

Wiley Computer Publishing

John Wiley & Sons, Inc.

NEW YORK · CHICHESTER · WEINHEIM · BRISBANE · SINGAPORE · TORONTO

Publisher: Robert Ipsen
Editor: Marjorie Spencer
Assistant Editor: Margaret Hendrey
Managing Editor: Marnie Wielage
Text Design & Composition: Benchmark Productions, Inc.

Library of Congress Cataloging-in-Publication Data:

Izzo, Paul, 1949–
  Gigabit networks : standards and schemes for next-generation networking/Paul Izzo.
    p. cm.
  Includes index.
  ISBN 0471-35235-7 (alk. paper)
  1. Computer networks—Standards. 2. Computer network protocols. 3. Internetworking (Telecommunication) I. Title.

TK5105.55 .I98 2000
004.6'2--dc21

Printed in the United States of America.

10 9 8 7 6 5 4 3 2 1

To: Jennifer, Carmella, and Mario

CONTENTS

ACKNOWLEDGMENTS

I would like to express my sincere gratitude to Deb Alford, a friend and colleague. She has been an invaluable resource in the composition of this book. Her breadth of understanding of current technologies is inspiring.

I would also like to express my gratitude to several other colleagues for their technical assistance, including Bob Dolliver, Todd Hill, Dennis Boas, and Al Rosen. A special thanks to Gary Kessler for his invaluable comments and suggestions.

In addition, I would like to thank Ronna Bauer-Sauerhoff and Lori Stimpson.

I would also like to acknowledge the editors Marjorie Spencer and Margaret Hendrey.

Over the years, I have been fortunate to work with countless intelligent, perceptive, and innovative individuals at Digital Equipment Corporation and Bay/Nortel Networks, all of whom have found the time to help me understand. Thank you all.

During the first quarter of the 1999 Super Bowl—with the Denver Broncos leading the Atlanta Falcons, 10–3—Victoria's Secret aired a commercial inviting viewers to its annual spring collection on the Web. Two days later, the high-profile fashion show, which was broadcast exclusively on the Internet, drew 1.5 million football fans.

This marketing ploy highlights several important points:

- The Internet is becoming an integral component of doing business.
- The Internet is no longer used to transfer data exclusively.
- The Internet is no longer the exclusive realm of the technically savvy.

The days of the Internet being used by only the technically astute professional for email and file transfers are gone. In fact, if one could view the type of traffic being carried on the Internet at any one time, one would see voice and video as well as data being carried within the packets that are traversing the Internet.

Local area networks, devised to provide traffic boundaries for workgroup environments, are being strained as they are required to support a new class of applications—applications with enormous throughput and low latency requirements. Also, cooperative computing is increasingly requiring that clients must cross a flow boundary to get to a server.

And from the users' perspective, the network is becoming a utility, and the boundary separating the local area network, the corporate network, and the Internet is becoming transparent.

For networks to keep pace with existing and forthcoming demands, they must become more reliable and more predictable, and they must provide more capacity. In an effort to meet these requirements, new technologies and schemes are being proposed and developed on a regular basis. These technologies and schemes are well documented. Over 20 IETF Draft documents discuss MPLS, and even more documents are dedicated to RSVP.

The intent of this book is to provide the reader with an understanding of the emerging enabling technologies. For some, the basic understanding provided here will suffice. For others, the next step is to actually delve into the draft or specification. For these readers, the intent of the book is to provide a knowledge baseline that will serve to make the actual document easier to read and understand. Often, a pointer to actual source document is provided.

The book is arranged in a manner that first addresses the local area network, then the wide area network, and finally the access points at which the local area network and the wide area network merge.

Throughout the book I have inserted personal commentary or pertinent information that is out of context by using a pencil icon.

The Denver Broncos won the football game 34–19.

The author can be reached at pizzo@networksIQ.com.

CHAPTER 1

Introduction

T he Internet is rapidly becoming as much a part of our lives as the telephone network or the highway system. In many regards, the Internet is already more critical to the world's business community than the telephone network or the highway system.

The Internet is an often-misunderstood *thing*. The primary focus of this book is the emerging technologies that *will* be implemented on the Internet and other networks to enable them to meet the ever-increasing number of users and diversity of applications they must support. Before examining these new technologies and schemes, let's look at how this critical component of our daily lives evolved.

Many people mistakenly believe that the Internet is a relatively recent creation that went from the imaginations of a handful of "propeller heads" in Palo Alto and Cambridge to the pervasive entity that we know today. Others think that it was invented by Bill Gates (whom, incidentally, they also credit with inventing computers and everything else that was not invented by Thomas Edison).

What exactly is the Internet? How does it work? Where did it come from?

Ancient Internet History

The early 1960s were troubled times. War in Southeast Asia was looming, the Berlin crisis was a daily news item, Cuba was threatening to deploy nuclear missiles 50 miles from the U.S. coast, the Soviet Union had detonated the most powerful weapons known to humans, and the Soviets had already launched the first Sputnik satellite into orbit. The Cold War was boiling over. Because of Sputnik and other successful space launches by both the United States and the U.S.S.R., it seemed apparent that this new missile technology would eventually be used to ignite an international war of catastrophic proportions. In preparation for the inevitable, America's foremost think tank, Rand Corporation, was tasked by the Advanced Research Projects Agency, Office of the Secretary of Defense, with devising a strategy that would allow American authorities to communicate with and control the military infrastructure after a preemptive nuclear attack. In 1972, the Advanced Research Projects Agency (ARPA) was renamed the Defense Advanced Research Projects Agency (DARPA).

In 1964, Rand proposed a network that would have no central authority. (The scheme was actually contrived by Rand's Paul Baran.) The decentralized network would be composed of devices that were all equal in terms of their ability to originate, terminate, and transmit messages. Each of the devices would act independently of other devices in the network, so that there would be no single point of attack capable of debilitating the whole network. Also, each message would be divided into components, called packets. Each packet would contain the address of the destination and would find its own way through the network independent of other packets that made up the original message. The path that a particular packet traversed through the network would be immaterial as long as it arrived at the destination. Effectively, the new network paradigm would render the network nearly indestructible. If a portion of the network were blown away, the packet would simply be forwarded to a surviving component. In this fashion, the packet would remain in flight and continue to be forwarded until it arrived at the destination.

This approach was significantly different from that for existing networks—most notably the conventional telephone network, which relies on a predefined path from source to destination and all information associated with a session traversing the same path.

Of course, there was a price to be paid with the new rugged approach. This rather haphazard delivery system involved additional overhead because each packet needed to contain addressing information. Also, to support this approach, several underlying conditions had to be met. First, all network devices needed to know how to forward the packet to ensure that it moved toward the destination. Second, the destination had to be able to reassemble the packets into the original message, even though the packets could arrive out of order because the individual packets might be taking different paths through the network.

During the mid-1960s, this concept of a decentralized, survivable, packet-switching network was investigated at Rand, the Massachusetts Institute of Technology (MIT), and the University of California at Los Angeles (UCLA). Also, during this same period, an independent packet-switching effort was under way at the National Physical Laboratory, under Donald Davies, in Great Britain.

Uncharacteristically, ARPA decided that the research should be unclassified, thus engaging some of the most creative minds in the computer science industry, and in 1967, ARPA issued a request for proposal (RFP) concerning creation of a packet-switching network, labeled ARPANET. Several people at UCLA, including Leonard Kleinrock, who had gone there from MIT, and Vinton Cerf expressed an interest in the RFP. The RFP postulated that the nodes of the network were to be high-speed computerized switches. In 1969, ARPA awarded the contract to build the computerized switches to Bolt, Beranek, and Newman (BBN), a small Cambridge, Massachusetts-based company. By fall of 1969, BBN delivered the Interface Message Processor (IMP) switch based on a Honeywell DDP 516 to UCLA. Subsequently, IMPs were also installed at Stanford Research Institute (SRI), U.C. Santa Barbara (UCSB), and the University of Utah in Salt Lake City. The IMPs were connected via 50kbps circuits. A variety of computers, including a Sigma 7 at UCLA, a SDS-940 at SRI, an IBM 360-75 at UCSB, and a DEC PDP-10 at the University of Utah were connected to the IMPs. The ARPANET was born, and scientists were able to remotely share computer facilities.

In April 1969, in an effort to share lessons learned on the new network, Steve Crocker, a graduate student at UCLA, issued the first request for comment (RFC). Because he was a graduate student, Steve reasoned that he did not have much credibility. The RFC approach was intended to be a nonimposing technique, basically saying, "Please comment on this, and tell me what you think."

By 1970, the ARPANET had grown to 15 nodes: UCLA, SRI, UCSB, University of Utah, BBN, MIT, RAND, SDC, Harvard University, Lincoln Laboratories, Stanford University, UIU(C), CWRU, CMU, and NASA/Ames. By 1972 there were 37 nodes participating in the ARPANET.

The original standard protocol for data transfer on ARPANET was known as the Network Control Program (NCP). NCP allowed communications between hosts connected to the *same* network. However, in an effort to allow diverse computers' networks to interconnect and communicate with each other, development of new protocol began in 1973. The protocol, later to be called Transmission Control Protocol/Internet Protocol (TCP/IP), was developed by a group headed by Cerf at Stanford and Bob Kahn at ARPA. In 1974, Cerf and Kahn published *A Protocol for Packet Network Internetworking*, which specified, in detail, the design of the TCP. Originally, TCP didn't distinguish between TCP, which provided for the assured delivery of the packets, and the IP, which provided for the forwarding of the packets through the networks.

In the mid-1970s, experiments were being conducted to transmit encoded voice through the packet-switched network. These experiments demonstrated that a protocol that ensured delivery of packets was not always desirable. Sometimes, if a packet is not delivered or is delivered corrupted, it is better to just ignore the lost or damaged packet and continue rather than attempt to retransmit the packet. This realization led to the separation of TCP from IP and made way for the development of User Datagram Protocol (UDP), which allows packets to be delivered across the network in an unreliable, yet efficient, fashion.

In 1982, it was decided that all systems on the ARPANET would migrate from NCP to TCP/IP protocols. The task was accomplished by January 1983.

During this time, there was another very significant research effort under way, the development of the local area network (LAN), which allowed computers connected to a coaxial cable, as opposed to telephone lines, to transmit data very rapidly. In 1976, Robert Metcalfe, with David Boggs, published a paper titled *Ethernet: Distributed Packet-Switching for Local Computer Networks*. The Ethernet is a system for connecting computers within proximity of each other, for example, within a building. Ethernet supports the same software that is used in the Internet (TCP/UDP/IP), but the connecting hardware is a coaxial cable to which the communicating Ethernet devices were attached. This is significantly different from the Internet, which connects computers separated by large distances via telephone lines.

In 1979, Metcalfe successfully convinced Digital Equipment, Intel, and Xerox Corporations to work together to promote Ethernet as a standard. Now an international computer industry standard, Ethernet is the most widely installed LAN today.

> I came to work one day at MIT, and the computer had been stolen, so I called DEC to break the news to them that this $30,000 computer that they'd lent me was gone. They thought this was the greatest thing that ever happened because it turns out that I had in my possession the first computer small enough to be stolen!
>
> —Robert Metcalfe on the trials and tribulations of inventing the Ethernet

Middle Ages Internet History

In 1981, the National Science Foundation (NSF) created the CSNET backbone network to enable institutions that were not connected to the ARPANET to experiment with network communications. In 1983, a gateway was established for communications between CSNET and ARPANET. By 1985, the extended ARPANET was congested enough that the NSF started evaluating new network designs. It constructed a network called NSFNET that initially interconnected six supercomputer centers with 56kbps lines. The TCP/IP protocol tied the network segments together and provided traffic forwarding through gateways or routers. The NSFNET formed a core network. NSF also supported regional or intermediate-level networks that would manage the demand of the universities and provide access to the NSFNET backbone. The regional networks were embraced enthusiastically by universities and other research institutions, which could now access the NSFNET supercomputers and exchange traffic with one another. The NSFNET did not own or manage the attached networks; it only provided the backbone to which these regional networks could connect. In this way, the NSFNET grew to become the foundation of the Internet as we know it today. The term Internet—*inter*connected *net*works—came to be used in reference to the NSFNET backbone and the attached regional networks.

There were several other significant developments during the late 1970s to mid-1980s that prompted an exponential growth in NSFNET traffic volume.

The Unix operating system that was developed at AT&T Bell Labs on DEC computers in the 1970s had become the most popular operating system implemented on workstations. In the mid-1970s, Unix-to-Unix Copy (UUCP), a facility for sending and receiving electronic mail, remote login, and file transfers, was developed and incorporated into the Unix operating system. In 1975, AT&T made Unix available on an open basis to universities and colleges for use in research and computer science programs. This was a major step in the popularization of the Unix operating system. The University of California at Berkeley did some of the most important work on Unix. Berkeley included the TCP/IP networking protocol and native Ethernet support into its workstation Unix operating system, which it labeled the Berkeley Software Distribution, or Unix BSD, and made publicly available in 1983. Thus, thousands of users on Unix workstations on local area networks with NSFNET access were able to communicate with each other.

In 1984, the Domain Name Service (DNS) was developed by Paul Mockapetris.

TCP/IP identifies systems using a 32-bit IP address. Prior to DNS, every computer in the network had a copy of the full list of names of computers on the network and their corresponding IP address. This approach worked while there were several hundred systems on the network, but as the NSFNET grew, this approach became unwieldy and unacceptable. DNS is a clever method by which computers can translate computer host names that are relatively human friendly (such as yourcompany.com) into an IP address (such as 192.128.12.9) that can actually be used by the network. More importantly, DNS supports a distributed database in which no one system knows all address to name associations, but any system can find the IP address associated with any given name. DNS employs a hierarchical naming scheme that consists of a sequence of subnames separated by a period. At the root, or top of the name structure, are the *root servers.* Every DNS server in the DNS domain knows the IP address of at least one server closer to the root. A server can resolve the IP address for any name by "walking" the DNS namespace.

DNS is still an integral part of the Internet. The familiar *company.com* type of names that have become familiar are actually DNS names that are resolved to IP addresses by DNS.

Also, the File Transfer Protocol (FTP), which specifies how directories of files are named and transported across the network between client and server computer systems, was developed. Another significant development was the Mail Transfer Protocol (MTP), which allows computers to send and receive electronic mail (e-mail) through mail servers, which store, copy, distribute, and forward messages to their proper destinations. The NSFNET was being used primarily to transport information between users rather than provide a mechanism whereby remote users could access the processing power provided by the attached supercomputers. In effect, the NSFNET provided the infrastructure for a utility that virtually everyone wanted to use. It was no longer the exclusive realm of researchers.

In 1986, the Internet Engineering Task Force (IETF) was formed. It is an all-volunteer group responsible for developing and endorsing the technical standards that run on the Internet. Over the years, the IETF has been the forum in which engineers and programmers have cooperated to solve a succession of crises caused by the Internet's phenomenal growth.

Realizing that management of the NSFNET was an enormous task, NFS helped create an agreement among MCI, Merit (a regional network operated by the University of Michigan), and IBM to form the Advanced Network Services (ANS), which assumed control of NSFNET in 1987.

By 1989, the number of nodes on the Internet exceeded 100,000, and the NSFNET backbone was upgraded to T1 (1.544Mbps, or million bits per second) circuits.

Soon after the completion of the T1 NSFNET backbone upgrade, traffic increased so quickly that plans to upgrade the network again immediately began. ANS began conducting experiments in high-speed networking.

In 1990, ARPANET ceased to exist, its role having been taken over by NSFNET. Until 1991, the primary focus of the NSFNET was not-for-profit research and development. The NSFNET had an "acceptable use" policy that restricted the use of the Internet to noncommercial activities. However, during the mid-1980s the National Science Foundation advised the regional networks that they would have to become self-sustaining. In 1991, this pressure culminated in the creation of the first commercial Internet providers. In March 1991, PSINet along with two other independent providers, UUNet Technologies and General Atomics (CERFnet), started the Commercial Internet Exchange (CIX). The CIX allowed access to the Internet without the NSF's restrictions for the first time. Commercial use of the Internet was now possible. The era of e-commerce had begun.

In 1992, the Internet Society (ISOC) was chartered to provide leadership in addressing issues that confront the future of the Internet. It is the organizational home for the groups responsible for Internet infrastructure standards, including the IETF and the Internet Architecture Board (IAB). The IAB, which was originated in 1983, provides oversight of the architecture for the protocols and procedures used by the Internet. It is responsible for editorial management and publication of the Request for Comments (RFC) document series and for administration of the various Internet assigned numbers.

By 1993, ANS had upgraded NSFNET circuits to DS-3 (45Mbps).

Modern Internet History

By 1992, NFS had defined a new architecture to support the rapidly expanding Internet. The key components of the new architecture were network access points (NAPs) and Internet service providers (ISPs).

Logically, the Internet is a hierarchical structure. At the top level are the national Internet service providers (national ISPs). These are the core ISPs such as AGIS, GTE, MCI, PSINet, and Sprint. The interconnecting point, or *Internet exchange point*, between national ISPs is a NAP. National ISPs connect into the NAPs to exchange traffic with other national ISPs in a process called *peering* and to sell transit service to other national ISPs. In 1993, NSF awarded NAP contracts to Ameritech in Chicago, Pacific Bell in California, MFS Datanet in Washington, D.C., and Sprint in the New York/New Jersey area. The NAPs were intended to provide NSFNET access to U.S. research and education sites. The national ISPs were invited, but not required, to use these NAPs as places to interconnect with other National ISPs. This invitation reflects the free-spirit nature of the Internet environment as totally open and distributed. There is no requirement to go to one place.

Although the four original NAPs were funded by NSF, many other Internet exchanges that were not funded by NSF are now in operation. The additional Internet exchanges are termed metropolitan area exchanges (MAEs). There are about 32 MAEs in the United States today.

The next level is the regional Internet service providers (regional ISPs). Two of the first super regionals were MERIT and BARRNet. Now companies such as AT&T WorldNet and Bell Atlantic are also involved at this level. Though users can connect at this level, the primary function served is to connect lower levels of ISPs.

The third level provides access for the end users, businesses, schools, and homes. These are the local ISPs. Local ISPs provide direct Internet access, POP mail, and news servers. Typically, the local ISP does no monitoring of connections for content, creating an open environment for transactions and information transfer of all kinds. Some of the players in the United States include AT&T, MediaOne, TIAC, and Ultranet.

Another type of ISP, called a content provider ISP, provides information such as e-mail, chat rooms, and Internet Web access. They may (and most often do) monitor content, impose e-mail limits/restrictions, and can limit Internet access. Many homes and some businesses in the United States connect here. The primary examples of content providers are America Online (AOL) and CompuServe.

The final level is homes, schools, and businesses that purchase access to the Internet and World Wide Web and in turn provide the information, products, input, and money that have turned the Internet and Web into the commercial influence it is today (see Figure 1.1).

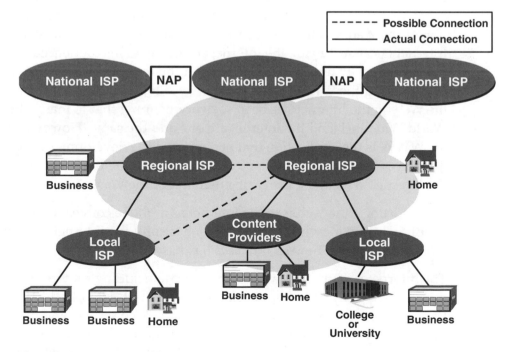

Figure 1.1   Internet architecture.

On April 30, 1995, the NSFNET was essentially shut down, and the NAP and national ISP architecture originally proposed by NSF became the Internet.

World Wide Web

By the early 1990s, the Internet had become a pervasive electronic infrastructure to which numerous businesses and universities, as well as individual users, had access. However, there was no easy way to access and assimilate the vast amount of information that was available on the Internet. Only the technically savvy could take advantage of the wealth of information using tools such as *Gopher* and *Archie*.

A significant development for the Internet occurred on April 30, 1993, when CERN placed the software for the World Wide Web (WWW) in the public domain.

Tim Berners-Lee developed the software at the European Laboratory for Particle Physics. The introduction of the World Wide Web (or Web) transformed the Internet from a passive environment utilized primarily by the technically oriented to an interactive, user-friendly universe filled with vast amounts of information accessible to countless users. The introduction of the Web was the single most important event in the history of the Internet because it made the Internet accessible to inexperienced users. It has dramatically fueled the popularity of the Internet to the point where many regard the WWW as the Internet's "killer application." The effect of the Web on the Internet has been so overwhelming that to many, the World Wide Web and the Internet are one and the same. However, in reality, WWW is the application that necessitated the development and introduction of new technologies and schemes within the Internet to enable the Internet to meet the increasing demand of the Web.

As an analogy, the Web is to the Internet as a phone conversation is to the telephone network wires and switches. Basically, the Internet is *communication* based while the Web is *information* based.

The Internet comprises a number of devices, including routers and hosts, that support a myriad of protocols, such as IP, TCP, DNS, and FTP. The Web relies on a different collection of devices: Web servers and browsers that support a number of protocols, namely, uniform resource locators (URLs), Hypertext Markup Language (HTML), and Hypertext Transfer

Protocol (HTTP). Of course, the Web server and browsers actually reside on Internet hosts. Web pages are created on Web servers, and the Web pages are delivered to Web browsers via the Internet.

The Web, like most applications on the Internet, is based on a client/server architecture. When users view pages on the Web using a Web browser, the machine is functioning as the client, and the computer hosting the data being viewed is the server. When users visit Web sites, the software running on their machines is the Web browser. A Web browser is the graphical interface that interprets the HTML and enables eye-catching visual content. The original Web browser was Mosaic, which was developed by Marc Andreesen.

HTML is the language that is used to create a file, which will generate a Web page. Basically, an HTML document consists of ASCII text surrounded by special markup codes, called *tags*. The tags provide instructions to the Web browser program viewing the file. Through the tags, the Web browser is told how text is to be presented to the viewer.

A real power of HTML comes from its ability to link text and an image to another document or section of a document. A browser highlights the identified text or image with color or underlines to indicate that it is a hypertext link (often shortened to hyperlink or just link). When a user "clicks" on the link, the contents of a remote Web page, referenced by the hyperlink, are displayed by the Web browser. Hyperlinks enable Web surfing. Web pages are retrieved within seconds without requiring complex searches or other tasks. Actually, the term "web" is derived from the extensive use of these interconnections between pages.

The location referenced by the Hyperlink, the URL, includes the type of resource being accessed (such as Web, mail, FTP), the address of the server, and the location of the file. The syntax is *http://webmaster@www .nameofcompany.com.* The protocol used to transfer the HTML file from its resident location to the Web browser is HTTP.

Note that www.nameofcompany.com will be an entry in DNS, where typically the *www* indicates that the corresponding IP address is the Web server for *company.com* domain.

Web search engines organize information on the Web to facilitate retrieval of the information. The user types a search keyword into the search engines, and the search engine program searches its database and returns a list of hyperlinks to the related databases. Search engines typically run a special program, called a bot, sculker, or spider, to gather the addresses of Web pages on the Internet. These programs index text on the discovered Web page, thus enabling the search to quickly associate the user's keyword query with the indexed Web pages.

The development of the Web has made the Internet a valuable and efficient resource by logically associating related information and making the information available to the masses.

Keeping Pace

Networks, from local area networks to the Internet, have grown so extravagantly over a short period of time because they provide a critical service. Networks are the vehicles that enable information to be shared without bounds or limitations.

On the local front, most corporations have standardized on Ethernet and the quest for network capacity, and throughput is increasing as more and more computers are connected to the LAN and work tasks require network-intensive processing. Factors driving the demand for higher LAN data transfer rates include enterprise resource planning (ERP) applications, e-commerce, and the pending convergence of voice and data, including LAN PBXs and Ethernet phones.

How do we meet these requirements?

Ethernet has proven to be a flexible, durable, and scalable technology. Since 1993, there's been a tenfold increase in Ethernet bandwidth every two years (Ethernet in 1993, fast Ethernet in 1995, and Gigabit Ethernet in 1997). Virtual LANs (VLANs) and 802.1p/802.1Q standards are supported in Layer 2 switches, providing mechanisms for prioritizing traffic. Layer 3 switches are now commonplace on the LAN. Layer 3 switches integrate routing and switching while offering more features than the Layer 2 approach. The options are many and varied. The Internet, as we know it today, comprises more than 7800 individual ISPs, each supported by a variety of devices and technologies. In fact, the only common component of the 7800 ISPs is that they all support TCP/IP. The ISPs exhibit different performance and reliability characteristics, accounting and billing schemes, underlying transport schemes, and scopes of penetration. However, all are part of the Internet, which, in recent years, has evolved into a global platform with the potential to become *the* unified network not only supporting data but also becoming an alternate voice carrier network, with the existing central office becoming an Internet access point.

In the following chapters, we discuss the emerging technologies and schemes that will enable networks, large and small, to meet the requirements of the forthcoming multimedia applications.

CHAPTER 2

The Ethernet Evolution

The Ethernet *local area network* (LAN) was introduced in the early 1970s and has been evolving ever since. Bob Metcalfe and David Boggs developed the technology at Xerox Palo Alto Research Center (PARC) with the help of Charles Thacker and Butler Lampson. In 1979, the DIX Consortium (Digital Equipment Corporation, Intel, and Xerox) was formed. In 1980, the original Ethernet specification was developed by the DIX Consortium and submitted to IEEE. In 1982, IEEE 802.3 for *carrier sense multiple access/collision detection* (CSMA/CD) (Ethernet) became the first IEEE standard for local area networks.

Over the years, IEEE has developed a series of clauses or modifications to the standard that support different types of media and different modes of operation. The IEEE 802.3 family is now supported by a variety of speeds, media, and extensions. Figure 2.1 illustrates the Ethernet family.

To some extent the CSMA/CD designations have undergone significant change, at least within the context of how they are interpreted. A typical CSMA/CD designation is 10Base-5 or 100Base-TX, where the first portion of the designation 10,100,1000 refers to the speed at which the signal propagates along the medium. The second part of the designation, *Base*, refers to the baseband transmission mode—effectively, the entire medium

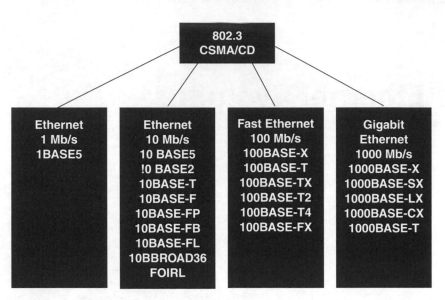

Figure 2.1 802.3 CSMA/CD.

is used for a discrete signal transmission. (This is in contrast to broadband "broad" signaling wherein the medium transmits multiple signals simultaneously, with each at a different frequency.)

The last portion of the designator initially referred to the distance that the signal could be driven without appreciable attenuation. The 5 (10Base-5) indicated that the signal could be driven for 500 meters over the 50 ohm coaxial cable without disruptive attenuation. Note that the 2 in 10Base-2 actually referred to driving the signal 185 (not 200) meters over the 75 ohm coaxial cable. In later 802.3 technologies, the last designation refers to the type of PHY (physical layer) rather than any signal/distance designation. The designation 100Base-T4 refers to a 100-megabit-per-second signal over a baseband medium where the PHY is specified as T4—4 pairs of UTP.

IEEE 802.3 Evolution

Figure 2.2 provides a chronology of the IEEE 802.3 standard. We discuss each of the modifications and clauses in detail.

IEEE 802.3 is based on the CSMA/CD technology. You can analogize the technology to a human conversation in which all stations are attached to a common medium and have an equal opportunity to access the medium.

ANSI/IEEE 802.3, 1996
Latest Base Standard

IEEE 802.3u, 1995
Suite of clauses relative to
100Base-TX and 100Base-FX

IEEE 802.3x&y, 1997
Defined full duplex and flow operation

IEEE 802.3 ac, 1998
Defined extension for VLAN tagging

IEEE 802.3z, 1998
Defined gigabit operation, including
1000Base-SX/LX/CX physical layers,
and 1000 Mbps repeater

IEEE 802.3ab, 1999
Physical layer specification for
1000 Mbps operation on 1000 Base-T

Figure 2.2   Evolution of the 802.3 standard.

When a station has a frame to transmit, it first listens to determine if another station is currently using the medium. If the medium is silent, the station proceeds with the frame transmission. If the medium is not silent, the station defers the transmission. After the station begins transmitting other stations on the medium, it will not detect the signal immediately because of signal propagation delay. If multiple stations begin transmitting simultaneously, a collision of the signals results, and both signals are corrupted. Subsequently, each of the transmitting stations involved in the collision backs off according to a prescribed randomization algorithm and then attempts the transmission again. The architectural layers of IEEE 802.3 and their relationship to the OSI Reference Model are represented in Figure 2.3.

Logical link control (LLC) defines the mode of the transmission. Because IEEE 802.3 is a connectionless, best-effort technology, the role of LLC in 802.3 is less important than in other LAN technologies. The LLC plays a more active role in IEEE 802.5 (token ring) technology where it is involved with some token access and frame delivery functions. The *media access control* (MAC) sublayer is effectively the conscience or brain of 802.3.

As Ethernet technology evolved, modification to the physical layer and modification to the conscience MAC layer were of equal and prime

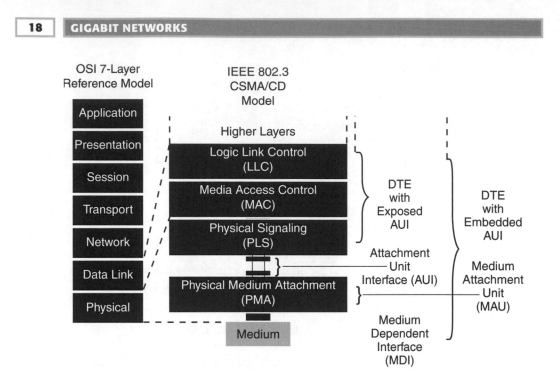

OSI 7-Layer
Reference Model

IEEE 802.3
CSMA/CD
Model

Figure 2.3 Relationship between the OSI and IEEE reference models.

importance. The physical layer components are primarily responsible for putting the signals onto and extracting the signal from the medium. In human conversation analogy, the physical layer acts as the mouth and ears, but the MAC layer actually processes what is heard and what gets transmitted.

Logical Link Control

The LLC (IEEE 802.2) protocol provides a layer of functionality above the MAC that provides addressing and control. The LLC protocol was developed later than IEEE 802.3 and is based on the *high-level data link control (HDLC) protocol*. HDLC is a general-purpose protocol that operates at the data link layer of the OSI reference model. The HDLC protocol provides either a best-effort or reliable communications path between the transmitter and receiver (that is, with acknowledged data transfer). LLC provides three different types of service or modes, and the type of service provided depends on the HDLC mode used: unacknowledged, connectionless service; connection-mode service; and acknowledged connectionless service. IEEE 802.3 uses unacknowledged, connectionless service and relies on a connectionless, best-effort mode of frame delivery. There is no form of acknowledgment or retransmission unless the frame has been involved in a collision. Ethernet relies on upper-layer protocols to detect and reschedule delivery of lost or corrupt frames.

LLC uses an extended 2-byte address in which the first byte indicates a *destination service access point* (DSAP) and the second byte indicates a *source service access point* (SSAP). DSAP and SSAP identify the network protocol entities that use the link layer service. A control field is also provided to indicate the mode type. It should be noted that the LLC protocol is not used in all implementations of Ethernet. In the original DIX Ethernet specification, the LLC layer was implied and not actually part of the frame.

Subsequent to the development of IEEE 802.2, the *subnetwork access protocol* (SNAP) was developed. Because IEEE 802.2 provided only one byte to identify upper-layer protocols, the SNAP scheme was developed to extend the protocol identification field. In a SNAP header, both DSAP and SSAP fields equal "AA" and CTRL equals "03." A 3-byte *organizationally unique identifier* (OUI) in the SNAP header following the *control byte* is used to identify an organization. For example, 080007 is Apple Computer, whose upper-layer protocol is identified in the next 2-byte field called the *protocol identifier* (PID), such as 809B—AppleTalk. See Figures 2.4 and 2.5.

Because the IEEE 802.3 frame does not support any upper-layer protocol differentiation, it was not incorporated into many Ethernet implementations. The most common implementation of IEEE 802.3 was by Novell. Folks at Novell probably reasoned that if you were smart enough to implement NetWare/IPX, you would recognize that there was no need to differentiate any other protocol (which was a bit presumptuous).

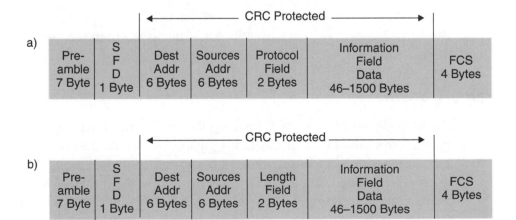

Figure 2.4 a) DIX frames b) 802.3 frames.

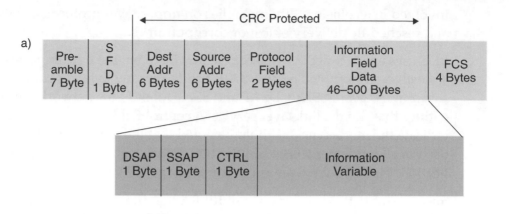

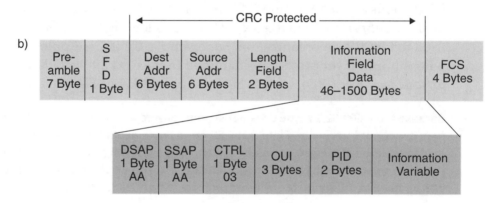

Figure 2.5 a) 802.3/802.2 frames b) SAP/SNAP frames.

The MAC has two primary functions: media access management and frame formatting.

Frame Transmit

The MAC is responsible for formatting the frame once it receives a frame to transmit from the LLC. This includes preappending the destination MAC and source MAC—including the length or protocol field—along with calculating and appending the *frame check sequence* to the frame. Media access management is accomplished by observing the state of the attached media as reported by the *physical signaling sublayer* (PLS). If the transmission channel is idle, the MAC initiates the transmission by first generating a 7-byte preamble with an alternating sequence "1,0,1,0..." The alternating sequence is used by the receiving end to synchronize to the incoming data stream. A one-byte *start of frame delimiter* (SFD) follows the preamble.

Note that there actually is another subtle difference between DIX and 802.3. In DIX, the preamble is specified as 62 bits followed by a 2-bit "synch" character—"11."

Next the MAC alerts the PLS that data is being transmitted via the *transmit enable* channel and commences to pass the frame bits to the PLS via the *transmit data* channel. This is illustrated in section A of Figure 2.6. The MAC transmits data serially in NRZ format. NRZ transmission is illustrated in section A of Figure 2.8. Clocking for the bit stream transmission is derived from a high-stability, crystal-based oscillator reference clock that is fed from the PLS component to the MAC—section B in Figure 2.6. After the frame transmission is complete—section C in Figure 2.6—the MAC initiates the *interframegap* (IFG), a 9.6-microsecond quiet time that allows the clock recovery circuitry within repeaters and DTEs to recover and relock to the known good local clock.

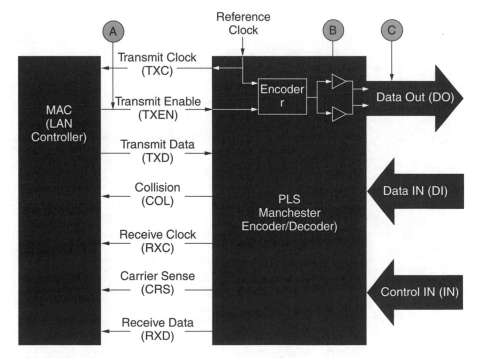

Figure 2.6   Transmit path for Manchester encoding.

The MAC recognizes that a collision has occurred if while it is transmitting data, the receive data channel becomes active. The MAC then stops transmitting the frame data and instead transmits a 48-bit jam signal to ensure that all MACs become aware of the collision. The MAC will then reschedule the transmission according to an exponential backoff algorithm.

According to the exponential backoff algorithm, the retransmission is attempted after the MAC has waited a random number of slot times (512-bit times) where the random number K progresses as follows: After one collision K is chosen from {0,1}. After two collisions K is chosen from {0,1,2,3,}, after three collisions K is chosen from {0,1,2,3,4,5,6,7}, and so on. After 15 unsuccessful attempts, the MAC abandons the frame transmission and notifies the upper layer of the failed transmission. See Figure 2.7.

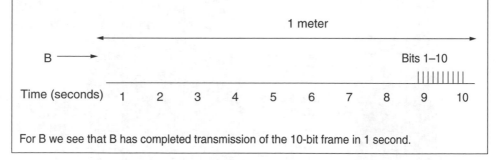

Slot time is dependent on the length of the frame, the diameter of the collision domain, and the rate at which the bits are presented to the medium. Of course, the speed at which the bits traverse the medium is an underlying constant—it is defined by the speed of light.

Assume that station A is operating at 10 bits/second and it has a 10-bit frame to transmit; also assume that station B is operating at 100 bits/second and also has a 10-bit frame to transmit:

For A we see that A continues to present bits to the medium (elevate voltage) for 10 seconds.

For B we see that B has completed transmission of the 10-bit frame in 1 second.

Figure 2.7   Slot time.

The PLS Manchester encodes the data that is transmitted over the AUI to the MAU using a differential signal technique (see Figure 2.8, section B). Manchester encoding allows both clock and data to combine into a single-bit symbol. Each bit symbol consists of two halves—the first half is the logical inverse of the data bit encoded, and the second half is always the logical value of the data itself (the inverse of the first half). Setting the voltage high during the first half of the interval and low in the second half of the interval sends a binary 1. A binary 0 is the opposite—the voltage is low in the first half of the interval and high in the second half of the interval. The encoding process guarantees that there is always a signal transition in the center of each bit symbol.

Differential Manchester encoding is a variation of Manchester. With Differential Manchester, a binary 1 is indicated by the absence of a voltage transition at the start of the interval. A binary 0 is represented by the presence of a transition at the start of the interval. Differential Manchester requires more complex equipment than Manchester, but it provides better immunity to noise. Differential Manchester encoding is illustrated in section C of Figure 2.8.

The two-wire differential signaling required by the AUI specification provides DC isolation between the DTE and the network medium. The MAU provides for the functional, electrical, and mechanical interface between the DTE and the network medium. For 10Mbps Ethernet, the MAC, PLS, and AUI functions are preserved regardless of the medium. Only the MAU is required to change.

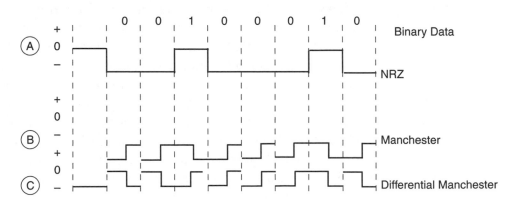

Figure 2.8 Digital encoding.

If the MAU detects a collision, the MAU reports the collision back to the MAC via the CI AUI pair. After the transmission completes, the MAU sends a *signal quality error* (SQE) test message over the CI pair to the AUI. The SQE feature notifies the MAC that the collision circuitry is operational and that the AUI cable is functioning properly. The SQE functionality must be disabled if the MAU is connected to a repeater because otherwise, the repeater will detect the SQE test as a collision.

The MAU also implements a jabber function used to prevent a node from transmitting for excessively long periods of time. If the DTE MAU receives a frame that is longer than the maximum length—1518 bytes—the MAU interrupts the transmission onto the network and indicates a collision to the MAC using the CI pair.

Frame Receive

The MAU detects activity (typically via an elevated voltage on the medium), validates that the signal amplitude is compliant with Manchester encoding, and passes the bits to the PLS for decoding and ultimate transfer of the NRZ signal to the MAC. The MAC then examines and validates the FCS and passes the frame to the proper upper layer client. If the frame is shorter than the minimum frame length (a runt frame), the MAC recognizes that a collision occurred.

Collision Handling

The CSMA/CD technology was designed as a half-duplex medium in which attached stations share and arbitrate for control of the medium. Vital to proper operation of the scheme is the concept of slot time. When a MAC commences to transmit a frame, it takes some amount of time for the elevated voltage to propagate throughout the medium. During this time, there is a chance that another station will also attempt to transmit a frame·that could result in a collision. The time it takes for a station to seize control of the medium is referred to as the collision window. More important than the collision window is slot time, or the time it takes before a station "knows" it has seized control of the medium and no longer needs to concern itself with a collision. Effectively, slot time is the same as round-trip propagation, although slot time is the round-trip propagation plus 32-bit jam time—an added safety margin. How does a station know when the frame it transmits gets involved in a collision and is therefore rendered corrupt and useless? A station knows when the collision condition exists because during a collision, the voltage on the medium is twice what the station contributes itself.

Remember that CSMA/CD was designed to operate in a half-duplex fashion over a coaxial cable. Consequently, the transmitting MAU sees its own transmission voltage along with any added voltage that is introduced onto the medium. The MAU acts as a voltmeter. The MAU must observe its own voltage as well as the voltage of the frame with which it is colliding to know that a collision occurred. Therefore, the length of the frame that the MAU transmits must be significant enough to propagate to the far end of the shared media and back. The two most important factors that determine the minimum size of a frame are the round-trip distance between the farthest stations and the propagation delay, which is the amount of time it takes for the signal to propagate along the media.

The Ethernet developers decided that a 64-byte frame (512 bits, and when transmitted at a rate of 10Mbps, it equals a total transmission time of 51.2 microseconds) was appropriate in terms of both the collision domain (or network diameter) supported and a reasonable smallest frame size that would not require an inordinate amount of waste; that is, padding.

The important Ethernet design constraints are signal attenuation characteristics of the medium (for example, 10Base-5, which specifies 50 ohm coaxial copper cable and requires that the signal not incur disruptive attenuation for 500 meters) and slot time, which takes into consideration both the minimum frame size and the network diameter (or collision domain). Maximum frame size is a measure of how long one station can seize control of the medium (arbitrary value chosen is 1518 bytes), so the maximum amount of time that one station may transmit before introducing the IFG quiet time is 12,064-bit times a, or 1200 microseconds. After the IFG, theoretically, all stations again have equal access to the medium.

Table 2.1 analyzes the delay characteristics associated with each component of a 10Base-5/2 network.

Of course, nothing's perfect. One problem with the 802.3 backoff algorithm is known as the capture effect, which occurs when two stations both have a large amount of data to send. The first station that wins the contention (draws the low backoff number) will transmit. That station will continue to transmit its next frame immediately after the IFG and will continue to transmit until the loser eventually completes its backoff algorithm. Then there may be another collision; however, in this

Table 2.1 Delay Characteristics of a 10Base-5/2 Network

ELEMENT	UNIT STEADY STATE DELAY	UNIT START-UP DELAY	# UNITS FORWARD PATH	# UNITS RETURN PATH	TOTAL DELAY
Encoder	0.10μs	0.10μs	5	5	2.0μs
Transceiver cable	5.13ns/m	0.00	300m	300m	3.08μs
Transceiver Transmit path	0.05μs	0.30μs	3	3	2.10μs
Transceiver receive path	0.05μs	0.60μs	3	0	1.95μs
Transceiver collision path	0.00	0.90μs	0	3	2.70μs
Coaxial cable	4.33ns/m	0.00	1500m	1500m	12.99μs
Point-point link cable	5.13ns/m	0.00	1000m	1000m	10.26μs
Point-point link driver	0.10μs	0.00	2	2	0.40μs
Point-point link receiver	0.10μs	0.00	2	2	0.40μs
Repeater repeater path	0.20μs	0.20μs	0	2	0.80μs
Repeater Collision path	0.20μs	0.20μs	0	2	0.80μs
Carrier Sense	0.00	0.20μs	5	0	1.00μs
Collision detect	0.00	0.20μs	0	5	1.00μs
Signal rise time	0.00	2.10μs	3	3	6.30μs
Collision fragment time tolerance	0.00	0.20μs	0	1	0.20μs
Total worst-case round-trip delay 46.38μs					

Adapted from Ethernet Specification Version 2.0

case, the playing field is not equal because the loser has a much wider range of random numbers it can select for its back off algorithm. For the winner, this is its first collision (that is, it will draw only a 0 or a 1). It's slim pickings for the loser. IEEE 802.3 defines the backoff time in terms of *slot time*, which is 512 bits. For 10Mbps Ethernet, this translates to 51.2 microseconds. The backoff time will be in integer number of slot times from zero to a maximum number. For slot time of zero, the time is not actually 0 bits but the minimum interframe gap (IFG). For 10Mbps, this is 9.6 microseconds. The actual number of slot times is a random number between 0 and the maximum number.

Suffice it to say that collisions are a way of life with Ethernet and, in fact, play an important role. Collisions and the subsequent backoff schemes provide an effective mechanism for congestion and flow control.

10Base-T

The *T* in the 10Base-T specification refers to the physical layer that supports *twisted pair wire medium*. The 10Mbps Ethernet system was designed to support segments using Category 3, voice grade, and unshielded twisted-pair (UTP) telephone wire. This system was a popular option because there is much Cat 3 wire in existing buildings. (New installations are wise to install Cat 5 UTP because doing so will enable the upgrade to 100Mbps Ethernet.) The 10Base-T system uses pairs of UTP, which are terminated in an eight-pin RJ-45-style connector. The transmit and receive data signals on each pair of the UTP segments are polarized; one pair carries the positive (+) signal, and the other pair carries the negative (–) signal. The 10Base-T Eight-Pin connector is illustrated in Figure 2.9. Remember that with Manchester encoding, each signal bit has a positive component and a negative component.

Local Pin Number	Local Signal	Remote Pin Number	Remote Signal
1	TX+	3	RC+
2	TX–	6	RC–
3	RC+	1	TX+
4	unused		
5	unused		
6	RC–	2	TX–
7	unused		
8	unused		

Figure 2.9   10Base-T Eight-Pin connector.

The most significant difference between the 10Base-T and 10Base2/5 technologies is that because the transmit and receive signal paths are separate, a collision is not detectable via an elevated voltage on the medium. However, if both transmit and receive pairs become active simultaneously, the MAU must indicate a collision to the MAC, which proceeds with backoff and retransmit. Also, because the transmit and receive signals are on separate physical paths, it is possible for one path to become faulty. The 10Base-T MAU continually monitors the receive data path for activity to ensure that the physical paths are working properly. When the MAU has no data to transmit, it periodically transmits a link integrity test signal that the remote MAU can observe on its receive path. The physical topology supported by 10Base-T is a star in which the link segments are connected to a repeater. The maximum distance 10Base-T link is 100 meters. In Figure 2.10, data received on any of the ports is repeated to all ports except the port on which the signal was received with amplitude and timing restored to the signal. If the repeater detects receive signal activity from more than one port, which constitutes a collision, the repeater will send a *jam* pattern on all ports including the active receive ports. In this way, the active devices will recognize that their transmission was involved in a collision.

Repeater

The repeater (or hub) is a physical layer device that provides signal amplification and retiming. The repeater enables the collision domain to extend beyond the signal attenuation limitations to the limits defined by the slot time. The repeater does allow different types of Ethernet seg-

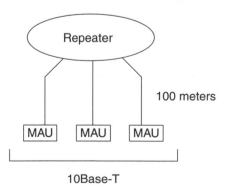

Figure 2.10   10Base-T topology.

ments to connect to ports and so participate in the same collision domain. Note that all interconnected segments must be of the same speed. For example, the repeater cannot be used to interconnect an Ethernet segment to a Fast Ethernet segment. Data received on one port is repeated with amplitude, and timing is restored to the signal on all other ports except for the active receiver port. If the receiver detects a collision on a segment connected to one of its ports or if it detects receive activity on multiple ports (a collision), the repeater sends a jam on all ports, including the ports responsible for the collision (see Figure 2.10).

When a frame is received at the repeater port, the repeater recovers clock by examining the signal transitions in the bit stream. As a result of the signal sampling, some preamble bits are typically lost. When the signal is retransmitted on another port, the preamble bits have to be restored. As a result of the loss and reintroduction of the preamble bits, the IFG shrinks. According to the IEEE 802.3 specification, the IFG must always be at least 6.8 microseconds (recall that initially it is 9.6 microseconds). Because of IFG shrinkage, it is specified that there exist no more than two repeaters between any two communicating stations in the same collision domain.

 Where the link between the repeaters is fiber, there is no IFG shrinkage because of a different clock recovery scheme. However, primarily for reasons of consistency, the two-repeater rule is specified even when there is a fiber link between repeaters.

Extending the LAN

Repeaters are physical layer devices that participate in the collision domain. Bridges are MAC layer devices that define or delimit the collision domain. Bridges do participate in the broadcast domain upon which, if a bridge detects a collision, it does not propagate the transmission onto any output port. Bridge operation is specified in the IEEE 802.1D standard.

Bridge forwarding is based on learning, filtering, and forwarding functions that are specified in IEEE 802.1D. The principal function of the bridge is to confine local traffic to a specific collision domain. The bridge forwards a received frame only on the port where the destination MAC is located. The MAC-to-port association information is stored in the bridge's forwarding database. When the bridge does not know where the destination MAC is located or when the destination MAC is either a broadcast or a multicast address, the bridge forwards the frame onto all ports (floods) that are participating in the same broadcast domain as the received frame. The bridge determines which broadcast domain the received frame is participating in by examining the received frame's source MAC address. It is imperative that the broadcast domain be free of loops because of the reliance on flooding unicast frames that the bridge has not learned and flooding multicast/broadcast frames. Another important reason that the broadcast domain be loop free is that there is no way to determine the number of bridges that a frame has traversed. There is no *time-to-live* field in the frame header.

The terms *bridge* and *switch* are used interchangeably; however, there are subtle differences. The device originally referred to as a bridge was a two-port device, and switches/bridges today typically have many ports. More important, bridge forwarding was a software operation, so it introduced delay. In addition, early bridges had a backplane that might be characterized as a piece of coax—the point is that there was contention in going from input port to output port—again introducing delay. Bridges and switches today typically support hardware (wire-speed) forwarding and also have a switch fabric with separate paths (usually the path is logical) between an input port and an output port. So there is much less delay associated with traversing a switch. Another important difference is that the switch can be configured such that some ports participate in one broadcast domain while other ports participate in a different broadcast domain. Effectively, the switch is divided into several logical bridges. The ports participating in the same broadcast domain are sometimes referred to as a bridge group or, more commonly, as participating in a port-based, virtual LAN (vLAN).

Spanning Tree Operation

The Spanning Tree Protocol (STP) is implemented in transparent bridges (and some source route bridges) and ensures that the broadcast domain topology resembles the branches of a tree. The branches do not loop and ensure that all LANs in the broadcast domain have a unique path to each other. Each bridge is configured with several elements of information that include:

Root bridge priority. The bridge with the lowest root bridge priority becomes the root of the spanning tree. In the event of a tie, the bridge with the lowest root bridge priority and the lowest MAC address becomes the root bridge.

Hello timer. This indicates the frequency with which the bridge will propagate BPDU messages.

Forward delay time. This element has several uses that include specification of the length of time a port should wait before forwarding frames on a port that has just become active. The delay is used to allow the bridge to learn which MACs to associate with the particular port.

Max age time. This has several uses that include specification of time to wait before timing out information learned from a root configuration BPDU.

Port cost. This is the cost associated with using this port—that is, going out of this port.

Long age timer. Times before dynamically learned entries are removed from the forwarding database.

Note that all bridges use the *hello timer*, *forward delay time*, and *max age time* values as specified in the root bridge.

The first step in the STP is election of the root bridge. Initially, each bridge believes that it is the root bridge, and each issues a Bridge Protocol data unit (BPDU) configuration message indicating its own root bridge priority (also its own hello time, forward delay time, and max age time). In Ethernet v2, BPDU messages were called *hello messages,* and frequently, the terms BPDU and hello message are used interchangeably. The BPDUs are sent on all bridge ports. A bridge that receives a BPDU with a lower priority than its own stops generating its own BPDU and forwards the received BPDU. BPDUs are not directly forwarded, but rather, information in the received BPDU is used in calculating the BPDU transmitted by the local bridge. Quickly, all bridges will agree on the root bridge. All the root's ports become designated bridge ports for the LANs to which they are attached.

After the root bridge election is complete, only the root bridge continues to initiate configuration BPDUs; all other bridges in the broadcast domain forward the BPDU only in response to receiving a BPDU from the root. The BPDU contains information that includes:

Flags. Used in the event of a topology change.

Root ID. The root bridge priority plus the MAC of a root bridge.

Root path cost. The cost of the least expensive path from a given bridge to the root bridge.

Bridge ID. The root bridge priority plus the MAC of the sending bridge.

Port ID. Identifier of the bridge port on which BPDU is sent.

Forward delay time. From root's BPDU.

Max age time. From root's BPDU.

Hello time. From root's BPDU.

All bridges operate with the same forward delay time, max age time, and BPDU time.

The next step in the STP is the logical elimination of loops within the broadcast domain. Enabling only one path to the root from each bridge allows this elimination.

Each bridge listens to the BPDU received on all ports. Each of the BPDUs will have a root path cost. The bridge adds the port path cost associated with the port on which the BPDUs arrived to the root path cost contained in the BPDU to determine its own root path cost associated with the port on which the BPDU arrived. By examining the root path cost of all received BPDUs, the bridge determines which of its ports has the lowest root path cost. The root port is put into the forwarding state. In the event that multiple ports have equal root path costs, a tie-breaker algorithm is implemented. The algorithm is based on bridge priority (the port that received the BPDU from a bridge with the lowest priority becomes the root port) and MAC address (if bridge priorities are equal, the port that received the BPDU with the lowest source MAC address will become the root port). Port priority and port number can also be used if further discrimination is required—typically port priority/number will be used only if a bridge has multiple ports connected to the same LAN.

The next phase of the STP selects one bridge to become the designated bridge for each LAN segment that is not attached to the root bridge. The designated bridge is the bridge that has the bridge port with the lowest cost path to the root bridge. If multiple bridges advertise equal lowest root path cost, the bridge with the lowest bridge ID becomes the designated bridge for the LAN segment. The designated bridge port attached to the LAN segment is called the designated bridge port and is put into the forwarding state. The bridge transmits only configuration BPDUs on designated bridge ports. All other ports are put into blocking state. While in the blocked state, a bridge port will neither send nor receive data and will not learn the MAC address on blocked ports. In addition, configuration BPDUs will not be transmitted on the blocked ports.

The root bridge sends a configuration BPDU every hello timer (default is 2 seconds). If a designated bridge does not receive a BPDU on its root port for max age time (default is 20 seconds), the designated bridge assumes that there is a link or device failure. If the bridge is still receiving configuration BPDU on any port, the bridge will simply switch its root port to a port that is receiving the best configuration BPDUs. If the bridge receives no BPDU for max age time, the bridge sends a topology change BPDU onto all ports and also sends a configuration BPDU with itself as the root bridge. Any bridge that receives the topology change notification examines all BPDUs it receives to determine if the root bridge has changed. If the root bridge has changed, the acting bridge forwards the topology change notification to all of its ports. In this manner, all bridges that need to take action will be notified, and the appropriate reconfiguration will occur.

After a topological change, it will take some time for the information to percolate throughout the broadcast domain. While the spanning tree is reconfiguring, there is a chance that the broadcast domain will become partitioned, and there is also the possibility that a loop will exist in the network. The chance of a temporary loop is minimized if, when a port transitions from the blocked state to a forwarding state, the port is required to wait a predetermined amount of time before it actually begins to transmit traffic on the port. There are two components to the waiting period. The first component is referred to as the *listening period*, and it ensures that the spanning tree configuration has stabilized. The second component, referred to as the *learning period*, occurs when the bridge learns which MACs correlate with which ports. In reality, both the listening period and the learning period are equal in time to the forwarding delay time (default is 15 seconds).

While the spanning tree is reconfiguring and ports transition from blocked to forwarding and vice versa, the port-to-MAC associations in the bridge might become incorrect. To remedy the situation quickly, once the bridge recognizes that a spanning tree reconfiguration is occurring by receipt of a topology change notification, the bridge begins to age the learned address using the *forwarding delay time* as the aging factor (instead of the long age time).

Cut-Through Bridges

The 802.1D standard specifies the behavior of *store-and-forward* bridges. The behavior signifies that when a frame arrives on a bridge port, the

Spanning Tree Reconfiguration Example

Initially, Chicago sends a configuration BPDU (C-BPDU) on LAN1 with "Chicago is root"; and London upon receipt of the C-BPDU from Chicago sends a C-BPDU onto LAN2 with "Chicago is root." In turn, Sydney sends a C-BPDU onto LAN3 with "Chicago is root."

Subsequently, a break occurs as shown in Figure 2.11.

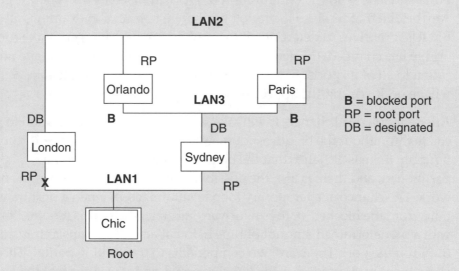

B = blocked port
RP = root port
DB = designated

Figure 2.11 A break occurs in a Spanning Tree network.

On LAN2

For 20 seconds after the break, no BPDU appears on the LAN2. After 20 seconds, London realizes that it is not receiving a C-BPDU from its root port and is not receiving C-BPDU on any of its other ports. London then sends onto LAN2 a C-BPDU and topology change flag set declaring itself the root. Because London believes that the root has changed, it also sends out topology change notification BPDU (TCN-BPDU) onto LAN2 (see Figure 2.12). As soon as Paris and Orlando receive the TCN-BPDU, they both forward the TCN-BPDU onto their root ports, which have since changed, as described in the next paragraph.

During these 20 seconds, neither Orlando nor Paris is receiving C-BPDUs on its root ports, but each of the bridges is receiving a C-BPDU from a nonroot port (the ports that are currently blocked). Each of the bridges will unblock its blocked ports, make them their root ports, and attempt to become the designated bridge on LAN2. Now Paris and Orlando are receiving a C-BPDU on LAN3 that specifies London as the root. Paris and Orlando are also receiving C-BPDU on their new root ports that specify Chicago as the root (obviously, Chicago is the preferred

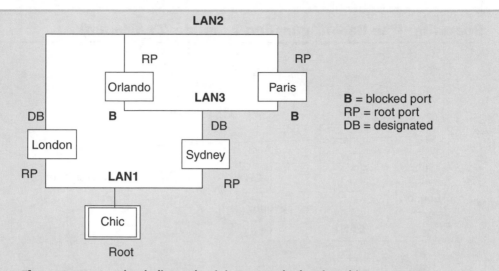

Figure 2.12 London believes that it is Root and advertises this on to LAN 2.

root because it was so designated before the outage). Both Orlando and Paris send onto LAN2 a C-BPDU specifying that Chicago is the root bridge. London, Orlando, and Paris all examine the C-BPDU that they have received on LAN2.

Based on information received (root path cost, root ID, bridge ID, and so on) London, Orlando, and Paris determine that, indeed, Chicago is the root bridge and Paris is the designated bridge for LAN2 (Paris now has the bridge port with the lowest-cost path to the root bridge). Because Paris is the designated bridge for LAN2, it sends a C-BPDU with *topology change acknowledge* bit set. Subsequently, Paris sends C-BPDU at 2-second intervals. After a bridge receives the TCN-BPDU, the bridge begins to age entries in its forwarding database using the forward delay time. Alternatively, the bridge can flush, or empty, its forwarding database. The bridge continues to use the forward delay time until notified by the root to stop using the short age timer (see Figure 2.13).

On LAN3

After the break, Sydney continues to send C-BPDU with "Chicago is root" every two seconds.

Sydney sees the two TCN-BPDUs but realizes that neither the root bridge nor its root path has changed because it is receiving C-BPDU from Chicago. Sydney sends a C-BPDU with "Chicago is root" and topology change acknowledge bit set onto LAN3. Now all LAN3 bridges are using the short age times on dynamically learned addresses. And, of course, the ports that went from blocked to forwarding are going through listening and learning delays before transitioning to forwarding.

Continues

Spanning Tree Reconfiguration Example *(Continued)*

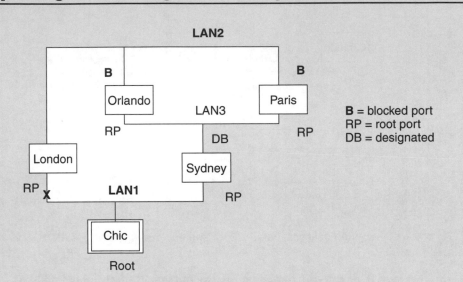

Figure 2.13   The Spanning Tree has restabalized.

On LAN1

Sydney transmits both TCN-BPDUs that it has received on its root port onto LAN1. Chicago sends a C-BPDU with "Chicago is root" and topology change acknowledge bit set. Chicago continues to set the topology change flag in its C-BPDU for a period of time (typically, max age plus forward delay). The time ensures that all bridges receive one or more with the topology change flag set. While bridges are in receipt of C-BPDUs with the flag set, they use the short age time to age out dynamically learned, forwarding-table entries.

entire frame is buffered. The buffered frame is then examined to ensure proper length and CRC integrity. Only valid frames are processed for filtering and forwarding—the process introduces delay. (Because of the delay, it is specified that no more than seven bridges exist between any two communicating devices.) However, a positive aspect of the store-and-forward device is that it prevents corrupt frames from forwarding onto an output port that would result in wasted overhead. Another favorable aspect of the store-and-forward bridge is that it permits interconnection bridge ports of different speeds. So it is possible to have 10Mbps and 100Mbps segments and participate in the same broadcast domain.

Another type of bridge that has received some degree of acceptance is called a cut-through bridge. When a frame arrives on a port of a cut-through bridge, the frame is buffered only long enough for the bridge to perform filtering and forwarding. Forwarding of the frame on the output port actually commences before the entire frame has arrived. This, of course, requires availability of the output medium. Consequently, if the frame is corrupt or is of invalid length, some or all of the frame will nonetheless be forwarded. The prime advantage of the approach is that the delay associated with the store-and-forwarded device is reduced significantly. Variations to the cut-through bridge theme have been introduced. For example, if a bridge realizes that a packet is corrupt because the CRC is invalid, the bridge will revert to store-and-forward for some period of time or until some criterion is met, at which time the bridge will resume cut-through mode. The idea is to minimize the amount of wasteful data introduced to a segment. However, with the introduction of many wire-speed devices that support both 10Mbps and 100Mbps ports, cut-through devices appear to be waning in popularity.

The term *cut-through* has been used lately to denote several different things. In a later chapter, we will see that cut-through Layer 3 mechanism has been introduced in both proprietary and standard-based protocols to expedite Layer 3 forwarding of packets. Additionally, many current switch manufacturers specify that they do cut-through switching so that latency through their devices is minimized. Often, what is meant is that the frame is forwarded to the switch fabric in a cut-through fashion; that is, forwarding of the frame to the fabric commences before the entire frame has arrived on the input port. However, the frame is usually not sent on the output port until it has been fully validated. Therefore, you may want to look at the entire device as a store-and-forward device although cut-through schemes were employed to minimize latency through the device.

Fast Ethernet (100Base-T)

Ethernet was already a pervasive LAN technology, far outdistancing token ring and FDDI, by the early 1990s. At the time, it made sense to upgrade the technology to support emerging bandwidth-intensive applications. In actuality, few people anticipated that 100Mbps would be required for an individual workstation. Yet with the rapid deployment of switches supporting improved performance and flexibility, it was obvious that higher bandwidth between switches would be required to support an aggregation of 10Mbps links. By keeping the essential characteristics of Ethernet technology unchanged, the developers and implementers of 100Mbps could benefit from the body of Ethernet expertise developed over the years and exploit the huge installed base.

The IEEE 802.3u Task Group was chartered with developing the enhancement of 100Mbps to the Ethernet suite. If 100Mbps Ethernet (which introduces bit signals 10 times faster than 10Mbps Ethernet) requirements dictate that it must operate within the CSMA/CD constraints specified in 802.3, it is necessary to decrease the collision diameter by a factor of 10. This is depicted in Table 2.2. The reason has to do with dynamics associated with slot time, minimum frame size, and collision-domain diameter The impact of the diminished collision diameter is demonstrated in Figure 2.14.

When it developed 100Mbps Ethernet, the IEEE 802.3u Task Group endeavored to meet certain goals that would ensure acceptance of the new technology. Of prime importance, the new technology would have to provide ease of migration and seamless integration with the installed base. The group focused on developing 100Mbps over UTP because UTP was the medium implemented most widely. Note that although support for Category 3 UTP was considered, it was determined that the physical characteristics of the medium were too restrictive, and support for Cat 3 UTP was deemphasized.

Another consideration was to keep cost consistent with the pricing model defined by the computer industry. Consequently, if the performance was to increase by a factor of 10, the price should increase by no more than a factor of 2. Developers decided early on to take advantage of existing technology so that they could provide a timely and cost-effective product. Developers leveraged the experience of FDDI and made use of the fully developed technology that operated at 100Mbps.

Another consideration weighed how readily vendors—including networking, systems, semiconductor, computer, integrator, and research companies—would adopt the new technology in their products. Wide-

Table 2.2   10Mbps versus 100Mbps Important Parameters

	10MBPS	100MBPS
Collision diameter	512 bit-times	51.2 bit-times
Bit-time (us)	0.1	0.01
Maximum round-trip delay (us)	51.2	5.12
Maximum network diameter with UTP (m)	2500	250

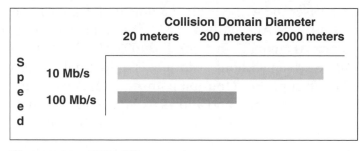

Figure 2.14   CSMA/CD constraints.

spread support is important to users because it ensures availability of interoperable products at competitive prices.

The 802.3u Task Force adopted a draft standard, consisting of 10 clauses that were added to the IEEE 802.3 specification as follows:

Clause 21: Introduction to 1000Mbps baseband networks

Clause 22: Reconciliation sublayer and *medium independent interface* (MII)

Clause 23: Physical—100Base-T4

Clause 24: Physical—100Base-X

Clause 25: PHY for 100Base-TX

Clause 26: PHY for 100Base-FX

Clause 27: Repeater for 100Mbps

Clause 28: Auto-negotiation

Clause 29: System considerations for multisegment 100Base-T networks

Clause 30: Management

Subsequent to the IEEE 802.3u Task Force recommendation, IEEE standards 802.3x and 802.3y were developed by the task force in 1996 for full-duplex, Ethernet operation and in 1997 for flow control in support of full-duplex operation, respectively.

Differences between 10Base-T and 100Base-T

As shown in Figure 2.15, the MAC is separated from the PHY by the MII. The MII performs essentially the same function as the AUI in 10Mbps: It decouples the MAC from the particulars of the underlying PHY and so permits the MAC, unchanged, to operate with the varieties of PHYs. There is one significant difference between the MII and AUI. With

10Mbps, data traverses the AUI one bit at a time with the AUI operating at a frequency of 10MHz. At 100Mbps, the MII would have to operate at 100MHz frequency. At an operating speed of 100MHz, the distance that the signal could be driven without distortion is quite small. Instead of a one-bit path, the MII supports a four-bit path, each clock cycle, in both transmit and receive directions, and allows the MII to operate with a 25MHz clock instead of 100MHz (required with a one-bit path).

Another consequence of increased signal frequency is that Manchester encoding is no longer used. Because Manchester encoding requires that data and clock be carried simultaneously in a single-bit symbol, at the increased speed, the negative effects of EMI and RFI become significant. Manchester encoding is replaced with NRZ over the short (<.5m) nibble-wide, MII-data path. Note that the type of encoding used on the link is predicated on the type of PHY implemented. In addition, to ensure ease of migration and the plug-and-play nature of 10Mbps Ethernet, the MII is capable of supporting both 10 Mbps Ethernet and 100Mbps Ethernet. The MII clock operates at 2.5MHz and 25MHz to support the two operating modes. The switch port should have the capability to support either a

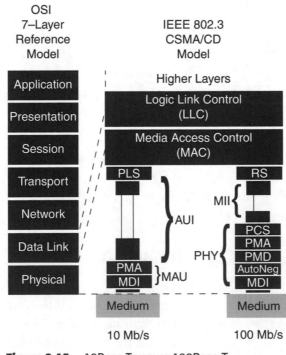

Figure 2.15   10Base-T versus 100Base-T.

10Mbps-attached device or a 100Mbps-attached device and determine the speed of the attached device automatically (known as auto-negotiation) with no user intervention. Auto-negotiation is specified only for 100Base-T PHYs. We will see later that auto-negotiation might also involve determining the full-duplex capability of the attached device. The MII consists of 18 pins divided into four groups: transmit data, receive data, network status, and device management. Note that because there is also a reduced MII (RMII) operating at 50MHz, only half of the data pins are required. The RMII is often implemented in switches to conserve space where port density is an issue.

Because the MAC has not changed, it might still present data one bit at a time to the lower layers. The function of the reconciliation sublayer (RS) is to assemble the MAC's bit stream into a nibble for simultaneous transmission across the MII (see Figure 2.16).

Fast Ethernet PHYs

Fast Ethernet combines the CSMA/CD MAC with several different specifications of physical layers. The physical layers are TX—twisted pair; FX—two pair of optic fibers; T4—four pairs of Category 3 UTP; and T2—two pairs of Category 4 UTP. Characteristics of each type of Fast Ethernet PHY are:

100Base-TX. 100Base-TX is by far the most common 100Base-T PHY and merges the FDDI PHY with the CSMA/CD MAC. 100Base-TX is similar to 10Base-T in that it operates over two pairs of UTP (UTP must be Category 5). While one pair is transmitting, the other pair is used to detect

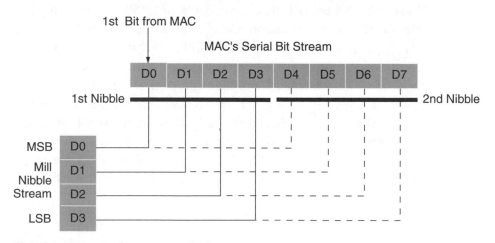

Figure 2.16 MAC byte to MII nibble.

a collision. The 100Base-TX signal is based on 4B/5B block coding technology originally developed for FDDI. The 4B/5B encoding technique maps the 16 possible 4-bit, data-nibble values to a subset of the 5-bit, binary-code groups. When the MAC transmits data, the PHY takes the 4-bit nibble from the MII and converts it to a 5-bit, FDDI-specified binary symbol. The 5-bit symbol is transmitted serially on the medium with an available frequency of 125MHz.

100Base-FX. 100Base-FX is a variation of 100Base-TX except that it operates on two pairs of optic fiber. (A major difference between the two is that unlike 100Base-TX, 100Base-FX does not support auto-negotiation.)

100Base-T4. 100Base-T4 is designed to operate with Category 3 UTP. This type of cable has poor RFI and EMI characteristics preceding 25MHz and does not meet FCC emission standards. Therefore, four pairs of wire are deployed to operate with Category 3 UTP. The signal is split among the wires, and six wires are used to carry the signal. The remaining pair of wires is used to detect simultaneous activity from the device at the other end of the link (indicating a collision). (In the 8B6T scheme, each of the 256 possible 8-bit values converts into one of the 729 possible 6-bit ternary values. The 729 values are derived when either a "+," "–," or "0" voltage on 6 of the 8 wires is presented.) The PHY collects 2 nibbles from the MII to form an 8-bit symbol and then converts the 8 bits to a 6-bit ternary symbol. The fact that 100B-T4 employs a completely new PHY layer encoding and signaling protocol means that special-purpose, integrated silicon has to be developed. The condition results in slow deployment relative to 100Base-TX and subsequently has not been implemented widely.

100Base-T2. 100Base-T2 PHY (completed in 1997) was not part of the original 802.3u specification and operates over two pairs of Category 3 UTP. Equalization and noise cancellation techniques are employed to achieve 100Mbps over two pairs of Cat 3 sophisticated, multilevel coding. The process requires sophisticated digital signal processing (DSP) techniques. The encoding, referred to as pulse amplitude modification (5x5 PAM), takes a nibble from the MII and maps the 4 bits into a pair of quinery symbols (there are 25), which are then transmitted using both pairs. This yields a 25MHz line rate—the same as the MII clock rate. Currently there are no implementations of 100Base-T2.

Full-Duplex Ethernet

Ethernet was by definition half duplex until 1996. The MAC was logically a half-duplex entity even when implemented over twisted pair with a separate transmit and receive path (see Figure 2.17). If the transmit and receive paths became active simultaneously, the MAC would cease transmission and perform its backoff algorithm. Full-duplex operation was never part of the Ethernet PHY or MAC specifications. However, the emergence of a predominantly UTP-based implementation, as well as the emergence of switching, meant that the transmission paths were primarily point to point and no longer shared by multiple users. The CSMA/CD algorithm is not required because there is no contention for use of the path. In 1997, IEEE Standard 802.3x was adopted to provide a modified MAC supporting full-duplex operation. A short time later in 1997, the IEEE Standard 802.3y was also adopted to provide a flow control mechanism in support of full-duplex Ethernet. Of course, with CSMA/CD, there was no need for flow control because the CSMA/CD algorithm provided access control and flow control. The MAC was modified to allow simultaneous transmit and receive operation, which involved disabling the normal CSMA/CD deferral process. In addition, the MAC control sublayer was added to the MAC to detect and process special MAC control frames or pause frames that affected the flow control operation. Figure 2.17 illustrates the modified MAC to support full duplex and flow control.

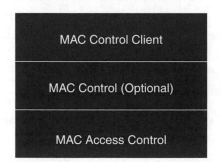

MAC Control Sublayer in 802.3 Layer Hierarchy

Figure 2.17   802.3x and 802.3y.

Auto-Negotiation

Auto-negotiation is a mechanism that seizes control of the link when a connection is established between network devices. It determines the various modes of operation each device supports and automatically configures the link for the highest-performance mode of operation. Auto-negotiation automatically switches to the optimal technology supported by both devices, such as 100Base-TX full duplex, 100Base-TX half duplex, 10Base-T full duplex, 10Base-T half duplex, or 100Base-T4. If the device at only one end of the connection supports auto-negotiation, that device will recognize that the remote device does not support auto-negotiation via its link integrity test signal. The local device will then automatically switch to 10Base-T operation. If the devices at both ends support auto-negotiation, each advertises its capabilities to the other. Auto-negotiation incorporates a reliable handshake mechanism to ensure data integrity. After each device is aware of the capabilities of the other device, it begins operating in the highest-performance common technology that they share.

Auto-negotiation relies on a key characteristic of 10Base-T, the *link integrity test*. If there is no frame to send, a link integrity test signal is transmitted. Auto-negotiation takes advantage of the link integrity test pulse by replacing the link test pulse with a burst of pulses called *fast link pulses* (FLPs). Each FLP consist of a series of clock and data pulses. Data in the FLP is used to form the 16-bit *link code word* (LCW). The LCW is transmitted on power-up or when requested by either of the devices. The FLPs are such that if the remote device is a 10Base-T device, the FLP will look like a link integrity test signal. However, if the remote side is a 100Base-TX device, its receive clock will be operating fast enough to interpret the individual pulses and so construct the LCW. In this fashion, the auto-negotiation mechanism is designed so that a single switch can support both 10M and 100M devices. By assembling and interpreting the LCW, the stations at either end of the link arbitrate the speed (10/100) at which to operate as well as negotiate half-duplex (CSMA/CD) or full-duplex and flow-control capabilities.

Auto-negotiation is defined only for 100Base-TX PHYs. Because the pulses do not translate directly into fiber, auto-negotiation is not used for 100Base-FX. However, auto-negotiation has been designed so that the basic approach of encoding and interpreting the LCW can be leveraged and interoperable with other technologies. (Later we see how Gigabit Ethernet encodes the LCW.)

Remember that an underlying objective was to ensure interoperability and ease of migration between 10Base and 100Base technologies. In this context, flow control becomes significant with 100Base-T because when the flow is going from a 100Mbps device to a 10Mbps device, it is quite conceivable that the 10Mbps device could be overwhelmed with data. Subsequently, either data must be discarded or we must control the flow of the data. Obviously, the latter is preferred.

Each device maintains a priority table. The priority is assigned by technology type and administered by IEEE 802.3 (see Figure 2.18).

The Pause bit (which was added by the 802.3x and 802.3y Full-Duplex and Flow-Control Standard) is supported only for full-duplex technologies and identifies if the device supports the Pause mechanism. The format of the Pause frame is illustrated in Figure 2.19.

Remote fault indicates the presence of a fault detected by the remote link partner. Typically, the RF bit is set if the device enters the *link fail* state, which might be the result of a broken receiver or cable. *Ack* indicates successful receipt of the previous LCW. After exchanging the LCW (that contains information to make a connection automatically), if both ends

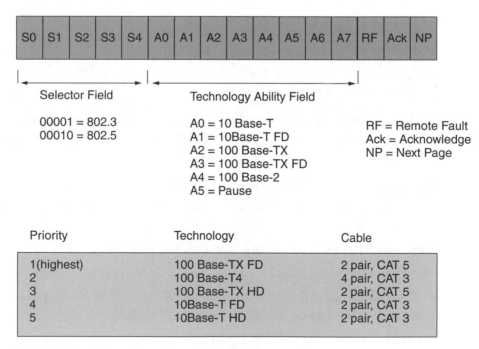

Figure 2.18 Link code word and PHY priorities.

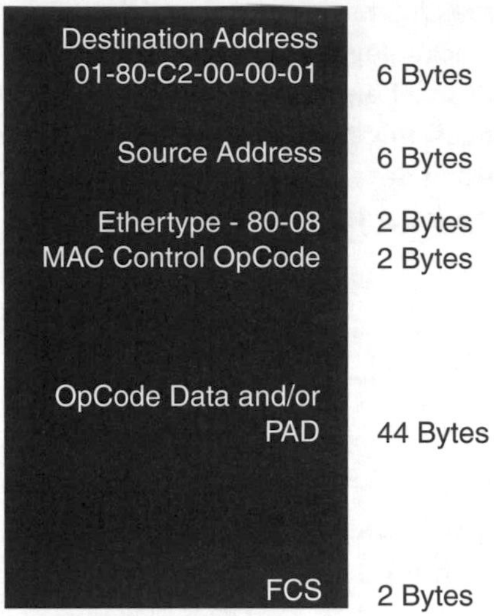

Destination Address 01-80-C2-00-00-01	6 Bytes
Source Address	6 Bytes
Ethertype - 80-08	2 Bytes
MAC Control OpCode	2 Bytes
OpCode Data and/or PAD	44 Bytes
FCS	2 Bytes

Figure 2.19 Flow control—Pause frame.

indicate support for the next page function, additional data can be exchanged. This allows extensions to the standard and proprietary extensions to exist without affecting operation. The next page function can be used to send information regarding an OUI where extra features can be implemented on a proprietary basis. Next page can also be used to indicate a remote fault type.

The MAC control frame consists of 64 bytes and can convey special information to the higher layers. The Pause is a specific MAC control frame. The following are elements of that frame:

Destination address (DA). Unicast or multicast—for Pause the value is 01-80-c2-00-00-01 (multicast)—although a multicast address is not forwarded.

Source address (SA). Unicast of the sending station.

Ethertype (88-08). Globally assigned to the MAC control frame.

MAC control OpCode. Determines how MAC control frame parameters are to be interpreted—for Pause equal to 00-01.

OpCode data. For Pause, contains a 2-byte pause timer.

Even when the MAC is paused, the MAC Control can generate a pause frame and send it where the pause frame might have a pause timer equal to 0 to indicate that the station can now accept transmissions—that is, stop the Pause.

In 100Base-T, the pause capability is symmetric—that is, both ends set the pause bit in the LCW. We will see that with 1000Base-T, pausing is asymmetrical.

The MDI

In addition to the MII, IEEE 802.3u specifies a media-dependent interface (MDI). The MDI refers to the type of connector and the signaling with regard to the particular connector pin-out. For 100Base-TX, an RJ45 connector is specified for Category 5 UTP with a straight through (MDI) or crossed over (MDI-X) for connection to a switch. Several MDIs are also specified in 100Base-FX.

Repeaters

100Base defines two separate classes of repeaters (unlike 10Base Ethernet, which has a single repeater definition for all media options) because of the necessity to optimize signal delays for Fast Ethernet and because there are significant differences between coding techniques employed for different media types. Class I repeaters allow more generous delays; they allow conversion between coding schemes, thereby allowing all media types to be connected to the repeater. Class II repeaters were defined with more stringent timing specifications, thereby allowing optimization for one specific coding scheme.

Fast Ethernet topology is a repeater-based star with two repeater types supported (Class I and Class II). Because of the more stringent timing specifications imposed, greater distances between repeater and the attached device are supported with Class II repeaters. Figure 2.20 illustrates the differences between Class I and Class II repeaters. With Class I, only a single repeater is allowed between any two devices. Class II repeaters allow two repeaters, or if used in a single repeater topology then Class II repeaters allow additional separation between devices.

Note that a switch port connected to a repeater must operate in CSMA/CD mode, and repeaters do not support full-duplex operation.

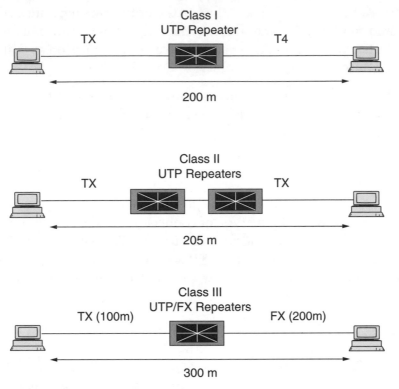

Figure 2.20 Repeater topologies.

Support for vLAN Tagging

Later we will explore IEEE 802.1Q, the standard that specifies how to identify vLAN between communicating devices. vLANs are identified by a 4-byte field inserted into the frame between the source MAC address and the Protocol/length fields. To accommodate the tags, or identifiers, IEEE 802.1Q actually modifies the frame-size parameters. The IEEE 802.3ac Standard was developed to align the work in IEEE 802.1Q and provide MAC-layer support for the modified frame sizes.

Gigabit Ethernet (1000Base-X)

The idea that 100Mbps would provide sufficient bandwidth for the ages was short-lived. By the mid-1990s, Fast Ethernet was widely accepted and implemented. The broad-scale deployment was fueled by the decreasing cost of 100Mbps equipment and its ability to interoperate and coexist with the exiting 10Mbps devices. However, a new class of applications was emerging. Bandwidth-hungry applications driven by intranet-based operations and Internet-based applications was increasing the demand for time-sensitive communication between networked users. Applications such as graphics and video, coupled with an increase in the number of network users, require higher network bandwidth. Fortunately, the next iteration of Ethernet, Gigabit Ethernet or 1000Base-X, began on the heels of completion of the 100Base-T Standard.

The design goals for 1000Mbps Ethernet were like those for 100Mbps Ethernet. The introduction of the new higher-speed, Ethernet technology must remain transparent to the user, and migration to the new technology must consist of a few nondisruptive steps. To be most cost effective, the new technology would have the capability of operating over the most widely deployed, physical media—rapidly becoming optic fiber and four-pair, Category 5 UTP. In late 1995, a study group was formed within IEEE 803.2 to investigate the feasibility of 1000Mbps Ethernet. The study group became known as the IEEE 802.3z Task Force.

Gigabit Ethernet Technology Goals

In addition to the 1000Mbps operating speed, there were several other technological goals established by the IEEE 802.3z Task Force. Use of the same frame format—including minimum and maximum size—would facilitate interoperability with 10Mbps and 100Mbps Ethernet installations.

Full-duplex operation would support switch-to-switch and switch-to-end station operations. It was decided that the flow control mechanism would be based on IEEE 802.3x, but that flow control would not be symmetrical as it was for Fast Ethernet. Rather, flow control would be asymmetrical, and only the switch would control the flow of traffic from the attached end station. The end station must have sufficient buffered space to accommodate traffic burst from the switch. Later we will see the rationale for this scheme.

The specification also supports half-duplex operation for shared connections using a single repeater and CSMA/CD operation. However, the MAC layer would have to be modified to compensate for inefficiencies associated with operating CSMA/CD at gigabit speeds. From a physical-medium perspective, it would be necessary for the new technology to operate over optic fiber and copper media. It was decided early on that

Fibre Channel technology would be leveraged to expedite the implementation of the Gigabit Ethernet technology.

Gigabit Hierarchy

Looking at the hierarchy from the top down, we see that the Data Link Layer hasn't changed, although the MAC has been enhanced to support CSMA/CD operation. The architecture of the Gigabit Ethernet is illustrated in Figure 2.21. The reconciliation sublayer (RS) is a transparent interface between the MAC sublayer and PHY and performs a function similar to that it performed in Fast Ethernet—that is, decouple the MAC from the PHY. However, the Gigabit RS collects 8 bits from the MAC for simultaneous transfer on the Gigabit Media Independent Interface (GMII), which contains 8-bit-wide transmit and receive data paths. In the migration from 10Mbps Ethernet to 100Mbps Ethernet, we saw that a new media-independent interface (MII) was required because the existing AUI could not scale to 100Mbps operation. Similarly, the MII used in 100Mbps Ethernet is not suitable for 1000Mbps operation. Therefore, GMII was developed with an 8-bit-wide data path and a 125MHz clock.

At the physical layer, we see the same components that were present in Fast Ethernet. However, in Fast Ethernet, we leveraged FDDI signaling and the physical sublayers were based on the FDDI specification. In Gigabit Ethernet, we rely on the physical sublayers specified for Fibre Channel because Fibre Channel operates at near gigabit speeds.

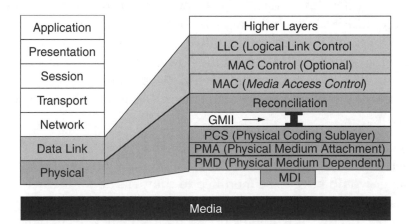

Figure 2.21   Gigabit hierarchy.

Gigabit Ethernet is generically referred to as 1000Base-X. However, this is a liberal interpretation. In fact, 1000Base-X applies only to Gigabit Ethernet implementations that use Fibre Channel's physical sublayers. Currently, all operating PHYs use Fibre Channel technology, although other PHYs are under development.

CSMA/CD Gigabit Ethernet

Modification to the MAC operation was required to support shared Gigabit Ethernet because when the speed of Ethernet is increased from 100Mbps to 1000Mbps, there is a corresponding decrease in the network diameter. The issue is similar to what was encountered in the increase from 10Mbps to 1000Mbps. As the transmission speed increases, the maximum distance between stations must be shortened so that all stations on the shared media can detect collision successfully.

It was reasoned that if the diameter of the network were limited to 20 meters, Gigabit Ethernet would not be widely implemented. Figure 2.22 shows the effect increasing speed and reliance on CSMA/CD has on the network diameter.

IEEE 802.3z introduced two enhancements to the MAC, carrier extension and frame bursting, that were designed to remove the distance limitation but keep the efficiency of Gigabit Ethernet reasonable.

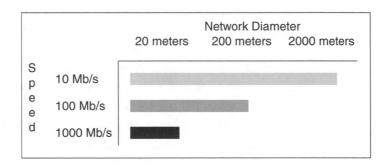

Increase work speed 10 times (100 Mb/s to 1000 Mb/s) = a corresponding decrease in network diameter (200m to 20m).

Figure 2.22   Half-duplex (CSMA/CD) issue.

Carrier Extension

Carrier extension serves to decouple the minimum frame size from the slot time. Recall that slot time is a critical component in CSMA/CD because it is instrumental in guaranteeing that a transmitting station will know if its transmission has been involved in a collision. To ensure detection of the collision, there is a mutual dependency on the minimum length of the frame and the farthest distance between stations within a collision domain. The mutual dependency is to prevent the situation in which one station begins a transmission and a station at the far end of the collision domain initiates its own transmission before the first bits from the first station arrive. In this scenario, a collision will occur, but the first station will not detect the collision unless the first station is still transmitting when the first bits from the far station's transmission arrive. If the first station is not transmitting when bits from the far station arrive, it will not realize there has been a collision because the first station will not see its transmit and receive links become active simultaneously. Slot time correlates the length of the shortest frame with the diameter of the collision domain or, more explicitly, the time it takes a bit to complete a round trip between the far ends of the collision domain. Obviously, as the bit time increases, the collision diameter must decrease accordingly.

If the minimum frame size were increased, the network diameter could also be increased. A change like this would necessitate a modification to IEEE 802.3 that would simply go against the grain of the specification because it would create many problems with existing 10Mbps and 100Mbps Ethernet implementations. It was reasoned that while it is necessary to increase the time that the transmit path remains active, it is not necessary to increase the minimum frame size. Minimum transmit time was increased to 512-byte times (4096-bit times) even though the frame size specification was not modified. A carrier extension symbol for 512-byte times was transmitted even though the actual frame may have been transmitted in as little as 64-byte times (512-bit times). With carrier extension, slot time is effectively increased by a factor of 8, and network diameter is increased to about 200 meters. In Figure 2.23, the carrier extension effectively increases the size of the frame to 512 bytes.

Carrier Extension—Transmit Operation

If the frame is 512 bytes or longer, there is no modification to the MAC. When the transmission is complete, the MAC sends a transmission completion indication to the upper layer. However, if the frame is shorter than

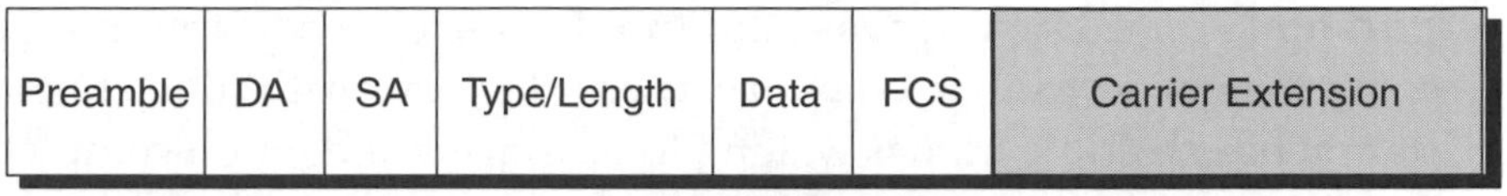

Preamble	DA	SA	Type/Length	Data	FCS	Carrier Extension

For Gigabit Ethernet, the 802.3 frame is extended, with the addition fo carrier extension bits. The frame on the wire is extended to a 512-byte slot time.

Figure 2.23   Carrier extension.

512 bytes, the MAC sends the frame to the physical layer and then, without interruption, signals the physical layer to continue transmission of carrier extension symbols. After 512-byte times, the MAC discontinues signaling the physical layer. The physical layer now proceeds with the interframe gap, and the MAC sends the transmission completion indication to the upper layer. The carrier extension symbol is a well-known symbol (Fibre Channel symbol).

Carrier Extension—Receive Operation

As the bits are buffered—except carrier extension symbols that are discarded—the *extend timer* is started. (The extend timer will run for 4096-bit times, which is the slot time.) If the extend timer has stopped running when the bits stop arriving, the slot time has been reached, and the receiver knows that the frame is valid. If the bits stop arriving before the slot time has expired, the receiver assumes that the frame has been involved in a collision and considers that the frame is a fragment. It is possible that the frame is not a fragment but instead a valid data frame and that the collision actually occurred during the transmission of the carrier extension symbols. Unfortunately, the frame is considered a fragment and is discarded. The receiving station's MAC will also notice that a collision has occurred and will initiate backoff and retransmission of the frame.

It should be obvious that carrier extension results in significant inefficiency in networks where there are many small-frame transmissions. To decrease the negative impact on performance, IEEE 802.3z introduced another modification to the MAC's operation called *frame bursting*.

Frame Bursting

As discussed earlier, after a station completes transmission of a frame, there is a quiet time called the interframe gap. The quiet time allows station-clocking circuitry to recover and stabilize and subsequently gives all stations equal (or near equal—recall the capture effect) access to the physical medium. Frame bursting was introduced to increase performance by lessening the impact associated with carrier extension. With frame bursting, if a station has multiple frames waiting to be transmitted, upon completion of the first frame transmission, the station keeps the channel occupied rather than initiating the interframe gap quiet period. So frame bursting prevents another station from capturing the channel. The net effect increases efficiency because only the first frame of the string of frames needs to have carrier extension applied.

With frame bursting, the station that has control of the path (instead of the interframe gap) transmits a control character. From the perspective of the other stations in the CSMA/CD collision domain, the path does not go idle, so the other stations continue to defer transmissions. Furthermore, the station controlling the path no longer has to be concerned with slot time because the physical medium has been active for a significant amount of time to detect any collisions. The station transmitting then sends a control frame (the same control frame is used for frame bursting that is used for carrier extension), and after 0.096 seconds (the interframe gap at 1000Mbps) transmits the next frame. So the transmitting station can transmit over 8000 bytes of data before relinquishing the physical medium. Also, regardless of the size of the frame in the string of frames, only the first frame has to be extended with carrier extension.

Frame Bursting—Transmit Operation

There is a MAC-controlled burst timer that is used to monitor frame bursting. When the MAC is ready to transmit a frame, it checks to see if the burst timer is running. If the burst timer is not running, the MAC sensed that the physical medium is not busy, and therefore, the frame is the first frame to be transmitted. The MAC starts the burst timer and commences to transmit the frame, including carrier extension, if the frame is less than 512 bytes in length.

If another frame is waiting to be transmitted, immediately upon completing transmission of the frame, the MAC signals the PHY to send a carrier extension symbol rather than initiating the interframe gap quiet time. The station commences transmission of the next frame in the burst sequence immediately after 0.096 microseconds of transmission of the carrier extension symbol. In Figure 2.24, the transmitting station inserts the carrier extension into the IPG, allowing the transmitting station to hold on to the media without relinquisning control for up to a burst limit of 8000 bytes—controlled by the *burst timer.*

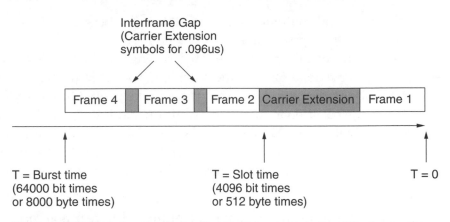

The transmitting station inserts the Carrier Extension into the IPG allowing the transmitting station to hold on to the media without relinquishing control for up to a burst limit of 8000 bytes—controlled by burst timer.

Figure 2.24 Frame bursting.

Why must we be concerned with IFG? Because it is possible that the frames are destined for a switch and will then be forwarded to a 10 or 100Mbps station. The carrier extension symbol is sent to indicate where the IFG belongs—so that the switch can apply the IFG—because the 10 or 100Mbps station can't understand the meaning of the symbol.

On the other hand, when the MAC is ready to transmit a frame and the burst timer is running, the MAC knows that the frame it is about to transmit is part of an existing burst sequence. The MAC also knows that it has control of the medium and that there is no chance of a collision. The MAC then transmits the frame with no carrier extension, regardless of the length of the frame.

Because the burst timer (64000 bit times and 8000 byte times) is examined only at the beginning of the transmission, the burst limit might actually exceed 8000 bytes. If the transmitting station has a 1500-byte frame to send before the burst timer has expired, the station might end up sending up to 9500 bytes in a single-frame burst.

Frame Bursting—Receive Operation

The receiving station collects the incoming bits, starts the carrier extension timer, and applies normal CSMA/CD rules. If upon reception of the frame the carrier extension timer has expired, the receiving station knows that this is a valid frame and continues with normal frame processing. If following the valid frame the receiver detects IFG symbols, then it knows that another frame that is part of a frame burst will be arriving and that it need not apply the carrier extend timer to the remaining frames in the burst. On the other hand, if upon receipt of the frame the carrier extend timer is still running, the frame has been involved in a collision and is discarded. In short, the receiving station must be concerned with a collision only during the slot time (or the first 512 bytes of the burst). Any carrier extend symbols that arrive after the slot time are interpreted as interframe gap.

In Figure 2.25 there are significant benefits when transmitting small frames. If we presume that we are transmitting 64-byte frames exclusively, the throughput is approximately 12 percent. When we introduce carrier extension and frame bursting, the efficiency is approximately 72 percent. The percentages are compared with the 76 percent efficiency we get when transmitting 64-byte frames with conventional Ethernet. A comparison of parameters for each Ethernet technology is shown in Table 2.3.

Flow Control in Gigabit CSMA/CD

As discussed in previous sections, CSMA/CD provides its own inherent flow control. However, when there is a switch supporting different-speed ports operating in half-duplex mode, there must be a mechanism to control the rate of traffic. For example, if a device (server) is connected to a

$$\text{No Carrier Extension: Throughput} = \frac{F}{F + 1 + P}$$

$$\text{Carrier Extension: Throughput} = \frac{F}{\max(S,F) + 1 + P}$$

$$\text{Carrier Extension + Bursting: Throughput} = \frac{F(1) + \sum\limits_{i=2}^{x} F(i)}{\max(S,F(1)) + \sum\limits_{i=2}^{x} (F(i) + p + I)}$$

F = frame size (bytes); S = slot time (4096 bits or 512 byte-times)
I = interframe gap (96 bits); p = preamble length (64 bits)
x = number of consecutive frames transmitted in Frame Burst
For example: F = 64 Bytes then:
            no carrier — throughput = 76%
            carrier extension — throughput = 12%
            carrier plus bursting (x = 93 frames) = 72%

Figure 2.25   Carrier extension and frame bursting efficiencies.

Table 2.3 10Mbps, 100Mbps, and 1000Mbps CSMA/CD Parameters

	10MBPS	100MBPS	1000MBPS
Slot time (bits)	512	512	4096
Bit time (us)	0.1	0.01	0.001
Interframe gap (us)	9.6	0.96	0.096
Transmit Attempts	16	16	16
Jam size	32	32	32
Maximum frame size (bytes)	1518	1518	1518
Minimum frame size (bytes)	64	64	64
Burst Size (bytes)	Not applicable	Not applicable	8192

switch at 1000Mbps and is transmitting traffic to another device (end station) connected to a switch at 10Mbps, at some point, it is likely that congestion will occur either at the switch or at the end station. The congestion would result in frame loss and throughput degradation. We demonstrated earlier that with full-duplex operation, IEEE 802.3z controlled the flow of traffic. To control the flow of traffic in a half-duplex situation, switches can rely on backpressure via carrier signal assertion. If traffic is arriving on a switch port at a rate in which the switch is becoming congested, the switch can assert carrier signal on the port. The remote MAC sees the link as busy and defers traffic. As the switch becomes uncongested or as the outbound port becomes uncongested, the switch can de-assert the carrier signal while the end station resumes transmitting traffic.

It should be reemphasized that carrier extension and frame bursting are enhancements to the CSMA/CM MAC and are not used when the MAC is operating in full-duplex mode. In addition, the use of back pressure to control the rate of traffic applies only to ports operating in half-duplex mode. Currently, there are no implementations of half-duplex Gigabit Ethernet.

Full-Duplex Gigabit Ethernet

Full-duplex Gigabit Ethernet supports only point-to-point connections. Because we are not operating in CSMA/CD mode, we do not need to be concerned with slot time, carrier extension, or frame bursting. Frame format and size constraints do not change; the interframe gap is still required; and, of course, we must still be concerned with distance limitation—that is, how far we can drive the signal—due to signal attenuation and distortion. Because we are operating in full-duplex mode, the MAC does not need to defer transmission during reception. Collision indication is ignored, and the MAC must support flow control.

Gigabit Physical Layer

There are several architectural differences between Gigabit Ethernet and Fast Ethernet (see Figure 2.26). One significant difference between the Fast Ethernet and Gigabit Ethernet architectures is how flow control is implemented. In Fast Ethernet, flow control is implemented in the auto-negotiation sublayer of the physical layer. Also in Fast Ethernet, auto-negotiation and flow control were specified only for 100Base-T. They were not provided for fiber links because the fast link pulse mechanism used for auto-negotiation was not well suited to optical signaling. With Gigabit Ethernet, auto-negotiation and flow control are specified for all physical media. In fact, because fiber is currently the preferred medium, it is especially important that auto-negotiation and flow control work over the fiber medium. In Gigabit Ethernet, auto-negotiation and flow control are specified in the PCS sublayer. It is leveraged from Fast Ethernet with modification to support direct in-band signaling. Whereas Fast Ethernet relied on out-of-band fast link pulses, Gigabit Ethernet relies on normal signaling using 8B/10B symbols, where a 10-bit symbol is used to represent an 8-bit character, to exchange *base link code words.* The symbols were necessary because link pulse used with copper does not translate directly onto fiber.

Another significant difference from Fast Ethernet is that IEEE 802.3x was modified to support asymmetric flow control. Asymmetric flow control means that the switch can control the flow of traffic from the attached device, but the attached device cannot control the flow of traffic from the switch. The intent is to stop traffic at the source so that additional buffering in intermediate switches is not needed. In addition, attached devices, endstation, routers, and so on will have to buffer frames until congestion eases. End devices and routers should have sufficient buffer capacity to accommodate the requirement. Also, switches should not flow control between them because doing so will aggravate head-of-line (HOL) blocking. HOL happens because the switch relies on first-in–first-out (FIFO)-input buffering. If the first frame in a queue is directed to a paused port, either frame behind the first frame (head-of-the-line) will be blocked, or a sophisticated forwarding scheme will need to be implemented.

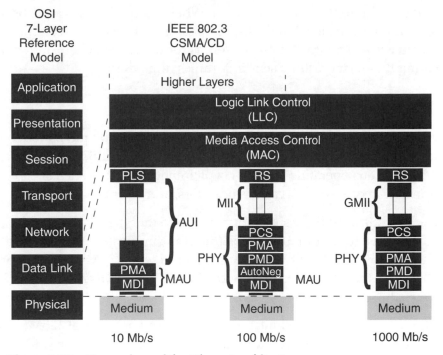

Figure 2.26 Comparison of the Ethernet architectures.

Flow Control Operation

Switches implement a flow control policy that is based on thresholds or watermarks. There is typically a high watermark and a low watermark in each input buffer. As frames arrive, they are accumulated in the buffer. If the frames in the buffer exceed the low watermark, a Pause is sent to the attached device. The Pause indicates a number of slot times that the device should wait before it resumes transmissions. After the attached device resumes transmissions, it is possible that the switch is still experiencing congestion, and consequently, frames may accumulate in the buffer such that the frame level exceeds the high watermark. In this case, the switch sends a Pause with a longer wait period. The watermarks should be configured with the expectation that it will take some period of time before the Pause reaches the attached device and during that period of time frames will continue to arrive. The watermarks should be such that the frames are not dropped. The Pause or number of slot times associated with each watermark is configurable.

Another algorithm that has been implemented specifies that whenever frames accumulate up to the high watermark, a Pause with a very long delay is sent to the attached station. When enough frames have been sent so that the frame level in the buffer is reduced to the low watermark, a Pause with a wait time equal to zero is sent to the attached station, indicating that it can resume sending frames immediately.

Mapping of GMII signals to PLS

As stated earlier, the reconciliation sublayer and gigabit media-independent interface interconnect the MAC sublayer and PHY entities. This includes an 8-bit data bus operating at 125MHz plus control signals, such as transmit/receive clocks, carrier indicators, and error conditions.

IEEE 802.3z specifies a signaling scheme so that the GMII provides signal support for 10, 100, or 1000Mbps (the chip supports both a MII and a GMII). For 1000Mbps the GTX-CLK is used with 125MHz. For 10 or 100Mbps, the TX-CLK is used with either 2.5 or 25MHz. Figure 2.27 illustrates the GMII interface signals.

RCV-CLK has function similar to TX-CLK's and operates at 125MHz for 1000Gbps. Carrier sense (CRS) is used to indicate the presence of a signal on a medium in half-duplex mode. Collision(COL) is used to indicate a collision in half-duplex mode. When the MAC wants carrier extension symbols sent, it notifies the PHY via TX-EN. RX-ER indicates that the carrier extension is active on the channel. *Management data clock/management data input and output* (MDC/MDIO) are specified for Fast Ethernet and have similar functionality in Gigabit Ethernet. Generally, the station management entity

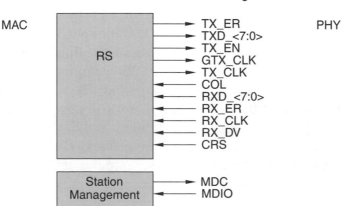

Figure 2.27   Gigabit media-independent interface signals.

is located in the MAC controller. The management frames are passed between the PHY Registers and MAC, and the *management data clock* (MDC) provides clocking for the transmission of the management frames.

There are four types of registers:

Management registers. Used to indicate auto-negotiation capabilities.

Control registers. Used to configure and reset the PHY.

Status registers. Contain status and condition of the PHY information.

Extend registers. Used exclusively for Gigabit Ethernet and contain status information for 1000Base-X PHYs.

Typically, there will be one RS per MAC. However, a single RS can support four or eight MACs (for example, quad MAC). In this case, the TX-CLK, which normally runs at 25MHz for FE, operates at 100MHz and multiplexes the four MACs.

Gigabit Ethernet Physical Layer

The Gigabit Ethernet standard supports a family of physical-layer implementations for various media. 1000Base-X implies that the *physical coding sublayer* (PCS) uses Fibre Channel FC-1 and FC-0 standard. The PCS contains the 8B/10B encoder/decoder for use with optical fiber and short-haul, copper links. When the 8B/10B encoding scheme transmits, 8 bits are represented by a 10-bit "code group." The transmission is DC-balanced to support electrical requirements. (There are two encodings for most bytes. Depending on where your DC level is, you'll pick from either column A or column B as to how you encode the particular byte.) The 8B/10B encoding ensures that enough transitions are present in the serial-bit stream for accurate clock recovery and error detection at the receiver. Figure 2.28 shows the Gigabit Ethernet architecture depicting the various supported PHYs.

The PCS also manages the auto-negotiation process that determines the link speed and mode of operation (full/half duplex). In half-duplex (CSMA-CD) mode, the PCS is responsible for carrier sense and collision detect. The *physical medium attachment* (PMA) sublayer performs 10-bit serialize/deserialize functions (referred to SERDES). The PMA receives 10-bit encoded data at 125MHz from the PCS and delivers a serialized data stream to the PMD sublayer. The PMA also receives serialized data from the PMD sublayer and delivers deserialized 10-bit data to the PCS sublayer. The *physical medium dependent* (PMD) sublayer and the *medium*

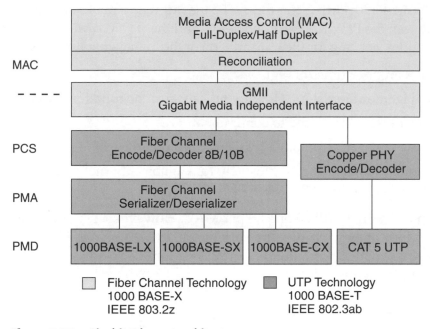

Figure 2.28   Gigabit Ethernet architecture.

dependent interface (MDI) provide the media transceivers and connectors for the various media. Both *long wavelength* (LX) and *short wavelength* (SX) optical drivers are supported as well as short-haul copper (25 meters over Category 5 UTP).

Fibre Channel was developed by IBM as a way to transfer data between storage devices, mainframes, and workstations over fiber cabling. The Fibre Channel architecture includes five layers; however, only the lowest two layers, FC-0 and FC-1, are used in 1000Base-X. FC-0 defines the physical link, including the fiber, connectors, optical, and electrical parameters, for various data rates. Surprisingly, the data rates specified for Fibre Channel are 133Mbps, 266Mbps, 532Mbps, and 1064Mbps. The FC-0 specification was modified to support 1250Mbps that is required for Gigabit Ethernet. The FC-1 defines the transmission protocol, including encoding/decoding rules, special characters, and error control. The conversion from 8B to 10B leaves a number of 10-bit patterns (code groups) unused. The additional code groups are used by 1000Base-X to support auto-negotiation, flow control, start-and-end-of-packet delimiters, carrier extension characters, and so on. The relationship between Fibre Channel and Gigabit Ethernet Physical Layer is shown in Figure 2.29.

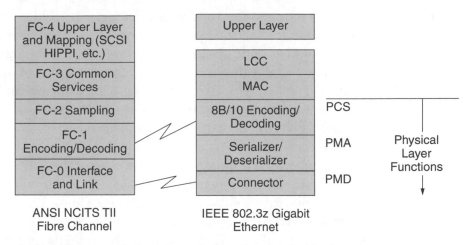

Figure 2.29   Use of Fibre Channel technology in Gigabit Ethernet.

Note that the data rate is 1250Mbps because we realize only 80 percent efficiency—a 10-bit code group represents only 8 bits of data. Figure 2.30 illustrates 8-bits being delivered from the GMII to the PCS. The PCS converts the 8-bit symbol into a 10-bit symbol for transmission.

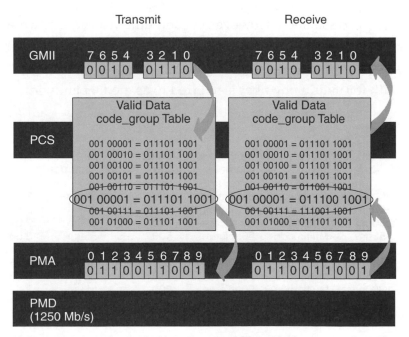

Figure 2.30   PCS encode/decode. 1000BaseX PCS leverages Fibre Channel (FC-1).

The PMD defines the standard for translating electrical signals to a suitable form for transmission of the specified physical medium, usually fiber optic. There are two types of fiber optic cabling: multimode (MMF) and single-mode (SMF). Light propagates through the core (central portion) of optical fiber. Multimode fiber, with a typical core diameter of 62.5 microns or 50 microns, is designed for coupling light from low-cost, LED-based transmitters. Single-mode fiber has a core diameter of 10 microns and is suitable only for laser-based transmission. Much of the installed base of optical fiber supporting LAN backbones is multimode because most of the current generation 10 or 100Mbps LAN equipment is LED-based. As mentioned before, 1000Base-X refers to those PMDs that utilize the Fibre Channel technology; that is, short wavelength optics (SX), long wavelength optics (LX), and coax (CX). There is another PHY that is currently under development (IEEE 802.3ab WG) called 1000Base-T, which operates over Cat 5 UTP. The 1000Base-CX PHY operates over twinax (two pairs of 150 ohm balanced coaxial) cable and is limited in run length to 25 meters.

The parameters that dictate the link distance—or how far the light signal can be sent—are the wavelength (frequency) of the light source, the diameter of the fiber, and the type of fiber.

Figure 2.31 summarizes the link lengths associated with each of the two fiber optic interfaces. Generally, fiber optic distances are limited by the power-budget dissipation. However, Gigabit Ethernet is not power-budget limited; rather, it is limited by distortion because of the high frequency.

The parameter used to indicate the distortion is the modal bandwidth. Bandwidth for multimode fiber is referred to as modal bandwidth

Transceiver	Laser	Fiber Type	Fiber Diameter	Model Bandwidth	Min Distance	Attenuation
1000Base-SX	850nm	Multimode	62.5 micron	160	220m	2.38 dB
1000Base-SX	850nm	Multimode	62.5 micron	200	275m	2.60
1000Base-SX	850nm	Multimode	50 micron	400	500m	2.37
1000Base-SX	850nm	Multimode	50 micron	500	550m	3.56
1000Base-LX	1300nm	Multimode	62.5 micron	500	550m	2.35
1000Base-LX	1300nm	Multimode	50 micron	400	550m	2.35
1000Base-LX	1300nm	Multimode	50 micron	500	550m	2.35
1000Base-LX	1300nm	Singlemode	9 micron		5000m	4.57

Figure 2.31   Physical medium-dependent sublayer (PMD).

because it varies with the modal field (or core diameter) of the fiber. Modal bandwidth is specified in units of MHz/km and refers to the total number of light pulses transmitted over some prescribed length of fiber that is still discernible at the far end. In other words, how fast can we inject individual light pulses into the fiber and still recognize the pulses when they emit the fiber? With multimode fiber, the light pulses take different paths. Because some paths are slower than others, pulse distortion (overlap) results at the far end. Pulse distortion is not an issue with single-mode fiber.

Fiber Overview

Most 1000Base-X implementations will be over fiber. The structure of the fiber is pictured in Figure 2.32. Optical fibers are made from a clear material, such as glass, in which two layers of the material are used: a core (through which light travels) and a cladding layer (that keeps the light in the core). The jacket provides protection from environmental factors.

Optic fibers transmit light via a phenomenon called Total Internal Reflection. There are two general types of fibers. Single-mode fiber has a core diameter that is small enough to limit the light transmission to a single path. Multimode fiber has a core with multiple paths. Because of differences in the refractive indexes of the layers, light that attempts to leave the core is reflected by cladding. Cladding allows signals to travel through the wire for long distances, even if the wire is bent, because

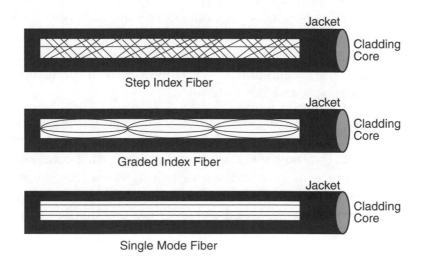

Figure 2.32 Fiber types.

cladding keeps the signal from "escaping." Each of the multimode fiber paths has a different end-to-end length. Consequently, light that travels in one path will take longer or shorter to reach the far end of the fiber. To compensate for the varying distances, the index profile of the fiber is varied such that light traveling the longer distance will travel faster. The intent is to have all light from the source pulse arrive at the far end at the same time. Typically, the light source used with single-mode fiber is a laser—a narrow, very defined source. The light source commonly used with multimode is a light-emitting-diode (LED), which is less expensive than laser but provides a more dispersed light source.

Differential Mode Delay Issue

Gigabit Ethernet operating at 1.25Gbps is too high a frequency for LEDs and requires the use of lasers. The 1000Base-X standard has introduced laser-based transmission over multimode fiber. The new type of transmission has introduced new types of physical layer issues.

Differential mode delay (DMD) is a phenomenon that results from using an extremely high-frequency light source over multimode fiber. For multimode fiber, the optimum index profile is nearly parabolic. However, precise control of the index profile is difficult to achieve and measure in production. One of the most common methods of manufacturing multimode fiber leaves a low index of refraction area in the center of the curve. In Figure 2.33, the optimum index profile is depicted on the left side while a problematic index profile is depicted on the right side. When a narrow laser source is used, it is possible that only the problematic portion of the multimode-fiber modes become excited; that is, it transmits the light. The transmission results in the signal's becoming distorted enough that it is unrecognizable at the far end of the fiber. However, the imperfections are normally not an issue with LED sources.

To address the DMD issue, the laser light source is conditioned or referred to as conditioned launch. The conditioned launch—usually implemented either internally to the transceiver or externally via a patch cord—is designed to introduce an offset to the laser launch that directs the laser beam away from the center of the multimode fiber. However, even with conditioned launch, gigabit transmission over multimode fiber is subject to the length limitation discussed previously.

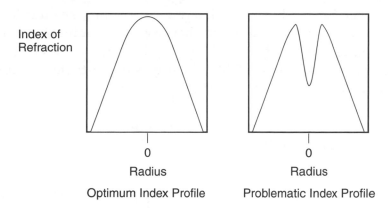

Figure 2.33 Graded index profile.

Conditioning either is built into the transceiver or can be external to the interface in the form of conditioning-patch cables. Conditioning is not required on long-haul, single-mode optics. However, conditioning patch cables are required when long-haul lasers (LXs) are used over multimode fiber across distances at the high end of the acceptable range for multimode. (Exactly when you start to need them depends on the installed cable plant and can be determined by measurement of the optical refractive index profile of a particular run or sometimes by trial and error; that is, does it work?)

Gigabit Ethernet Interface Carrier

The transceiver is typically incorporated directly into the gigabit interface and becomes a permanent part of the interface. The transceiver can support a particular physical medium (for example, 62.5 µm multimode or 50 µm single-mode fiber). The interface is not interchangeable or compatible with another type of fiber or copper link. The *Gigabit Ethernet interface converter* (GBIC) modular technology interface allows a Gigabit Ethernet port to support short-wave and long-wave lasers as well as copper physical interfaces. The technology comes from the Fibre Channel environment. Multiple transceivers are incorporated into a single, pluggable module. The configuration allows switch vendors to build a single physical switch or switch module that the customer can configure for the required laser/fiber topology. GBICs offer equipment designers and system users increased flexibility and ease of migration by allowing hot-swappable, system-configuration changes and upgrades in the field.

As stated earlier, Gigabit Ethernet initially supports three key media: short-wave laser, long-wave laser, and short copper. In addition, fiber optic cable comes in three types: multimode (62.5 μm), multimode (50 μm), and single mode. With the GBIC, the user is not restricted to particular physical medium.

1000Base-T (Gigabit Ethernet over Four-Pair 100 Ohm Category 5 UTP)

Largely because of the success of Fast Ethernet, Four-pair, 100 ohm, Category 5 UTP is the most widely deployed cabling system in high-speed LANs, especially for equipment in the network computing center and between computing centers. It is obvious that supporting Gigabit Ethernet over UTP could leverage the widespread deployment and provide a solution to the dramatic increases in bandwidth demands driven by desktop computing and Internet-based applications. A separate working group, IEEE 802.3ab, was chartered to support gigabit operation over UTP cable. A new working group was needed to provide the UTP solution because digital signal processing (DSP) expertise was required. The technical expertise had not been required in previous Fibre Channel–based, gigabit implementations. IEEE 802.3ab adds a new physical-layer, signaling system based on DSP to the basic technology defined by 1000Base-X.

Transmitting 1000Mbps over four-pair of Category 5 UTP presents several design challenges. The challenges are due to both the physical characteristics of the UTP cable and the dual-duplex, transmission technique deployed by 1000Base-T. Dual-duplex transmission means that signals will be sent in both directions simultaneously on all four wire pairs. When the signal is introduced onto the wire, a portion of the signal is reflected or returned because of impedance mismatches within the link, called echo. The unwanted portion of the signal (noise) must be removed from the attenuated signal that is arriving from the far end of the circuit. The echo (or network return loss) characteristics of the circuit become more important at higher frequencies, and at high frequencies, echo cancellation becomes quite difficult. Complex integrated circuit techniques that can effectively cancel the reflected energy must be introduced. Additional complexities include signal attenuation and cross talk as well as electromagnetic emissions and susceptibility.

Attenuation is the decrease in signal amplitude during transmission from one point to another. Attenuation also increases with frequency, so the challenge is to find the smallest frequency that can support the 1000Mbps data rate with the highest-quality data transfer for the desired distance (100 meters).

Cross talk is interference caused by the signal traveling in the opposite direction. Because 1000Base-T uses the same cable for the signal traveling in the opposite direction, the cross talk issue is even more significant than in conventional UTP implementations. Near-end cross talk (NEXT) is described as the relationship between the power presented on one pair of UTP and received as noise on the other pair at the same end. Far-end cross talk (FEXT) is the noise on the far end of the wire pair caused by leakage from the adjoining wire pairs. In addition, the transmission system operating over UTP is susceptible to energy radiated from other sources, such as AM, CB, cellular, and other external transmitters.

The characteristics of UTP cabling identified previously create a significant challenge in specifying 1000Base-T. To summarize, the high-signal frequency makes the signal attenuation significant. Additionally, cross talk and echo become enhanced because of the signal frequency, and in combination with ambient external noise, they all serve to further mask the signal. Fortunately, some recently developed digital communication techniques can make 1000Mpbs over UTP feasible. 1000Base-T utilizes DSP techniques to transform the desired-bit rate (data) into an acceptable baud rate (signal) for operation over four-pair Category 5 UTP.

The maximum rate at which data can be transmitted over a circuit is called channel capacity. Channel capacity can be increased through use of a multisignal encoding system. Typically, signal encoding involves two signal levels: one to represent 0 and another to represent 1. 1000Base-T uses five signal levels: Four signal levels are used to represent data, and the other level is used for error detection/correction.

Therefore, 1000Base-T uses all four pairs operating at 125MHz and five-level *pulse amplitude modification* (PAM), which transmits data as symbols. Each symbol represents 2 bits of information. With five-level PAM, each transmitted symbol represents one of five different levels (–2, –1, 0, +1, +2). For example, signal level –2 could represent bit combination 0,0, and –1 could represent 0,1 and so on. With this technique, 8 bits are transmitted every clock cycle (8 bits × 125MHz = 1Gbps). DSP hybrid circuits are used to enable bidirectional transmission over single-wire pairs by filtering out the transmit signal at the receiver end. Figure 2.34 illustrates the DSP hybrid circuit configuration that is used to support 1000Base-T.

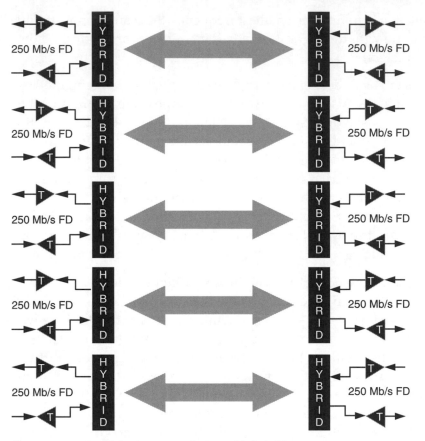

Figure 2.34   Dual duplex transmission with hybrids.

Gigabit Repeater

As in other CSMA/CD environments, the collision domain of the 1000Mbps LAN segment is constrained by the round-trip propagation delay characteristic of the network components. IEEE 802.3z defines two types of gigabit repeater environments called *transmission system model 1* and *transmission system model 2*.

Transmission system model 1 defines rules for DTE-to-DTE direct connection as well as rules for a single repeater connecting different physical signaling (1000Base-LX, 1000Base-SX, 1000Base-CX, 1000Base-T) segments into a single-collision domain. The allowed configurations have been validated under conservative rules. The model relies on these rules rather than calculating the round-trip propagation time on a case-by-case basis. Table 2.4 illustrates length limitations while Figure 2.35 illustrates the configuration for Transmission System Model 1 without a repeater.

Table 2.4   Transmission Model 1—Two DTEs Directly Connected—Distance Limitations

LINK	CAT 5 UTP	CX	LX OR SX
DTE to DTE	100m	25m	320m

Table 2.5   Transmission Model 1—a Single Repeater—Distance Limitation

LINK	CAT 5 UTP	CX	LX OR SX	CAT 5 AND LX OR SX	CX AND LX OR SX
One repeater	200m DTE to DTE	50m DTE to DTE	220m DTE to DTE	210m (a) DTE to DTE	220m (b) DTE to DTE

(a) Assumes 100m link of Cat-5 and 110m link of fiber
(b) Assumes 25m link of CX and 195m link of fiber

Table 2.5 illustrates length limitations while Figure 2.36 illustrates the configuration for Transmission System Model 1 with a repeater.

Transmission system model 2 specifies a single repeater and requires that the round-trip propagation time between any two DTEs does not exceed 4096-bit times. The user has more flexibility, but the user is responsible for ensuring that round-trip propagation constraints are not violated (see Table 2.6).

Round-trip propagation equals (Slink delay + (repeater delay + DTE delays + safety margin). Note: Safety margin is equal to 32-bit times by default.

The following illustrates the DTE A to DTE B round-trip propagation delay calculation in a transmission system model 2 network:

DTE A = 432 bit times

110m fiber link DTE-repeater = 1111

Repeater = 976

DTE   DTE

Figure 2.35   Transmission Model 1: Two DTEs directly connected.

Table 2.6 Transmission Model—Two Distance Limitations

COMPONENT	ROUND-TRIP DELAY BIT TIMES/METER	MAXIMUM ROUND-TRIP DELAY IN BIT TIMES (MAX LENGTH)
Each DTE		432
Cat 5	11.12	1112 (100m)
CX	10.10	253 (25m)
LX or SX	10.10	1111 (110m)
Repeater		976

100m CAT 5 link repeater-DTE = 1112

DTE B = 432

Safety margin = 32

The total = 4095-bit times (because less than a 4096 configuration is compliant)

The configuration is compliant with transmission system model 2 because when the delays contributed by all components are added together, the total is less than the 4096-bit time that is specified for the slot time (round-trip propagation). See Figure 2.37.

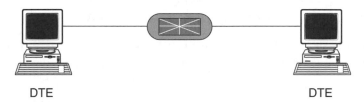

DTE   DTE

Figure 2.36   Transmission model 1: Single repeater.

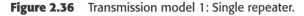
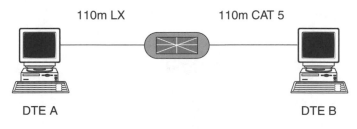

110m LX   110m CAT 5

DTE A   DTE B

Figure 2.37   Transmission system model 2.

Conclusion

Since its introduction Ethernet has proven to be an adaptable and resilient technology. Some would argue that the technology has evolved to the point that it bears little resemblance to the original Ethernet technology. After all, collision detection has been widely replaced by flow control, coaxial cable has been replaced by fire optical or unshielded twisted pair cable, the repeater has been replaced by the buffered distributor, the signaling protocol seems to change with each iteration of the technology, and, of course, the bit rate has gone from 10Mbps to 1000Mbps. However, regardless of these modifications, the format of the Ethernet frame has remained constant so that applications have not had to be modified as newer iterations of the technology have been introduced. Portions of the network can be upgraded as required with no impact to the users, except an increase in performance.

Ethernet evolved because of a need presented by a plethora of new applications that place increasing demands on the network. In the next chapter, we discuss some schemes that have been developed to better control the traffic and to allow prioritization of traffic within the Ethernet network.

These schemes allow the new applications to operate effectively and efficiently on the network. The next few chapters discuss some of these schemes and their individual advantages and disadvantages.

CHAPTER 3

Virtual Local Area Networks

In this chapter, we discuss virtual LANs (vLANs). vLANs provide one technique to manage traffic on Ethernet networks to accommodate new and increasingly demanding applications. As noted in the last chapter, Gigabit Ethernet has breathed new life into local area networks. At a time when real-time applications are emerging, Gigabit Ethernet provides an alternative to ATM to meet the response and bandwidth requirements of these applications. Initially, Gigabit Ethernet will be deployed at aggregation points such as between switches and server connections, but eventually Gigabit Ethernet may be used throughout the local area environment. Until Gigabit Ethernet is fully deployed, other techniques, such as vLANs, are needed.

Before addressing specific aspects of the switching evolution and virtual LANs in particular, let's examine the evolution to switching and vLANs from a historical perspective (see Figure 3.1).

During the early to mid-1980s, computing was dominated by the mainframe and to a lesser extent by minicomputers. It was during this time that bridges emerged. Bridges were developed primarily to eliminate the physical constraints of the local area networks and to provide some isolation from broadcast storms.

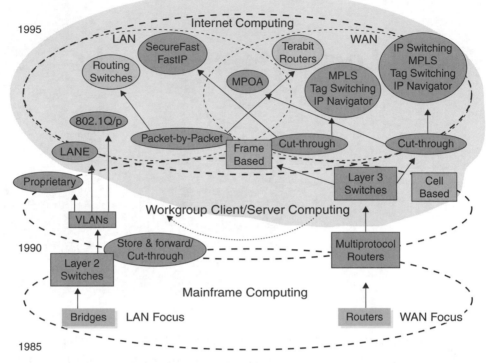

Figure 3.1 The switching evolution.

Also during this time, routers were introduced primarily to provide connectivity across the wide area and to provide connectivity between different technologies on the LAN; for example, between Ethernet and token ring. Routers at this time were software-driven devices. They typically supported a single routing protocol, such as IP, and a limited number of wide area technologies, such as X.25.

The desire to support multiple broadcast domains within a single device and to decrease the latency associated with bridges inspired the evolution from bridges to Layer 2 switches. To further decrease the latency associated with store-and-forward devices, the cut-through Layer 2 device emerged. At about the same time, routers began to support multiple routing protocols as well as bridging. However, the router was at this time still a software-interrupt–driven device.

During the early 1990s, the computer landscape began to shift. This shift was driven primarily by a new class of applications that were based on a client/server model of distributed computing. Client/server is a modular computational architecture that involves client processes requesting service from server processes. With client/server computing, the client component and the server component need not execute within the same memory space. The client/server model was further characterized on a workgroup basis in which clients of a particular workgroup are more inclined to access a particular server or set of servers.

This new compute model altered the traffic patterns and presented more stringent demands on the network to provide acceptable response times. The desire to categorize users into workgroups and to provide a degree of segmentation and isolation on a workgroup basis while allowing multiple workgroups to share the same physical network inspired the development of virtual local area networks, or vLANs. A vLAN may be defined as a set of devices that belong to the same broadcast domain yet are not constrained by their physical location. Because vLANs remove physical constraints of the Layer 2 domain and eliminate the requirement for routers to contain broadcast, there was much anticipation early on that vLANs could replace, or at least limit, routers. Since the workgroup client and servers are in the same broadcast domain, there is no need to traverse a router, and the delay associated with traversing the software-based router is avoided.

In the early 1990s, vLAN capability was an integral feature of switched LAN solutions from every major LAN equipment vendor. However, deployment of vLANs was slowed by the fact that mechanisms used to define and extend the vLAN between multiple switches were proprietary. And, of course, proprietary approaches are deployed with reluctance in multivendor/open network environments. Also, people realized they still had to route between vLANs, thereby diminishing some of the attractiveness.

Later, in the mid-1990s, standardized vLANs, using ATM Forum LANE or IEEE 802.1Q, emerged, and vLANs began to receive a broader acceptance. Ironically, during this same time frame, wire-speed hardware-based routers also emerged. The ability to perform routing without the latency typically associated with routers infringes on some of the benefits of vLANs.

Layer 2 Frame Switching and vLAN

Layer 2 frame switches forward frames based on the frame MAC address, and typically the forwarding is hardware assisted. There is a separate path between input and output ports. Because of these aspects, frame switches exhibit very high throughput and low latency characteristics. Layer 2 devices are typically inexpensive and are easily introduced into the network. In fact, Layer 2 switches are transparent to other devices attached to the LAN. Layer 2 devices support the IEEE 802.1D Spanning Tree protocol so that alternate physical paths can be created to provide redundancy in the event of failure, yet loops in the data path will be avoided. Most modern Layer 2 frame switches possess vLAN capabilities.

vLAN Types

As noted, a vLAN consists of a group of devices that are members of a common broadcast domain; that is, the devices communicate with each other as though they were attached to the same physical segment. Initially, vLANs were confined to a single switch, and ports on the switch were manually configured to participate in a specific broadcast domain. What types of vLANs are there, and how does a device become a member of a particular vLAN? Several approaches have been widely implemented. The most common type of vLAN is the port-based vLAN. A particular port is explicitly (and manually) specified to be a member of a specific vLAN, essentially defining the vLAN. Port-based vLANs are static; they are created manually, and the port will continue to participate in the vLAN until it has been manually reconfigured out of the vLAN.

Typically, vLANs are identified with a numeric assignment—for example, vLAN #20 or vLAN #91.

Later, when IEEE 802.1Q is discussed, we will see that some aspects of the vLAN have been standardized. However, IEEE 802.1Q does not currently specify how a vLAN is created.

Note that the vLAN exists solely from the perspective of the switch port. That is, the device attached to the port has no knowledge of the vLAN.

Figure 3.2 shows that when a device that is connected to a port configured in vLAN 22 sends a broadcast frame, that frame is sent by the switch on all ports that are configured in vLAN 22. The end device has no knowledge itself about any vLAN—the vLAN exists solely from the perspective of the switch. Another important point is that devices connected to ports configured in vLAN 22 cannot directly communicate with devices attached to ports configured in vLAN 33. Since these are separate broadcast domains, a router is required.

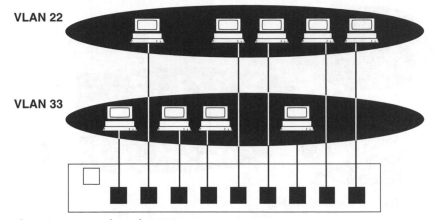

VLAN 22

VLAN 33

Figure 3.2   Port-based vLANs.

Another important point about port-based vLANs is that typically, a port can belong to only one port-based vLAN. (This is reasonable because it would not be possible for a port to simultaneously be connected to multiple real LANs.) Also, there should be an instance of the spanning tree protocol supporting each port-based vLAN. Since port-based vLANs must be manually configured, they do not exhibit some of the administrative advantages that are realized with dynamic vLANs.

With MAC-based vLANs, membership is based on the MAC address of the attached device (see Figure 3.3). Ports are assigned to MAC-based vLANs dynamically; that is, the port is assigned to a particular vLAN only after it has received a frame that matches the particular vLAN criterion. A table is manually constructed within the switch that associates each MAC address with a specific vLAN. When the workstation transmits a frame to the switch, the switch examines that frame's source MAC address and references the table to see which vLAN this MAC address should be associated with. The vLAN port is then put into that particular vLAN. After the initial manual configuration, a workstation may be moved to a different physical location (that is, a different port on the switch), and the workstation will automatically retain is vLAN membership. MAC-based vLANs are generally small because of the administrative overhead of defining the tables that associate a MAC address with a vLAN. Some vendors have devised schemes to simplify the construction of the MAC-to-vLAN tables. An advantage of MAC-based vLANs is that they do provide considerable security because it is difficult to spoof a MAC address. Typically, devices that support MAC-based vLANs allow a port to belong to only one MAC-based vLAN at a time; thus, MAC-based vLANs should not be implemented in shared environments.

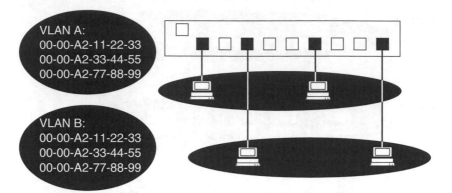

Figure 3.3   MAC-based vLANs.

Protocol-based vLANs are Layer 2–based vLANs. They are defined by the Ethernet frame's Ethertype (or Protocol Type) field. These vLANs are generally used to segment broadcast domains in environments in which there are multiple Layer 2 protocols—for example, NETBIOS and LAT. Although supported by some vendors, protocol-based vLANs based on routable protocols, such as IP and IPX, are typically implemented only to meet specialized requirements.

Policy-based vLANs are defined by Layer 3 information, such as an IP subnet. These vLANs are also dynamic. Policy-based vLANs provide user mobility (see Figure 3.4).

Again, a table is constructed within the switch that associates some Layer 3 information, such as an IP subnet, with a particular vLAN. When the switch receives a frame on a port, it examines the source IP subnet and references the table to determine to which vLAN the port belongs. Users can physically move their workstations without having to reconfigure

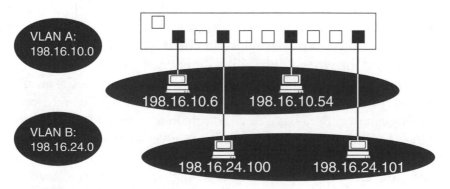

Figure 3.4   Policy-based vLAN.

their workstation's IP address. As soon as the workstation sends a frame, the switch will automatically configure the attached port into the vLAN broadcast domain.

Unfortunately, IP subnet-based vLANs may actually create problems in networks where Dynamic Host Configuration Protocol (DHCP) is used to administer workstation IP addresses. Subnet-based policy vLANs support location-independent broadcast domains whereas DHCP dynamically allocates IP address to workstation for fixed periods of time. When DHCP recognizes that a workstation has moved, it simply allocates a new IP address that is consistent with the workstation's new physical location. In this fashion, DHCP allows the workstation to move from subnet to subnet without the network administrator's involvement. In other words, when a workstation moves within a policy-based vLAN, the physical topology of the broadcast domain is modified.

DHCP handles changes by reconfiguring the client while a vLAN-capable network handles the change by reconfiguring the network port the client is moved to. DHCP dynamic configuration requires a DHCP server and DHCP client software in the workstation. Subnet-based vLANs are not standardized. vLAN support is proprietary, and any vendor interoperability is probably coincidental. Also, note that when the vLAN spans multiple switches (we will talk about this shortly), all switches throughout the network must be vLAN capable, and each must support the same vLAN schemes.

Although DHCP assigns an IP address to the workstation while IP-based vLANs enable a port to participate in a broadcast domain, DHCP- and IP-based vLANs are not compatible. They should (generally) not be used together. (Some vendor implementations of vLANs in concert with DHCP enhancements do support simultaneous operation of DHCP and Subnet vLANs.) The issue with trying to use DHCP and subnet-based vLANs at the same time is that the vLAN-capable network determines the workstation's vLAN based on the workstation's source IP address. Doing so assumes the workstation is already configured with an IP address, which precludes the use of the network to get the configuration information from a DHCP server.

When should policy vLANs or DHCP be used? Generally, DHCP is aimed at giving "easy moves" capability to networks that are divided into subnets on a geographical basis or on separate physical networks. vLANs are generally aimed at allowing network managers to set up subnets on some basis other than geographical; for example, instead of putting everyone in one office on the same subnet, putting on a subnet each person who has access to the servers that that person requires. Since DCHP is an IP-based protocol in situations where it is desirable to contain broadcasts from non-IP protocols, vLANs are preferred to DHCP. Also, in situations where Layer 2 access is more critical than confining the broadcast domain, policy-based vLANs are preferred. For example, if latency is an issue such that the primary concern is that workstations be able to access a server without traversing a router regardless of the workstation location, the policy-based vLAN is preferred. However, in a well-defined purely IP environment where there are a limited number of workstations and few subnets and the need to dynamically create independent logical workgroups is diminished, DHCP provides a simple approach to IP address administration.

Although DHCP and policy-based IP subnet vLANs are generally mutually exclusive, DHCP may work in a complementary fashion with other types of vLANs. With port-based vLANs, the workstation IP address must be reconfigured when the workstation moves to a new port-based vLAN. Implementing DHCP with a DHCP "scope" defined on the port-based vLAN basis allows this address reconfiguration to happen automatically.

Extending vLANs

The real benefit of vLANs is realized when the vLAN is extended beyond a single switch. In order to extend a vLAN beyond a single switch, there must be a way of conveying vLAN membership between vLANs. Switches must be able to determine to which vLANs the attached stations belong and how to forward frames arriving from a remote switch. Generally, the vLANs are manually configured on each switch and on each intervening switch. And vLAN membership information is carried within each frame, either explicitly or implicitly.

In this scenario, as shown in Figure 3.5, switch 1 and switch 3 have attached devices (ports) that belong to vLAN A. When the station attached to switch 1 sends a broadcast, the broadcast frame must be forwarded through switch 2, even though switch 2 has no attached devices that are members of vLAN A. This operation is straightforward for static port-based vLANs but is more complicated for dynamic vLANs. Also, processing at switch 2 and switch 3 can be reduced when the frame is

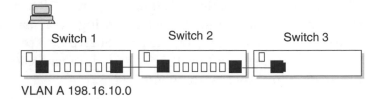

VLAN A 198.16.10.0

■ VLAN A

Figure 3.5 vLAN membership between switches.

tagged with a vLAN identifier (VID) so that the frame may be forwarded without having to be reprocessed to determine vLAN membership. With implicit tagging, vLAN membership is conveyed via some field within the frame; for example, the Source MAC or the source IP address, or, in the case of ATM, the implicit tag may be a VPI. With explicit tagging, vLAN membership is generally conveyed via some additional field within the frame. Prior to IEEE 802.1Q, vLAN membership was conveyed in a proprietary manner, and the vLAN tagging scheme was also handled proprietarily. Besides the proprietary vLAN tags, some other interoperability issues are raised. One is that vendors differ in the way they deal with frames that are larger than the acceptable maximum MAC-layer frames that result from the introduction of the explicit VIDs. Also, these larger frames increase the amount of overhead in the network, and the modified frame format may impact network management and troubleshooting methods that are currently being used.

IEEE 802.1p and IEEE 802.1Q

Although 802.1p and 802.1Q are often used together, there are differences and distinctions worth understanding. Basically, 802.1p is an enhancement to (and now a part of) 802.1D. In 802.1D, traffic forwarding is based on what the bridge has learned; that is, a MAC address is associated with a given port, and traffic is filtered and forwarded accordingly. Also with 802.1D, multicast frames are generally forwarded on all ports. There is no mechanism for the switch to determine whether or not there is a station attached to a port that needs to receive the multicast frame. The enhancement that 802.1p provides to 802.1D is the ability for bridges to dynamically and proactively modify the filtering database so that multicast traffic is forwarded only onto ports that have a station either directly attached or further downstream that needs to receive the multicast frame. A common use would be for an end station to join an IP multicast group, and the switch would set a filter in its forwarding database to ensure that the multicast is propagated on the port. 802.1p also provides a frame prioritization scheme to support the expedited transmission of time-critical information in LAN environments.

802.1Q extends the concepts proposed and defined in 802.1p in order to provide a set of capabilities to support the definition and management of vLANs. For example, 802.1Q extends the priority handling aspects of 802.1p to make use of the ability of the vLAN frame format to carry user priority information end to end across any set of underlying MAC services.

 The uppercase *Q* and lowercase *p* are significant. IEEE 802.1p is an extension to IEEE 802.1D. It does not stand alone. In fact, IEEE 802.1p is actually referenced as IEEE802.1D/p. IEEE 802.1Q is an independent specification that stands alone and separate from any other specification, although it certainly does make numerous references to IEEE 802.1D/p.

IEEE 802.1p (1997) Concepts

In the mid-1990s, IP multicast applications began to take hold. There was a new interest in videoconferencing, distance learning, and other applications that could benefit from a one-to-many delivery scheme. However, IP multicasting was devised as a Layer 3 protocol. On LANs, there was no way of directing the multicast frames explicitly to stations that requested to participate in the multicast group. (See the next chapter for a discussion of IP Multicast.) When the IP multicast frame arrives at the MAC-bridge, it is flooded onto all ports. Also, these multimedia applications present a new challenge for the network in that they require real-time, or near real-time, response. The IEEE 802.1p Working Group was devised explicitly to address these issues.

IEEE 802.1p defines the Generic Attribute Registration Protocol (GARP). It is used to communicate generic attribute information between switches and clients and servers. The services provided by GARP are at the Link Layer and are similar to those provided by IGMP at the Network Layer. GARP associates a set of properties, or attributes, with a Group MAC address and defines the port forwarding and filtering behavior of frames destined for that Group. Because GARP is a Layer 2 transport mechanism, it can be used with any Layer 3 protocol.

With GARP, a device asks to receive a specific attribute and forwards the request to the adjacent bridge. (Actually, GARP is a generic protocol. Other protocols that we will discuss shortly specify the exact attribute—for example, frames from a certain vLAN.) The bridge propagates the request throughout the network, and each GARP-capable device updates its MAC forwarding database, indicating that the attribute (should it have or receive it) must be forwarded in the direction of the requestor. In Figure 3.6, end station A requests to receive an attribute and the request is propagated through the network so that when any switch receives a frame with attribute A, the switch will forward that frame in the direction of the end station that requested to receive it.

When a second device declares that it wants to receive the same attribute, that request too is propagated throughout the network, the MAC forwarding tables are updated accordingly, and a path is created between the two stations.

When either of the stations sends the particular attribute, that attribute is forwarded in the direction of the other station only (see Figure 3.7).

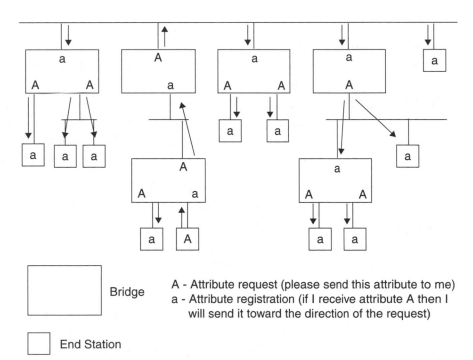

Bridge

End Station

A - Attribute request (please send this attribute to me)
a - Attribute registration (if I receive attribute A then I will send it toward the direction of the request)

Figure 3.6 GARP operation—attribute propagation from one station.

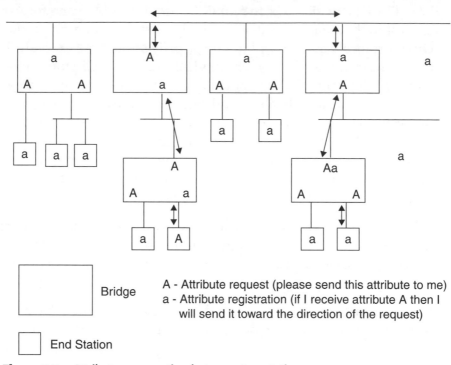

Bridge

A - Attribute request (please send this attribute to me)
a - Attribute registration (if I receive attribute A then I
    will send it toward the direction of the request)

End Station

Figure 3.7   Attribute propagation between two stations.

GARP is a generic protocol. In addition to GARP, IEEE 802.1p specifies a specific implementation of the GARP framework called the GARP Multicast Registration Protocol (GMRP). With GMRP, IP multicast group membership is the attribute that is propagated using the GARP protocol. GMRP is a GARP application that performs a function loosely analogous to the Internet Group Management Protocol (IGMP) in that it is a mechanism by which end stations join and leave a particular multicast group. (Of course, GMRP operates at Layer 2 whereas IGMP operates at Layer 3.)

An end station issues a GMRP message requesting to participate in a particular IP multicast group. In Figure 3.8, the GMRP message is propagated throughout the network, and the MAC forwarding tables are modified so that when the server generates a message in the multicast group, that message is forwarded only in the direction of the station that is participating in the multicast group.

In order to participate in GMRP, the end station must have the capability to generate the GMRP Join Request. A more common way, albeit not as sophisticated, to prune the Layer 2 multicast tree is via IGMP Snooping. We discuss this technique in the next chapter.

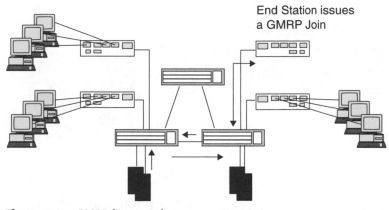

End Station issues
a GMRP Join

Figure 3.8 GMRP in operation.

Although IEEE 802.1p does not explicitly specify the frame format that supports frame prioritization (this is part of 802.1Q), 802.1p does specify the algorithm for forwarding frames according to the frame's traffic class. For each port, frames are selected for transmission on the basis of the traffic classes that the port supports. For a given supported value of traffic class, frames are selected from the corresponding queue for transmission only if any queues corresponding to numerically higher values of traffic class supported by the port are empty at the time of selection. The specification does allow support for additional implementation-specific algorithms.

IEEE 802.1Q (1998) Architecture

Despite the promise of vLANs to provide an effective solution to overwhelmed routers, to contain broadcast storms, and to help free up bandwidth, vLAN acceptance has been slowed for several reasons, most importantly because multiswitch vLANs are proprietary. IEEE 802.1Q provides a standardized approach to extending the vLAN between switches. The IEEE 802.1Q Architecture is illustrated in Figure 3.9. It also provides a mechanism to propagate vLAN registration among switches. IEEE 802.1Q also defines a frame format that supports a standardized tagging scheme to support multiplexing vLANs over physical links and a field to specify a frame's priority.

Configuration

Configuration specifies which vLANs are defined and how they are configured. For example, a specific priority may be associated with a given vLAN. This information may be stored in the switch's Management Infor-

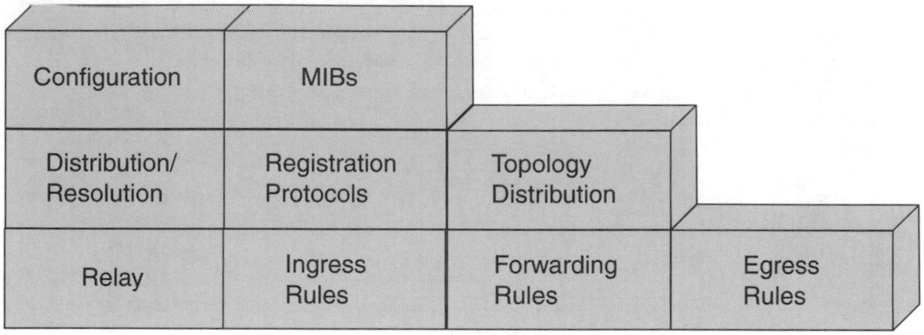

Figure 3.9   802.1Q vLAN architectural framework.

mation Base (MIB) and be accessed via SNMP. However, these are only suggestions. How this information is stored and accessed is implementation specific, and the actual determination is beyond the scope of 802.1Q. Note that 802.1Q is not concerned with types of vLANs or how the vLANs are defined. The only type of vLAN mentioned in the specification is a port-based vLAN. The specification does not preclude other types of vLANs. It is simply not concerned with vLAN definitions. Although the specification is not directly concerned with vLAN definitions, the user must certainly be aware of vLAN definition specifics, especially where a vLAN is being extended between different vendor switches.

Distribution/Resolution

The distribution and resolution component of the architecture is responsible for distributing vLAN information to all switches so that the switch will be able to determine to which vLAN a received frame should be classified. Reliable operation of the vLAN infrastructure requires vLAN membership information to be consistent across all vLAN-capable switches in the LAN to ensure proper forwarding and delivery of frames. The information may be manually configured in the switches or the GARP vLAN Registration Protocol (GVRP) may be used to automatically disseminate it.

GVRP is a GARP application that provides a vLAN registration service that allows GVRP-aware devices to dynamically establish and update their knowledge of the set of vLANs that currently have active members and through which switch ports those members can be reached. vLAN-aware end stations may participate in GVRP. GVRP provides a way for the end station to inform the switch to which it is attached that it is participating in a particular vLAN. The vLAN is identified with the VID numeric value.

GVRP propagates the VID information to other switches. Doing so ensures that switches will forward frames to all vLAN members, even though the switch itself may have no active participants in the vLAN.

Non-vLAN–aware end stations have no need (or capability) to register vLAN membership via GVRP. (This is a subtle aspect of 802.1Q. Prior to 802.1Q, end stations had no knowledge of vLANs. The vLAN existed solely from the perspective of the switch. With 802.1Q, end stations that are GVRP capable may actually register to participate in vLANs, and they may also generate 802.1Q frames specifying vLAN membership and priority.) Non-vLAN–aware end stations receive their vLAN registration requirements by means of a Port VID and possibly other implicit tagging mechanisms. After the non-vLAN–aware end station has been identified by the switch as belonging to particular vLAN, this vLAN membership information is propagated to other switches via GVRP.

In Figure 3.10, end station A is vLAN aware and issues a GVRP registration message for VID 101. This information is propagated to the other switches. However, only when end station B also registers for the same vLAN is a path created, and frames tagged with VID 101 are allowed to flow between end station A and end station B. Note that it is possible that a non-vLAN–aware end station may have evoked the same action. We will see how this could happen shortly. Also, GVRP supports proactive deregistration from a vLAN whereby an end station indicates that it no

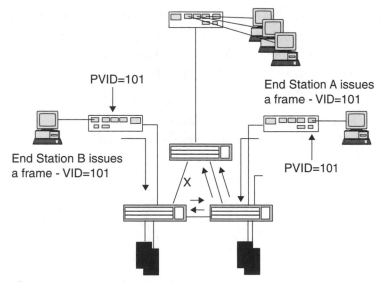

Figure 3.10   GVRP in operation.

longer wishes to receive frames destined for a particular VID. Of course, this information is also propagated to other switches.

IEEE802.1Q does not mandate that a switch implement GVRP. In fact, to date, there are few implementations that propagate vLAN membership using GVRP. Most implementations rely on manual configuration of the vLANs at each switch. This approach is allowed by the specification, and switches that manually configure may still be compliant with the 802.1Q specification.

Relay

The Relay component of the architecture is concerned with the mechanics of:

- Classifying frame to vLANs—ingress rules
- Making decisions related to where the frame should be forwarded—forwarding rules
- Mapping frames for transmission through the appropriate outbound port and queue and in the appropriate format (tagged or untagged)—egress rules

IEEE 802.1Q Concepts

IEEE802.1Q defines several different types of links. A trunk link allows multiplexing of different vLANs between 802.1Q devices. In Figure 3.11, the frames that traverse the trunk line will have 802.1Q tags identifying to which vLANs they belong. All devices that connect to a trunk link must be 802.1Q aware. All frames, including end station frames, on a trunk link are explicitly tagged as belonging to a specific vLAN.

Access links are used to multiplex one or more vLAN-unaware devices onto a port of an 802.1Q switch. All frames on an access link are untagged. They inherit a vLAN only after they are processed at the 802.1Q switch. Also, all frames sent to the end station will be untagged;

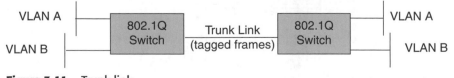

Figure 3.11   Trunk link.

even if the frame has a tag, the switch must remove it before forwarding the frame to the end station. Usually, end stations will connect to an 802.1Q switch via an access link. However, 802.1Q end stations are emerging, and these devices are capable of explicitly tagging frames that they send onto the link. In this case, the link to the switch would have to be either a trunk link or a hybrid link.

A hybrid link supports both tagged and untagged frames. Note that all frames belonging to the same vLAN that are traversing a particular hybrid link must be either all untagged or all tagged and carrying the same VID.

There can be a mix of tagged and untagged frames, but they must be for different vLANs. In Figure 3.12, all frames for vLAN A are tagged on the hybrid link, and all frames for vLAN C are untagged on the hybrid link. On the hybrid link the decision to tag or to not tag a frame is a function of the vLAN and not a function of the link itself because both frame formats are allowed. The port that accesses the hybrid link will be configured as untagged for vLAN C, yet for vLAN A, the same port will be configured as tagged.

Typically, switch ports are untagged by default, and the links are access or hybrid links. Making the ports untagged ensures that the 802.1Q switch can interoperate with 802.1D switches and also so that spanning tree messages may be freely exchanged.

All switch ports, except trunk ports, belong to a single port-based vLAN. The port-based vLAN to which the port belongs is identified via a PVID

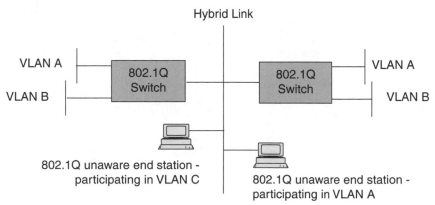

Figure 3.12 Hybrid link.

numeric value. Initially, all ports belong to a default port-based vLAN (PVID = 1), but the port may be reassigned to a different port-based vLAN. Any untagged frame that enters the switch becomes a member of the vLAN identified by the PVID for the port through which the frame entered. Conceptually, the port itself does not belong to a vLAN; rather, the frame that enters the port belongs to the vLAN, and the frame inherits the PVID.

Also associated with each switch port are one or more VIDs, which identify all the vLANs in which the port is participating. When a frame arrives at the switch, the frame will be identified as belonging to a vLAN (either by a VID within the frame or via the port on which the frame arrives), and the frame will be forwarded onto all ports that have a matching VID.

In the diagram, Figure 3.13, each of the three access ports belongs to a different port-based vLAN, and each is configured with a different PVID. Also, each of the ports is configured to receive frames from other vLANs. For example, the leftmost port is configured with a PVID=2. So when ES1 sends a frame (it will of course be untagged because the link is an access link), the switch will assign the frame to vLAN 2, and the frame will be forwarded onto the middle port because the middle port is configured to receive frames with a VID=2. When station S1 sends a frame, the untagged frame will be assigned to vLAN 4 (PVID=4) and the frame will be forwarded on the leftmost and the rightmost ports because each of these ports is configured to receive frames that belong to the vLAN with a VID=4.

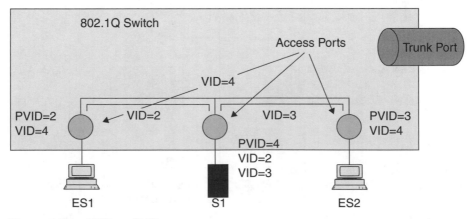

Figure 3.13 PVID and VID.

Also associated with each port is a priority. The priority is a numerical value (0–7). A higher numeric value corresponds to higher-priority frame. Frames of a given priority are forwarded as specified in 802.1p; basically, higher-priority frames are transmitted before lower-priority frames. It is allowable for a switch to modify the priority of a received frame according to a manually configured User Priority Regeneration Table.

IEEE 802.1Q Frame Header

A tagged frame is one that has an 802.1Q header. Typically, the header is added by the switch, but the header could be added by an 802.1Q-capable end station. In some situations, the header will be removed, for example when the frame is delivered to an 802.1Q-unaware end station. The 4-byte 802.1Q header is positioned after the Destination MAC and Source MAC address. (Note that the specification provides for insertion of the 802.1Q header into token ring frames; it will be inserted after the RIF field. The specification also provides for translation and encapsulation to accommodate going between different media. Our discussion focuses on Ethernet v2 frames.) After insertion of the tag, the FCS must be recalculated.

The IEEE 802.1Q frame header is illustrated in Figure 3.14. The Tag Protocol Identifier (TPID) is 2 bytes in length. It carries the value 8100, which is used to notify the receiving station that the frame contains an 802.1Q header and should be processed accordingly.

The Tag Control Information (TIF) field is also 2 bytes in length. The "priority" is a 3-bit field that indicates the priority level (0 through 7) of the

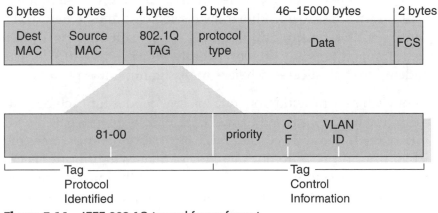

Figure 3.14 IEEE 802.1Q tagged frame format.

frame, with 0 representing the lowest priority level. The use of this field is actually defined in 802.1p.

The Canonical Format Identifier (CFI) is a single-bit flag value. CFI, when set, indicates that a RIF field is present and that MAC data carried by the frame is in canonical format; when unset, it indicates that there is no RIF and that the carried data is in noncanonical format—that is, Ethernet format.

The VID is a 12-bit value that uniquely identifies the vLAN to which the frame belongs.

802.1Q Frame Processing

Upon arrival at the switch port, the switch classifies untagged frames to specific vLANs according to ingress rules. This generally means that the frame is assigned to the vLAN that is identified by the PVID. However, as we will see later, this need not be the case. IEEE802.1Q does not preclude the switch from assigning the frame to a different vLAN (for example, a MAC-based vLAN) based on some information within the frame. Minimally, in order to be 802.1Q compliant, the switch must have the ability to classify the untagged frame into the vLAN specified by the PVID. If the frame is already tagged, the switch will not modify the VID.

Next, the switch applies filtering rules. The filtering rules ensure that frames are not propagated onto the port from which they arrived. The filtering process also examines the destination MAC address carried in the frame and information in its forwarding database for that MAC and VID to ensure that frames do not cross a vLAN boundary. Remember that vLANs are separate broadcast domains, and a router is required for movement between vLANs. The switch then classifies the frame into an 802.1p traffic class to expedite transmission of frames generated by high-priority or time-sensitive applications. Here again, the priority assigned to the frame is typically the port priority. However, 802.1Q does not preclude more sophisticated schemes for assigning frame priority.

The switch may provide from one to eight queues for each output port. The frame will be assigned to one of the output queues based on the priority of the frame and switches mechanism for queuing frames of the particular priority; a one-to-one mapping of queues to priorities is not required. Also, before submitting the frame to the output queue, the switch must ensure that the frame is either tagged or untagged, depending on the type of link, or in the case of hybrid link, the type of frames supported for the given vLAN on the hybrid link.

The concept of multiple output queues to support different traffic classes is appealing, but one must be careful. Vendors are allowed to map priority tagged frames to output queues in any fashion they devise. For example, if two switches from different vendors support the same number of traffic queues, one switch might map priority 3 traffic into a low-priority queue while the other maps priority 3 traffic to a high-priority queue. The result is that the same class of traffic would be forwarded differently by each switch. Even though an application may require top-priority service, it may end up vying for bandwidth with lower-priority traffic. The situation becomes more complex when one switch supports eight output queues while another switch supports three output queues.

802.1Q Walk-through

In Figure 3.15, two vLANs are supported. VID 1 is a default vLAN; all ports are untagged, the PVID=1, and the priority=0. When ES1 sends a broadcast (or multicast) frame, that frame is forwarded without a tag onto

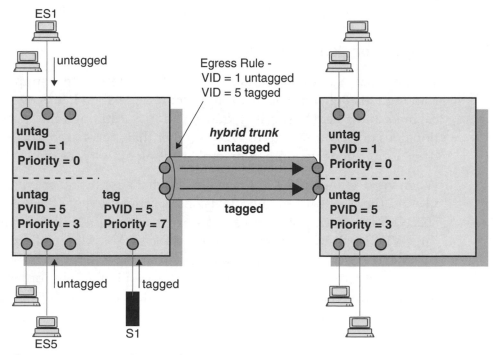

Figure 3.15   802.1Q in operation.

the trunk link to the other switch. Since the frame is untagged, it will be forwarded onto all ports in the default vLAN. The remote switch will update its forwarding database associating the ES1 MAC address with VID 1 and the trunk link port.

When ES5 sends a broadcast (or multicast) frame, the switch will assign VID=5 and a priority=3 to the frame. The 802.1Q header will be inserted into the frame, and the frame will be put onto the proper output queue for the trunk link. At the remote switch, the 802.1Q header is removed before the frame is delivered to the remote end-station.

When S1 sends a broadcast (or multicast) frame, the frame will be tagged with VID=5 but with a priority=7. In the example, S1 may be a video server generating multicast video frames to clients that have registered (for example, via 802.1p) to receive the particular multicast group. Since the video stream requires expedited delivery of its frames a priority=7 has been assigned. Actually, in the diagram, the video server is capable of delivering tagged frame, and the server itself has tagged the frames with priority=7. Because of the high priority, the frame will be put into a high-priority output queue and will likely be delivered without delay. The tag will be removed from the frame before delivery to the clients, assuming that the clients are connected to untagged ports on the switch.

Support for Other vLAN Types

The primary focus of 802.1Q is to define a frame format that supports a standardized tagging scheme to support multiplexing vLANs over physical links and a field to specify a frame's priority. Although the specification does not discuss types of vLANs (other than port-based vLANs), it does not preclude vendors from implementing other types of vLANs.

When vendor implement different devices that support other types of vLANs, there are several important considerations, even if the devices are 802.1Q compliant. First, as always, ensure that the vLAN is given the same VID on all switches participating in the vLAN. Also, make sure that each device uses the same criteria for determining to which vLAN the frame belongs and that the criteria are processed in the same order. The following sequence of questions should be asked about an incoming frame to determine to which vLAN it belongs:

■ Is the frame tagged?
■ Does the frame belong to a MAC-based vLAN?

- Does the frame belong to a Subnet-based vLAN?
- Does the frame belong to some other Layer 3 policy-based vLAN?
- Does the frame belong to Layer 2 protocol-based vLAN?
- Does the frame belongs to the vLAN specified by the port's PVID?

An important consideration is timing: "When does the port actually begin to participate in the vLAN, and when does the port stop participating in the vLAN?" For example, usually a port is enabled for a particular vLAN, say IP protocol vLAN, but only after the station that is attached to the port actually transmits an IP frame does the port begin to participate in the vLAN. That means that when an IP broadcast frame arrives at the switch, the switch will transmit the frame onto that port. Also, at some point, the port should dynamically be removed from the vLAN—for example, if the attached station has transmitted no IP frames in 30 seconds.

Another important consideration is to understand how vLAN information is propagated through the network. Although 802.1Q does specify a mechanism for the automatic propagation of the vLAN information via GVRP, this aspect of 802.1Q is not widely implemented. Most vendors rely on manual configuration for vLAN definition. If both types of switches are implemented in the same network, understand how they interact with regard to vLAN membership.

In Figure 3.16, the server port is configured into (or enabled for) several protocol-based vLANs. Assume the server wishes to communicate with the device that has the IP address 128.8.8.1. The server issues an ARP for the IP address. When the ARP (IP broadcast) arrives at the switch, the switch will determine that the frame belongs to vLAN 8. The switch then examines the egress rules and determines that the frame is to be tagged and sent on the trunk link to the remote switch. The remote switch receives the frame and delivers it untagged to the port configured to receive vLAN 8 frames.

If the server were to transmit an IPX broadcast to the switch, similarly, that frame would be delivered to the remote port configured to receive vLAN 9 frames. However, if the server were to transmit a LAT broadcast frame, that frame would be put into vLAN 5, and it would be delivered to both stations at the remote switch.

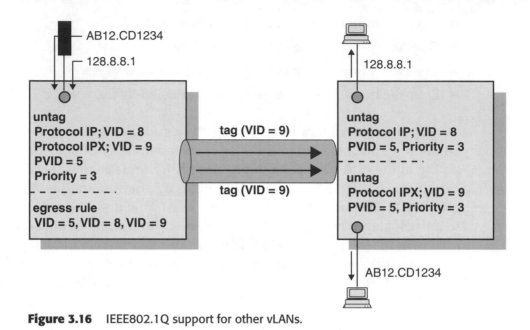

Figure 3.16   IEEE802.1Q support for other vLANs.

vLAN Forwarding Databases

The above discussions raise an issue that has received much attention by the 802.1Q Working Group, namely whether to support independent vLAN learning (IVL), in which there is a separate forwarding database for each vLAN, or shared vLAN learning (SVL), which uses a single forwarding database with shared learning. In Figure 3.17, the intent is to allow each end station to communicate with the server yet ensure that the end stations cannot communicate directly with each other.

With SVL, when ES1 transmits a frame to the server, the Switch 2 associates ES1 MAC address with vLAN 2 and Port 1, but this information will be available to other vLANs. When the server (S1) responds, the frame will

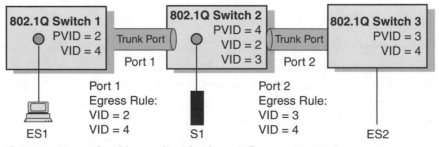

Figure 3.17   Style of forwarding database influence on switch operation.

Table 3.1   Shared Forwarding Database

MAC ADDRESS	PORT NUMBER
ES1 MAC	1
ES2 MAC	2

have the same destination MAC address as ES1 MAC, but the frame will have a vLAN ID=4. Since the forwarding database is shared, the forwarding process will know that ES1 MAC is on Port 1 and that Port 1 is configured to receive vLAN 4 frames, so the frame is delivered directly on to ES1 on Port 1. Effectively, the forwarding process examines a universal database that looks something like that in Table 3.1.

At first look, it might appear that this approach allows a frame to be switched between vLANs. However, this is not the case. The frame is being sent on Port 1 because of the egress rules. Because the forwarding process views all learned addresses, it actually forwards the frame onto only Port 1, even though the egress rules imply that the frame should be forwarded onto both Port 1 and Port 2.

The issue with this approach arises when multiple end stations have the same MAC address. Because the forwarding database is shared, the MAC will be associated with only a single port, which may create end-station-to-server communications problems (see Figure 3.18).

With IVL, an independent database for each vLAN is created. When ES1 transmits a frame to the server, the switch associates the ES1 MAC address with vLAN 2 and Port 1. This information is not available to other vLANs. When the server (S1) responds, the frame will have the destination MAC address ES1 MAC, but the frame will have a VID=4. The forwarding process examines that vLAN 4 database and finds no entry for ES1 MAC. So the forwarding process does what it is supposed to do

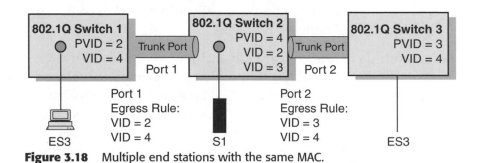

Figure 3.18   Multiple end stations with the same MAC.

Table 3.2 vLAN 2 and vLAN 3 Forwarding Databases

	MAC ADDRESS	PORT NUMBER
vLAN 2	ES3 MAC	1
vLAN 3	ES3 MAC	2

when it receives a frame with an unknown destination MAC address. It floods the frame onto all ports in the vLAN according to the Egress Rules. So the frame is sent on both Port 1 and Port 2, and ES1 receives the frame. Obviously, both approaches work, but in this scenario, the former approach is more efficient. The latter approach ensures proper communications when end stations with the same MAC address do exist. (See Table 3.2)

IEEE 802.1Q supports both shared and independent learning, and some switch implementations provide a way for management to determine the specific type of learning to be used.

Conclusion

In the early 1990s, many vendors believed in the promise of vLANs to provide a solution to network management problems, but it has not materialized. There are several reasons for this failure to deliver. The most important one is that the standard just took too long to be ratified. During this time, most vendors implemented proprietary vLANs. In many cases, these approaches incorporated a frame format that later proved not to be compliant with the specification. As we shall see later, during the time that the standard was being finalized, the nature of workgroup computing had been changing, resulting in traffic patterns that were less localized. This mandates that vLANs overlap in order to access centralized servers and gateways. Finally, although vLANs are supposed to simplify network management, they may actually add a level of complexity to the troubleshooting of network problems.

Because vLAN definitions typically include multiple LAN switches, it can be more difficult to troubleshoot problems affecting a virtual workgroup. Another vLAN issue is that each vLAN has two views associated with it: a physical view and a logical view. The physical view may include a number of LAN switches interconnected in a variety of ways, whereas the logical view is a simple shared-media LAN topology. When a problem occurs, the network manager must be able to separate the physical manifestation of the problem from the logical. Identifying and isolating problems across a large building or campus LAN infrastructure may involve correlating information from multiple switches and multiple views. Thankfully, other techniques and technologies were being developed concurrently with these vLAN standards. New flow control algorithms were developed, new switching products were introduced, and new vendors began sprouting up like wildflowers. Routers, which had grown seriously congested, started adding switching functionality, high-speed ASICs, and new software to better manage traffic and support new applications. Next, we take a closer look at the evolution, or revolution, in the routing marketplace.

CHAPTER 4

Routers Evolve to Keep Pace

A vLAN standard, Gigabit Ethernet, and the steadily falling prices of Layer 2 switches provided the impetus for LAN traffic to grow at very high rates through the early 1990s. The workgroup client/server computing model relied on predictable traffic patterns. The general rule was that 80 percent of the workgroup traffic was between the client and workgroup server. This premise encouraged network managers to create localized vLANs with client and server collocated in the same broadcast domain. Since only 20 percent of the workgroup traffic was for a device not within the workgroup broadcast domain, this was no problem for the routers that had to handle this traffic.

In the mid-1990s the 80/20 principle that had been guiding network managers for several years began to change. In fact, the rule began to reverse itself so that as little as 20 percent of the traffic remained local to the workgroup. Many network managers had become unwitting architects of their own biggest headaches. Those high-speed switches and gigabit links that they so cleverly deployed began to overwhelm their software-interrupt–driven routers, resulting in bottlenecks. The vLANs that they deployed resulted in the bottlenecks being moved to a different part of the network rather than being eliminated.

Also, network designers have traditionally tried to minimize router hops whenever possible. However, today's unpredictable traffic flows can undermine this basic design premise.

The router bottleneck problem is compounded on the Internet where traffic in recent years has been steadily growing by a factor of five each year. But that's not all. The nature of traffic being carried on corporate networks, as well as the Internet itself, is changing steadily. This new traffic requires a network that provides a higher level of performance and reliability than was envisioned even only a couple of years ago.

The situation has created a new opportunity for creative startups and innovative thinkers at established companies. In an effort to alleviate the router bottleneck, they began to develop new schemes. Some schemes are focused on addressing the problem within the campus or corporate environment while others are focused on the Internet backbone. Some of these schemes are based on frames, and others are cell based. Some schemes are based on expediting router performance, and others are based on avoiding routing: "route once, switch many." This is the approach implemented in Ipsilon's IP Switching, Cisco's Tag Switching, 3Com's Fast IP, Ascend's IP Navigator, Cabletron's SecureFast, and the emerging IETF standard Multiprotocol Label Switching (MPLS). Some of these schemes are designed so that they support either frames or cells. Also note that Multiprotocol over ATM (MPOA) developed by the ATM Forum is a cut-through—route once, switch many—scheme.

Some of the schemes will be accepted while others fade away. Some of the schemes will become de jure standards, and others will become de facto standards. In this chapter, we examine the new class of switches and routers and technologies that attempt to meet the requirements of our evolving networks. Figure 4.1 illustrates the evolution of routing technology.

Layer 2 Issues

As the nature of the applications changes, so does the LAN switching paradigm. LAN traffic being generated by sophisticated applications and modern PCs and servers is increasing steadily. More importantly, most of this traffic is now destined for other LAN segments, increasing the relative percentage of intersubnet traffic and, consequently, decreasing the usefulness of vLANs. The traditional 80/20 rule that had influenced

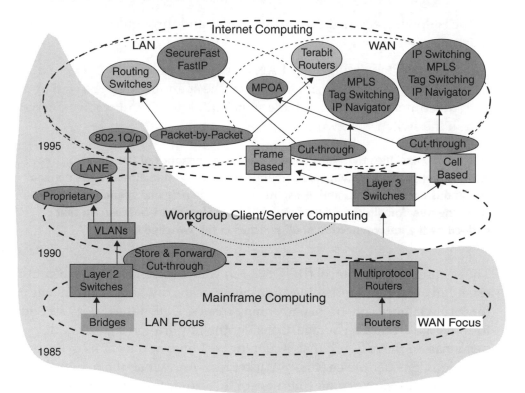

Figure 4.1 Evolution of routing.

many network designs has been reversed. Traffic that remains local to the workgroup vLAN is now the exception rather than the rule. There are many reasons for this dramatic change in traffic patterns, most notably:

- Internet and intranet applications are becoming dispersed throughout the enterprise, which itself may be distributed to far corners of the Internet.

- Multimedia applications and services that are more sophisticated and more demanding of the network are becoming more common.

- Enterprises have come to appreciate the benefits of centralized secure computing centers. Server farms where Web servers, file servers, application servers, and gateways are localized facilitate management and maintenance. They also provide economies of scale by providing load sharing and fault tolerance of these critical corporate resources.

This change of the network paradigm is forcing more and more traffic through the routers located at the core. An ever-increasing percentage of traffic is flowing across the entire enterprise and through the Internet, as illustrated in Figure 4.2.

Another important issue with vLANs is that since the vLAN defines a Layer 2 broadcast domain, it is reliant on the spanning tree protocol to both determine routes through the switched network and resolve outages within the switched network.

IEEE 802.1Q specifies that there should be a single instance of the spanning tree protocol per port-based switched domain. There may be numerous vLANs defined within this domain, but nonetheless, there should be only one spanning tree. That spanning tree domain should be defined by the default port-based vLAN that is defined by the interconnection of all switches in the switched domain.

The spanning tree protocol (IEEE 802.1D) was created at a time when Ethernet ran at 10Mbps and applications were primarily data transfers with few or no latency constraints. Spanning tree typically takes 30–40 seconds to converge around an outage. Consider the implication a 30-second delay has on the network that is running real time applications over gigabit links. Consider the enormous packet loss. And when the network has restabilized after an outage, there is apt to be an influx of millions of packets and more lost packets. Gigabit-connected servers may well be

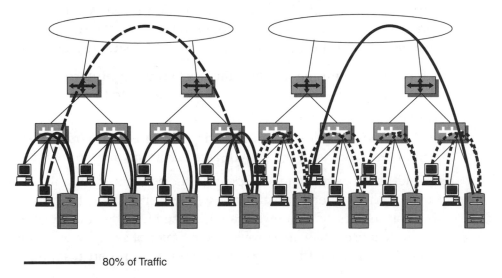

———————— 80% of Traffic

- - - - - - - - - - 20% of Traffic

Figure 4.2 The 80/20 rule has been reversed.

incapable of handling the influx of packets, resulting in precipitous degradation in network performance.

Some New Terms

The term *Layer 3 switching* has become rather fashionable and ubiquitous over the past several years. Unfortunately, unlike Layer 2 switching, which has a fairly consistent definition, Layer 3 switching has a different interpretation with each vendor and implementation. The following sections define some terms that are commonly used in discussions on the various Layer 3 switching techniques and strategies.

Routing Switch or Switching Routers

Router switch generally refers to a device that forwards packets based on the Layer 3 information contained within the packet, like a conventional router. However, the forwarding is done in hardware via Application Specific Integrated Circuits (ASICs) with throughput and latency characteristics that greatly exceed the performance characteristics of conventional Layer 3 routers. Figure 4.3 illustrates a conventional router, where the router is involved each time a packet is transmitted between subnets. Prior to the new class of routers, or routing switches, the decision on how to forward the packet was done via processor interrupts and software processing. Routing is assisted by hardware in making the forwarding decision.

Multilayer Switching

Multilayer switching is perhaps the most difficult term for which to find a consistent definition. Basically, a multilayer switch combines Layer 2 and Layer 3 functionality in a single box. It removes the requirement that every inter-vLAN and intersubnet packet traverse a conventional IP router. The multilayer switch can be positioned between the switches and the router. The multilayer switch learns all MAC-to-IP address associations. How this is done is an implementation issue; snooping on ARP-Request and ARP-Response messages is a commonly used scheme. (Although the illustration in Figure 4.4 is of IP subnets, the same principle is applied to vLANs or to other Layer 3 protocols.) The first packet between subnets traverses the router so that the router may apply any access control or security rules that have been configured for communications between the source and destination. The multilayer switch will cache the IP, MAC, and port infor-

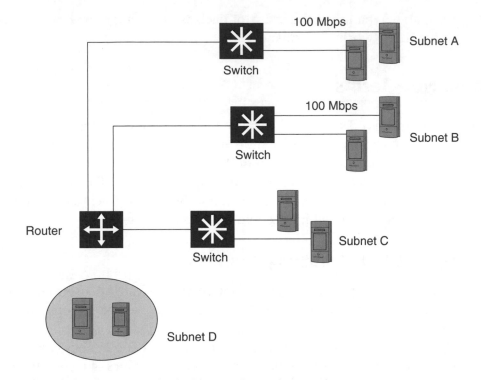

Figure 4.3 Router involved with every intersubnet packet.

mation as the packets pass between source and destination. Basically, the multilayer switch identifies a flow. When subsequent packets for the same flow arrive at switch, the multilayer switch will intercept the packet (the packet is actually addressed to the router's MAC) and switch it directly to the destination. The packet does not traverse the router. The multilayer switch, of course, must modify the packet header—change the destination MAC, modify the TTL, and so forth—because the multilayer switch is transparent to the end devices.

Flow

In the broadest sense, a flow is a collection of packets that have something in common. They may have the same source address, the same destination address, the same destination address, and the same TCP port number. The most common interpretation of a flow is all packets associated with the same application and session, which would be identified by the source address, destination address, and destination port number tuple.

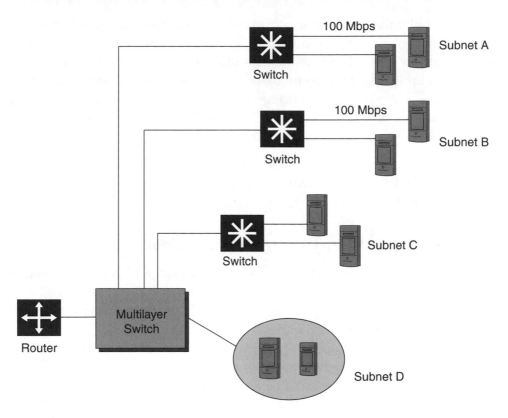

Figure 4.4 Multilayer switch front-ending a router.

Cut-Through Layer 3 Switch

The biggest bottleneck on a conventional router is the header processing and next-hop determination. Basically, cut-through Layer 3 switching schemes map Layer 3 paths into Layer 2 circuits, eliminating the header processing and performing the next-hop determination in hardware. For the most part, all aspects of cut-through Layer 3 switching are propri-etary. The idea is to first identify flows at Layer 3. Once a flow is identi-fied and its destination determined, the packets of the flow avoid or short-cut the Layer 3 process and are switched directly at Layer 2. Cut-through Layer 3 routing is synonymous with short-cut routing.

There are many variations on cut-through switching, but two characteris-tics that all varieties have is that they forward some or all packets at Layer 2, and they all separate the forwarding functionality from the route calcu-lation functionality. The routing protocol continues to be software driven;

usually there is a separate route processor that is responsible for the routing protocol and building the route forwarding table. But after the routing table is created, the switch uses this information to establish a Layer 2 virtual path. At some point, usually after the flow has been identified or after some flow threshold has been exceeded, all packets belonging to this flow are forwarded at Layer 2 via hardware. Thus, the timely software interrupt is eliminated from the packet-forwarding process.

There are two generic types of cut-through switches: topology driven and traffic driven. Both switch packets at Layer 2 and yield very high throughput and low latency characteristics.

Topology-Based Cut-Through Layer 3 Switching

With topology-based cut-through schemes, the Layer 2 path is created independently of any user data. After the routing table is built, a separate proprietary algorithm is invoked, which associates an identifier (usually the identifier is called either a label or tag) with the Layer 3 route entry. This association, Layer 3 route and Layer 2 identifier, is propagated throughout the network. When data packets enter the network, the Layer 3 address is mapped to a Layer 2 identifier and is added to the header of the packet. The Layer 2 header is used to forward the packet through the network at Layer 2. With this approach, because the Layer 2 path is created independently and prior to any user data, all packets of the flow are switched at Layer 2. There is no criterion (threshold) that must be met before the Layer 2 path is used.

Cisco's Tag Switching, IBM's ARIS, Ascend's IP Navigator, and IETF MPLS are popular topology-based schemes that we examine.

Traffic-Based Cut-Through Layer 3 Switching

With traffic based cut-through schemes, the Layer 2 path is created with not only the topology information. Rather, the Layer 2 path is created in response to user data. Typically, the user data is switched through the network at Layer 3 until the flow meets some criteria or some threshold is exceeded. These approaches rely on the switch's ability to identify characteristics of the flow and to establish a Layer 2 path in response to the characteristics. Some switches are programmed such that flows of a particular protocol are classified as being long-lived. For example, a Web download might be classified as a long-lived flow. Upon identifying that the flow is long-lived, the switch uses the Layer 3 information to establish a Layer 2 path through the network. Subsequent packets are switched through the network at Layer 2 Ipsilon's IP Switching scheme and ATM Forum MPOA are traffic based. The top portion of Figure 4.5 shows the forwarding path with conventional routing. In the bottom portion of Figure 4.5, the first packet is routed in the conventional fashion, but subsequent packets are forwarded independent of the Layer 3 processing. Typically, these subsequent packets are forwarded by hardware.

Cut-Through Routing Schemes

Recently, MPLS has gained much momentum and is being touted as the technology that will enhance the speed, scalability, and service-provisioning capabilities of the Internet. It defines a mechanism that enables IP devices to forward packets at Layer 2. It does this by replacing the standard Layer 3 destination-based, hop-by-hop-forwarding paradigm with a Layer 2 label-swapping technique. The technique has the benefit of simplifying packet forwarding—the routing table does not have to be examined at every hop, enabling easier scaling to gigabit and terabit network links. Additionally, because the forwarding component is decoupled from the routing control component, the existing Internet routing protocols and network manage-

Packet Forwarding—Packet-by-Packet Routing Switch:

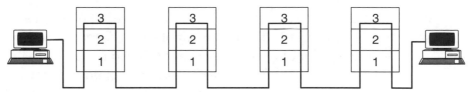

Packet Forwarding—Cut-through Layer 3 Switch:

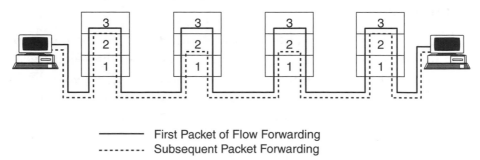

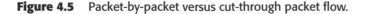

——————— First Packet of Flow Forwarding
----------- Subsequent Packet Forwarding

Figure 4.5 Packet-by-packet versus cut-through packet flow.

ment strategies do not have to be replaced. Instead, the existing routing protocols and network management strategies can be used in concert with the new MPLS protocols to introduce new specialized routing services (for example, explicit forwarding) without requiring change in the forward-path calculation.

Another benefit of MPLS is that it is possible to associate many flows with a label or a single flow with a label, thus enabling a time-critical application to achieve the quality of service it requires. MPLS facilitates traffic-engineering applications (like load balancing across multiple links) and control so that resources can be allocated in a manner that provides both efficiency and utility. This feature can be used by network managers to associate a specific path through the network with a specific user or address, enabling class-of-service differentiation. The technology is not totally original; its roots are in such technologies as IP Switching developed by Ipsilon Networks (Nokia), Cisco's Tag Switching, Cascade's (Ascend/Lucent) IP Navigator, and IBM's ARIS. It can be stated that MPLS is a consolidation of several proprietary schemes developed to do the same thing: Switch IP packets at Layer 2 and introduce traffic engineering and control on the Internet.

Background

Why did these new ways of handling data evolve? The exponential growth in Internet traffic did not go unnoticed. The realization that existing networking technologies were never designed to deal with the volumes of traffic that the Internet was handling inspired innovative schemes. IP Switching was the first scheme introduced to attempt to alleviate the Internet under siege.

IP Switching

In 1996, Ipsilon Networks (a startup) introduced an innovative approach for supporting IP over ATM. The basic premise of the scheme was that ATM is a connection-oriented switching technology whereas IP is a connectionless routing technology. This mismatch led to inefficiency and duplication of functionality when asynchronous transfer mode (ATM) was used to support IP networks. Although ATM is a very effective multiplexing and switching technology, the signaling, routing, and discovery mechanisms defined by IETF and the ATM Forum to facilitate IP over

ATM were overly complex and not well suited for the Internet or other large networks. IP Switching is basically a scheme to implement IP directly on top of ATM hardware while preserving the connectionless nature of IP, eliminating complex routing, discovery, and signaling and instead using IP for the functions. Figure 4.6 illustrates that the IP Switching Architecture incorporates the IP routing functionality of a conventional IP router and the ATM forwarding functionality of an ATM switch. It is a traffic-based scheme in which the decision to forward data at Layer 2 or Layer 3 is determined solely by the flow's own characteristics. The Layer-2-switched path is created only in response to data traffic and never created before there is data or traffic.

The IP Switch is composed of three components: an ATM switch, an IP switch controller, and two specialized-management protocols. The IP Switch is an ATM switch with all software above the AAL-5—ATM signaling, discovery, and routing protocols—removed and an IP router with all components below the IP layer removed. The IP Switch controller functions as a standard IP router with software enhancements that allow it to communicate with the ATM switch hardware component. Ipsilon Flow Management Protocol (IFMP) RFC1953 is used to convey IP switching information between adjacent IP switching devices. General Switch Management Protocol (GSMP) RFC1987 defines how the IP Switch controller communicates with the ATM switch hardware.

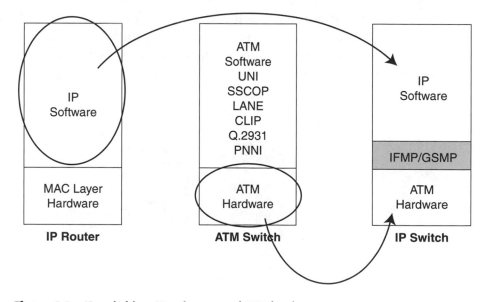

Figure 4.6   IP switching, IP software, and ATM hardware.

IP switches run an IP routing protocol, and an IP route-forwarding table is constructed and maintained at each of the IP switches. When the IP Switch is initialized, a default forwarding virtual circuit (VCI=15) is created automatically between the IP Switch devices. (The Virtual Path Identifier [VPI] is typically set to 0.) The end stations are attached to an IP Switch Gateway that has an ATM connection to the ingress IP Switch. The IP switch is preconfigured with criteria to determine if a flow is long-lived. The criteria can be based on source IP address, destination IP address, source port number, destination port number, or some other field within the packets. (Typically the port number is used to identify a flow that is likely to be long-lived, such as a Telnet or FTP session.) When the end station sends a packet to the gateway, the gateway SARs (segmentation and reassembly is the process of segmenting the frame into cells and the subsequent reassembly of the cells into a frame) the packet using VCI 15 and sends it to the ingress IP Switch. All VCI 15 cells that arrive at the IP switch are forwarded to the IP switch controller where they are reassembled into frames (using the AAL-5 PTI field to identify the last cell of a frame). The IP switch controller then examines the frame to determine if it matches any of the long-lived flow criteria that have been configured at the switch. If none of the criteria are met, a routing decision is made based on the packet-destination IP address and the IP routing table, and the packet is SARed using VCI 15 and sent to the next hop IP Switch. In this case, the packet is forwarded through conventional IP store-and-forward routing. The idea is that if the flow is short-lived, there is nothing to be gained by setting up a switched path, so simply route the packet. Of course, the egress IP Switch Gateway receives the VCI 15 cells, reassembles the packet, and delivers the packet to the end station. Figure 4.7 illustrates a case where the packet is not part of a long-lived flow. Because it is not associated with a long-lived

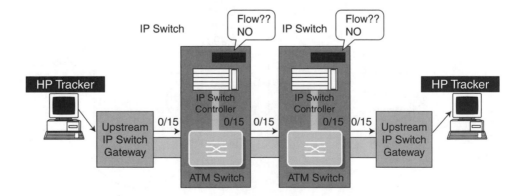

Figure 4.7 IP switch forwarding.

flow, the packet is actually routed through the network and it never receives the benefit of cut-through forwarding.

The real benefit of IP Switching comes when the flow matches the long-lived criteria configured at the switch. In this case, the IP switch controller assigns a VCI value (not 15) to the flow. The IP switch controller then notifies, via IFMP, the preceding (upstream) IP switch of the new VCI value along with the criteria that should be used to associate packets with the flow. Now whenever packets from the flow arrive at the upstream device, the new VCI value will be used when the packets are SARed. The IP switch controller also configures, via GSMP, the ATM switch VPI/VCI forwarding table with the new VCI. An IP routing decision is then made on the packet; it is then SARed with VCI 15 and forwarded to the next IP switch device.

Assuming that the next switch has the same flow criteria, a new ATM hardware at the switch obtains updates with a new VCI value for the flow. After the initial packet has made its way through the network, all forwarding is via the ATM switch hardware. The cells are switched directly by the ATM hardware. There are no cell reassembly and hop-by-hop, route-forwarding decisions. As is shown in Figure 4.8, the VPI/VCI values are associated with the flow, and subsequent packets are forwarded as cells. In effect, IP Switching has used IP as the ATM signaling, routing, and discovery protocol.

Note that the flow criteria decision is made independently at each IP switch. It is a local decision, and it is not necessary that the flow criteria in all switches are identical. If the flow criteria are not the same, the cells will have to be buffered and packets reassembled. This is because an IP

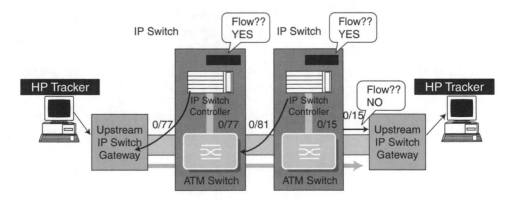

Figure 4.8 IP switch forwarding.

route-forwarding decision will have to be made; that is, the forwarding decision is not made by the ATM hardware at the switch where long-lived criteria are not met for the flow. After the next hop has been determined, the packet is SARed with VCI 15 and forwarded to the next device.

IP Switching is a soft-state machine. The per-flow state information is maintained locally and refreshed periodically. In other words, the VPI/VCI table entries associated with a flow have a lifetime and are timed out upon expiration. Failures are routed automatically around because when an IP route forwarding table entry changes due to a routing update message, the IP switch controller automatically removes the VPI/VCI entry, and the switch reverts to the default VCI 15 until new flow information is established.

IP switching easily and efficiently deals with multicasting and employs Internet Group Multicast Protocol (IGMP) and Distance Vector Multicast Routing Protocol (DVMRP). The multicast flows are handled in the same way as ATM multicast. In other words, the incoming flow can be directed to more than one downstream interface with either the same or different VPI/VCI values on each of the downstream interfaces.

> **Why did IP Switching fail? Simply put, technology fuels the industry, but marketing drives technology. There were shortcomings with IP Switching (for instance, per-flow VCs), but what really doomed IP Switching was the negative marketing campaign waged by other vendors—most notably, Cisco. Very few IP switches were actually sold.**

Tag Switching

Tag Switching is Cisco's response to IP Switching. It is Cisco's approach to address scalability and flexibility issues. Tag Switching is topology driven, meaning that all data traffic is switched at Layer 2, and switching paths are created prior to and independent of any data traffic. The switched paths are typically based on the network topology independent of any traffic characteristics within the topology.

Tag Switching fuels the technology of routing with the performance of switching by allowing packet routers and ATM switches (with specialized hardware) to support gigabit forwarding rates. In addition, Tag Switching supports traffic engineering and provides quality of service (QoS) capabilities because tags can be assigned administratively to distribute network load and provide policies and different QoS paths. The basic idea is to apply a tag (either implicit or explicit) to a frame or cell and then forward the data element based solely on the tag. The forwarding is done in hardware without hop-by-hop referencing of the route-forwarding table.

IP Switching caught router and switch vendors off-guard. Everyone realized that the Internet was strained and that something needed to be done. Most approaches were focused on quicker and more intelligent routers and/or an overlay model wherein routing was pushed to the periphery of the network and traffic through the core was primary-switched, primarily using ATM. IP Switching introduced a new paradigm and quickly caught everyone's attention. Cisco's response to IP Switching, at least in the literature, was so rapid that one might wonder if the response was hurried and the approach not very far along in the implementation stage. Conjecture can be further substantiated by the fact that it took an inordinately long time before Tag Switching was actually available in products.

Tag Switch routers (TSRs) support a network layer routing protocol (EIGRP, OSPF, BGP) and implement two additional fundamental components: a forwarding component and a control component. The forwarding component applies the tag to the data element and switches the data element through the switch or router based on the tag contained in the data element. The control component binds tags to an IP network and distributes the tags between the TSRs. (There is no reason that Tag Switching could not be modified to support routing protocols other than IP.) The forwarding component is decoupled from the control component, enabling the forwarding component to be implemented in hardware while allowing the control component to be software driven.

Three different types of tags are supported. In IP V4 (Version 4), the tag is a 4-byte field inserted in the frame between the Layer 2 header and the Layer 3 header. In IP V6 (Version 6), the tag is carried in the Flow-Label field of the Layer 3 header. In ATM, the VCI is used as an implicit tag.

Two other components of the Tag Switching architecture are the Tag Information database (TIB), which is the table that stores tag bindings within the TSRs, and the Tag Distribution Protocol (TDP), which relies on a connection-oriented protocol, typically TCP, to distribute, request, and release tag bindings between TSRs.

As part of the architecture, TSRs run a routing protocol and build a routing database. The routing table becomes the basis of the TIB. Tags are then associated with the routing table entry, and tag binding is distributed to

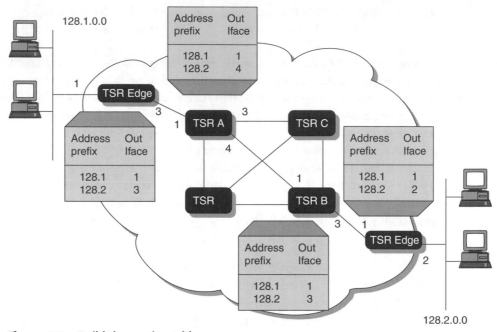

Figure 4.9 Build the routing table.

adjacent TSRs. In Figure 4.9, each Tag Switch element has built an IP forwarding table.

After Tag bindings have been distributed (shown in Figure 4.10), the TIB is pushed into hardware, and forwarding is accomplished through the switching of labels according to the TIB. The results are a simple and quick forwarding decision, decreased latency, and increased throughput (see Figure 4.11).

When a data element arrives at a TSR Edge Switch, the switch references the TIB and inserts the tag associated with the destination-IP route. (Other optional information could be examined and QoS applied to the flow. This would mean that a different path and TIB entry would be created for each QoS supported.) The data element is then forwarded to the next TSR that extracts the tag from the data element and uses it as an index into the local TIB. Each entry in the TIB contains an incoming tag that is mapped to a set of forwarding information used for all data elements arriving on the same interface with the same tag. For unicast traffic, the outgoing information consists of the outgoing tag, the outgoing interface, and perhaps information on other outgoing data elements such as the MAC address of the downstream node. For multicast traffic, the

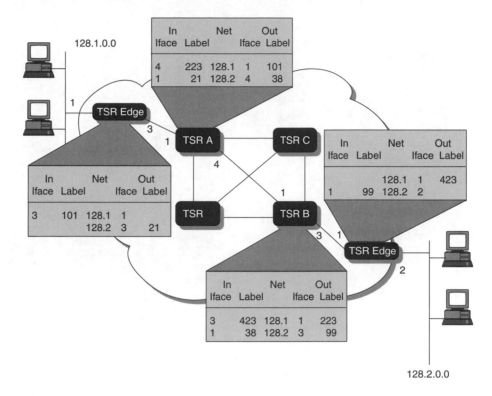

Figure 4.10 Bind and distribute the tags.

outgoing information can contain multiple tags and multiple interface information. The approach is protocol independent so that it is feasible that Tag Switching could be used to support protocols other than IP.

There are three different ways that the tags can be allocated. With downstream tag allocation, the tag binding is initiated by the downstream node, or the node closest to the IP network. This will probably be the TSR Edge device that has an interface to the destination IP network. The TSR Edge will determine what tag it wants to bind to in the IP network and informs its upstream neighbor. The upstream neighbor will record the tag in the outgoing tag field of the TIB entry associated with the destination IP network. The TSR will then choose an inbound tag value to associate with IP destination. The TSR may or may not choose to associate a different tag with each of its interfaces. The TSR will then notify each of its upstream neighbors of the tag it wants associated with the IP destination. In this manner, binding information will be distributed from the downstream node outward or in the upstream direction. Downstream tag allocation is the most common implementation and it is the allocation scheme that was used in Figures 4.10 and 4.11.

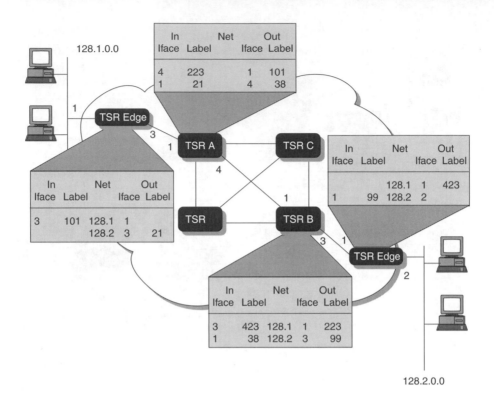

Figure 4.11 Forwarding via the TIB.

Another approach is downstream tag allocation on demand, in which the tag is distributed only when it is requested. In the approach, the TSR Edge device associates a tag with the attached IP network but notifies the upstream TSR Switch of the binding only when the upstream switch actually requests it and has data destined for the destination IP network. The approach results in smaller TIBs at the expense of a small delay in data delivery.

The final approach is upstream tag allocation. With this approach, the upstream TSR initiates the tag binding. After the routing table is created, the upstream TSR will notify the downstream TSR of the tag it will associate with a particular IP network.

When the downstream TSR receives the binding notification from its upstream neighbor, it places the tag in the incoming tag field of the TIB entry associated with the route. With upstream tag allocation, the TSR generates the tag binding for outgoing traffic and into the downstream TSR of the tag that it will receive. The TSR receives from its upstream TSR the tag that will be on incoming traffic. The advantage of the approach is that it gives the upstream TSRs the opportunity to associate multiple tags with flows that have the same criteria. This is important in ATM TSRs because it provides a mechanism to prevent interleaving of ATM cells that arrive from different upstream TSRs but are forwarded to the same downstream TSR. With ATM TSRs, the tag is carried implicitly in the VCI field of the ATM cell. The upstream TSR notifies the downstream TSR of multiple VCI values that are to be sent to the same destination. Basically, a different VCI is created for each of the flows, so cells from each flow are on a different virtual circuit (see Figure 4.12). (Downstream-on-demand tag allocation can also be used to prevent the cell-interleaving problem.)

Note that an ATM TSR must implement a routing protocol and Tag Distribution Protocol.

Tag switching also supports hierarchical tags or tag stacks. When a TSR receives a frame containing a tag stack, it swaps tags, adds a tag, or removes a tag. This is useful when a routing domain traverses a tunnel and both routing domain and the tunnel network support tag switching.

In the illustration in Figure 4.13, a data element that arrives at TSR A destined for TSR F will be tagged according to TSR A's TIB. However, when the data element arrives at TSR C, it must push a new tag onto the tag stack to ensure that the data element is forwarded to the tunnel's egress TSR, TSR D. At TSR D, the top tag will be removed, and the tag to TSR F will be·exposed so that the TIB at TSR E will forward the data element properly. In this way, the tunnel is truly transparent from the perspective of the routing domain.

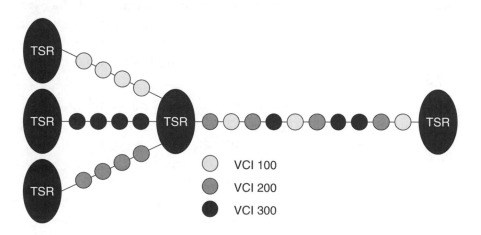

VCI 100
VCI 200
VCI 300

Figure 4.12 Upstream tag allocation allows a different VC for each flow.

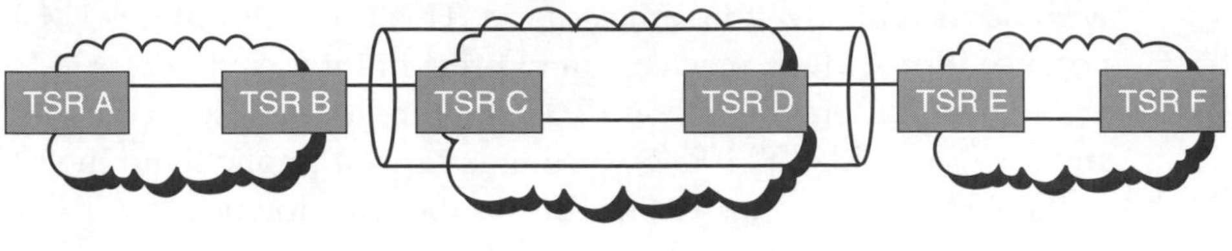

Figure 4.13 Support tag stacks.

IP Navigator

In 1996, Cascade Communications introduced a new approach to support the expanding needs of IP service providers. Each of the schemes discussed so far has scaling limitations in terms of the number of IP routes that it can store and process and the number of flows that can be monitored and maintained. IP Navigator addressed the scaling limitations by offering support for numerous IP addresses and by offering a new and different overlay approach. Cascade recognized that typical overlay schemes require an inordinate number of circuits. This is because typical overlay approaches rely on a full mesh of point-to-point circuits. This well-known problem is referred as the $O(n^2)$ "order of n-squared" scaling problem where n is the number of sites that must be interconnected. In other words, if the network must support n sites, the formula to calculate the number of virtual circuits required is n*(n–1). As n gets larger, the resultant number approaches n^2, hence the term. Therefore, if five sites are to be fully interconnected, 20, or 5*(5–1), unidirectional virtual circuits must be created and maintained, as illustrated in Figure 4.14. As the number of sites increases, the number of circuits increases exponentially. Considering the number of sites in the Internet (or even a large individual Internet service provider), the problem becomes obvious. As traffic from remote sites approaches the core of the provider's network, it is easy to see that the number of virtual circuits required might exceed the capacity of the core device.

Two important components of IP Navigator are Virtual Network Navigator (VNN) and Multipoint-to-Point Tunneling (MPT). Prior to 1996, Cascade had already developed VNN to support establishment of switched-frame relay circuits. VNN employs a Cascade proprietary link-state routing protocol that is similar to OSPF, but with proprietary enhancements, so that QoS information about the physical links is also propagated in the link-state advertisements. VNN keeps track of all links, bandwidth, and existing circuits, and when a switched frame relay circuit

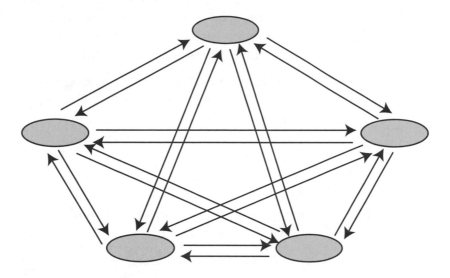

Figure 4.14 O(N²) problem.

is to be established, the VNN database is referenced to ensure the service level of the frame-relay, virtual circuit. The VNN architecture has been refined and extended to support ATM and IP networks.

Because each switch in the network runs VNN, each has a topological view of the network. In other words, each switch knows about all other switches in the network. Each IP Navigator switch creates a multipoint-to-point path to itself in a treelike structure with itself as the root of the tree. Each switch uses its VNN database to create a path based on a sequence of switches from itself to all other switches. The path is based on the best-path information in the VNN database. After the root switch builds the path, it propagates MPT packets that specify a unique identifier for the path between itself and each of its neighbors. The neighbors then determine and propagate their unique path identifiers to their neighbors, and so on. The unique identifiers become the labels used in going from a leaf switch to the root switch. The multipoint circuit now functions as a reverse-forwarding tree for data destined to the root. Because full-meshed connectivity is achieved with n circuits instead of n*(n–1), the scheme is very scalable.

With IP Navigator the ingress and egress devices function as IP routers while the core devices function as Layer 2 switches. When traffic arrives at an ingress switch, the switch references its IP routing table to determine the switch associated with the destination IP address and affixes the corresponding label. The ingress switch also validates the packet's time-to-live (TTL) to ensure that the number of intervening switches does not exceed the TTL. TTL validation prevents routing loops and allows existing IP diagnostic tools to be used (for example, traceroute).

The ingress switch then forwards traffic to the switch using the MPT circuit in the opposite direction. The egress switch makes a routing decision to determine which outbound port goes to the destination IP address. Each packet requires only two routing decisions, regardless of the number of switches that must be traversed. In Figure 4.15, the switch adjacent to subnet 198.20.20.0 initiates a multicast tree to all other switches. When a packet arrives with a destination IP address of 198.20.20.2, the packet is forwarded along the reverse direction of the multicast path that was established from the switch that is adjacent to the 198.20.20.0 subnet.

IP Navigator is designed to function with both ATM and frame-relay networks. It is topology-driven because the MPT paths are pre-established independent of any data traffic. As a result, every packet receives the benefit of switching.

IP Navigator supports end-to-end QoS across the core, allowing Internet service providers (ISPs) to provide tiered-service offerings. Different MPTs could be created, each providing a different QoS. In addition, because VNN is fully aware of existing network resources and throughput, characteristics-informed QoS decisions can be made. IP Navigator supports several IP multicast routing protocols. IP multicast packets designated to particular Class D addresses are delivered over a multicast MPT.

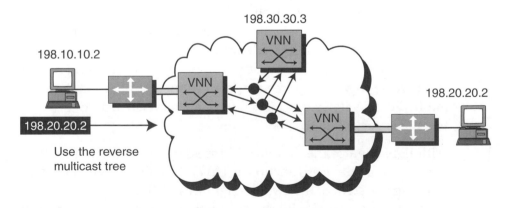

Figure 4.15 Delivering a packet with the reverse multicast tree.

ARIS

In 1996, IBM introduced a scheme called Aggregate Route-Based IP Switching (ARIS). ARIS is also based on multipoint-to-point trees rooted at the edge of the network, but ARIS uses route aggregation to further reduce the number of paths and state information that the core switches must support. ARIS also provides a means of mapping network-layer routing information to link-layer switched paths, enabling traffic to traverse a network at media speeds. An Integrated Switch Router (ISR) is a switch (typically frame-relay or ATM) that has been augmented with standard IP-routing support. The ARIS protocol establishes switched paths through a network of ISRs by mapping network-layer routing information directly to data-link-layer switched paths. A switched path is created for an egress identifier that identifies a routed path through a network. Egress identifiers can be extracted from information existing in the routing protocols or can be configured by an administrator.

The provisioning of network resources is managed at the edge (egress) of the network and not at each device in the entire network. Routes that are populated in a router's forwarding table are extended to include a reference to an egress identifier with a corresponding switched path. ARIS supports switched-path granularity ranging from end-to-end flows to the aggregation of all traffic through a common egress node. The choice of granularity is determined by the choice of the egress identifier. Because multiple routes can map to the same egress identifier, the number of switched paths needed in a network is minimized. Switched paths for different levels of aggregation can exist simultaneously. The premise is that all traffic flowing to a specific common destination and belonging to the same Forward Equivalence Class (FEC)—having the QoS requirements—eventually merges and arrives at the destination on a single virtual circuit.

The egress switch (typically the switch that has an interface in the IP subnet for which the ARIS switched path is created) initiates the path establishment by sending an Establish message to each of its neighbors, Reverse-Path, Multicast style. The Establish message is a control message and contains a hop-count set to 0 if the egress is the switched-path endpoint; otherwise, the hop-count is set to 1. This will happen if the ARIS domain is contained within a set of routers that do not support ARIS. The router-ID list is set to the egress ISR's router-ID, and the upstream label to be assigned for this IP subnet is inserted in the message. Each ISR that receives an Establish message for an egress identifier verifies that the message was received from the correct next-hop for the given egress identifier as indicated by its Forwarding Information Base (FIB), an extended routing table, and verifies that the path is loop free. The ISR receiving a new valid Establish message populates the FIB with the given downstream label and replies to the sender with a positive Acknowledge message. The ISR then allocates a label for each of its ARIS upstream neighbors (where the downstream neighbor is the ISR from which the Establish was received). Each ISR forwards the Establish message to the upstream neighbors with an incremented hop-count, the ISR's router-ID appended to the ISR list if loop prevention is configured, and the allocated upstream label. In this manner, the Establish message is propagated out to all other ISRs.

When a data packet arrives at the ingress switch, it examines the destination IP address and references its FIB to determine the label to associate with the IP destination. The label is attached to the packet and is forwarded on the outbound interface according to the FIB. The path follows the reverse path of the Establish control message to the destination.

In Figure 4.16, switch ISR-X advertises Net7 with a Label equal to 100. Switch ISR-C associates a Label equal to 107 with Net7 and advertises this association to its adjacent switches. This process continues until all

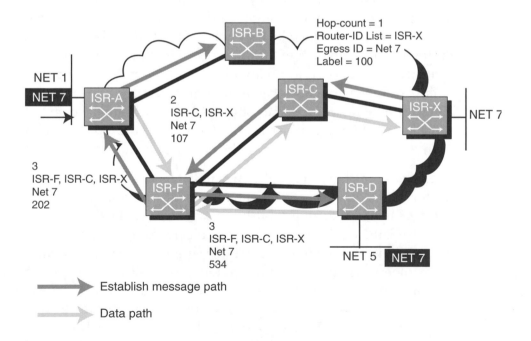

Figure 4.16   Switched path establishment and data flow.

switches have a label to associate with Net7. On the left side of the illustration, when a packet arrives at the ingress switch with a destination IP address equal to Net7, the ingress switch assigns the corresponding label—in this case the label equals 202—to the packet and the packet is then forwarded through the network via a label switching process at each ARIS switch.

When the ISRs are ATM switches, there are two approaches to prevent cell interleaving. If the switched paths are VC-based—called VC merging—the label is a VCI. In this case, the ISRs must ensure that cells are not interleaved. They do this by transmitting all cells from a frame before any other frame cells are transmitted on the VCI. Another approach is VP merging where the label is based on the VPI. With VP merging, cells from different flows will have different VCIs, although they would have the same VPI. In this situation, cell interleaving is not a concern because the VCI differentiates the flows.

Merging switched paths enables ARIS to create a full mesh of switched-path trees without n^2 switched paths. In addition, ARIS is topology-driven so that paths are determined independently of data traffic, and every data packet in the flow gets switched at Layer 2.

What Is MPLS?

Each of the preceding approaches to address scaling and throughput problems associated with the Internet or large intranets has been a private proprietary undertaking. Most of the schemes have been incorporated into RFC drafts (in some cases, numerous drafts; just because it's an RFC does not mean that it is an Internet standard), but none has been adopted by any standards organizations. In fact, it could be reasonably argued that each of the proprietary schemes is designed to leverage the implemented technology and/or the installed base of the vendor that created the scheme. The MPLS Working Group within the IETF is chartered with developing an architecture and protocol suite that defines a standardized mechanism for IP devices to switch packets.

In this context, switch means to forward packets based on some information (label) contained within the individual packet and not on a destination IP address. This approach eliminates the time-consuming and complicated process of referencing the routing table and making a forwarding decision that is required with conventional packet routing. MPLS will assign locally significant identifiers to provide easy forwarding of packets. The identifiers will be consistent with the routed path through the network. In other words, a routing protocol will run to establish the paths through the network, and the routing table will be referenced when the local identifiers are established. Effectively, MPLS will create IP-level virtual circuits by assigning Layer 2 labels according to Layer 3 paths through the network. It is expected that the forwarding (switching) will be at or very near wire speed, implying that it will likely happen in hardware. The net result is that MPLS-enhanced Layer 3 routers will provide throughput, scalability, and service-level characteristics that have been the realm of frame relay and ATM networks.

 Although MPLS is protocol independent, most efforts by the MPLS Working Group focus on IP.

The MPLS Working Group is certainly influenced by work that has been done by the individual vendors. The relationship to Tag Switching, IP Navigator, and ARIS is obvious.

Probably one of the more difficult tasks for the MPLS WG is dealing with political influences. Basically, everyone has the same idea on what needs to be done, but there is little consensus about how to do it. The vendors that have created proprietary schemes have much to gain by influencing the WG to adopt their schemes, if not in their entirety, at least partially. Note that some people separate the MPLS architecture from the MPLS protocol. They argue that the MPLS architecture describes a behavior and that this behavior can be manifested with other existing protocols such as Tag Switching. The argument continues that Tag Switching or ARIS is MPLS. The remaining discussion presented here examines MPLS.

The Virtual Circuit

Vital to MPLS and to its predecessors is the creation of the virtual circuit. The virtual circuit might be called different names by different schemes, but the concept is consistent. To support an abundance of traffic between numerous locations and at the same time provide different levels of service, a connection-oriented protocol is required, and virtual circuits must be deployed. The concept has been demonstrated and validated by frame relay and ATM.

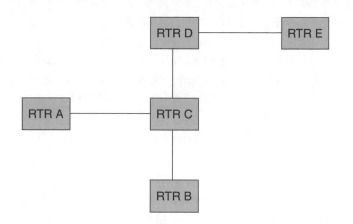

Figure 4.17 Routers interconnected with point-to-point links.

To illustrate the concept, consider the network shown in Figure 4.17 and assume that the links are T1 circuits.

In a conventionally routed network with TDM circuits, it is conceivable that traffic from Rtr A to Rtr E will consume so much of the bandwidth (Rtr C to Rtr D) that traffic from Rtr B to Rtr D will be deprived of sufficient bandwidth required for some desired service level. The problem becomes significantly more important when one is trying to aggregate traffic from 50 or 100 sites. Early ISPs configured in this manner were inhibited from implementing any sort of traffic control or engineering, which is why they were quick to implement frame relay and later ATM. The technologies enabled traffic control and traffic engineering. The connection-oriented, virtual-circuit-based technologies enabled ISPs to allocate some portion of resources between sites even though the physical links were aggregated.

A goal of MPLS is to enable traffic control and traffic engineering at Layer 3 independent of the underlying physical technology. Basically, in a way not unlike frame relay or ATM, MPLS relies on Layer-3 forwarding at the edge and label (Layer 2) forwarding in the core.

MPLS Physical Components

MPLS identifies two basic types of nodes: a Label Edge Router (LER) and a Label Switching Router (LSR). Both the LER and LSR implement an IP-routing protocol (RIP, OSPF, BGP) and participate in the Label Distribution Protocol (LDP). The LER and LSR can be either frame or ATM switches that implement MPLS.

The LER is located at the edge of the MPLS domain. It is effectively the ingress (or egress) MLPS switch. As the ingress switch, it examines the packet header, determines the destination and Forward Equivalency Class (FEC) of the packet, inserts the appropriate label onto the packet, and forwards the packet to the outbound interface. When functioning as an egress switch, the LER receives a labeled packet on a label-switching interface and extracts the label before forwarding the packet over a non-MPLS interface.

The LSR is in the MPLS core, and all of its interfaces are label-switching interfaces. The forwarding decisions are based on labels. An LSR looks at the label of the packet on the incoming interface. It performs a look-up in a table to find the associated outgoing interface and label. It then either swaps the label to the correct one for the outgoing link or adds another label on top of the existing label and then forwards the packet over the out-going interface. MPLS will support "*label stacking,* an ordered set of labels, so that multiple labels can be carried simultaneously within the packet. This practice enables simultaneous support of interdomain and intrado-main labels so that one set of labels can be used within a domain and another set of labels used between the domains, as shown in Figure 4.18.

When LER and LSR are implemented, it is likely that both logical components are in the same device. In other words, the same node can perform both simple forwarding on label information and label-switching-edge functionality and forwarding at Layer 3.

Label Distribution Protocol

LDP is the protocol used to establish labeled paths through the network. LDP comprises a set of procedures and messages used by LSRs to establish Label Switched Paths (LSPs), distributing labels and binding labels to

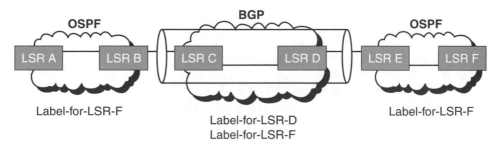

Figure 4.18   Label stacking.

the appropriate FEC. The same protocol, LDP, distributes the labels between the MPLS devices and binds the labels to FEC.

The term *Forward Equivalence Class* was introduced by MPLS to denote packet-forwarding classes of service. A forwarding equivalence class will typically be associated with a particular destination (IP address). However, it may be more specific, like constricting traffic to a destination with distinct service requirements.

Thus, each MPLS device creates and maintains a FIB that is a table with one-row-per-forwarding equivalence class.

FEC implies a set of packets being sent to the same place and receiving the same general type of treatment. We have to be careful when we say the same type of treatment because the idea is that an MPLS label corresponds to an FEC. But the label itself contains *Class of Service* bits, so it is possible that packets have different Class of Service requirements within the same FEC. The MPLS WG is finding that getting the definition of FEC and determining how to use it is a tricky task.

Two Label-Switching Routers using LDP to exchange label-binding information are called *LDP peers*. An *LDP adjacency* is created between the peers. An LDP adjacency is a bidirectional relationship that allows each peer to learn the other's labels and streams.

There are four categories of LDP messages:

Discovery messages. Used to announce and maintain the presence of an LSR in a network.

Session messages. Used to establish, maintain, and terminate sessions between LSR peers.

Advertisement messages. Used to create, change, and delete label mappings for FECs.

Notification messages. Used to provide advisory information and to signal errors.

Discovery messages are used by LSRs to continually advertise their presence to the network. The messages are transmitted as UDP packets using a special "all LSR routers" group-multicast address. Upon discovery of a neighbor, the LSR begins an initialization procedure using LDP Session messages. Session messages are transported with TCP transport to ensure delivery. Upon successful completion of the initialization procedure, the two LSRs are said to be LDP peers. The LDP peers can now exchange label-binding information using the LDP Advertisement messages. Advertisement messages also rely on TCP for reliable delivery. Correct operation of LDP requires reliable and sequential delivery of binding information.

Label-switched paths are controlled in a distributed fashion. Each LSR negotiates a label for each forwarding equivalence class with its upstream and downstream neighbors along the path. There are several methods supported by MPLS that can be used to assign and distribute label information between the LSRs. The method to be used is negotiated during the initialization phase.

With Downstream label allocation, the downstream LSR—the one that will receive traffic from its upstream neighbor—binds labels to the IP-destination address and FEC and informs the upstream LSR of the bindings. (It is also possible for the labels to support levels of granularity. For example, the same label can be associated with multiple IP-address prefixes.)

The upstream LSR will then insert the labels into its *label information base* (LIB). The LIB maps the relationship between the link-specific label of each label-switched path and the corresponding forwarding-equivalence class. With this approach, the downstream TSR ensures that the labels it receives are within an acceptable range. (It might be that the downstream TSR assigns label values in a way that expedites lookup, or the label value can have some other internal representation.)

Another method for label allocation is Downstream on Demand Label Allocation. The ingress node of each label-switched path initiates the label-binding requests that are propagated along the route to the egress node. The label-switched path is created as label bindings are propagated in the reverse direction (downstream allocation on demand). The approach also allows the upstream neighbor to associate multiple labels with the same IP destination or FEC. This can be very useful when ATM switches are used as a way to prevent ATM cell-interleaving problems. (See the discussion on Upstream Tag allocation in the *Tag Switching* section for an explanation of the cell interleaving issue.)

The MPLS architecture also supports Upstream Label Allocation in which the upstream neighbor informs the downstream TSR of label bindings, but the consensus is that upstream label allocation is less desirable than the downstream methods.

It is expected that first generation of MPLS technology will be deployed in ATM switches. Therefore, the default mode of operation will be Downstream on Demand Label Allocation. However, it is very possible that Downstream Label allocation will be used with frame-based MPLS networks.

Whenever a change occurs in the forwarding information base, the MPLS application renegotiates the label-FEC binding and updates the label information base.

Data Flow in MPLS

Using fields from the packet header as a key, the forwarding function looks up data stored in the forwarding information base to determine the next hop, what link to use, and which queue to use for the link. Figure 4.19 illustrates the forwarding table constructs and the subsequent date flow using MPLS. When a packet arrives at LER1 with a destination IP address of Net.1, LER1 puts a label equal to 0/35 on the packet and forwards it on interface 1. At LSR1, the packet arrives on interface 1 with a label equal to 0/35, so LSR1 changes the label to 0/34 and forwards the packet on interface 2, and so forth.

Traffic Engineering

The advantage that virtual circuits (frame, relay, ATM) provide to ISPs is the capability to control resource allocation and the flow of traffic. They

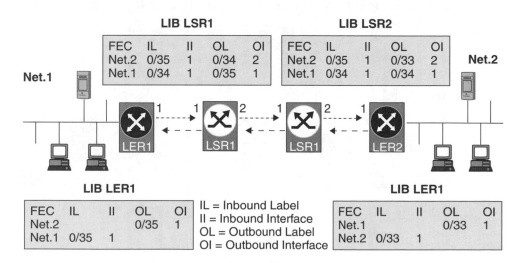

Figure 4.19   Data flow with MPLS on ATM switches using VPI/VCI defined labels.

define VCs in terms of where they go, the resources allocated to each VC, and who can use what VCs. Administrators may designate some traffic to traverse one path while other traffic traverses a different path. There may also be some QoS characteristics associated with the different paths. For example, an ATM circuit between two locations may be allocated as CBR (Constant Bit Rate) Service Category. ATM CBR Service Category supports real-time applications such as circuit emulation and voice.

To provide similar capabilities, MPLS will have to associate QoS with FECs, such that a separate path will need to be created to support FECs, each having a specified QoS associated with it. A packet arriving at an ingress MPLS switch will then be directed to a particular switched path, either administratively or dynamically, after the incoming packet header is examined and some criteria are applied to direct the packet onto one switched path or another (see Figure 4.20). The MPLS WG is currently investigating ways to assign resources and to associate QoS with MPLS switched paths. The current hypothesis is that some variant of RSVP will be used to convey the QoS information between the MPLS routers. The RSVP flow semantics and syntax, and RSVP resource semantics and syntax, will likely be adopted by the MPLS WG. In other words, the reserving resources and identifying who is entitled to those resources will probably be derived from RSVP work that has already been done.

MPLS Recap

MPLS will define a method for building switched paths through an IP-based network. The switched paths, although based on IP-routed paths, will move

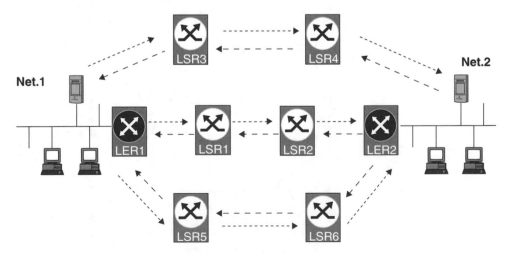

Figure 4.20   Multiple paths through the MPLS network.

traffic in a way that is independent of the standard IP-forwarding algorithm. The forwarding will be based on labels and hardware assisted.

> **The core MPLS switches are actually MPLS-enhanced IP routers, but we are assuming that they behave as core switches. The distinction is that when we think of frame relay or ATM core switches, we don't usually expect that there will be any end stations or IP networks directly attached. But if the MPLS core switches happen to support attached IP networks, they by default must be LER and thus must make IP-routing decisions.**

MPLS uses LDP for establishing IP-routing-based, label-switched paths through the network. In the early implementations, the switched path reflects what the routing protocol determined to be the best path through the network. Routed paths are not suited to provide traffic engineering and control and thus lack QoS capabilities. If the routed path changes, the switched path will respond to the change and a new switched path will be created. Later, as the protocol and implementations become more refined, the paths through the network may incorporate QoS-sensitive path selection. The MPLS WG is investigating the feasibility of incorporating some aspects of RSVP into MPLS to support QoS. However, the intrinsic problems associated with RSVP will also be a burden to MPLS— soft-state refreshing, control-resource authorization, limited-explicit-route support, and so forth.

Another approach to provide QoS in an MPLS that is being investigated is to incorporate some of the Diffserv functionality into MPLS. Perhaps the Diffserv codepoint could be carried in the MPLS label field. This may be problematic because of the different size of the Diffserv codepoint and the MPLS label fields.

In summary, despite the hurdles to overcome, MPLS will happen. How Diffserv and MPLS and RSVP are ultimately used depends on a variety of factors. However, there is certainly enough support—technical and political—behind the MPLS effort to overcome any amount of challenge.

Cut-Through Layer 3 Switch Issues

There are many variations of the cut-through theme; all variations of cut-through switches are focused on the convergence of Layer 2 and Layer 3. All are intended to relieve router congestion and latency and to expedite the path between switched subnets. The convergence of Layer 2 and Layer 3 is nontrivial. The OSI 7-layer model was intentionally developed with well-defined separation between Layer 2 and Layer 3. The idea is that Layer 3, the network layer, should be very independent of Layer 2, the datalink layer so that a single Layer 3 protocol could be supported by a variety of Layer 2 protocols such as IP (Layer 3) over Ethernet, token ring, and frame relay (Layer 2). This natural separation between Layer 2 and Layer 3 creates some interesting problems for cut-through switching schemes.

A fundamental concept with all cut-through schemes is that each revolves around an attempt to give the Layer 3 connectionless environment more of a connection-oriented switching atmosphere. In Layer 3's connectionless universe, packets move hop by hop from one router to the next until they arrive at their destination, and different packets in the same data stream might follow different paths through the network as each router along the way contends with constantly changing network conditions. In contrast, connection-oriented Layer 2 switching establishes a dedicated circuit between two end stations. All packets in that traffic stream follow the same path, and complex routing decisions don't have to be made at every node along the way. But because Layer 3 protocols such as IP are designed to operate in a connectionless, datagram environment, making them abide by Layer 2's connection-oriented switching methods presents a new set of issues.

Typically, Layer 3 protocols make forwarding decisions on a packet-by-packet basis. Each packet that arrives at the Layer 3 switch is treated independently. The destination address is examined in conjunction with the internal routing tables and forwarded accordingly. These internal routing tables are updated automatically with the aid of routing protocols that exchange reachability information between the Layer 3 switches. The Layer 3 devices maintain no per-flow state information, and in the event of an outage, the packets are forwarded around the outage as soon as the routing table has been updated. With link state routing protocols, this frequently happens within one or two seconds.

By contrast, the cut-through schemes are slow to react to routing changes. Most cut-through switching schemes rely on a routing protocol to determine a disruption in the network. However, only after the internal routing table has been updated does the process of building the Layer 2 switching table begin. The process of building the Layer 2 switching table is a slow switch-by-switch process. (To date there is no way to expedite the construction of the Layer 2 switching table; there is nothing analogous to a link state protocol that supports this.) Until the switching table has been stabilized and the new switching information propagated to the edge of the network, the "tagged" frames (or cells) continue to follow the broken path and, of course, at some point, are discarded. There is no chance that they will arrive at the intended destination.

Many cut-through schemes, in fact, provide no way for the Layer 2 switch path to respond to changes in the Layer 3 path. When there is a change in the network, the Layer 3 routing protocol responds, and the internal routing table gets updated, but there is no proactive way to notify Layer 2 of the change. Instead, these schemes periodically flush the Layer 2 information and then rebuild it. Between the time of the outage and the time the Layer 2 path is reconstructed, the frames using this Layer 2 path are sent into a "black hole." Management approaches usually allow configuration of the lifetime of the Layer 2 path. Of course, if the path lifetime is very short, fewer packets will be sent into the black hole but at the expense of much overhead to constantly reconstruct the Layer 2 path. If the Layer 2 path lifetime is longer, there is less overhead in reconstructing Layer 2 paths, but more packets are apt to be discarded when there is a failure. Even the more sophisticated cut-through schemes rely on Layer 2 path table rebuilds. With these schemes when there is an outage, Layer 3 notifies Layer 2, and the rebuilding of the Layer 2 path table commences. However, the important thing to note is that there is no Layer 2 protocol. The Layer 2 table is constructed based on information in the Layer 3 internal routing table.

With topology-based schemes, the Layer 2 path is constructed independently of any traffic. To construct the Layer 2 table requires a rich signaling, or path distribution, protocol. To accommodate signaling, an additional protocol is introduced into the network, and typically, signaling protocols are rather complex with much overhead. The advantage to pre-establishing the path is that all traffic, including the first packet in the flow, uses the cut-through path.

With traffic-based schemes, the path is created only in response to some traffic, and probably the first several packets rely on the conventional Layer 3 path because the Layer 2 path is not yet constructed. The signaling required to construct the Layer 2 path is much simpler. Usually some sort of path set-up message simply follows the Layer 3 path to the destination. With these schemes, there is the issue of when to establish and subsequently tear down the cut-through path.

Regardless of the cut-through scheme that is used, there will be new protocols introduced into the network. There will be new and different packets to support these protocols, and there will be new management issues. For example, it is likely that new tools will need to be developed to trace a packet's path through the network, and new management tools will be required to monitor the flows, network, and switch resource utilization. Also, since these cut-through schemes are not standardized (there may be an MPLS standard in 2000), there is no, or very limited, interoperability. To take full advantage of the cut-through scheme's efficiencies, the same type of cut-through device will need to be deployed end to end. This may involve an enormous investment in a protocol with a limited future.

Routing Switches

Each of the schemes just described is designed to avoid packet-by-packet routing. Each requires buying into a new technological architecture that may or may not become an industry standard. Each may require the deployment of new switches or edge devices. Some may even require new adapter cards and upgraded or reconfigured client software.

All the issues and complexities associated with router throughput and latency have led many in the industry to ask the obvious question: Why don't we just fix the problem rather than avoid it? Recognizing that cut-through switches evolved because of the limitations of conventional routers, vendors sought to develop high-performance devices that are fast enough to prevent the bottlenecks yet require no modification to the existing infrastructure or management strategy. These devices have inherited different names: Layer 3 switches, packet-by-packet Layer 3 switches, wire-speed routers, and routing switches are several of the more common names used in reference to these high-performance devices. Unlike cut-through and learning bridge techniques, these devices route all packets. They examine each packet's Layer 3 information. Using advanced ASICs to perform Layer 3 forwarding in hardware, they implement routing update protocols such as OSPF and RIP and often go beyond basic IP routing to support IP multicast routing, vLAN segregation, and multiple priority levels to assist in QoS. Unlike the cut-through techniques, wire-speed routing does not introduce proprietary technology into the network, so it offers full interoperability and avoids excessive administrative overhead. In effect, these intelligent, feature-rich devices are true routers capable of operating at speeds formerly associated only with Layer 2 switches.

Wire Speed

Routing switches are sometimes called Layer 3 switches or wire-speed switches. Wire speed is an ambiguous description. In the late 1980s to early 1990s, when wire-speed routers first appeared in the market, their fundamental characteristic was that they could transmit frames onto a link at a rate that would saturate the link. For example, if a router port was connected to a T1 link, the router could actually transmit frames at the full T1 rate. Of course, since the router has to process the packet header and make a routing decision, there is some amount of delay between the time that a packet arrives at the router and when the router actually transmits the packet. This delay (latency) is represented by the curved line in Figure 4.21. With early routers, the amount of latency was substantial, typically in the order of 10s of milliseconds. The delay associated with today's routing switches is typically in the order of nanoseconds.

With wire-speed devices, packets arrive at wire speed and depart at wire speed. Within the device, there is some amount of delay (referred to as latency). The amount of latency depends upon the particular device.

Also recognize that traffic is bursty and that the amount of queuing delay is related to the utilization of the outbound link. Of course, if more packets are destined for the output link than the link can accommodate, there will be long queuing delays. If the data rates are sustained long enough (beyond the internal buffering capacity of the link), packets will need to be discarded.

The diagram in Figure 4.22 also demonstrates an important concern. Network latency implies how long a user has to wait, and it increases as network utilization increases (in fact, it increases exponentially). However, that does not mean that if utilization of a network is kept low, the latency will not be an issue. This is because of the delays associated with traversing the box. When wire speed is used to describe a modern Layer 3 switch (or routing switch), the implication is that the delay internal to the device is very small.

At this point, here's a slight digression to discuss the distinction between delay and latency.

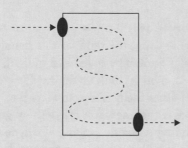

Figure 4.21   Wire Speed Device.

Continues

Wire Speed (*Continued*)

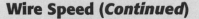

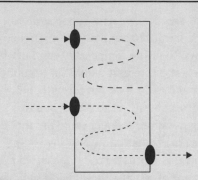

Figure 4.22   Oversubscribed link results in long queue delays and packet discard.

One might look at *delay* as a metric that measures how long something is not happening (for example, a packet waiting in a queue). *Latency* is a metric that measures how long it is between things happening (the time between when the packet arrives at the device and leaves the device).

Basically, latency is the time to transit a network component. We observe latency because of delay. There are many types of delay, including queuing delay, disk I/O, and processing time, within a device.

Network latency, or *end-to-end latency*, is a result of the summation of component delays (latencies) and propagation delays.

As the speed of the network increases the latency associated with each device (the time it takes a packet to traverse the device) becomes a more important concern.

For example, the time to transmit a 1 Mb file across the United States on a 50 Kbps link will be 20 milliseconds propagation delay (due to the speed of light) and an additional 20 milliseconds (1 Mb × 50 Kbps) for transmission time. However, with a 1000 Mbps link the propagation delay remains 20 milliseconds, but the transmission time is now only 1 millisecond (1 Mb × 1000 Mbps).

Consequently, the device latency is much more significant in a high-speed network than it is in lower speed networks.

This example illustrates that the propagation delay is the same regardless of the link speed (or bandwidth). How is that so? Because the time for the signal to propagate down the wire (*propagation delay*) is limited by the speed of light, but *bandwidth* isn't limited by the speed of light. One might look at bandwidth as representing *bit density*—or how close to each other the bits are. To increase bandwidth all we have to do is put the bits closer together—not make them go faster. Simply stated, the first bit of the transmission begins arriving at the destination at the same time—regardless of the bandwidth. However, as the bandwidth increases the subsequent bits arrive quicker.

Routing Switches Advantages

Most enterprises have adopted routing as the basis for their enterprise networks. Routers use the information in network protocols to intelligently forward packets through the network. Routers support arbitrary mesh topologies of virtually any diameter, and they support highly sophisticated dynamic adaptive routing algorithms that provide the capability for the network to recover from link and node failures. With routing switches, this distributed routing model remains intact.

Modern routers are capable of much more that the basic IP routing functions. One of the primary advantages of a router is that it creates a logical environment over the physical infrastructure. Routers are capable of using this logical network view to automatically select optimal paths through the network. Routers support different routing protocols, which allows users to create routing environments that suit their specific requirements. These protocols are standardized and provide tunable routing parameters to further meet the needs of specific network requirements. Newer routing protocols also provide load balancing where there are multiple links and paths. Most modern routers provide traffic prioritization, typically with multiple output port queues. This capability ensures that mission-critical or real-time traffic takes precedence over less important traffic. Many routers support routing protocols that have broadcast and multicast capabilities, which reduces broadcast traffic proliferation and provides directed multicast traffic. Both schemes conserve valuable bandwidth and router resources. Most routers support a way to control access to different portions of the network. Router filters, screens, and router-supported firewalls are methods commonly employed by routers to provide a form of security.

Routing switches minimize or eliminate the performance penalty previously associated with packet-by-packet traffic forwarding. The throughput of these devices is typically on the order of millions of packet per second, whereas software-based routers peak out at less than 1 million packets per second. Consequently, there is significant advantage to implementing routing switches rather than cut-through devices. Routing switches typically run the standard routing protocols, including RIP, OSPF, and IPX-RIP. As a result, there is no vendor lock-in when routing switches are deployed. One vendor's routing switch will be able to interoperate with another vendor's switch. Not only is the routing protocol standardized, but so is the management protocol. The tools that have been used in the past to monitor and troubleshoot the network will continue to work. This means that there is no learning curve. The operations and management staff will be able to resume their responsibilities without disruption.

No new protocols are introduced into the network because there is no convergence between Layer 2 and Layer 3. There is no need to maintain flow related state information or to modify the existing subnet structure. Because the traffic patterns are not being modified, the existing network design need not be modified.

Because routing switches forward packets on a packet-by-packet basis and each packet is processed at Layer 3, the router's network layer, it is possible for the routing switch to continue to provide the enhanced features that were described above.

Routing Switch Techniques

All routers have two components. They run a routing protocol and they forward packets. Routers run routing protocols to construct a routing table, and for every packet they receive, they must look up the route in the table and then forward the packet accordingly. As the size of the routing table increases, so does the time to look up the entry in the table. Routers incorporate various techniques to minimize the size of the routing table and to expedite the look-up process. Many summarize the route table entries to allow an arbitrarily large and complex network to be described in a bounded table, but this makes routing table searching somewhat more complex. A common technique employed in some products is to use a "route cache" of frequently seen addresses. This route cache is searched like a bridging table at high speeds. If the destination address isn't found in the cache, these products default to the conventional software interrupt-based route look-up (sometimes described as a *slow path*).

Caching routers can be useful in simple networks that don't connect directly to the public Internet or even in workgroups within large networks. In enterprise backbones or public networks, the combination of highly random traffic patterns and frequent topology changes tends to eliminate any benefits from the route cache strategy. Consequently, the performance is bounded by the speed of the software driven slow path, which may be many orders of magnitude lower than the caching *fast path*. Important considerations with caching routers are the size of the cache, the way the cache is maintained, and the performance of the slow path because at least some percentage of the traffic will take the slow path in any application.

Modern routing switches actually perform full routing at very high speeds. Instead of using a route cache, these products perform a complete routing table search for every packet at high speeds. Typically, they do this via a separate ASIC that is located on the line card. By eliminating the route cache, these products fully eliminate the slow path. Now, performance is predictable for most traffic in even the most complex internetworks.

The secret to their speed is that they separate the forwarding process from the routing table calculation process. Typically, there is a central processor that runs the routing protocol, builds the forwarding table, and handles a small portion of the actual forwarding. Typically, a copy of the central forwarding table is kept on the line cards, and this line card resident copy of the forwarding table is used by the ASIC to determine how the individual packets are to be forwarded.

Routing Switch Architectures

As previously emphasized, routing switches were developed to address the performance limitations imposed by conventional routers. In order to remove these limitations, the routing switches need to be designed in a way that maximizes throughout and minimizes latency. The devices that have emerged incorporate a variety of architectures. Figure 4.23 depicts a high-level switch architecture. As packets arrive they are put into input buffers and subsequently transferred across a backplane to an output buffer before being transmitted onto the output link. The most important aspects of a switch's architecture are the switch backplane characteristics, the buffering scheme, and the processor type.

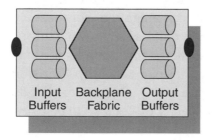

Figure 4.23 Switch architecture.

Switch Backplane

The data elements may be transferred across the backplane as either variable-length frames or fixed-length cells. Of course, with cell-based fabrics, there is additional work that needs to be done initially. When a frame arrives, it must be segmented into cells before the cells are switched across the fabric, and then the cells must be reassembled before they are presented to the output link. However, because there are significant advantages with cells, most modern routing switches employ a cell-based backplane. With fixed length cells, the latency associated with transferring the cell across the fabric is predictable, as is the time to transfer the cell from the input buffer to the fabric. Because of these consistencies, the scheduling of cell transfers is simplified and made more efficient. This is contrasted with unpredictably sized frames where the latency associated with transfer from input port to output port is dependent on the size of the frame. Also, with unpredictable frame sizes, a small frame associated with a real-time application may be detained in a buffer waiting for delivery of a longer frame to complete. The variable frame size contributes to interframe transfer variations or "jitter" as the frames traverse the switch. Fixed-length cells also simplify switch resource allocations. The fixed size eases buffer allocation and management and reduces the complexity of cell processing within VLSI chips.

Another important consideration with regard to the switch's backplane is its throughput, or transfer capacity. If the backplane throughput is not at least as large as the sum of the theoretical maximum speed of all the ports, the switch is considered a *blocking switch*. Many implementers assume that the added expense of a nonblocking switch is always justified. Vendors that manufacture nonblocking switches have done much to popularize the benefits of a nonblocking architecture. Certainly, there are places within the network that can benefit from a nonblocking switch. However, often nonblocking switches are only required at the core of the network and at other points where there is a lot of traffic aggregation. For most other places in the network, a blocking switch that has reasonable throughput will usually suffice. In order to appreciate the implications of a nonblocking architecture, consider a switch that has eight 100Mbps ports. Each port can theoretically handle 200Mbps (full duplex). This means that this switch would require a throughput capacity of 1.6Gbps to be truly nonblocking. However, in most networks, it is unlikely that the average per-port utilization would exceed 50 percent. So a 0.8Gbps blocking switch would be adequate. Thus, the criticality of a nonblocking architecture involves many criteria that should be evaluated on a case-by-case basis.

The terms *blocking* and *nonblocking* are sometimes used in a slightly different context. A nonblocking switch sometimes refers to a switch with no internal blocking. That is, once the cell or frame enters the backplane, it will pass undeterred through the backplane. There are switches, such as Banyan switches, for which the backplane is composed of stages, and there may be contention, and limited blocking, at an internal stage.

Conventional switch backplanes can generally be categorized as time-division or space-division based. With time-division schemes, all data elements flow across the same physical fabric that is shared by all input and output ports. Time-division schemes can be further divided into shared memory or shared bus. The general approach is that when frame arrives at the input port, it is processed and then transported via a bus structure to either shared memory or the destination output port. The bus is usually logically separated into time slots, which are shared by the ports in a time-division multiplexing fashion. With space-division–based backplanes, there is a separate path between input and output ports.

Crossbar switches are typically nonblocking switches with a fully interconnected structure. The general architecture of a crossbar switch is shown in Figure 4.24. Each input port is effectively connected to each output port. The effective capacity of the switch fabric increases as line cards are added

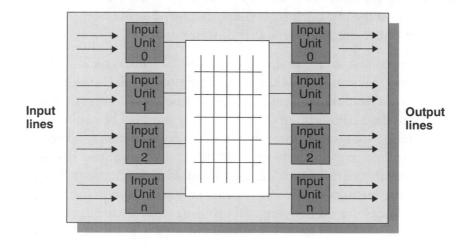

Figure 4.24 Crossbar switch design.

and more of the fabric becomes active. The density of the backplane—that is, the number of crosspoints required—is the square of the number of slots in the switch. A major drawback to most crossbar designs is the well-known head-of-line blocking (HOLB) issue. HOLB is a consequence of input buffering, which is used in many crossbar switches. With HOLB data, elements at the front of the input port queue (head of the line) that are destined for a busy output port will block traffic destined for a nonactive output port. Eventually, data is discarded as the input buffers fill. Head-of-line blocking introduces delay and delay variation and creates artificial and unnecessary congestion into the network. Some modern switches implement sophisticated and costly buffering schemes, such as per-flow buffering or virtual output queuing in which each input port maintains a separate queue for each output port, to minimize the effect of HOLB.

Another issue with crossbar designs is that inbound traffic that is destined for multiple output ports, such as IP multicast, must be replicated multiple times and transported to and stored in multiple output locations. Also, the combined effects of HOLB and replicated packets make it difficult to deliver prioritized traffic on a port basis.

For crossbar switches to support gigabit speeds, enhancements must be made to the basic crossbar design to counter the HOLB. Modern switches not only implement sophisticated buffering schemes, but they also employ very fast crossbar switching fabrics. If the crossbar is sufficiently undersubscribed, it can compensate for the relative inefficiency of the design. For example, if there are two inputs with data contending for the same output port and the fabric operates twice as fast as the link speed, both cells at the input buffers will be delivered to the output before another data element arrives at the input ports.

Shared memory switches, as shown in Figure 4.25, are typically time-division structured. All ports access the central memory pool. Data elements are transported from the line cards to the memory pools via a shared bus. Access to the bandwidth of the shared medium may be arbitrated dynamically among the switch ports on a demand basis, which can provide efficient multiplexing of interfaces with different access rates. This scheme eliminates the HOLB problems associated with the crossbar designs and utilizes the memory system in a highly efficient manner, facilitating efficient multicast frame delivery and enabling traffic prioritization. The shared memory switches are obviously limited because of their dependence on a bus and the associated bus arbitration. Another limiting factor

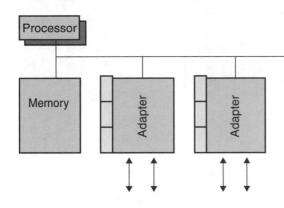

Figure 4.25   Conventional shared memory switch.

is that each data element must be placed onto the bus two times. At gigabit speeds, it is difficult to achieve nonblocking performance with this design.

If a shared memory switch is to support gigabit speeds, enhancements must be made to the basic shared memory design. The bottleneck with shared memory architectures is the traditional bus. At gigabit speeds, a shared bus capable of supporting more than a few ports is difficult to design. With modern shared-memory–based routing switches, all ports share the same memory space; however, unlike with the traditional bus-based shared-memory architectures, each port has a dedicated path with which to directly access the shared memory (see Figure 4.26). This approach removes the limitations imposed by the shared bus. When coupled with a nonblocking shared-memory switching fabric, this design is capable of supporting full wire-speed performance on all ports, even during periods of heavy traffic.

With *distributed shared memory switch* (shown in Figure 4.27), each line card is effectively a miniature switch, and all switch functions are per-

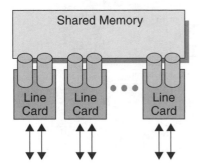

Figure 4.26   Modern shared memory switch.

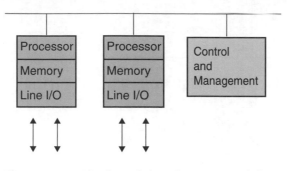

Figure 4.27   Distributed shared memory switch.

formed on the line card. Data is transferred between line cards via a back-plane bus. The control processor typically maintains a central forwarding table that is distributed to each line card. This design avoids HOLB, and it is effective for multicast because one copy of the frame can be placed onto the bus and tagged so that it will be copied onto several destination line cards. With this design, there is considerable overhead in arbitrating for control of the bus. And the effective utilization of the bus is a function of the length of the bus, so only a few line cards are supported.

Distributed shared memory architectures are not commonly found in gigabit routing switches.

Multistage (Banyan) switches (shown in Figure 4.28) are space-division switches with a separate physical path between each input port and each output port. However, the fabric is composed of multiple stages, and each stage has a number of switching elements. Each switching element has two inputs and two outputs. The number of stages and switching elements per stage is a function of the number of slots in the switch. With

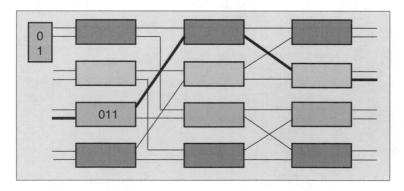

Figure 4.28   Multistage switch.

this design, there is a unique path from each input port to each output port. There are two ways of specifying the path through the switch. With self-routing, each switching element examines the data element to determine on which of its outputs to send the data element. With label routing (as shown in Figure 4.28), the traffic is examined at the input port, and the path to the destination output port is specified with a label.

In the diagram, the input port specifies that path as "011," indicating that the first switch sends the data element on it port 0, the second switch element sends the data on it port 1, and the third switching element sends that data on its port 1. However, there could be contention at any of the internal switching elements. For this reason, it is said that this design exhibits "internal blocking." Also, there can be HOLB at each of the switching elements, further contributing to inefficiencies of this design. Batcher-Banyan switches provide an enhancement to the Banyan Multistage design and implement an algorithm at the input port that minimizes internal blocking. In general, multistage switch design has proven to be ineffective for high-speed data switches.

Multistage switching architectures are not commonly found in gigabit routing switches.

Buffering Schemes

There are two fundamental switch-buffering schemes. Input buffering occurs between the input port and the switch fabric, and output buffering occurs between the switch fabric and the destination port. The term *input/output buffering* is somewhat misleading. In reality, both input and output ports have some amount of buffer. Input/output buffering is more realistically an indication of where buffering is preferred and also where flow control is initiated. With input buffering, the flow of data across the switch fabric is determined by buffer availability at the output port. When a data element arrives at the input port, it is detained on the input side of the fabric, until the output port indicates that it is ready to receive the data. (Obviously, there must be some buffering/queuing capability at the output port; otherwise, the output port would never be able to present a continuous flow of data onto the link.)

As mentioned earlier, HOL blocking is a significant issue with input buffering; data elements at the front of the input port queue that are destined for a busy output port will head-of-line block traffic destined for a

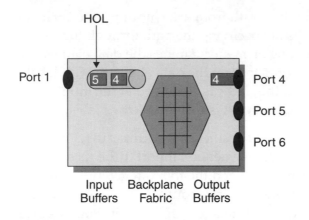

Figure 4.29 Input buffering with HOL blocking.

nonactive output port. In Figure 4.29, a packet that is destined for output port 5 is waiting on input port 1, behind a packet that is destined for output port 4. Output port 4 is busy. This problem instigates other problems because as the input buffer becomes saturated, data may be delayed or discarded even though there are available resources at the output port and link. Or as the input buffers become filled, a flow-control message may be sent to the switch at the end of the link. The result is that the flow of data is quenched even though there is an available resource on the path between the source and the destination—except at the HOLB blocked input buffer.

With output buffering (shown in Figure 4.30), most of the buffers are located at the output side of the switch fabric. As data elements arrive, they are immediately switched to a buffer serving the output port. Data flow across the switch fabric is controlled at the input side of the fabric; when data arrives, it is sent. There is no HOLB.

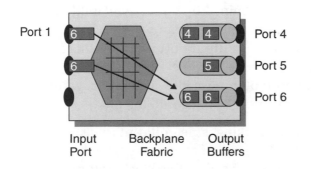

Figure 4.30 Output buffering.

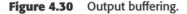

But there are issues with output buffering as well. Because data arriving simultaneously from several input ports may be destined for the same output port, many more buffers are required with output buffering. As the data accumulates in the output buffers, delay and delay variation are being introduced into the flow. If the output buffers overflow, the data that is discarded will have already been processed and switched across the fabric. This is a waste of the resource.

Some switches attempt to leverage the advantages of input buffering and output buffering. They use a combination of input and output buffers along with a *backpressure* technique that delays cells at the input when congestion occurs at the output port. The downside of input/output buffering schemes is that they tend to increase delay and delay variation, and they can limit the throughput when congestion occurs.

Buffer Algorithms

Not only is the position of the buffers important, but effective buffer management is instrumental to the overall operation of the switch. Buffer management plays an important role in providing quality of service, flow control, discard schemes, and congestion control. Typically, the buffer space is physically, or logically, allocated to queues. These queues serve to separate the physical locations within memory of the data from the logical view of the data's position or relative importance, as shown in Figure 4.31.

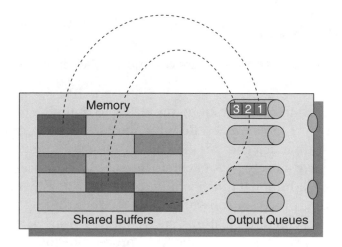

Figure 4.31 Buffers and queues.

Buffer space can be allocated in a number of ways. Three of the more common approaches are buffer separation, partial buffer sharing, and common buffer with push-out.

With buffer separation a fixed portion of buffer space is allocated to each of the output queues. With switches that support traffic prioritization, there will be more than one queue associated with each output port. Each queue will support traffic of a different priority. This scheme is easy to implement, but because of the lack of sharing, it may result in unnecessary congestion and data discard. If there is a great deal of traffic of a particular priority destined for an output port, this queue may overflow, resulting in data discard, even though there is, in fact, unused buffer space allocated to a different queue.

Partial buffer sharing schemes are more efficient than buffer separation. Generally, with this approach, the buffers are allocated on a port basis rather than a queue basis. If a high-priority queue becomes filled, it can utilize buffers allocated to a lower-priority queue. Some implementations of this scheme allow management to adjust the various thresholds to compensate for various system loads.

The common buffer with push-out scheme offers the most sophisticated buffering approach. With this scheme, all queues share the common buffer pool. However, if there are no buffers available when high-priority traffic arrives, lower-priority data is discarded, and the buffers are made available to the higher-priority data. This scheme is very efficient, but it is the most complex and difficult to manage.

Processors: RISC and ASIC

The following two types of processors are commonly used in routing switches:

RISC processors. Used to run the routing protocols, to build the routing tables, and to forward some frames. Reduced instruction set computer (RISC) processors are much cheaper than the customized counterparts that are designed exclusively for switching. Because RISC processors are programmable, additional functionality can be added with an upgrade to the RISC processor software. Many modern routing switches implement enhanced features, such as security, support for vLANs, and traffic prioritization, on the RISC processor. However, the RISC processor introduces more delay than ASIC processors.

Application-specific integrated circuit (ASIC) processors. Customized for a particular operation, with all of the functionality in the hardware. Typically, routing switches will implement an ASIC processor on each line card, and the ASIC is responsible for most data forwarding. Although the ASIC is much faster that the RISC processor, extra functionality cannot be added via software. To enhance the supported features of the ASIC processor requires development and a new processor "spin" or build.

Modern routing switches usually employ both RISC and ASIC processors. The RISC processor usually resides on a centralized control module. The RISC will distribute information, such as routing tables and filters, to the line cards. Resident on each line card is one or more ASIC processors responsible for functions such as referencing the distributed line card tables for data-forwarding information, prioritizing traffic, and managing traffic. Where possible, the data is forwarded without involvement of the centralized RISC processor.

Switches Support Enhanced Features

Much of the enhanced functionality found in modern conventional routers is also implemented in routing switches. Routing switches not only understand the network topology and dynamically adapt to network topology changes, but they typically provide the traditional features such as security, access policies, manageability, and broadcast containment. Many routing switches also support IEEE 802.1p priorities via multiple output queues. Many also provide a management tool that allows the network manager to configure port services, routing functions, link-level load sharing, SNMP traps, RMON information, multicasting and IGMP snooping techniques, and Virtual Redundant Router Protocol (VRRP) support. Many also support IEEE 802.1Q vLANs. Because vLANs provide flexibility of membership to network devices without regard to the physical connection, it is important to secure communications between vLANs. Generally, vLAN security is provided through packet filtering provided by the routing switch.

Routing switches typically route several Layer 3 protocols in hardware, usually IP and IPX, at least. They also typically support several routing protocols; RIP, RIP2, OSPF, and IPX-RIP are supported by most. Routing switches may also support other protocols via conventional software interrupts. For example, a routing switch may support DECnet in software, such that whenever a DECnet packet arrives at the switch, the input port forwards the packet to the central RISC processor. The RISC processor understands the DECnet protocol and provides forwarding of the DECnet packet. Of course, there is a significant delay penalty associated with the protocols that are supported with the centralized RISC processor.

Many routing switches also support extensive redundancy and resiliency features such as redundant and hot-swappable line cards, redundant and hot-swappable power supplies, redundant and hot-swappable cooling devices, redundant fabrics, and extensive fault- and alarm-monitoring systems.

A Typical Routing Switch Walk-Through

The following steps demonstrate how a packet is forwarded through a routing switch, as shown in Figure 4.32. In this example, the routing switch also supports IEEE 802.1Q VLANs.

1. As a packet enters the line card, the first 48–64 bytes are collected by the ASIC. The ASIC examines these bytes and makes switching and routing decisions, vLAN determination, and priority determination. The line card ASIC has local access to a forwarding table that is created and maintained by a centralized system processor.

2. If the Destination MAC address on the incoming frame is other than the MAC address associated with the routing entity for the vLAN, the packet is handled at Layer 2. (If the packet is to be routed, it is addressed to the router's MAC address. Normally an end station determines the router's MAC address by ARPing for the Default Gateway IP address.)

3. If it is determined that the incoming packet should be handled at Layer 2, vLAN processing commences.

    a. Does the frame have an 802.1Q tag?

    b. Does the frame belong to a MAC-based vLAN?

    c. Does the frame belong to a subnet-based vLAN?

    d. Does the frame belong to a policy-based vLAN?

    e. Does the frame belongs to the port-based vLAN configured on the received port?

4. If the packet is a routing update packet (for example, a RIP packet) it is sent to the central control processor, which is responsible for maintaining and distributing the routing table.

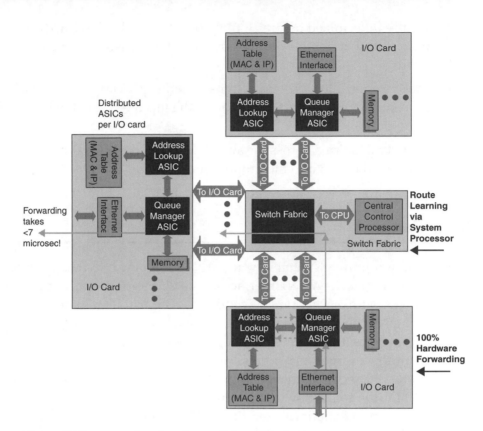

Figure 4.32 Example of routing switch architecture.

5. If the packet is to be handled at Layer 3, the ASIC examines the forwarding tables for the destination IP address. If there is no host entry in the table, the ASIC determines if the destination IP network is in its table. If there is a network entry in its table, the ASIC next determines if the IP network is local; that is, is one of the switch ports configured into the same IP subnet that the frame is destined for.

   a. If the destination IP network is local, the ASIC sends the packet to the central control processor, which will ARP for the host.

   b. If the destination IP network is not local, the ASIC forwards the packet to the next-hop router.

   c. If there is no network entry in its table, the ASIC looks for a default route.

   d. If there is no default route in the table, the ASIC sends the packet to the central control processor.

6. After the ASIC evaluates the Layer 2 and Layer 3 information and has determined the priority associated with the packet (this information is

usually determined before all the bits of the packet have arrived at the input ports), it notifies the system control processor that a packet is coming.

7. The system control process assigns a memory location and signals the appropriate output port and informs the input ASIC to begin transfer of the data.

8. Data is transferred across the switch fabric to the output port ASIC that puts the data into the proper output queue.

Terabit Routers

The original routing switches were LAN-only devices that supported no wide area network (WAN) interfaces. This was appropriate because the largest WAN links were typically 45Mbps (DS3) and could not take advantage of the gigabit capacity. Also, because routing switches supported many features that were not found on conventional routers with WAN interfaces, such as priorities and vLANs, there was no impending requirement to connect them directly to the conventional WAN routers. So initially, the routing switches were deployed in the LAN and were connected to a conventional router via an Ethernet link to provide access to the WAN from the LAN.

Recently, the WAN landscape changed considerably. More users, faster access rates, and longer session times have provoked a perpetual cycle of escalating demand for bigger WAN pipes. Carrier and service providers are racing to meet the demand by providing enormous amounts of new transmission bandwidth. Wavelength-division multiplexing is increasing the bandwidth capacity of existing fiber optic networks by orders of magnitude. Although bandwidth alone is not the solution to the Internet's congestion problems, it is certainly a significant step in the right direction.

As we have seen, routers of the late 1990s are significantly faster, more powerful, and more intelligent than those from just a few years earlier. Today's routers, routing switches, and switching routers are capable of allocating bandwidth, creating wide-ranging vLANs, and providing much more flexibility for network managers than could have been imagined just two years ago. New vendors, new technologies, and enhanced software functionality are even beginning to address the needs of real-time applications. However, one major aspect that still must be considered is the requirement of many new applications to communicate one to many or many to many. This need calls for multicast and broadcast capabilities that are just starting to emerge and be standardized.

Conclusion

This chapter examines standards and schemes that are being implemented or proposed to address increasing bandwidth requirements. The networking landscape is changing dramatically. Not only is the number of users increasing exponentially, but the types of applications that are being run across the Internet and private networks are also changing. Increasingly, multimedia applications are being introduced onto networks. These applications have more stringent throughput and response times requirements.

Subsequent chapters examine emerging techniques designed to provide network requirements demanded by this new breed of applications.

CHAPTER 5

IP Multicast

As more and more applications demand communication among predefined user groups, the need to effectively manage this traffic has increased. While routing and vLANs can accomplish some of the goals, there are still areas that need to be defined, including how to address and distribute the traffic. In this chapter, we explore the various multicast issues and techniques.

When operating in a LAN environment, IP multicast groups are sometimes categorized as multicast vLANs. Although the fundamental concept of defining a broadcast domain still applies, the manner in which the broadcast domain is defined is significantly different. With vLANs, we enable switch ports for a vLAN, but the port begins participating in the vLAN only when a frame that matched the enabling criteria arrives at the port. The vLAN usually exists solely from the perspective of the switch, and the end station knows nothing about the vLAN. (Of course, if the end station is 802.1Q aware, this is not the case.) Also, although vLANs do support multicast frames, most of the frames transmitted in a typical vLAN are unicast frames.

Contrary to the vLAN situation, all the frames transmitted in an IP multicast group are multicast frames. By default, multicast frames are sent on all ports in a vLAN. With IP multicast groups, the end station must explicitly request to participate in the multicast group. The end station joins the multicast group by responding affirmatively to a broadcast notification, which signals the multicast group's existence. The switches will listen for this affirmation from the end stations, and the switch will forward the multicast only on ports that have processed an affirmation to receive the particular multicast. As a result of this action, the forwarding database is "pruned"; that is, the multicast is not forwarded on all spanning tree active ports but rather only on spanning tree active ports that have received an explicit affirmation for the multicast.

Multicast groups are dynamic in that the end station remains a member of the multicast group for a period of time and must reaffirm its desire to continue participating in the multicast group. As a result, the multicast group has a high degree of flexibility and application sensitivity. Another very important distinction between vLANs and multicast groups is that vLANs by default constrain the broadcast domain, so they should not span bandwidth-limited wide area links. On the other hand, multicast groups are inherently designed to span wide areas. Several routing protocols are explicitly designed to support multicast groups across the wide area.

Multicast Concepts

Until recently, most applications were based on a unicast distribution model that relies on point-to-point transmissions between a unique source and a single destination. Today's emerging applications often involve communications between one or more sources and many receivers. These applications include multimedia conferences, stock quotes, and distance learning for which the audio and/or video signal is digitized, compressed, and transmitted as a sequence of packets.

The applications that transmit information from one computer to many other computers present a new set of challenges for the data network.

First, it would certainly be inefficient and resource demanding to create a point-to-point session between the source and each of the destination workstations, as depicted in the left side of Figure 5.1. It would be significantly more efficient for the source to send a single packet stream and then have network devices distribute the stream intelligently as duplicate streams only when necessary, as shown in the right side of Figure 5.1. This is the goal of IP multicasting.

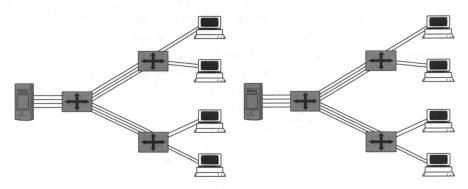

Figure 5.1   IP multicasting.

> Primarily because of multimedia applications, there is another consideration that is addressed in later chapters. There has been considerable effort lately to deliver an enhanced quality of service to this class of application. The video and audio applications are much more demanding in terms of delay and delay-variation tolerances than are conventional file transfer applications. To carry this thought further, if all applications—including telephony—were to converge on IP and the Internet, a mechanism to prioritize traffic would certainly be required.

The benefit of multicast is not new. It was first realized in the LAN environments where a particular class of Layer 2 MAC addresses is defined as multicast addresses. These multicast addresses are used to send a single frame to multiple stations simultaneously. Layer 2 multicast frames are used in RIP, OSPF, NetBIOS, IPX, and DECnet to transfer data efficiently to multiple stations on the LAN. IP multicast is basically an extension of this approach. The original intent of IP multicast was to allow stations that are not collated on the same LAN to realize the benefits of multicast. IP multicast provides an efficient Layer 3 transport for delivering multimedia traffic to groups of IP addressable devices.

Originally proposed in 1989 (RFC 1112), IP multicast permits a host (source) to transmit a single IP packet that is delivered to multiple IP hosts (receivers) that are participating on the IP multicast group. Associated with each multicast group is a unique IP multicast address. The packet is addressed to an IP multicast group address that determines the set of receivers. Hosts may simultaneously participate in a number of multicast groups and hence select the multicast packets they wish to receive. Hosts may join and leave multicast groups dynamically. Multiple sources may transmit to the same group, thus permitting many-to-many communications.

Although IP multicast was originally intended to support multicast in the wide area network, the concept has been enhanced (via *snooping*) to provide support for multicast groups in the LAN. Consequently, comprehensive IP multicast requires modifications within end stations, switches, and routers.

IP Multicast Addressing

IP multicast uses IP class D addresses. Each multicast application is assigned a class D IP address or a group address. When the source sends a multicast packet, the sender addresses the IP packet to the class D group or multicast address instead of an individual IP host address. In effect, the class D group address represents the collection of hosts that want to receive the particular multicast (in other words, hosts participating in the multicast group). The hosts can receive the multicast by registering to join the multicast group. Joining the group informs the network that the host wants to receive packets addressed to the particular class D IP address. Conversely, a host can leave a multicast group at any time.

The class D address used by IP multicasting ranges from 224.0.0.0–239.255.255.255 where the first four bits of the address contain 1110 (see Figure 5.2). The remaining 28 bits identify a particular IP multicast group. The address represents a multicast group identifier that can be used only as a destination IP address (never a source IP address) and does not provide any further information such as origin of group or subnet. In addition, multicast packets cannot generate ICMP error messages such as destination unreachable, source quench, or echo reply. However, some addresses within the address range have special significance.

Address range 224.0.0.0–224.0.0.225 is reserved for administrative functions and system-level routing tasks. For example, OSPF uses 224.0.0.6, the *all-designated-routers* multicast, to send link state advertisements to the LAN's designated router. The designated router uses 224.0.0.5, the *all-OSPF-router* multicast, to forward link state information to all other routers on the LAN. Address range 224.0.1.0–238.255.255.255 is specified for multicast applications that traverse the Internet while 239.0.0.0–

1	1	1	0	IP Multicast Group

Figure 5.2 IP Multicast address format.

239.255.255.255 is reserved for locally administered or site-specific multi-cast applications.

Because frame delivery on the LAN relies on Layer 2 (not Layer 3) addressing, IP multicasting provides a mechanism for translating Layer 3 multicast addresses to Layer 2 multicast addresses. IEEE 802.3 reserves a portion of the IEEE 802.3 MAC address space (01-00-5E-00-00-00 to 01-00-5E-7F-FF-FF) for IP multicasting. The low-order 23 bits of Layer 3's multicast address are mapped to the low-order 23 bits of Layer 2's multicast address. For example, IP multicast address 224.0.0.1 becomes Ethernet multicast address 01-00-5E-00-00-01.

The hosts that are participating in the multicast group enable the MAC address that corresponds to the IP multicast address on their *network interface cards* (NICs). In Figure 5.3, hosts ES1 and ES2 are participating in an IP multicast group. Consequently, the IP address of the multicast group (the IP Class D address) is translated into a MAC address (01-00-5E...) on the NIC. The NIC now accepts frames with the MAC address that corresponds to the IP multicast group.

Note that the mapping is not guaranteed to be unique. Because IP multicast group addresses have 28 bits (the first 4 bits are always 0111) with only the low-order 23 bits mapped, multiple Layer 3 multicast addresses have the same Layer 2 multicast address. For example, 224.12.1.2 and 225.12.1.2 both map to 01-00-5E-0B-01-02. In fact, 32 different Layer 3

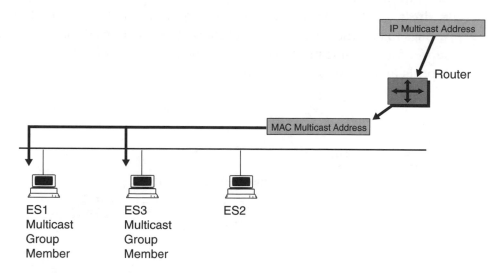

Figure 5.3   On LAN frame delivered via MAC multicast address.

addresses will map to each MAC. The consequence is that a host will receive delivery of some multicast packets even though the packets were not destined for the host. All incoming packets must be checked by IP software and discarded if delivery was unintended. Note that a host running a multicast application has two IP addresses: its own unicast IP address and the group IP address associated with the multicast application.

Internet Group Management Protocol

A host wishing to participate in a multicast application is configured with the class D address associated with each multicast application for which it wants to receive traffic. *Internet group management protocol* (IGMP), RFC1112 and RFC2236, is the protocol used by multicast routers to learn the existence of host group members on their directly attached LAN segments. To determine if any hosts on a local segment belong to a multicast group, one multicast router per subnet periodically multicasts an IGMP host membership query on each LAN to which it is attached. If there are multiple multicast routers on the LAN, one of them is elected the IGMP designated router and only it sends out the query. IGMP provides a mechanism to elect the IGMP designated router. All hosts wishing to participate in a multicast group accept the query. The query is sent to the all-hosts group (network address 224.0.0.1) with a TTL of 1 so that it is not propagated beyond the LAN. Each host sends back one IGMP Host Membership Report message per host group. The report is sent to the group address, so all group members see the report. If another host on the LAN wishes to join the same multicast group, there is no need for it to send a report for the same multicast group—thus, only one member of the LAN reports membership (see Figure 5.4).

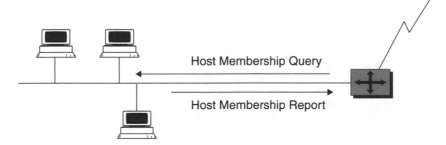

Host Membership Query

Host Membership Report

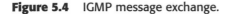

Figure 5.4 IGMP message exchange.

If a new multicast process is started on a host, it signals that it wants to participate in the multicast group by immediately sending an IGMP host membership report with the group address on the LAN. The host's NIC maps the IP multicasts group address to the MAC address and begins to accept frames for that MAC and forward them to the multicast process.

Periodically, the local multicast router sends an IGMP host membership query to the all-hosts multicast group to verify current memberships. If all member hosts reported memberships at the same time, frequent traffic congestion might result. It avoids this congestion by having each host delay its report by a random interval and send the report only if it has not seen a report for the same group from another host. As a result, only one membership report is sent in response for each active group address, although many hosts may have memberships.

Hosts can also leave the multicast group at any time. When the multicast application terminates, the host sends a host membership leave message (network address 224.0.0.2). The message informs the router that the host is no longer a member of the multicast joining and informs the router to forward the multicast onto the LAN.

IGMP Snooping

As we have seen, IGMP provides a mechanism for hosts to convey their desire to participate in an IP multicast group to their adjacent router. But what if the host is on a large switched network? By default, multicast frames are flooded throughout the broadcast domain, but in a large switched network, it is likely that only a limited number of end stations actually participate in the multicast.

When the host sends the IGMP report, it will find its way to the router because it is a multicast frame. Upon receiving the IGMP report, the router will create an internal filter such that IP multicast frames for the multicast group will be sent onto the LAN. However, all the multicast group frames will be multicast frames and consequently will be flooded throughout the LAN—very inefficient indeed (see Figure 5.5). What is needed is a mechanism to prune each switch's forwarding table so that the multicast is delivered only on ports that have received an IGMP report message for the multicast group.

IEEE 802.1Q provides this functionality with GMRP. The GARP *multicast registration protocol* (GMRP) is used to communicate multicast group

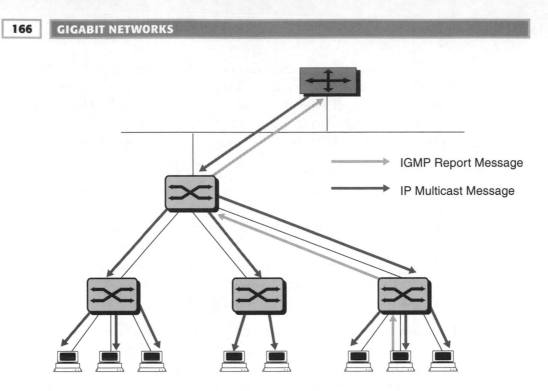

IGMP Report Message

IP Multicast Message

Figure 5.5 Inefficiencies of IP multicast on the switched network.

membership information between switches and multicast clients and servers. However, as mentioned in the last chapter, GMRP has not been widely implemented.

In contrast to the limited host support for GMRP, IGMP client support is built into the TCP/IP protocol stack of many common operating systems, including Windows 95/98, Windows NT 3.51+, and most Unix implementations.

Capitalizing on the general acceptance of IGMP, many switch vendors have implemented an IGMP snooping scheme to enable switches to automatically set up multicast filters so that the multicast traffic is directed only to the segments that have participating hosts. With IGMP snooping, the switch floods IGMP queries on all switch ports and forwards IGMP reports on ports in the direction of a router. But the switch will monitor (snoop on) the IGMP reports and create a multicast address entry in its forwarding table so that multicast frames are forwarded only onto segments that have members participating in the multicast group. In Figure 5.6, the switch will forward the multicast only on the ports from which it has received a report. The other switch ports will not receive the multicast.

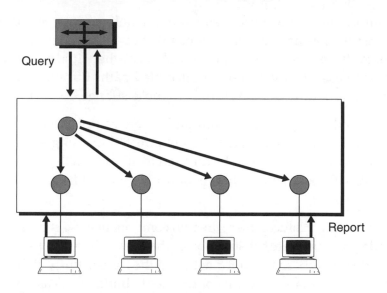

Query

Report

Figure 5.6 IGMP snooping switch.

Many switches that support IGMP snooping also feature additional enhancements. Some switches snoop on multicast routing protocols, such as *distance vector multicast routing protocol* (DVMRP), *multicast open shortest path first* (MOSPF), *protocol independent multicast–dense mode* (PIM-DM), or *protocol independent multicast–sparse mode* (PIM-SM), to determine which ports lead to routers. The switch must forward all multicast packets to the routers because the routers may have multicast receivers on other ports. IGMP query messages cannot be used to determine ports that lead to routers because a single router is elected the IGMP designated router. Switches that do not have this capability must be manually configured so that the switch knows which ports lead to routers. Another feature usually found in IGMP-capable switches is that report messages are not flooded, but rather, they are forwarded only on the router ports. Regardless of the number of report messages received by the switch, only a single report for each multicast group is forwarded to the router.

Multicast Routing

Because IGMP is concerned only with forwarding multicast traffic from the local router to group members on local networks attached directly, IGMP provides the final step in delivering the multicast packet. Multicast routers must run a multicast routing protocol so that they can exchange multicast information and subsequently build a delivery tree to ensure that multicast packets are delivered efficiently between routers. At the same time, multicast routers must avoid delivery where it is not needed. The delivery tree is effectively a set of calculated paths through the network that deliver multicast packets only to those subnets requiring them.

Delivery of a multicast packet is significantly more complex than delivery of a unicast packet because the packet is not directed to a single IP address. Rather, the multicast packet must be directed to all routers that have received an IGMP host membership report for the particular IP multicast address.

As with any routing protocol, there are two components: the sending of routing updates to facilitate construction of the forwarding database and forwarding decisions based on information in the forwarding database and the routing protocol in use. Several approaches to build multicast delivery trees exist, but they all require protocol extensions beyond standard IP functionality. There are two general types of multicast routing protocols. Dense multicast routing protocols are designed with the expectation that multiple receivers are nearby and that bandwidth is plentiful—typical of a campus broadcast. Sparse multicast routing protocols assume that group members are far apart and interconnected by wide area links where bandwidth is not abundant—more typical of an intranet or Internet broadcast.

Multicast Concepts

Dense-mode multicast routing protocols are simpler to implement because they can take advantage of abundant bandwidth and limited distances. The protocols can use flooding algorithms where the router examines destination multicast addresses. If the router has not seen the packet before, the router forwards the packet on all interfaces except the interface on which the packet arrived. Routers can rely on the TTL field of the packet header to constrain looping of the multicast. The algorithms are simple to implement because the router does not have to maintain a multicast forwarding table and needs to keep track only of the most recently seen packets. However, flooding does not scale for Internetwide applications; flooding generates a large number of duplicate packets and sends packets on all paths across the network instead of only a limited number of paths. Generally, protocols implement enhancements to the flooding scheme to prune the delivery tree so that packets are not flooded in a direction they are not needed. Sparse multicast routing protocols must be more selective in dispersing packets.

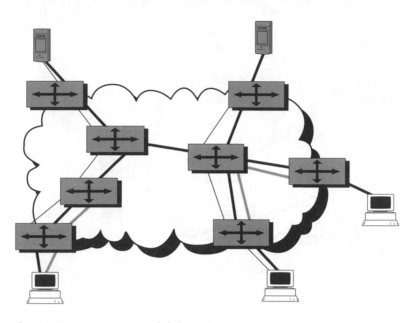

Figure 5.7 Source-rooted delivery tree.

Because flooding every packet is inefficient, both dense and sparse-mode multicast routing protocols rely on delivery trees, of which there are two types. The source-rooted delivery tree is rooted at the sender with one tree per sending host, as illustrated in Figure 5.7. For example, if a multicast group has five members and each member sends multicast data, there are five source-rooted delivery trees. The approach results in routers having to maintain state information based on the number of senders times the number of groups. Dense-mode multicast routing protocols rely on a source-rooted delivery tree.

Shared delivery trees are better suited for multicast groups populated sparsely that are apt to have low-bandwidth network connections. Shared delivery trees have per-group delivery trees rooted at a core router, meaning that all multicast groups are rooted from the same core router. Sources initially unicast their multicast packets to the core router that then forwards the packets via a shared tree to the members of group. The significant difference between the source-rooted tree and the shared tree is that the shared tree has a single tree between all sources and receivers of a given multicast group (see Figure 5.8). Consequently, there is less reliance on flooding. Thus, routers in the network other than the core router need to maintain state information only on the number of multicast groups in the network. (The PIM multicast routing protocol refers to the core router as the Rendezvous Point.)

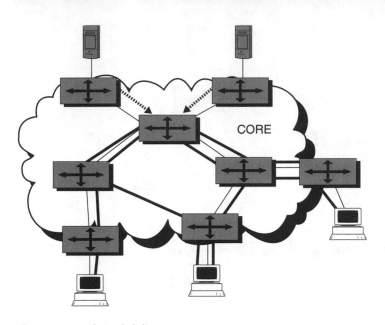

Figure 5.8 Shared delivery tree.

Shared tree schemes are much more network efficient. However, all multi-cast data must flow through the core, and if the multicast data is congested or unavailable, a problem results. Unlike data-driven, dense-mode proto-cols that respond upon receipt of a multicast packet, sparse-mode protocols rely on a receiver-initiated mechanism. Construction of the shared tree on the core router is initiated when the core receives a unicast join message from one of the local hosts requesting membership in a particular group. The intermediate routers construct their multicast-group forwarding table by associating the interface on which the join message arrives as part of the group's delivery tree. In reality, the unicast is forwarded to the core router IP address via the router's forwarding database. The database was con-structed by the particular routing protocol that the router is running, like OSPF. In effect, the router's forwarding database is used in reverse to con-struct the multicast-group forward database.

Distance-Vector, Multicast-Routing Protocol

Distance-vector, multicast-routing protocol (DVMRP) is specified in RFC1075. DVMRP supports forwarding multicast packets and is derived from the *routing information protocol* (RIP). Unlike RIP, which calculates the next hop to a particular IP address, DVMRP is concerned with computing the path back to the source of a multicast packet. DVMRP uses a source-rooted delivery tree in which each multicast member is the source of a rooted tree for a particular multicast group. DVMRP implements the *reverse path multicast* (RPM) algorithm. The RPM forwards packets based on the destination multicast IP address and the packet's source IP address (source, group) pair. When a source sends its initial IGMP Host Membership Report and declares membership in a multicast group, the adjacent router first broadcasts the packet on all interfaces except the interface providing the shortest path back to the source. The latter interface may or may not be the one on which the packet was received. It becomes the parent interface on the router for the particular multicast group. The initial packet for any (source, group) is forwarded across the entire network, provided that the packet's TTL does not expire. Each receiving router identifies the parent interface for the multicast group and then broadcasts the packet on other interfaces.

During the flooding process, a downstream router might receive a multicast packet addressed to a group for which there are no members on any of its attached subnetworks. In this case, the router sends a "pruned" message on the interface to its upstream neighbor. The pruned message results in removing the branch from the tree for the particular multicast group. Because the pruned message is group specific, a branch can be blocked for one multicast group yet pass another. It is the pruning process that results in a source-rooted, shortest-path tree.

Because group membership and network topology are dynamic, DVMRP provides a mechanism for pruned branches of the tree to "grow back." Periodically, the pruned information is removed from the router's multicast forwarding tree, and the next packet (source, group) is forwarded on all of the routers' interfaces—it is flooded. This flooding results in a new burst of pruned messages and construction of a new source-rooted tree for the multicast group.

DVMRP also employs a mechanism to add new members to a multicast group quickly, to "graft" a new branch onto the multicast delivery tree. When a router receives an IGMP host membership report from a receiving host on a pruned branch, it forwards messages upstream. When the upstream router receives the graft message, the upstream router overrides the previously received pruned message and effectively grafts a new branch—a previously pruned branch—onto the tree. The graft message is cascaded upstream toward the source, restoring all previously pruned branches as part of the multicast delivery tree.

Although the creation of source-rooted multicast trees via RPM algorithms is significantly more efficient than flooding, there are scaling issues. DVMRP scalability is affected adversely by the need to flood multicast traffic periodically throughout the network. In addition, because each router must keep state information in the form of (source, group) and prune information, DVMRP becomes a resource-intensive protocol. However, DVMRP is implemented in most routers, and it is by far the most widely used multicast routing protocol. Note that the inefficiencies of DVMRP are usually not a significant detriment in dense-mode networks where bandwidth and capacity are typically abundant.

MBONE, the multicast overlay on the Internet, runs mostly on DVMRP. However, because the Internet is not fully multicast capable, multicast tunnels are deployed frequently. The approach is exceedingly inefficient and contributes to poor performance on the MBONE.

Multicast Extensions to Open Shortest Path First

The multicast extensions to the popular OSPF routing protocol are defined in RFC1584. Multicast extensions to open shortest path first (MOSPF) leverages OSPF, the link-state, routing-topology database, to build multicast delivery trees. As with DVMRP, MOSPF relies on IGMP as the protocol used by hosts to join a multicast group. When the MOSPF router receives an IGMP host membership report, it generates a group membership *link-state, advertisement* (LSA) message that is propagated to all MOSPF routers in the local OSPF area. The MOSPF router then incorporates the group membership information into its own link-state database, enabling the MOSPF router to build a detailed map of the multicast topology.

When a multicast data packet arrives at the router, the router knows the routers and interfaces in which particular groups exist because the router already has a picture of the entire OSPF topology. The MOSPF router runs the Dijkstra algorithm to build a source-rooted delivery tree dynamically to every group member. It is not necessary to flood the packet throughout the OSPF domain; the MOSPF routers perform RPM computations in memory. Additionally, all MOSPF routers maintain the same topology information and therefore calculate the same delivery tree for each multicast group. These aspects of MOSPF make it quite network efficient.

The Dijkstra algorithm is a mathematical calculation that enables routers to find an optimal path through a mesh of network connections based on information contained in router advertisements, which are flooded throughout the domain.

To convey group membership information between areas, MOSPF relies on an *inter-area multicast forwarder* (IAMF), an MOSPF enhancement to the *area border router* (ABR) functionality. The IAMF forwards group membership information from the nonbackbone areas into the backbone area (0.0.0.0). The operation is asymmetric; the IAMF does not advertise group membership information from the backbone area into the nonbackbone area.

It is possible for a multicast group to extend between nonbackbone areas but not include the backbone. In other words, there might be members of the same multicast group in the nonbackbone areas while there are no members of the group in the backbone areas so that the multicast group is segmented. To support the forwarding of multicast information between nonbackbone areas, the ABR must be configured as a *wild card multicast receiver* (WCMR) that is another MOSPF enhancement to ABR functionality. The WCMR is a router to which all multicast traffic in the area is forwarded. The WCMR is effectively a member of all multicast groups in the area. Because the backbone has complete knowledge of all areas' group membership information, when the MCWR receives a multicast packet, it forwards the packet to all areas having group membership. When the multicast packet arrives at the ABR, the ABR runs the Dijkstra algorithm to create a source-rooted discovery tree for all members in the group. The ABR is the root of the source-rooted discovery tree for all multicast traffic coming into the area from remote areas. Propagation of multicast traffic in an MOSPF network is illustrated in Figure 5.9.

MOSPF is compatible and can interoperate with OSPF routers that are not MOSPF routers. The introduction of multicast capabilities into an OSPF network is seamless. During the transition period, MOSPF routers can route multicast traffic around noncompliant routers. However, if there are many multicast groups—and thus many Dijkstra calculations—CPU use can be significant.

Protocol Independent Routing

Protocol independent routing (PIM) is a new multicast routing protocol developed by the *inter-domain multicast routing* (IDMR) working group of

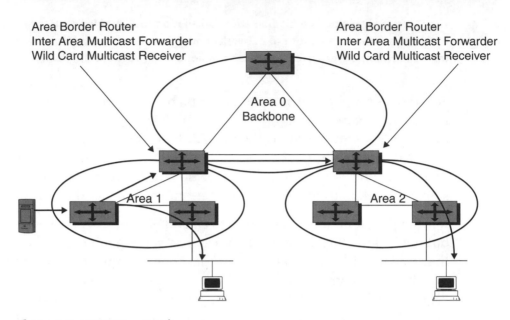

Figure 5.9 MOSPF network.

the IETF. As the name implies, PIM is intended to be routing protocol independent. The only requirement is that the router runs a routing protocol that provides a routing table and adapts to topology changes. PIM maintains protocol independence by using the native unicast routing protocol to establish a router-to-router dialog. PIM supports two different modes of operation. PIM dense mode is designed to operate in environments in which work groups are relatively densely packed and bandwidth is plentiful. PIM sparse mode is optimized for environments in which work group members are dispersed across many parts of the Internet, and bandwidth is not necessarily abundant.

PIM Dense Mode

PIM dense mode (PIM-DM) is similar to DVMRP in that it also uses RPM to create a source-rooted, multicast delivery tree. Unlike DVMRP, which calculates a set of child interfaces for each (source, group) pair and uses the information to limit the amount of multicast packet flooding, PIM-DM relies on multicast packet flooding and simply forwards all multicast packets on all downstream interfaces until a pruned message is received. PIM-DM is actually less efficient than DVMRP because it relies on multicast packet flooding. PIM-DM accepts the multicast packet duplication to eliminate any routing protocol dependency. PIM-DM, like DVMRP, also employs a grafting mechanism to add previously pruned branches to the delivery tree.

PIM Sparse Mode

PIM sparse mode (PIM-SM) is a multicast routing protocol that provides efficient communication between members of sparsely distributed, multicast groups. PIM-SM implements a shared delivery tree rooted at a core router called a rendezvous point (RP). Rather than flood multicast packets with PIM-SM, a router must request to receive group multicast data explicitly before the router receives the multicast data. Therefore, traffic is not forwarded on any link unless the link is part of a group-specific, shared delivery tree rooted in the RP router. The RP router controls the process of building the shared delivery tree. When a PIM-SM router receives a IGMP host membership record message from a host desiring to join a multicast group, the PIM-SM router sends a PIM join message to the RP router, enabling the RP router to create a shared delivery tree rooted at itself for the multicast group. There is one RP root-shared delivery tree for each multicast group defined by a multicast group (class D) address. Typically, the PIM-SM routers are configured with the IP address of the RP router (alternatively, there is a dynamic, bootstrap mechanism enabling a PIM-SM to locate a multicast group's RP router dynamically). When the local RP router receives multicast data from an adjacent host, the local RP router encapsulates and unicasts the packet to the RP router. The RP router then de-encapsulates the packet for distribution on the shared delivery tree.

The scheme is highly efficient because there is no packet flooding, and the routers must maintain information only on the multicast groups that actually pass through the router. The router does not care how many senders there are because the router supports only the shared tree rooted at the RP router (see Figure 5.10).

Conclusion

IP multicast routing protocol and IGMP alone aren't enough to meet all the requirements of IP multicast applications. The larger issues in running multimedia multicast applications over packet networks have to do with meeting the bandwidth and latency requirements of these applications.

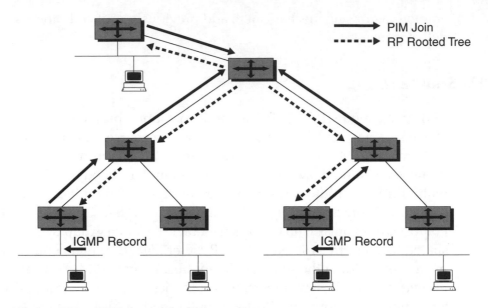

Figure 5.10 PIM join and the RP rooted tree.

Certainly, the multicast routing protocols and IGMP help, but what's needed is a network capable of discriminating between traffic streams that have different service-level requirements and then prioritizing the traffic through the network based on those requirements. In Chapter 6, "Quality of Service Issues," we address some of the current efforts designed to meet the real-time traffic needs.

Quality of Service Issues

We have seen how vLANs, routing, and IP multicast can support a degree of traffic management. However, with today's more complex networks varying from corporate intranets and extranets to the Internet itself, there is a demand for more fully defined and measurable levels of service that can be directly affiliated with users or user groups.

The Internet and most corporate intranets are built with the familiar IP routing protocol. IP, which transmits packets asynchronously, is a connectionless protocol that provides no guarantees about the timeliness or relative order of the delivered packets. Routers receive an incoming packet, reference a forwarding table, and put the packet into an output queue for the selected interface. The packets are moved from the output queue onto the transmission link in a *first-in–first-out (FIFO)* fashion. Transmission links are constrained by bandwidth. If packets are placed into the queue faster than they are moved from the queue to the transmission link, congestion occurs; packets are delayed, and eventually, packets may be discarded.

Because of this inherent behavior, the Internet has historically offered a single level of service, that of "best effort." Best effort implies that all packets are treated with equity on the Internet, but this does not mean that all packets receive the same level of service or service quality; certainly, some portions of the Internet are less congested than others. Best effort means that IP does not differentiate packets. Generally, all packets are forwarded in a FIFO fashion.

For many years, the Internet was exclusively used to support noncommercial data-based applications, such as e-mail and file transfer. These applications are capable of dealing with lost packets and are tolerant of packet delay.

In the early 1990s, curious minds began experimenting with transmitting real-time video applications over the Internet. Using IP multicast, they were able to transmit a video stream simultaneously to several receivers dispersed through the Internet. The experiment proved that the Internet, and IP, could support real-time applications. However, the quality of the reception was not consistent across the receivers. In fact, at some sites, the quality was quite poor. These early experimenters recognized the need to differentiate types of traffic and to provide a preferred service based on traffic type. Nonetheless, the MBONE was born, and it has grown steadily since its inception. Interest in supporting multicast communications across the Internet has been a significant motivating factor for developing quality of service schemes.

More recently, significant advances have been made in digitizing and packetizing voice. Because voice is very sensitive to delay and delay variation, packet-based phone conversations over IP networks will require a preferred quality of service.

The Internet is growing exponentially, but before global organizations consider the Internet a full-fledged business partner and begin using it to support critical business applications, the Internet will have to be able to provide predictable end-to-end levels of service quality.

Terms and Definitions

A stream of packets that has the same quality requirements is a flow. A flow may be classified in a number of ways. It could be defined by an application, for example, all the packets of a particular file transfer. However, a flow does not necessarily refer to packets of an application; it could refer to the aggregation of packets from several applications that are to receive the same quality requirements, such as all the packets traversing a specific virtual circuit.

Quality of Service is a vague term that has been used and overused recently to categorize the performance characteristics of the network traffic generated by an application. All network traffic can be categorized with three parameters that we refer to as quality parameters.

Quality Parameters

The three quality parameters are:

Delay. The total elapsed time for packet to go from the sender to the receiver.

Delay variation. The variation in the arrival time of consecutive packets.

Loss ratio or reliability. The average error rate, or the ratio of the number of packets that arrive and are usable at the destination to the number of packets that either don't arrive or are unusable at the destination. An example of an unusable packet is one that arrives too late to be of any value to the recipient application.

Not all applications require the same level of quality parameters. The tolerance of the quality parameters varies from application to application. For example, a file transfer application is much more concerned with reliability than with delay variation, but a video application is much more concerned with delay and delay variation than with reliability. Generally, video applications can tolerate lost packets occasionally. The quality parameters that are critical to a particular application are quality requirements. Table 6.1 characterizes the Quality of Service requirements for some common applications.

In addition to the quality parameters, another component impacts the quality of a connection. Bandwidth, which is the maximum data transfer

Table 6.1 Quality of Service Requirements

	DELAY	DELAY VARIATION	RELIABILITY
Mail	Low	Low	High
File transfer	Low	Low	High
Database	Low/medium	Low	High
Video (MPEG)	High	Medium	Low
Telephony	High	High	Low
Videoconference	High	High	Low

rate on a network link, is an important consideration. Although bandwidth impacts quality, it does so in an indirect manner. It is a resource that is shared by all traffic; it is an unwitting participant in the quality of a connection. There is nothing that can be done to the data after it is put onto the link. Bits are transferred on the link in the same order that they are presented to the link. However, quality is significantly affected within the router. It is the router that determines the order in which data is put onto the link. Conventional routers have a single output queue for each interface, and traffic is handled on a purely FIFO basis.

Quality of Service really means providing preferential treatment (defined by quality parameters) to specific flows based on the quality requirements of the specific flow. This preferential treatment must be provided within the router (or switch) and occurs via sophisticated buffer management, queuing, and scheduling schemes.

Quality requirements are specified on a per-flow basis. The quality requirements that are applied to a flow are determined by the nature of the flow—that is, how do we want the network to treat the packets that make up the flow?

Whereas quality requirements specify the desired behavior of the packets in the flow, quality parameter defines how the network attempts to meet the flow's quality requirements.

Ideally, the quality parameters are such that all quality requirements are met.

If we accept these definitions, Quality of Service and Class of Service are both based on quality parameters. From now on, the word *quality* is used interchangeably with the term *quality parameters*. In either case, it means how the network is attempting to meet a flow's quality requirements.

In general, there are three different types of quality parameters, as discussed in the following sections.

Predictive Quality

Predictive quality is a consequence of overprovisioning the network. The underlying premise with overprovisioning is that if there is no congestion, there is no need for concern with quality of service; rather, monitor the network, and increase the capacity as the demand increases. Keeping utilization low enough should make it possible to minimize queuing delays for delay-sensitive traffic (such as interactive voice and video). By sizing bandwidth for the most delay-sensitive traffic, the network should meet latency as well as bandwidth requirements for all types of network traffic. With the emergence of Gigabit Ethernet and routing switches, this is a reasonable approach on the LAN. The promise of dense-wave-division multiplexing and terabit routers make this approach a possibility for the WAN, albeit a remote and costly possibility. Another advantage of Predictive QoS is that policy administration, accounting, and billing could be eliminated if everyone were charged a flat fee and the network provided whatever service individual applications might require. In this scenario, there would be no need to differentiate at any level.

Flow-Based Quality

Flow-based quality implies that a portion of network resources is allocated to a particular flow for the duration of the connection. Flow based requires a signaling protocol and devices that maintain some state information about each of the flows. There are several significant issues. This approach would work best when the flow is long-lived (for example, video streams and large file transfers); however, most flows across the Internet are relatively short-lived—on the order of 10–20 packets. This means that there is little return on the flow set-up process. In addition, because state information on each flow must be kept at each device, the approach is difficult to maintain in large networks. Consider the amount of state information an Internet switch would have to keep in order to support tens of thousands of connections simultaneously.

Class-Based Quality

Class-based quality marks or labels the packets to indicate the type of quality of service that they should receive. Network resources are allocated on a class, or group, or a flow aggregation basis. When a packet arrives at the router/switch, it is categorized as belonging to a particular class/group/flow and treated accordingly. The category is usually indicated with a marking or label in the packet. Within the particular class, all packets are treated in a best-effort manner.

The difficulty with this approach is in establishing policies: What packets get what priority label? Also, how does the device doing the marking know if the quality requirements associated with the label it is applying to the packet are available? For example, suppose that a quality requirement called gold implies that packets will be delivered within some delay tolerance. When a packet arrives at the ingress device, the device references some table to determine which quality requirement to apply to the packet. The packet warrants gold-quality requirement and gets marked. How does the ingress switch know if the resources are available in the network to ensure the delay tolerance specified for the gold quality of service? How does the ingress switch know if the quality parameters necessary to meet the quality requirements are available?

Obviously, there is no simple or comprehensive approach to deliver quality of service. There are many protocols or schemes that can be implemented. Some schemes are more appropriate for one portion of the network or another, and other schemes try to work across all components of the network. First, we look at the general makeup of each of the network components and talk about the type of quality of service that can be appropriate for that particular component. Next, we examine each of the schemes in some detail. Finally, we examine options for creating connections of varying quality of service end to end.

Quality of Service (or Is It Class of Service?)

For now, we do not differentiate between Quality of Service and *Class of Service* (CoS). Generally speaking, Quality of Service refers to performance characteristics of the computer network system. Few people are concerned with the performance of the local area network, wide area network, or Internet or of computer processing power or database characteristics; however, all of these considerations are involved when the performance of a system is characterized. When we attempt to access another computer system, we are concerned with how long a delay there is between systems, transfer rate, and so forth.

The two networks most familiar to us, the *public switched telephone network* (PSTN) and the Internet, operate on very different standards as far as Quality of Service is concerned. When a call is placed through the public telephone network, we expect that the call will complete with an optimal quality through all the connections and rarely be rejected. This represents premium quality of service. This type of service is markedly different from the quality of service that we might expect when communicating across the Internet.

When we dial into the Internet, we are fairly confident that the connection will complete, but we are unsure of the quality of the connection. Even worse, we have no control over the quality of the connection. If our connection uses a congested path through the network or if many other users are accessing the same server that we are trying to access, we can expect an inferior quality of service. This is best-effort quality of service.

With the public telephone network, quality of service is an expectation that usually does not present a problem because there are enough resources available for all users. Of course, from an application perspective, the telephone network is really simplistic compared with that of the Internet. The telephone network was designed to support a single application, the phone conversation, and all instances of the conversation require the same types of resources: 64Kbps bandwidth and well-defined resources within each switch. The telephone network is a circuit-switched network, meaning that resources are allocated in support of the particular conversation before the conversation flows. All switches keep state information on all connections and are aware of available resources. The switches reject additional connections when resources are exhausted. Therefore, the existing connections maintain their high quality of service. Telephone networks were designed based on the premise that reliability in completion of and quality of connection are paramount and that people are willing to pay for such service. One might say that telcos know the habits and expectations of their customers.

The rationale behind designing telephone networks contrasts markedly to that for the Internet and most any other data network. Data networks (for our purposes, we assume that data networks are IP based) support a myriad of applications, each with its own characteristics and network requirements. A file transfer has very different resource requirements from those for a transaction processing application, which in turn are quite different from the requirements of a real-time, video application. Quality of Service on data networks is best effort and connectionless by nature. Currently, there is little control over the number of connections traversing a switch or a particular link in the network. In addition, there is little in the way of differentiation. The switch (or router) moves the packets according to the destination IP address only and shows no preference to an application based on importance or requirement characteristics. The Internet evolved from a best-effort, nondifferentiated model with low and inexpensive barriers to entry. One might say that Internet service providers (ISPs) do *not* know the habits and network requirements of their customers.

Today, many pundits believe that conventional telephone traffic can be transported more economically in packets. As a result, eventually all traffic—voice, video, and data—will traverse the Internet. The rationale is based on the premise that today's voice traffic is digitized and compressed and that circuit-switched networks are wasteful because of their reservation policies: 64Kbps for each call. If a voice bit is no different from a data bit, why not transmit voice in a packetized format? Furthermore, packetizing and transmitting voice over an IP network is economical, and an integrated network is effective in terms of management and utility.

How do we meet Quality of Service requirements in different applications? How do we assess the requirements of a particular application and then differentiate the traffic based on delay, latency, delay variation, and other Quality of Service parameters from another application's requirements?

> **It could be argued that there is really no distinction between Class of Service and Quality of Service; the difference is semantics. Both deal with a service level that traffic receives as it traverses the network. Quality of Service is generally used to describe connection-oriented networks, such as PSTN and ATM, while Class of Service is generally used to describe packet switched networks, such as the Internet. In reality, the difference is not in *what* is provided but rather in *how* it is provided.**

Class of Service

With Class of Service, the quality parameters are specified within the router/switch. The router/switch is preconfigured to allocate resources and to provide preferential treatment to some class of traffic. Resources are allocated to some identifiable portion of traffic. No signaling is required, and resources are not allocated on a per-flow basis. The router doesn't retain any information about individual flows (state information). The router/switch expects that the amount of traffic arriving that is to receive a preferred treatment will be controlled and that router/switch resources allocated to the preferred traffic will not be overextended. The router/switch itself does nothing to ensure this.

Generally, class of service is used to categorize types of traffic. Class of Service deals with the treatment of groups of flows. It can be interpreted as a method to differentiate traffic and to provide preferential treatment to some arbitrary portion of network traffic. That is, rather than all traffic being treated in a best-effort manner, there may be several class of service categories. All traffic within a particular CoS category receives the same treatment as all other traffic in that same category, but all traffic in a particular CoS category may receive better or worse treatment than all other traffic in a different CoS category.

There may be specific quality parameters associated with each of the CoS. In Figure 6.1, CoS-1 may be configured such that it provides some quality parameter, such as delay variation or delay tolerance, while CoS-3 is for all traffic that does not meet CoS-1 or CoS-2 criteria.

Any traffic that arrives at the router and meets the criteria for CoS-1 is placed into the CoS-1 Queue. The criteria that define the type of traffic may be a source or destination IP address, a port number, a type of service marking, or any other information that may be carried in the packet. All CoS-1 traffic is aggregated and shares the CoS-1 bandwidth. This is very important in that the information that the router must maintain—state information—is minimal. Because each packet is treated independently, the router does not need to maintain information about each individual connection. Basically, the connectionless nature of the communication is maintained.

As long as the amount of CoS-1 traffic remains below some threshold, all traffic will receive the prescribed quality parameter. But if the amount of CoS-1 traffic exceeds the critical threshold, either CoS-1 must take resources that have been allocated to different CoS or the traffic no longer receives the desired quality requirement. This is obviously a situation that is best avoided. How can the network be engineered to prevent this oversubscription? There are three approaches. First, the network could be overengineered such that sufficient router and bandwidth resources are allocated and there would never be oversubscription. Several years ago this approach was not conceivable. However, with the emergence of new technologies such as Gigabit Ethernet and dense wavelength division

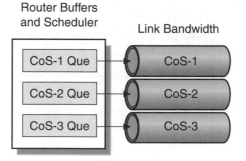

Figure 6.1 Router buffers and schedulers.

multiplexing, some maintain that overprovisioning resources is becoming a feasible approach.

Second, a signaling protocol could be used to request resources prior to sending traffic on the path. If the resources are available, they are reserved for the particular connection. If the resources are not available, the connection is refused. The final approach is to create an omniscient policy server, which monitors all resources within the network. When a connection is needed, the request is sent to the policy server. The policy server determines whether a path exists that provides the requested service quality. If the path does exist, the policy server allocates the resource, updates its own information, and notifies the requester to proceed.

Quality of Service

With Quality of Service, *quality requirements* are specified for a flow, or a particular connection. Then an agreement is reached with the network to ensure that the quality parameters will meet the quality requirements of this flow. Signaling is required, and resources are allocated on a per-flow basis. The router retains information about individual flows (state information).

Quality of Service (QoS) is used to categorize a particular connection or flow. QoS deals with the treatment of packets within flows. Each connection has its own dedicated resources, similar to the circuit-switched environment used by telcos and ATM networks. QoS generally implies that quality requirements are guaranteed.

QoS is much more granular than CoS. QoS implies that a connection's traffic will receive a consistent and predictable service level, which may include specific bandwidth, delay, delay variation, and reliability parameters. There is no aggregation. Each connection has its own resources reserved. The quality parameters applied to a connection can then be much more granular. Rather than associating a service level with a queue and then placing packets in the queue based on information within the packet, as is done with CoS, each connection may request particular service levels, with its own queue, buffer, schedule, and bandwidth assignment. Generally, QoS requires a signaling protocol, and because there is no aggregation, much state information about each connection must be maintained at the router/switch.

QoS versus CoS—In the Eyes of the Beholder

Conventional wisdom says that CoS and QoS are distinct. Both use the same parameters to define the service level that packets receive. There are differences, but ironically, the differences are in perspective. With QoS, quality is viewed from the perspective of the flow. With CoS, quality is viewed from the perspective of the network. QoS and CoS are terms that are used to define the same thing. Generally, QoS implies a more predictable service level, but there is overlap. In fact, it is possible that the CoS connection will receive a better and more predictable service level than the QoS connection. So although CoS and QoS define the same thing, they are used at different times and under different circumstances. In later sections of the chapter as we examine different protocols and schemes that have been devised to provide predictable service levels, we use the appropriate term. The difference is not in *what* is provided but rather in *how* it is provided.

Also, CoS and QoS are significant in name only. The four service level parameters—delay, delay variation, bandwidth, and predictability—are the true topics of the protocol and schemes discussed in this section.

Also, there are only two ways to determine if a path meets the quality requirements of a connection: via signaling or via the omniscient policy server.

Table 6.2 characterizes the differences between CoS and QoS.

Table 6.2 Class of Service versus Quality of Service

SERVICE	CHARACTERISTICS
Class	Policy server (constraints applied only at network edge)
	Flow aggregation
	Stateless
Quality	Signaling required (constraints applied at every switch)
	No flow aggregation
	Much state information kept

A Quick Look at ATM

Before discussing Quality/Class of Service, we look at Quality of Service from the perspective of ATM. This is appropriate because ATM was developed from the ground up with focus on quality of service and the ability to provide high-speed, low-delay, low-jitter on a per-flow basis, enabling ATM to support virtually all types of traffic, such as voice, video, and data applications, simultaneously. ATM sets the standard for all quality/class of service endeavors.

 Members of the *Internet Engineering Task Force* (IETF) who are developing quality/class of service schemes are aware of ATM capabilities and in some respects strive to emulate them.

ATM defines five different service classes. Each of the service classes has a set of Quality of Service parameters that serves to provide variability within those classes. Quality of Service is defined in terms of rate guarantees, delay guarantees, and loss guarantees. Table 6.3 defines the ATM Service Categories, their QoS characteristics, and the applications that they are designed to support.

Associated with each flow is a *virtual circuit* (VC) with a prescribed service category and set of parameters. There are two different types of virtual circuits. *Permanent virtual circuits* (PVCs) are configured manually and require manual intervention at each switch that the virtual circuit traverses. *Switched virtual circuits* (SVCs) are established dynamically via a call-setup mechanism. In either case, PVC or SVC, the VC must be established and the requested resources allocated before data is transmitted on the VC. The resources (bandwidth, buffers, and so forth) are allocated for

Table 6.3   ATM Service Categories, QoS Characteristics, and Example Applications

SERVICE CATEGORY (BROADBAND-BEARER CAPABILITY)	PARAMETERS (ATM TRAFFIC DESCRIPTORS AND QUALITY OF SERVICE INDICATORS)	EXAMPLE
Constant bit rate (CBR)	Peak cell rate (PCR) Cell transfer delay (CTD) Cell delay variation (CDV) Cell loss ratio (CLR)	Voice circuit emulation
Real-time variable bit rate (rtVBR)	PCR, CTD, CDV, CLR, sustained cell rate (SCR)	Packetized voice and video
Non-real-time VBR (Nrt-VBR)	PCR, SCR, CLR	Frame relay
Available bit rate (ABV)	PCR, minimum cell rate (MCR)	IP/data
Unspecified bit rate (UBR)		IP/data

the duration of the VC. Each switch validates that the requested resources are available via *connection admission control* (CAC).

If the requested resources are not available, the user is informed and may request a lesser quality of service. After the VC has been established, the switches provide a policing function to ensure that the traffic is not in violation of terms that were established at VC creation. ATM is designed to operate end to end; the resources are allocated from end station to end station. In a simplified example, if a phone call were placed across the ATM network, the source (for example, a PBX) would associate the target telephone number with an ATM address. The source would then create a set-up message that would specify CBR service category with a PCR of 64Kbps and some acceptable delay tolerance. The setup message would be addressed to the target ATM address and submitted to the ingress ATM switch. The ingress switch would access a table to determine the path to the target ATM address and then ensure that 64Kbps bandwidth is available on the link to the next switch in the path to the target.

The ingress switch allocates the bandwidth and buffer resource to accommodate the delay tolerances to the particular flow. In this fashion, the setup message makes its way to the target; the target returns an acknowledgement to the source, and the conversation commences. The resources have been allocated, and a toll-quality conversation results. (Note that ATM was designed from the beginning to provide the delay and delay-variation characteristics that are necessary for real toll-quality voice.) Subsequent VCs may or may not (depending on the specific service category) reserve portions of the network. An email connection will likely request the UBR service category, indicating that no resources are allocated and that the application will rely on a best-effort delivery mechanism.

A couple of key concepts were oversimplified in the previous example. First, although ATM addressing is flexible and scalable, it is not directly compatible with the E.163, or plain old telephone system (POTS), address used in today's telephone networks. Therefore, it is necessary to translate between the target telephone number and the target ATM address. This might be nontrivial. Second, the connection described is an SVC, so signaling and routing must be implemented at several different levels. Both the end station and the ingress switch must support *user-to-network interface* (UNI) signaling. *Private-network-to-network interface* (PNNI) must be supported between the switches. The ingress/egress switches must be able to translate between UNI and PNNI signaling. PNNI is a complex and rich protocol; it provides signaling along with dynamic routing, using a complicated algorithm to construct a path through the network that meets the Quality of Service requirements specified in the setup message. PNNI is a link-state protocol that dynamically advertises routes and quality-of-service capabilities associated with different routes throughout the network.

SVCs are the preferred type of VCs because they provide real-time connections without the need for manual, preprovisioning of the connection. Another big advantage of SVCs is they provide the ability to make connection bandwidth available for new and existing network applications whenever and wherever it is needed. With SVCs, users establish a connection with the desired quality-of-service parameters applied to the VC on a call-by-call basis. When the application completes, resources are returned and available for other VCs.

Currently, there is only limited support of SVCs in the public sector. Most public ATM environments today merely take advantage of ATM's multiplexing capabilities and rely on nailed-up PVCs.

Another important ATM concept involves *virtual paths* (VPs). A virtual path is a virtual connection between two points that can carry multiple *virtual circuits* (VCs). VPs provide ease of configuration and routing from the provider or network administrator's perspective and flexibility in how the bandwidth between the locations is allocated. It is possible to provision a VP between two locations and subsequently configure SVCs of varying bandwidth and Quality of Service within the VP. Of course, the amount of aggregate bandwidth that can be allocated to the SVCs is limited by the amount of bandwidth allocated to the VP. In addition, SVCs cannot be of a higher (better) Quality of Service than is provisioned for the VP. Figure 6.2 illustrates the relationship between a virtual path (VP) and a virtual circuit (VC).

Figure 6.2   ATM VP/VC/transmission path.

Defining the Problem

There are many components to consider when one is providing a Quality of Service. Before attempting to address quality of service from the end-to-end perspective (which is what we are really after), we need to look at the different components and how quality can be characterized and achieved within each of the components. Figure 6.3 provides a high-level view of the network components of several corporate networks and the connectivity between the corporate networks via the Internet.

The Enterprise LAN

It is fairly simple to assess types of applications and bandwidth requirements on the LAN. There are a finite number of users and a limited number of applications. However, we must be concerned with broadcast and multicast containment. In addition, we can divide the LAN logically into vLANs to isolate traffic on a workgroup or multicast group basis. We could also separate the LAN via routing switches.

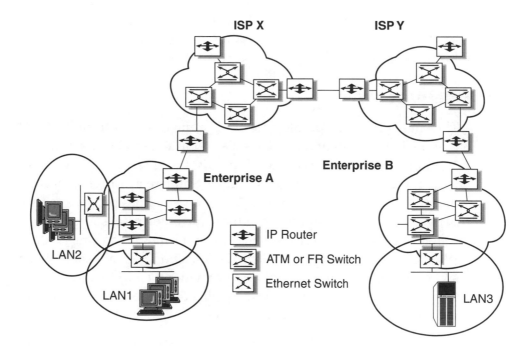

Figure 6.3   ISP interconnected enterprise networks.

There have been many LAN QoS innovations within the last few years. Gigabit Ethernet has been a significant contributor to the innovations, and ATM was the impetus behind the Gigabit innovations. Although the promise of ATM has yet to be realized, the ATM QoS threat has certainly not gone unnoticed. ATM has found significant presence on the LAN, but there are several reasons the ATM promise has not been realized. ATM LAN presence is based primarily on ATM forum *LAN emulation* (LANE) for which there is an ATM proxy device that establishes SVCs across the ATM network to other LANE proxy devices. The attached devices—workstations, servers, and so forth—are equipped with conventional LAN NICs (Ethernet or token ring), so the ATM connection is not really end to end. The other issue with LANE (Version 1.0) is that the SVCs are UBR VCs so that there are no Quality-of-Service parameters established. The VC provides best-effort delivery only. LANE Version 2.0, beginning to roll out, provides QoS SVC capabilities.

Options available to achieve quality of service on the LAN include using gigabit and routing technologies to overprovision the network; using IEEE 802.1p/Q to assign priority levels on a port or vLAN basis; using a differentiated service with policy management (such as the DIFFSRV scheme) to allocate some portion of available resources to classes of traffic and then assign packets to a particular class via a label; using a per-flow reservation protocol to reserve resources on a per-flow basis (such as RSVP); and using LANE V2.0 to create SVCs.

The Enterprise WAN

The enterprise or corporate network is quite different from the LAN in that the bandwidth of the links is usually much smaller than the 10,100,1000Mbps of LAN links. Typically, the enterprise network relies on leased lines or reserved circuits—either frame relay or ATM, or more recently *virtual private networks* (VPNs). Leased lines provide connectivity between different components of the same enterprise, such as between different business campuses, sales offices, or manufacturing facilities. With leased lines, a circuit-switched connection is established. In a circuit-switched connection, resources are permanently allocated to the connection, and access to the circuit is through a dedicated/private device; therefore, security is not a critical issue.

On the other hand, a VPN is a private network that uses a public IP network or an individual ISP as the basic transport. Typically, enterprise networks are not designed and coordinated from a centralized location. Rather, enterprise networks tend to evolve over time and adapt to the organization as the organization matures, grows, and diversifies. In addition, it is not uncommon to find many different networking technologies within the network. When we consider that the enterprise network provides support for myriad corporate functions, it is not surprising to find many different applications, each with different Quality-of-Service requirements within the same enterprise network. The applications were probably created to work with a specific network protocol (such as IP or NetBIOS) and conform to different network architectures.

Quality of Service within an enterprise network is complicated because of the different topologies, applications, and traffic patterns associated with the network. The major issues involve the type of transport and corresponding QoS capabilities for the transport (such as frame relay, ATM, and so forth) along with QoS requirements on an application basis. For example, should an enterprise network support real-time video? Is the real-time video between different LANs within the building or campus where bandwidth is apt to be private and significant, or should we support the video application between different sites that compose the enterprise?

The ISP

The Internet comprises a collection of ISPs surrounded by customer enterprise networks. ISP networks are bandwidth constrained. The modus operandi is to keep up with bandwidth requirements. Any overprovisioning of bandwidth is short-lived because it is consumed soon afterward. ISP networks deal with many customers simultaneously. Each customer has different requirements and expectations for a myriad of applications, from e-mail to transaction processing to videoconferencing. Each ISP component— every switch and every link—has numerous applications to support at any one time. Each ISP needs to communicate with numerous enterprise networks and numerous other ISPs. The problem with supporting a consistent level of QoS for any one flow to other ISPs is monumental, especially considering that each ISP might have different transport and physical layers. No standard currently available supports policy or quality encoding between an enterprise network and an ISP or between individual ISPs. The problem is compounded when the communicating networks are based on different underlying technologies such as ATM (cell based) and frame relay (frame based). The way that ISPs are providing QoS today is by provisioning nailed up ATM or frame relay PVCs.

ATM and frame relay provide the transport infrastructure. Typically, there is a router on the edge of the ISP network. The router connects to ATM or frame relay switches that are internal to the ISP network. Switches are configured with VCs to every other edge switch. If the ISP is providing *service level agreements* (SLAs) to offer QoS support, typically, there will be multiple VCs between the edges and a QoS level associated with each of the VCs. The number of VCs required for each QoS level is equal to the number of edge devices times the number of edge devices minus one (N * (N–1)). Another concern with QoS SLAs is how to assure customers that their traffic is getting preferred service. If the ISP cannot demonstrate that a quantitative amount of customer traffic is receiving the prescribed QoS, the QoS implementation is worthless. The other problem with nailed-up VCs is that the approach reduces flexibility and cost effectiveness significantly. Figure 6.4 is an illustration of the many virtual circuits that may be required between network components in order to provide different QoS connections.

Because of the vast number of flows that ISPs support simultaneously, it is unlikely that an ISP can provide QoS on a flow basis. The amount of state information that would have to be stored and processed is prohibitive. It appears likely that ISPs can offer some sort of differentiated service like DIFFSRV, for example. The strategy removes the complexity from its core and places it at the edge; the edge device would need to know about policies and who can make what sort of resource reservation. The edge device would also need to know about the resources available.

It appears likely that ISPs will provide differentiated service levels via DIFFSRV and/or QoS offering via *multiprotocol label switching* (MPLS), ATM, and frame relay.

ISP

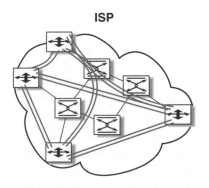

Figure 6.4   An Internet service provider (ISP).

Numerous ATM proponents would argue that ATM is the only technology capable of QoS on a per-flow basis and that per-flow QoS is required for some applications like real-time video. Therefore, if the Internet is going to become the global, multimedia network that many envision, ISPs would be wise to design their networks with ATM today. If ATM does become the transport of choice, it will likely be based on virtual paths with support for dynamically configurable QoS-capable SVCs.

Access (from the Enterprise to the Internet)

As stated earlier, quality of service is really an end-to-end proposition; network users are not concerned with QoS as it relates to any component of their connection. Users are concerned only with the quality of the connection. In delivering end-to-end QoS, one of the most difficult aspects is to convey a particular QoS between different networks. The most important demarcation is between the enterprise network and the service provider.

There are three components to end-to-end QoS: enterprise QoS, access QoS, and ISP QoS. At the access, typically, there is a broad range of traffic types from a diversity of applications with different QoS schemes supported on the enterprise. The numerous and varied applications must be mapped to the QoS types supported on the ISP network. As noted in the previous discussion, there will likely be a more limited number of QoS types within the ISP.

Access QoS has already been implemented to control user access onto the Internet via an access link; many corporations implement intelligent firewalls that control user access to the Internet. Control techniques are also employed in Web farms to determine which Web servers can consume which portion of the access bandwidth. However, currently QoS is very limited on the Internet so it is not being passed across the access into the Internet. Many believe that differentiated services provide the ideal demarcation indicator between enterprise QoS and Internet QoS because DIFFSRV is a Layer 3 scheme. It is independent of the underlying transport technology—in that it can work between networks that are based on ATM, or frame relay, MPLS, or *packet over SONET* (PoS). (SONET is *Synchronous Optical Network* from Bellcore.) Regardless of the transport technology operating within the network, DIFFSRV can be used to convey QoS information between the networks. Because of this capability, DIFFSRV can also be used between two ISPs. Again, the ISPs may be using different backbone technologies. With DIFFSRV, the QoS information is carried within the Layer 3 portion of the packet. Therefore, the QoS indicator is not modified as the packet passes between different ISPs, even if they are based on different technologies. Of course, the underlying premise is that within each of the ISPs, some amount of resource is allocated to each of the classes that the particular ISP supports. There is also the related policy issue; QoS information is passed between the ISPs, but at each ISP ingress, the flow must be validated to ensure it is privileged to receive the indicated class of service.

Another point to consider is from which layer of the OSI architecture the QoS is derived. Some schemes provide QoS parameters at Layer 2, and others provide QoS parameters at Layer 3. The primary distinction is that when QoS has been defined at Layer 3, the type of QoS that a packet receives is based on some higher-layer criteria, such as the destination IP address. When the QoS has been defined at Layer 2, the type of QoS is based on some Layer 2 designation, such as an ATM VPI/VCI.

There are obviously some interdependencies. However, theoretically, for true ATM applications communicating across an ATM network, there cannot be any Layer 2–Layer 3 interdependencies. Another distinction is that QoS at Layer 2 requires either manual configuration at each device or a signaling protocol. A Layer 3 QoS may or may not require an explicit signaling protocol. In either case, the key components are an admission control policy to determine if the resources requested are available and a policy control scheme to ensure that the user has the administrative privilege to reserve the resources. The following section examines the more popular schemes proposed for supporting QoS.

Integrated Service

Since its start in 1992, the *multicast backbone* (MBONE) network has supported multicast applications on the Internet as an "overlay" network. The MBONE has provided invaluable information on Internet support of multimedia applications and has proven itself an experiment with high visibility. The MBONE has demonstrated that there is a great deal of interest in running real-time applications over the Internet, and it is likely that the trend will increase as computers become more powerful, multimedia applications become more popular, and programmers become more innovative.

Undeniably, there are significant issues with running applications that traditionally subsisted on connection-oriented, circuit-switched networks over a best-effort packet network. Packet-switched networks that route individual packets independently across shared resources were designed to support data that by its very nature brings the concepts of delay and delay variation (jitter) in the packet stream into the forefront. When data alone was transported, people did not care about delay or delay variation unless the delay resulted in an application timeout, but this generally did not happen. The conditions of delay and delay variation are byproducts of queuing and scheduling variable-length packets at the router and of congestion leading to packet loss. Because typically real-time packets are useless if they not delivered within some prescribed time period—although the network has no way of knowing this—the negative impact of congestion and packet loss is even more detrimental with real-time applications.

MBONE is termed an *overlay* network because it actually includes only a subset of the Internet routers. The routers support the multicast routing protocol independent of and in addition to conventional Internet routing. To connect individual routers or an island of routers that support the multicast routing protocol, a form of virtual links through the general IP network called tunnels is employed. A tunnel is created between routers that support multicast routing. The multicast packet is encapsulated with the unicast address of the multicast router at the other end of the tunnel, allowing the packet to traverse routers that do not support multicast routing. The receiving multicast router unwraps the encapsulated packets and multicasts them on the local subnet, giving the subnet access to the MBONE. The scheme allows subnets to establish "MBONE tunnels" that flow seamlessly over older routers; however, the packet must be encapsulated, adding to the overhead and bandwidth consumption. In addition, encapsulation might result in strange failure modes when there is an outage and the network topology changes.

To encourage the MBONE to implement DVMRP, the concept of default route was introduced into DVMRP. Default route aggregates all routes coming from an interface into 0.0.0.0 address. Thus, updates from MBONE, which might flood 6k-to-8k routes, can be funneled into one advertisement. Each downstream router sees only one route, yet it can reach all 8k routes.

The Integrated Services (intserv) initiative, spawned in 1994, was driven primarily by the desire to have the Internet support real-time multicast applications. The Integrated Service Architecture asserts that the underlying

Internet architecture does not need to be modified to support MBONE type of applications. It suggests that extensions to the existing architecture could be devised to provide capabilities beyond the traditional best-effort service.

Integrated Service Architecture

The Integrated Services architecture provides a set of extensions to the best-effort, traffic-delivery model currently used on the Internet. The approach provides special handling for certain types of traffic and a mechanism for applications to identify traffic and delegate the traffic to the appropriate service level. The basic premise is that the Internet does not need modification to provide customized support for the different classes of applications. Instead, enhancements to the existing architecture can meet the new requirements.

The proposed architectural extensions include an integrated services model and a reference implementation framework. Simply stated, the integrated services model specifies QoS capabilities and behaviors that routers in the traffic path must exhibit. The reference implementation framework provides a mechanism for applications to communicate their QoS requirements to adjacent routers. Additionally, it provides a mechanism for routers to communicate per-path QoS capabilities between them.

Quality of Service in the intserv model is concerned primarily with the timely delivery of packets. Per-packet delay is the parameter around which networks have the ability to make quantitative service guarantees. The only quantitative service commitment intserv determines relates to specifying actual minimum and maximum acceptable delays.

Integrated Service Characteristics

How does intserv determine QoS to various applications? The intserv model defines two classes of applications by distinguishing the application's dependence on timely delivery of packets. Elastic applications are those that do not have strict requirements for timely delivery of packets; the packet arrival rate is not critical. Elastic applications wait for data to arrive and process the data as it arrives. There is no need to detain the data before delivering it to the application. The application is insensitive to variation in the interpacket delay. (Keep in mind, the applications are not totally insensitive to delay; significant delay would result in packet retransmission or session termination, depending on which upper-layer protocol the application uses, but usually the application has enough flexibility to withstand substantial delay variation.) Examples of elastic applications include Telnet, bulk transfer (FTP), and asynchronous transfer (SNMP). Elastic applications can be characterized as belonging to the best-effort traffic class.

The other class of application specified by intserv is called inelastic or real-time applications. There are two categories of real-time applications. Real-time applications that can tolerate some amount of delay and delay variation in their traffic are handled with the controlled-load service. The applications that tolerate delay and delay variation in packet delivery are called adaptive applications. The other category of real-time traffic is guaranteed-load service. Guaranteed-load service is intended for applications that require bandwidth guarantees and have stringent bounds on the delay and delay variation that they can tolerate.

> **Typically, real time implies that there is a common synchronized clock at source and destination. Intserv does not have the ability to maintain a synchronized clock.**

Integrated Service Controlled-Load Service (RFC2211)

Controlled-load service is intended for real-time applications that require no firm quantitative guarantees. The application requesting the controlled-load service provides the network with an estimate of the peak traffic rate that it will generate. The application does not specify parameters that include information about packet delay or loss. Controlled-load provides the application with a QoS that is slightly better than best effort. The controlled-load service does not accept or make use of specific target values for control parameters such as delay or loss.

The router supporting controlled-load ensures that the flow receives a QoS no worse than a real best-effort application would receive on a lightly loaded network. In other words, the flow could likely experience progressively deteriorating service as the network load increases, but the network load is bounded. Consequently, the level of deterioration is also bounded.

The router ensures the enhanced best effort by checking the flow's packets and validating that the packet rate does not exceed the original peak traffic rate estimate. Any nonconforming, controlled-load data flows will not be allowed to affect the QoS offered to other conforming controlled-load flows. However, the router should attempt to deliver the nonconforming packets, provided the packets do not impact the QoS of other conforming flows negatively.

Fundamental to controlled-load service is the playback buffer. Adaptive applications are generally more tolerant of delay than of delay variation. An example of an adaptive application is packetized video. The amount of delay and delay variation encountered by the packets en route to the destination is a function of many factors, most notably the amount of congestion that the packet encounters. The receiver depacketizes the data and attempts to play back the signal at the same rate that it was played at the transmitting end. To compensate for any delays introduced by the network, data is buffered before it is replayed, introducing some additional delays but minimizing delay variations. (Delay variation is a much more critical parameter than delay when it comes to replaying data.) The length of time or offset delay that the signal is held in the buffer before it is played is called the playback point. Data arriving before the playback point is held in the buffer until the playback point arrives. Data arriving after the playback point is useless, must be discarded, and obviously should not be retransmitted.

The challenge for the host is to determine the correct playback point, or how long before delivering or playing data to hold it in the buffer. Because the application knows its own traffic characteristics and receives (via RSVP, as we will see) information on router queue depth, the application has a priori knowledge of the flow's delay characteristics and can therefore calculate an appropriate playback point. After determining the amount of delay, the application must determine if it can tolerate the associated playback point.

Intserv also defines adaptive playback applications. Delay characteristics in the network are apt to change with time. An application that is capable of modifying its playback point dynamically is called an adaptive playback application. (The dynamics associated with adaptive playback are indeed complex. Recently, Ethernet-based [or IP-based] telephones began to emerge. Generally, these devices exhibit adaptive playback behavior.)

Integrated Service Guaranteed-Load Service (RFC2212)

Guaranteed service is intended for real-time applications that have intolerant real-time requirements. Guaranteed service ensures that packets will arrive within the guaranteed delivery time and will not be discarded due to queue overflows, provided the flow's traffic stays within its specified traffic parameters. This service is intended for applications that need a firm guarantee that a packet will arrive no later than a certain time after it was transmitted by its source. For example, some audio and video playback applications are intolerant of any packet arriving after a very brief playback time. Applications that have intolerant real-time requirements will also require guaranteed service.

Although a policy scheme is not explicitly specified as part of intserv, the expectation is that one will exist within the host. This is necessary to control which user/ applications are allowed to request a specific QoS; otherwise, an application could simply request an arbitrarily large peak-traffic rate and effectively deprive other users of network resources, defeating the very purpose of intserv. Additionally, if the application is prone to traffic bursts, the host should implement a shaping scheme so that traffic is presented to the routers at a conformant rate.

Delay has two parts: a fixed delay (transmission delays, and so forth) and a queuing delay. The fixed delay is a property of the chosen path, which is determined not by guaranteed service but by the setup mechanism. Only queuing delay is determined by guaranteed service. Guaranteed service does not control the minimal or average delay of packets; it controls merely the maximal queuing delay. Furthermore, to compute the maximum delay a packet will experience, the latency of the path *must* be determined and added to the guaranteed queuing delay. Guaranteed service does not attempt to minimize the jitter (the difference between the minimal and maximal packet delays); it merely controls the maximal queuing delay.

The router that supports guaranteed-load service allocates a portion of bandwidth to the flow and ensures a firm end-to-end delay bound with no packet loss as long as the packets conform to the peak traffic rate specified for the flow.

Guaranteed-load service is subject to admission control. The flow must be shaped and policed. The ingress router polices flow to ensure that it conforms to the requested traffic rate. Packets not conformant are treated as best-effort packets by the router. Reshaping is an attempt by the router to restore the flow's traffic rate. The traffic rate might skew because of queuing-delay variations and subsequently deliver in a manner that exceeds peak traffic rate—an effect referred to as *clumping*. Reshaping mechanics schedule or shape the delivery of clumped packets so that they conform to the peak packet rate.

Integrated Service Traffic Control

Once the appropriate reservation has been installed in each router along the path, data flow can expect to receive the QoS commitment requested, provided there is no path change or router failure and that data flow conforms to the data rate specified. To ensure that data packets receive the contracted QoS, the intserv architecture identifies three additional router components. The function of the components—packet classifier, packet scheduler, and packet dropper—is to provide a traffic control mechanism. Figure 6.5 shows the components of a router supporting the intserv architecture.

The packet classifier maps each arriving packet (belonging to a particular flow) to the appropriate output queue that provides the packet with the QoS specified for the flow. Packet classification is generally more complicated with connectionless-mode protocols (IP) than with connection-oriented approaches (such as ATM) because typically, IP packets must be processed at every node. In other words, the classifying criteria (such as destination IP address) must be examined at every node. One approach to reduce the overhead associated with consistent packet classification might be to provide a *flow-id* field in the IP packet header. The flow-id would persist with the packet and expedite packet classification considerably at each router. With connection-oriented protocols, an imbedded identifier (implicit or explicit) typically removes the need for consistent packet classification.

The packet scheduler's basic function determines queue-servicing order: when to deliver a packet from a particular queue onto the output link.

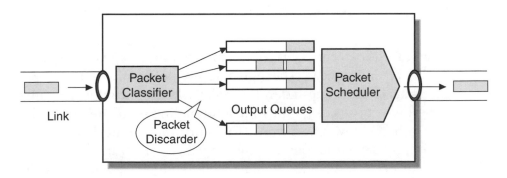

Figure 6.5   Integrated service router.

There are many approaches to packet scheduling (some are discussed later in this chapter). A classical router uses a simple FIFO scheme and consequently makes preferential treatment to a particular flow impossible. Another approach is simple priority queuing in which the highest-priority queue is emptied before other queues are serviced. Applying the approach, if enough packets arrive and are placed into the high-priority queue, other queues might become starved, which means they are never emptied. An alternative approach is round robin or some round-robin variant (such as weighted fair queuing, which is discussed later) that grants all packets some access to the link bandwidth while offering a preferential service to the higher-priority queues.

Packet dropping is a very important component of traffic control. Obviously, at times, the routers' buffers become full, which might be the result of an outage or a reconfiguration. A simple approach to handle the condition is to drop packets that arrive when the buffers are full, although this could result in very detrimental effects. Consider a case where there are 10 TCP applications traversing the congested router. If a packet from each of the applications arrives at the congested router so that one packet can be discarded from each application, all TCP applications will have to retransmit their packets as a result. More importantly, all TCP applications will go into TCP slow-start mode at the same time in an overreaction or incorrect reaction, resulting in wasted bandwidth and router resources. It would be much more efficient to discard 10 packets from the same TCP application.

When a TCP connection starts up, the TCP specification requires the connection to exhibit conservative behavior and assumes that the available bandwidth is small. TCP relies on a closed-loop, feedback algorithm to determine the rate at which it should transmit packets. The algorithm is called *slow start* and is quite simple, though some argue quite inefficient. At the start of the TCP session, the source sends one TCP segment and waits for an acknowledgment. Upon receipt of the acknowledgment, the source sends two segments and expects a single acknowledgment for both segments. The source continues to increase the number of TCP segments sent until a segment is lost and interprets the loss as a sign of congestion. The source then reduces its transmit window, typically to one packet, and restarts the slow-start process. The inefficiency arises because a stable state is never realized. In addition, TCP has no way of distinguishing losses as a result of congestion from losses due to transmission errors. It would be prudent not to close the window in response to transmission losses.

As another example, if a real-time application's packet is in a congested router's queue, it is possible that the packet can experience delay sufficient to make the packet useless to the real-time application—the packet arrives too late. In this case it would be wise to discard such packets from the queue. There is obviously much to be gained by implementing intelligent packet-dropping controls.

In the context of real-time services, dropping directly correlates to achieving desired QoS. If a queue builds up, dropping one packet reduces the delay of all the packets behind it in the queue. The loss of one packet can contribute to the success of many. There are several schemes (for example, *random early discard* [RED], discussed later in this chapter) that address the issue of intelligent packet dropping.

RSVP (RFC2205)

As stated previously, integrated services define an architecture that provides a framework for applications to select a controlled service level for delivery of their packets. There are two basic requirements. The first requires routers to support the QoS capabilities and traffic-control algorithms referred to previously. The second requires a mechanism through which applications can communicate their QoS requirements to an adjacent router and routers can communicate with each other about QoS requirements provided for in particular traffic flows.

The *resource reservation setup protocol* (RSVP) (RFC2205) enables senders, receivers, and routers of unicast or multicast applications to communicate with each other by setting up necessary host and router states that support QoS and traffic control requirements of application flows. It is the network control protocol specified by the intserv architecture.

Because the primary focus of intserv is to support multicast applications, RSVP is designed to support multicast environments and heterogeneous service needs. RSVP provides flexibility in the way that multicast applications share branches of the multicast delivery tree. RSVP also provides flexibility in the way that new members join the multicast delivery tree and as a graceful way for a host to leave the multicast delivery tree. RSVP is robust and scales well to large-multicast groups. RSVP provides for advance reservation of resources to support QoS and associated traffic-control mechanisms.

RSVP is not a routing protocol; it relies on unicast and multicast routing protocols to determine an appropriate destination path. Unicast relies on IP routing while multicast relies on the multicast delivery tree. RSVP is the vehicle that transmits QoS requests to all routers along the transit paths of the traffic flows. RSVP establishes and maintains a soft state in the routers along the flow's path, meaning that it is maintained by periodic refresh messages sent along the flow's transit path. The traffic-control state is torn down in the absence of a refresh message. In other words, the router's resources allocated to the flow's resources are returned to the router's general resource pool.

Because traffic-control state information is created and maintained by periodic updates, resource allocation is termed soft state. This is markedly different from the type of state tables created to support connection-oriented sessions known as hard state connections. Typically, soft-state connections are more reactive to change and require less router resource to maintain the state at the expense of constant updates and associated bandwidth consumption. Conversely, hard-state sessions conserve on updates at the expense of consuming router resources. In hard state connections, if an outage occurs, there must be some mechanism in place for routers to rebuild the state table. RSVP adopted the soft-state approach to maintain the simplicity and robustness that has long been demonstrated by connectionless protocols such as IP. With soft-state connections, if a route change occurs, the refresh messages automatically make the necessary changes in the state tables.

RSVP Operation

RSVP is the network control protocol used to set up reservations for network resources. RSVP identifies a communication session by combining destination IP address, transport-layer protocol, and destination port number. The information, along with QoS parameters associated with the session, constitutes the session's flow. Because each RSVP operation applies only to packets of a particular flow, every packet in the flow must include all details (that is, destination IP address, transport layer protocol, and destination port number) of the session to which it applies.

Because the transport layer protocol information is examined at each RSVP router, it is important to ensure that the maximum transfer unit (MTU) or packet size is negotiated when the end-to-end transit path of the flow is established. If the packet were to be fragmented, the transport layer information would be lost because it is not part of each fragment.

Because support for unicast RSVP is a simplification of RSVP for a multicast session, our discussion is limited to the multicast environment where the application is associated with a multicast address. Let us further assume that the multicast delivery tree has been established.

RSVP sessions are initiated by the receiver. Periodically, the sender, or source, advertises the application along with service levels supported by the application to the multicast delivery tree. After learning of the application, the receiver initiates the session by requesting resources in the path from itself to the server. Receiver-initiated reservations are used because different receivers might want (and be willing to pay for) a higher or lower quality of service. For example, a video source might offer a movie at three different service levels: a home video quality compressed at 64Kbps, a broadcast quality compressed at 1.5Mbps, and a high definition at 5Mbps. The receiver selects the level of service and makes a request to have the appropriate bandwidth allocated to the path from the sender to itself. Obviously, the higher the bandwidth the more expensive the connection. Differences between reservations from different receivers are resolved ("merged") within the network by RSVP.

RSVP Path Message

When a server or sending application starts up, an advertisement is sent to the multicast address and then delivered to all members of the multicast group. The advertisement carries information describing the data stream that the application generates. The RSVP message is called a PATH message. PATH messages provide each router in the path with a reverse path to the source of the PATH message. In addition, PATH messages provide receivers with information about the characteristics of the sending application and capabilities of the routers making up the path from the sender to the receivers.

PATH messages have three components. Previous hop (Phop) is the IP address of the last RSVP-capable router to forward the PATH message. The flowspec specifies characteristics of the flow, including QoS information, and the filterspec identifies the sending application, such as the sender's IP address and port number. Filterspec defines the data flow that receives the QoS specified by the flowspec.

The flowspec is further subdivided into the Transmit Specification (Tspec), which specifies the transmission characteristics of the sending application. The adspec contains information regarding the router's capabilities along the path and provides the receiving applications with information regarding QoS available on the path to the sender. Tspec is not modified by intervening routers, although Adspec is modified at each RSVP router on the path. Phop is also modified by each of the RSVP-capable routers in the path. Figure 6.6 illustrates the format of an RSVP PATH message.

Each RSVP-capable router along the delivery tree processes the PATH message. The Phop address is stored and used to construct the reverse path back to the sender. The cleanup timer is also stored. Expiration of the cleanup timer triggers deletion of PATH information within the router. The router updates the Phop field (with its own IP address) and modifies the adspec before forwarding the PATH message to the next router in the multicast delivery tree.

The adspec advertises the capabilities of the end-to-end communications path to the receivers; that is, adspec information fields are used by the receiver to determine the levels of service achievable on the path from the sender. The initial adspec always includes the service-level capability— either guaranteed service or controlled-load service—because currently, RSVP does not support heterogeneous service levels between senders and receivers. All receivers must request the same service. Adspec information for guaranteed service includes minimum bandwidth of any link in the path, number of RSVP routers in the path, minimum MTU in the path, latency approximation, and a bit indicating if any routers in the path are not RSVP-capable routers. If any routers in the path are not RSVP-capable, the end station should infer that the adspec information might be invalid. A router should never upgrade an adspec service level. Additionally, an

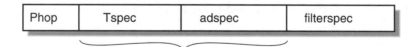

| Phop | Tspec | adspec | filterspec |

flowspec

Phop	IP address of the previous RSVP-capable router
Tspec	The transmission characteristics of the sending application, for example, 100 Kbps average transmission rate, with a 200 Kbps burst rate
	cleanup timer—how long information is valid
	refresh timer—frequency the sender will transmit PATH messages
adspec	GoS capabilities of routers in the path, for example, MTU size, maximum bandwidth available
filterspec	Uniquely identifies the sender flow, for example, 130.1.1.2 port 345

Figure 6.6   PATH message format.

RSVP router should never increase the bandwidth-available field or MTU field because doing so would provide erroneous information to the receiver.

RSVP RESV Messages

After receiving the PATH message, each receiver knows about the sender's application and resources available in the path from itself to the sender application. The receiver uses the information to determine bandwidth and network resources required for the communication. The receiver can generate an RESV message and direct the message to the sender. The RESV message includes a reservation specification (Rspec) that specifies resources reserved for the flow, a style specification that provides routers in the path with information concerning how to merge the flow path, and a filterspec used to identify the sender. Figure 6.7 illustrates the format of an RSVP RESV message.

The RESV message is sent in the reverse path from the receiver to the sender. Each router that receives the RESV message validates the request (admission control) and determines if resources are available to provide the requested bandwidth and delay characteristics. If resources are not available, the router refuses the request and notifies the requestor of the denial. If resources are available, the router allocates the bandwidth, installs the queuing policy necessary to meet delay tolerance of the flow, and forwards the RESV message to the next router in the path. When the RESV messages pass downstream to the sender they might merge with other RESV messages arriving on the same interface to provide efficiency to the flow. Table 6.4 shows the transmission characteristics and the reservation characteristics that are typically specified for each of the RSVP service categories.

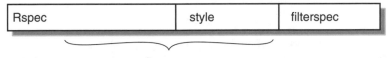

Rspec	style	filterspec

flowspec

Rspec   Resources reserved for the flow—most resources are the same as those specified in Tspec of the PATH message, for example, bandwidth = 120 Kbps; maximum delay = 5 ms

style   FF, WF, SE—specifies how the flow can be merged with other flows

filterspec   Uniquely identifies the sender flow, for example,130.1.1.2 port 345

Figure 6.7   RESV message format.

Table 6.4 Quality Requirements Specified for Each RSVP Service

	GUARANTEED SERVICE	CONTROLLED LOAD	BEST EFFORT
Rspec			
Packet loss	Specified	Not specified	Not specified
Packet delay	Not specified	Specified	Not specified
Delay variation	Not specified	Not specified	Not specified
Tspec			
Peak rate	Optional	Not specified	Not specified
Token bucket	Specified	Specified	Not specified

Figure 6.8 summarizes RSVP operation:

1. The end station (receiver) issues an IGMP message to register for a specific multicast group.

2. The RSVP Path multicast message that the source (sender) is transmitting now reaches the receiver—presuming, of course, that a multicast protocol, such as DVMRP, is running in the network.

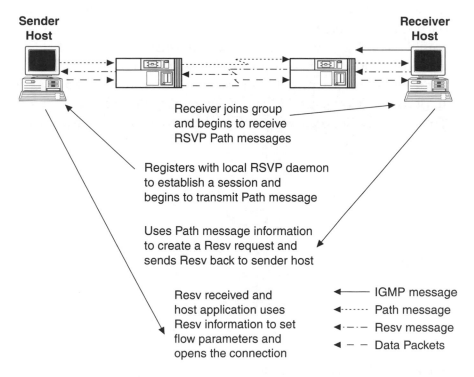

Figure 6.8 RSVP operation.

3. The receiver examines the RSVP Path message and determines the transmission characteristics of the source application (Tspec), and the Quality of Service capabilities of the routers in the path (adspec) from the sender to itself.

4. The receiver then sends an RSVP Resv message to the sender. The RSVP Resv message indicates to each intervening router the resources (Rspec) that are to be reserved for this flow. When a router receives a reservation request, it checks to see whether it has enough reservable bandwidth available on the circuit it must use to route the data. The total amount of reservable bandwidth is configured on a per-circuit basis, and is allocated to reservation requests on a first-come, first-served basis. Once all the routers between the sender and the receiver have allocated the requested bandwidth, that amount of bandwidth is guaranteed to that application flow until the application finishes.

5. Data is forwarded from the sender to the receiver along the established RSVP path.

How individual RSVP routers merge RESV messages to achieve the QoS requested is the task of the QoS control mechanism resident in each of the routers. RSVP specifies merging behavior yet how the behavior is accomplished is implementation specific. RSVP provides vehicles to transport requirements but does not specify explicit behavior. It is said that QoS data is opaque to RSVP. When flows are allowed to merge, the more stringent request must receive priority. For example, in Figure 6.9, if R5 requests 10Mbps and R6 requests 5Mbps, the merger results in R4 reserving 10Mbps. Consequently, R6 receives better QoS than requested, which is fine.

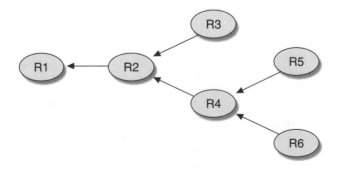

Figure 6.9   RESV message merging.

Flow Merging: Reservation Styles

RSVP provides several reservation styles to fit a variety of applications. The RSVP RESV request includes options that are called the reservation style. The styles define how reservations are treated from different senders within the same session and whether or not the requests need to meet specific criteria.

Reservations can be either distinct or shared. A separate distinct reservation can be created for each upstream sender, or a single reservation can be created that's shared among all packets of selected senders.

Within the selection of senders, an explicit list of all selected senders may be created to match a session, or a wildcard may be given, selecting all senders to the session. With an explicit list, each filter specification must match exactly one sender, but wildcard filters need no filter specification.

There are three reservation styles defined by RSVP. Only packets from the same application and only flows specifying the same style can merge. Figure 6.10 provides an illustration of how the Wildcard Filter style merges traffic. The router pathstate is established in R1, R2, R3, and R4 when GM1 sends its RESV. A wildcard reservation uses a filterspec that is not source specific. When GM2 joins the same multicast group, GM2 sends a RESV to the same filterspec, and the message merges with GM1 RESV at R3. In fact, GM2's RESV never goes beyond R3 unless the resources requested by GM2 are greater than what's been allocated by GM1. Effectively, GM1 and GM2 participate in the same multicast group and use the

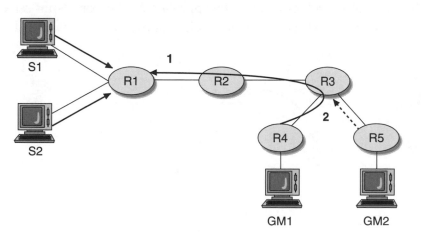

Figure 6.10 Style: Wildcard Filter (WF).

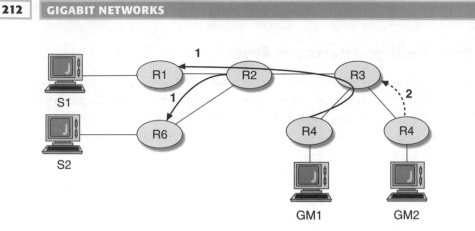

Figure 6.11   Style: shared explicit (SE).

same router resources. The approach works for audio conferences in which there is only one speaker at a time.

Filter style shared explicit (SE) is similar to style WF, except the filterspec specifies a unique sender, and only packets from the explicit sender are merged on the RESV path. It uses explicit sender selection and shared reservations. In Figure 6.11, GM1 sent an RESV that explicitly specified S1 and S2 in its filterspec. When GM2 issued an RESV with the same filter-spec and style, the messages merged, conserving router resources and bandwidth. The style is useful for subscription to a movie or an Internet channel (CNN, for example).

With filter style fixed filter (FF), the RESV specifies the explicit IP address of the senders from which it wants to receive data. It uses explicit sender selec-tion and distinct reservations. A separate path is established to each of the senders, as shown in Figure 6.12. The approach works from "split-screen" reception so that GM1 sees speakers at GM3 and GM4 simultaneously.

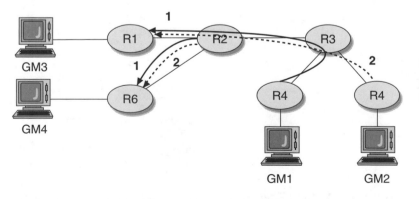

Figure 6.12   Style: fixed filter (FF).

Traffic-control mechanisms at each router must allocate the most stringent QoS parameters specified by each receiver.

RSVP Issues

Scalability is the primary concern in wide-scale deployment of RSVP. The fact that RSVP must maintain state information, albeit soft-state information, requires processing control messages and consuming memory to store state information. Therefore, the amount of router overhead consumed is in direct proportion to the number of RSVP flows that traverse the router. Additionally, router forwarding might be impacted because of packet classification and sophisticated scheduling mechanisms required to provide the appropriate level of service. Interestingly, as bandwidth on router links increases, the number of RSVP sessions that the link supports also increases. Consequently, more state information must be maintained and managed. All routers in the flow's path must support RSVP; otherwise, QoS information received by the receiver might be inaccurate. Another significant consideration is the length of a typical Internet flow. If the flow is not sufficiently large (in other words, for a long duration), the relative amount of overhead in setting up the RSVP path becomes more of a concern. If you consider the enormous bandwidth and number of possible paths through an Internet router, it is easy to see that RSVP implementation on the Internet might not be forthcoming.

RSVP is not widely used because it is not supported on many of the installed host applications and operating systems. Other issues are with prioritizing and authorizing reservation requests. RSVP operates on a first-come, first-served basis. If a critical application needs to reserve resources and the resources are unavailable, the application will not be able to obtain the QoS it needs. Further, there is no way to prioritize incoming requests. If a request for a lower-priority application is accepted, there may not be any or enough resources to meet the needs of a higher-priority application. Once a session is established, it cannot be stopped by the network, although the hosts can dynamically redefine their service needs during an active session. There is no mechanism within RSVP to reprioritize traffic.

RSVP requires signaling to be deployed end to end in order to provide the requested type of service. Though RSVP is transparent through routers that do not support it, RSVP can not guarantee the type of service provided by non-RSVP routers.

Intserv imposes a circuit-oriented model on a packet switching network, such as the Internet. This circuit-oriented model forces the network to behave in a way that it was not originally designed to do, and it becomes difficult to ensure the services requested. To implement a circuit-oriented model, heavy hop-by-hop signaling is required. This signaling uses up not only precious bandwidth but also device processing cycles for reservation requests, state updates, and traffic control.

How about running RSVP in an intranet environment? Many of the issues cited above are less important on an intranet than on the Internet, but there are concerns. Integrated service architecture does not define a policy control scheme, and there is certainly no mechanism to transport policy information between routers. In other words, there is no well-defined approach to control who is authorized to reserve what portion of resources. Consider the case in which 5Mbps of a 10Mbps link is allocated for guaranteed service RSVP sessions. If a user allocates the 5Mbps, all other users are locked out.

In addition, because RSVP reservations are made on a hop-by-hop basis, it is possible that one router would accept a request while another router somewhere further in the path would deny the request, resulting in wasted resources. Another issue arises because the RSVP request follows the routed path that was devised by a routing protocol optimized for number of hops or bandwidth. It is possible a path exists having the requested resources but that it is not the path in the router's routing table. There is no way for RSVP to know of or revert to another path. Another concern is encryption. Typically, encryption algorithms encrypt the flowspec portion of the packet, making it problematic for the RSVP router to provide the proper level of service.

The underlying premise of integrated services architecture is to provide quality of service but not at the expense of providing service.

Differentiated Services Architecture (RFC2475)

There are several significant concerns that will likely prevent deployment of RSVP on the Internet and probably confine RSVP deployment to corporate intranets. Most notably, the issue for the Internet is the requirement for a signaling mechanism to establish per-flow traffic states in each router that the path traverses, resulting in an important scaling limitation. However, several significant issues might even discourage RSVP's deployment in intranet environments. Because applications must be RSVP capable to signal for participation in an RSVP flow and because all routers in the path must be RSVP–capable to reserve resources on a per flow basis, means that RSVP requires nontrivial modification to the network.

The differentiated services architecture (diffserv) provides a class of service to a flow aggregate. In other words, at diffserv boundaries, packets are classified and marked. Within the diffserv domain, resources—bandwidth and buffers—are allocated for each classification. Packets with the same classification use the resources allocated for the classification. When a stream of packets with the same IP destination and class marking arrive at a diffserv router, the packets exit in the same order in which they arrived. However, if the packets were destined for the same IP address but had different class markings, they would exit according to priorities assigned to the different class markings. The service level is differentiated not on a per-flow basis but rather on a per-class basis wherein class represents the aggregation of all individual flows meeting the same classification criteria. Collectively, the aggregate of flows receives different levels of service, but there is no differentiation on the service level received by the individual flows within the Class of Service.

Diffserv simplifies the forwarding path by moving the complexity of classifying traffic to the edges of the network. Diffserv relies on edge-based, packet marking, and per-class management of routers in the network to support multiple service levels.

Diffserv takes advantage by prioritizing traffic, a capability that many existing Internet routers have already. Priority or packet differentiation is achieved within the router via queue management and scheduling mechanisms. Diffserv uses the bits in IPv4 ToS field or IPv6 *traffic-class field* for marking packets. The mark indicates a packet's priority or drop preference such that if congestion occurs in the network, the packet would drop before others. Routers, firewalls, or other network edge devices provide packet marking. Note that neither host nor application is required to do packet marking. Therefore, nothing has to change at the host for the host to participate in diffserv. Additionally, modifying routers is not overly complex.

Diffserv has renamed the ToS field the *differentiated services codepoint* (DSCP field).

Diffserv uses no signaling protocol. The DSCP indicates the particular behavior a packet is to receive at each router. How a packet gets marked is based on a policy administered and configured into the network. (A number of Internet drafts suggest various encodings of the DSCP field to achieve a specific behavior from the routers.) There are several ways to administer the policies. For example, one network provider might mark all packets going from one source IP network to a specific IP network destination as "high priority" while another ISP might mark all HTTP traffic as "high priority." The policy definition is up to the network provider.

Maintenance of flow-state information within routers is not required with diffserv. In addition, there is no explicit signaling protocol that establishes session paths and maintains state tables within the routers. Packets carry "state" information in their IP headers. Each router treats the packet according to the information in its DSCP field. This is referred to as per hop behavior (PHB).

By using the DSCP in each packet and applying PHB at each router, diffserv provides differentiated Classes of Service without requiring signaling and per-flow state information at every router. Packet classification via examination of fields within the packet is done at the edge of the network. The scheme is much more efficient and scalable than RSVP for the Internet core routers because diffserv routers examine only the IP header to determine the output port/queue to which the packet belongs. Forwarding path decisions are made separately from any quality-of-service considerations. All packets having the same DSCP receive the same behavior. Therefore, the forwarding component of the router must not only look at the destination IP address but must also examine the DSCP bits. Because the bits are within the IP header anyway, the high-speed router can still take advantage of hardware-based forwarding. Additionally, because the router examines only the IP header, that is not encrypted, the encryption dilemma encountered with RSVP is avoided.

Diffserv is a Layer 3 protocol. Unlike RSVP, there is no per-flow requirement for diffserv to communicate with link-layer drivers for allocating bandwidth and scheduling packet delivery. Decoupling diffserv from Layer 2 enables diffserv to interoperate with various Layer 2 protocols. For example, if the underlying network is ATM, a CBR PVC could be configured and the premium diffserv traffic (traffic with the same DSCP) directed to the PVC. However, if the packet is being forwarded over an underlying network without QoS support, then the packet may be adversely delayed or dropped due to congestion regardless of its DS designation.

Service Levels

Currently, diffserv defines three service levels: premium, tiered, and best effort. Associated with each service level is a corresponding PHB. Figure 6.13 shows an ISP composed of three routers. A portion of each router's resources is allocated for premium traffic. In other words, some portion of bandwidth on the outbound links and some portion of high-priority buffers are also allocated to premium service; the internal schemes used by the router to provide such allocations are not specified.

Another portion of the router's resources is allocated for tiered service. Tiered service allows traffic to be categorized with different levels of precedence. The precedence information will be conveyed to the router from a policy server. The tiered service will provide the most flexibility. It is, effectively, a "better than best effort" delivery mechanism. The balance of router resources is reserved for best-effort traffic.

As packets arrive at the edge device, they are classified according to source, destination, or any combination of fields in the header. The DSCP of the packet's IP header is marked accordingly, and the packet is forwarded into the network. Rather than deal with per-flow traffic control and maintain per-flow state information, routers simply forward the packet according to the DSCP bits. The router treats the packet with a PHB—expedited forward (EF), assured forward (AF), or default forward (DF)—that corresponds to its DSCP.

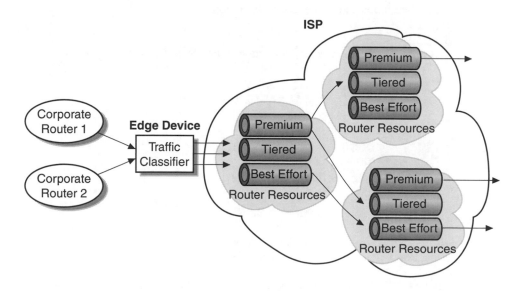

Figure 6.13 Diffserv defines three service levels: premium, tiered and best effort.

IETF Diffserv Recommendations

An IETF diffserv document (IETF assured forwarding PHB group) makes the following recommendations.

Premium service traffic that is to receive expedited forwarding PHB receives a DSCP equal to 101110.

Tiered service traffic receives one of the following DSCPs:

AF11 = 001010	AF21 = 010010	AF31 = 011010	AF41 = 100010
AF12 = 001100	AF22 = 010100	AF32 = 011100	AF42 = 100100
AF13 = 001110	AF23 = 010110	AF33 = 011110	AF43 = 100110

The first three bits represent the class, and the next three bits represent the drop precedent, with three levels of drop precedence currently defined. In the case of congestion, the marking of the DSCP field allows the diffserv node to determine the relative importance of the packet within the AF class. A congested diffserv node tries to protect packets with a lower drop precedence value from being lost by preferably discarding packets with a higher drop precedence value.

The drop precedence bits can be used to indicate if a packet is "in profile." It is used to identify packets that are not compliant with a service-level agreement (SLA). These packets should be dropped before any other tiered service packets.

Figure 6.14 shows the relationship between the DSCP value and the per hop behavior.

DSCP
Differentiated Services Codepoint, six bits of the DS field are used to select the PHB a packet experiences at each node.

CU
Currently Unused, a two-bit field that is currently reserved for future use.

Differentiated Services Field (DS)

DSCP	Per Hop Behavior
Premium Service	Expedited Forward (EF)
Tiered Service	Assured Forward (AF)
Best Effort	Best Effort (BE)

Figure 6.14   Relationship between the DSCP value and the Per Hop Behavior.

Within a diffserv node exhibiting assured forward (AF) PHB, the level of forwarding assurance of an IP packet thus depends on:

- The available forwarding resources that have been allocated to the AF class to which the packet belongs
- The current load of the AF class
- The drop precedence of the packet (in case of congestion within the AF subclass)

The Edge Device Functions

Fundamental to diffserv architecture is the service level agreement (SLA). The SLA is a contract between the service provider (the network) and customer (a user) that describes the behavior characteristics that traffic receives end to end. With a premium SLA, the customer specifies the peak-bit rate for the flow or aggregation of flows—all traffic that has the expedited forward bits set. The network portion of the contract specifies an availability of bandwidth and that premium traffic traverse the network with negligible queuing delay. For tiered traffic, the form of the SLA is currently not well defined. The terms are arbitrated between user and provider. Not specified in the diffserv architecture is the network management component that defines how the user validates the level of service that is actually received.

The differentiated services architecture is based on a simple model in which traffic entering the network is classified and possibly conditioned to ensure compliance with the SLA. This happens not only when traffic from a host enters the diffserv domain but must also occur when the flow traverses different diffserv domains. For example, a situation might occur where an end-to-end path crosses ISP boundaries, each of which is an autonomous diffserv domain.

The classifier is the component of the edge device that examines the fields within the packet to determine which PHB bits get set. Which fields are examined depends on the policies configured on the edge device. A situation might occur in which all TCP packets destined for a particular IP subnet receive premium service. The classifier component examines each packet to see if the packet meets premium service criteria. The process is consistent with the original premise of diffserv, which is that all packet processing or classification occurs once and at the diffserv domain boundaries. Currently, classifying traffic is quite simplistic: the packet meets some set of static and predefined criteria and receives premium service, the packet meets some less stringent criteria and receives a tiered service, or the packet receives best-effort service. The traffic is classified independently of the current condition of the network. That is, the classifier has no knowledge of outages or congestion when traffic is being classified. In the future, directory-enabled networking and policy servers will work in concert to dynamically determine the status and availability of network resources, and this information will be conveyed to the classifier.

After the packet has been classified, the marker function within the edge device sets the DSCP bits. Packets marked premium are placed in a queue with the expectation that the queue is relatively short and service very quick. Premium traffic should maintain significantly lower levels of latency, packet loss, and delay variation than best-effort traffic. The packet scheduler should be designed in a way that tiered traffic receives a reasonable amount of resources and that best-effort traffic is not starved. In other words, best-effort traffic should not remain in a buffer so long that it is useless.

Another component of the edge device is the shaper. The shaper ensures that the traffic rate to the ISP router is compliant with the traffic rate specified in the SLA. For example, there might be numerous flows passing through the edge device into the ISP. The SLA specifies the allowable traffic rate for the premium traffic and allowable rate for best-effort traffic. It is possible that as flows from the user network are classified and aggregated at the edge router, the rate of premium traffic sent to the ISP exceeds what has been specified in the SLA. The shaper should buffer the premium traffic and deliver the traffic to the ISP at a rate compliant with the SLA. The ISP can discard noncompliant packets, or possibly, the SLA is structured such that there is a burst allowed so the traffic rate might burst to some level for some brief period of time. However, there will be a charge associated with the increased traffic level. Figure 6.15 illustrates packets arriving at a diffserv Edge Device. The packet is examined by the Classifier to determine the priority of the packet, and the DSCP is then set by the Marker. The packet is then placed in the appropriate output queue and then scheduled for transmission onto the output link.

Work is in progress to explore the implication of using the currently unused (CU) field to indicate explicit congestion notification (ECN) in a manner similar to frame relay's FECN. Currently, the CU bits are set to zeroes, and the field is ignored by diffserv-capable routers.

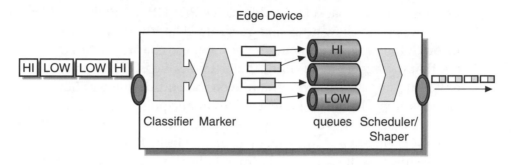

Figure 6.15 Preferential packet forwarding.

PHB

Diffserv routers implement PHB used to forward traffic of different service levels with differing behavior. The DSCP determines how routers handle each packet. The service level for each class is ensured by the combination of admission control functions (shaping) and core functions (provisioning bandwidth).

The PHB, designed to support the differing service levels, is generally implemented via queues, queue management, and schedulers that reside at the router's egress interfaces (see Figure 6.16). Packets experience loss, latency, and jitter all because of queuing at the transit routers. From the perspective of the diffserv router, when a packet arrives, the routing table is referenced to determine to which egress port the packet is sent. The packet is sent to the proper output queue for the egress port based on PHB bits set in the DSCP of the packet header, making diffserv highly scalable. Router processing involves simply examining the IP header. This enables the router to implement hardware-based packet forwarding. However, diffserv routers must support some form of queue management and scheduling.

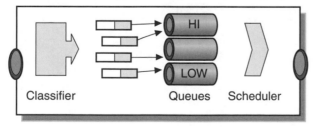

Figure 6.16 Components of the DS router.

Premium service packets should receive EF PHB. EF PHB provides low loss, low latency, low jitter, and guaranteed bandwidth end to end through the diffserv domain. Providing these characteristics means ensuring that the aggregate of traffic that is to receive EF PHB experiences little or no queuing. The forwarding rate on the output queues should meet or exceed the packet arrival rate. Until dynamic policy servers are available, providing EF PHB will be very inefficient. Effectively, the EF PHB service provider will have to implement a "virtual leased line" mentality. That is, the resources will need to be permanently allocated. Without dynamic policy servers, this is the only way that the desired behavior can be guaranteed. Consequently, premium service traffic should be kept to a very small fraction of the total network traffic until policy servers are available to dynamically allocate resources for EF PHB.

In Figure 6.17, assume that all links are 10Mbps. Assume that we want to configure our network such that whenever Host 1 communicates with application (x) on Host 4, it receives premium service. In other words, the service will feel the same as a point-to-point connection. This implies that resources need to be preallocated on Rtr1 such that 4Mbps of the bandwidth between Rtr1 and Rtr3 is committed to the connection. In addition, queue management within Rtr1 must ensure scheduling to accommodate the connection. Now assume the same for Host 2; that is, premium service between Host 2 and Host 4. Again, 4Mbps of bandwidth and queue resources are committed. If we wanted to do the same for Host 3, we could not because there is not 4Mbps left on the Rtr1-to-Rtr2 link; only 2Mbps remains. If we were to expand the approach to provide premium service to numerous users across the Internet, the task of traffic engineering would be immense. Simply stated, until policy servers provide network resource

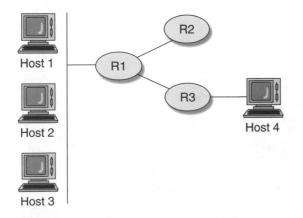

Figure 6.17   Example configuration.

information dynamically, premium service is prohibitively expensive for ISPs. However, in small intranets, expect to see premium service implemented, especially in networks supporting real-time applications.

Tiered service packets receive AF PHB. AF PHB provides a way to prioritize best-effort traffic. Currently, four AF classes are defined. Each AF class is allocated a certain amount of forwarding resources (buffer space and bandwidth). The edge device is configured to categorize and mark (set the DSCP) IP packets according to precedence rules. The value of DSCP provides different levels of forwarding assurances; basically, the DSCP value specifies a drop-order in the event that a packet experiences congestion at a subsequent diffserv router.

There is now no standard way of associating traffic requirements with a specific tiered service level. It is a reasonable expectation that proprietary service classes will be implemented before there is a standard. For example, the SLA might specify that HTTP traffic going from network(x) to network(y) will experience a specified packet loss ratio and incur on average some specified amount of delay. Another more subtle issue that is equally important has to do with expectation. There are certainly cost and administrative gains made by supporting real-time applications on the data network. Is it realistic to expect a premium class of service, and is a premium class of service required? If we want premium service, it appears that a signaling protocol is probably a better approach, as in RSVP or ATM. Currently, it is impractical to expect premium service from a diffserv network. However, if the user is conditioned to expect (and not be annoyed by) an occasional "click" during a phone conversation, the benefits realized by the diffserv network may well be acceptable.

Prioritizing Traffic

With connection oriented schemes, such as RSVP and ATM, network resources are allocated at the time that the path is established through the network. If the requested resources are not available, the connection is denied. When the connection is accepted, the requested resources are reserved for the duration of the particular flow. Typically, this means that some portion of buffer space is reserved for the flow, the flow is scheduled to be placed onto the output link in a fashion that is consistent with the request, and an appropriate portion of bandwidth is reserved on the link. Unscheduled traffic that arrives at the router/switch will not impact the service level allocated to the connection-oriented flow. With connection-oriented schemes, when there is a network failure, the connection and resource allocation have to be renegotiated. Traditionally, traffic in a connection-oriented environment is linear and nonbursty. Even if the source application generates traffic in a bursty nonlinear fashion, the traffic is shaped, or smoothed, before it is allowed into the connection-oriented network. Connection-oriented networks typically have another component called policing, which validates that traffic submitted to the connection-oriented network is in compliance with the service agreement.

In a connectionless environment, bursty unpredictable traffic is the norm. In a diffserv network, this unpredictable bursty traffic will share resources with linear predictable traffic, such as voice. In order to provide different assured service levels in a connectionless network, we must rely on mechanisms that prioritize traffic, smooth or shape the bursty traffic, provide clever traffic scheduling, and implement intelligent traffic discard policies.

The diffserv ingress device is responsible for four key tasks: classifying traffic, marking, shaping, and policing. The ingress device is configured with admission control policies. Ideally, these policies relating to the requirements will come from the dynamic policy server, but initially, they will be static.

Within the diffserv network, packet scheduling, buffer management, and packet discard are the functions required to provide the differentiated services. Scheduling, buffer management, and packet discard are the methods by which the network and each individual switch enforce policies. Scheduling, or queuing, is a fundamental requirement of connectionless packet-based networks and is the primary contributor to the superior efficiency and lower bandwidth cost of packet-based networks. Scheduling controls the rate at which users gain access to bandwidth. Scheduling ensures that each user transmitting at a rate that is conformant with the SLA will not be denied service by a user who is not transmitting in a conformant manner. Obviously, a more sophisticated scheduling scheme than FIFO is required.

The first attempt at a more sophisticated scheduling scheme was called priority queuing (PQ). With this scheme, the buffer space is prioritized. Packets are queued or placed into the buffer space according to the packet priority. High-priority packets are sent on the output link before lower-priority packets. The problem with the scheme is that it is possible that lower-priority packets are delayed too long to be useful, or possibly, they are discarded.

Class based queuing (CBQ) is an enhancement to PQ. CBQ attempts to provide fairness by allocating portions of link bandwidth to specific types of traffic. Instead of providing absolute service to the high-priority queue, it deploys a more equitable scheme. With CBQ, the user configures the preference with which each queue will be serviced and the amount of traffic that will be delivered from the queue to the link on each pass. This method permits the user to assign buffer space to defined traffic classes, thus reserving link bandwidth. However, there are limitations with CBQ. In this manner, CBQ attempts to provide fairness by not allowing any class of traffic to get an inordinate amount of resources. Typically, the buffer allocation is static, and the user must configure sufficient buffers in each router along each potential path to accommodate each of the traffic classes.

Buffer management is necessary because even the best packet scheduling algorithm can not ensure that buffer space will be fairly allocated to packets waiting to be transmitted. Ideally, buffer space will be managed in a way that makes all buffer space available to all traffic but does so in a manner that ensures higher-precedence traffic will not be deprived of buffer space by a lower precedent or nonconforming packets. This is exactly why an intelligent packet discard scheme is required.

Weighted fair queuing (WFQ) with random early discard (RED) is a technique that attempts to intelligently manage buffer space by influencing the type of traffic (priority) that is allowed into the network. WFQ provides bandwidth allocations and delay bounds to specified traffic types. It does not require users to configure router buffer allocations. Rather, it uses a servicing algorithm that attempts to provide predictable delays. As packets arrive, the buffer space is sorted in a way that attempts to ensure that each packet is delayed the appropriate amount of time. Basically, WFQ forwards packets just before the packet reaches the maximum delay value for its priority. This approach can significantly improve response times and decrease the delay variation for interactive traffic, resulting in more predictable round-trip delays. Obviously, as more and more packets arrive, the task of timely packet delivery becomes more complex, and eventually, it becomes impossible.

WFQ needs a mechanism for controlling traffic that enters the network. During high traffic periods as the router becomes too congested to provide acceptable delays, RED begins dropping packets. RED selectively drops single packets from multiple flows, forcing the TCP sessions to go into slow-start mode and reducing network traffic at its source.

Unfortunately, WFQ with RED cannot produce performance guarantees by only reacting to congestion. Each router can only attempt to dynamically allocate buffer space and juggle packets to maintain performance and fairness. In a large complex network, traffic must be proactively controlled at ingress. Otherwise, it is possible that many priority packets will arrive at a router, making it impossible for the router to deliver packets in a timely manner.

Traversing Diffserv Domains

As stated earlier, the SLA is fundamental to the diffserv architecture. The SLA is a contract between a service provider and a customer that describes the behavior characteristics marked traffic receives end to end. However, it is quite possible that end to end means traversing several ISPs. Certainly, customers will not be willing to negotiate SLAs with each of the ISPs (in fact, customers won't know or care about the other ISPs). To deal with the scenario, ISPs need to reach agreement on the support of PHB and the interpretation of codepoints. Until PHB for various service levels is standardized, it is expected that different service providers will offer different levels of service and that different service providers will probably use different codepoints (DSCP) for equivalent service. As a simplification, it is possible that one service provider will designate the highest level of service that it offers with a codepoint of 11110 while another may represent the best service that it offers with a codepoint of 000001. The "best" services may be quite different in terms of what they offer and how they are measured. Even after codepoints are defined in standards, it is quite possible that some providers might want to use some PHB privately for their own purposes within their own diffserv domain.

Problems associated with interoperation between two diffserv domains should now be obvious. If we consider two ISPs (diffserv domains), ISP(x) and ISP(y), an agreement between the two domains must be reached regarding the support of PHBs and the interpretation of the codepoints. This involves two agreements: how to handle flows from ISP(x) into ISP(y) and how to handle flows from ISP(y) into ISP(x). Consider the traffic passing from ISP(x) into ISP(y).

Note that the egress device (that is the last device that the packet passes through in ISP(x)) is now considered the edge device from the perspective of ISP(y). Therefore, it should exhibit the edge device behavior discussed earlier. ISP(y) is oblivious to the fact that the packet is coming from another ISP.

The diffserv router in ISP(y) that receives the packet from ISP(x) must modify the codepoint in the packet in such a way that the packet receives the same behavior within ISP(y) that it received in ISP(x). There are several ways to achieve this. The resolution is trivial if both ISPs use the same codepoints for the same behavior. In this case, nothing needs to be done to the packet when it enters ISP(y), except to police it to make sure that it is compliant with the service level agreement between the ISPs.

The situation is a little more complex when the ISP provides the same service levels but uses different codepoints to represent the particular service level. In this case, ingress router to ISP(y) would have to be configured so that it would modify the PHB bits in the appropriate way to ensure that the packet receives the desired behavior within the ISP. A corollary to this approach would be for the egress router at ISP(x) to modify the packet before forwarding it to ISP(y). In either case, the same result is achieved. The more complicated scenario is when the two ISPs use different codepoints and have different ways of defining service levels, or perhaps one ISP is ATM-based while the other is IP-based. For example, the IP-based ISP may define a service level in terms of a peak traffic rate and a delay while the ATM-based ISP may provide nrt-VBR connections where the delay is minimal but not measured. In these situations where there is no direct mapping of service levels between the ISPs, care must be taken to use a codepoint at the receiving ISP that provides a per-hop behavior at least as good as the PHB in the sending ISP. The primary reason not to allow the service level to be diminished is that it is quite possible additional ISPs are downstream. Furthermore, accumulation of small amounts of decreased service levels may result in significant end-to-end performance degradation.

As mentioned above, the mapping decisions must be made for traffic in both directions. In other words, we must also provide a mapping when going from ISP(y) to ISP(x). Initially, these decisions and mappings will be done manually. When codepoint designations have been standardized, it is possible that a dynamic protocol will be designed and implemented that will assess the performance characteristics of individual ISPs and provide information across ISP boundary devices so that mapping decisions can be made automatically.

At some point, diffserv classification and marking procedures will be standardized, ensuring that there will be some level of QoS commonality between ISPs. Certainly, service providers will continue to sell and price combinations of service classes as they wish.

Policy-Enabled Networking

With diffserv, QoS classification is happening at the edge of the network. Thus far, we have assumed that the edge devices were preconfigured with the criteria needed to make QoS decisions. We have further assumed that careful traffic engineering has been implemented to ensure that the QoS characteristic (for example, bandwidth, delay tolerance) is available to provide the packets with the QoS that is indicated in its DSCP. The implication is that all the network devices are acting independently (with no knowledge of what is happening at the other network device). However, we are expecting that together, the network devices will provide the desired behavior. We have relied on traffic engineering to make sure that all network devices are preconfigured (bandwidth, buffers) so that each individual packet that arrives at any network device in the diffserv domain will receive the QoS that the edge device has assigned. This might be a reasonable expectation if an army of traffic engineers is supporting a network that is limited in size and the network supports only a couple of traffic classes.

What if the network is large and supports multiple service levels and user profiles? What if only a certain group of users is granted access to privileged information? What if service levels that a group of users is entitled to varies depending on the time of day or time of year? What if available resources have to adapt to particular events, such as a network broadcast to announce that the company has just been bought? It is easy to manually configure policies such as filters and access lists into an edge component. Yet there is significant benefit to having a mechanism that supports networkwide availability of the policy information, such as a tool that could be used to deposit the policy information onto a central repository or directory accessed by all of the edge devices.

In addition, it would be advantageous to have some control mechanism built into the network such that the edge devices have a sense for the resources that are available within the core of the network dynamically. The edge devices could then use the information to make intelligent QoS decisions. The mechanisms to support monitoring and distributing the information (bandwidth available, buffer delay) on a per-interface basis through the diffserv domain is nontrivial. The issues become more significant and complex when we consider that often the end-to-end connection traverses several ISPs. The bottom line is that for diffserv to truly scale, profile, policy, and resource information must be known throughout the network. Several working groups within IEFT are investigating approaches, including the RSVP admission policy (RAP) WG.

Bandwidth Broker

The primary goal of the differentiated services architecture is controlled sharing of bandwidth and router resources. Developers achieve the goal by implementing policies that define who can access what portions of the network resources and when. The approach proposed for diffserv involves two components: the policy client that resides in each of the edge devices and the policy server, the repository for policies and network resource availability. In diffserv, the policy server is called a bandwidth broker. The bandwidth broker can configure with organizational policies to monitor available bandwidth and other network resources, interpret service-level requests from clients, and keep track of the current allocation of marked traffic. The bandwidth broker can also proactively reconfigure the router with regard to DSCP, marking a flow, and can communicate with bandwidth brokers in other diffserv domains (another ISP, for example) to ensure viability of end-to-end traffic agreements.

As an illustration, the router can inform the bandwidth broker of available bandwidth for each of its links and can further specify some percentage of bandwidth available for premium (EF) service. The router can also support five different classes of service, each with an associated DSCP marker. The router can specify support of some amount of traffic rate (packet per second) on each service (the router would have to make internal calculations based on queue depth, queue management, and scheduling policies). When a client wants to make a connection, it specifies a peak and perhaps a burst-traffic rate and/or a delay tolerance and a time period (9:00 A.M. to 5:00 P.M., for example) for the connection. The policy server resident in the edge device constructs a policy request and forwards the request to the bandwidth broker. The bandwidth broker examines the destination address and validates the user profile to ensure that the user is privileged to make the request, and the resources remain on the connection. If everything checks, the bandwidth broker sends a confirmation to the client with the specified DSCP marker to apply to the packets for the flow. The bandwidth broker then recalculates available bandwidth and queue depths for the QoS queue and uses the updated information for subsequent client requests. Additionally, at 5:00 P.M., the bandwidth broker can proactively inform the router that the DSCP marker for the flow is no longer active.

In the event the connection traverses DSCP domains, the local bandwidth broker informs the adjacent region's bandwidth broker, which then recalculates available bandwidth and network resources and configures the remote-edge device with the appropriate packet flow information. Typically, the process entails a secure association between the bandwidth broker peers. Of course, this presumes that some bilateral agreement exists between the two-DSCP domains.

As an enhancement to bandwidth-broker functionality, the bandwidth broker might reside on a router that is running a QoS-sensitive routing protocol, such as QOSPF. When a request for a service level arrives at the bandwidth broker, the QoS-sensitive routing protocol could determine the end-to-end path of the request and reference the QoS-enhanced routing table to determine the bandwidth and delay associated with the path. It would respond with the appropriate marker. As the flow's marked traffic started to flow, consuming the router and bandwidth resources, the router would send an update and include the new QoS parameter availability. The bandwidth broker would learn the update information as a result of running the QoS-enabled routing protocol.

Working groups within IETF have identified several protocols and devices to support policy-enabled differentiated services.

Directory Enabled Networking

Policy-based networking is closely related to directory-enabled networking (DEN). DEN is a scheme to create a common framework for storing management information, called objects, about various network elements and services in a directory. Associated with each object is a set of parameters called attributes. Objects can include network equipment, such as routers, switches, applications, and even vLAN information. Also in the directory is a set of attributes for each object. For example, a router object would contain information normally found in the router's configuration file plus some additional information, such as bandwidth on each link, bandwidth on the link available for the different service levels, and queue buffers available for each of the service levels.

Directories certainly are not new; DNS and DHCP databases have been used for years. The problem is that there is no consistency between the different databases. Because DEN can store all sorts of information, DEN will possibly become a universal standards-directory framework. Despite the sophistication of the database, the database becomes useful only when there is a standard protocol for accessing directory information and defining operations that can perform using the information. For this, the entire industry has already embraced the LDAP standard. Unfortunately, directories alone are insufficient to make policy-based networking feasible. Even though directories store policy and profile information, directories are basically static and lack knowledge about the current state of the network. If a user were to query a directory server about setting up a connection, the directory server might have the ability to determine if the user has privilege. However, the directory server would have no way of knowing if the resources requested were available. DEN work is being done by the Desktop Management Task Force (DMTF) of IETF.

Lightweight directory access protocol (LDAP), RFC1588, is a "lightweight" version of the directory access protocol (DAP) and part of X.500. LDAP is a directory scheme with a simple goal of letting directories communicate. The protocol is used to access directories and make multiple directories in an enterprise interoperable and manageable from a single point. LDAP support is being implemented in Web browsers and e-mail programs to allow them to query LDAP-compliant directories.

Policy-based networking requires a policy server (a generic term; the diffserv initiative adopted the name *bandwidth broker*) to obtain information from the directory server using LDAP, but the policy server updates the information and maintains the state of the network. The policy server will make policy decisions. The protocol used for communication between the edge device and the bandwidth broker is common open policy server (COPS). COPS is a client/server protocol that uses TCP as the transport. TCP connection is the responsibility of the edge device. The edge device uses the connection to send policy requests to the bandwidth broker. The bandwidth broker validates the requests and responds with rejections or DSCP. The bandwidth broker can initiate a COPS message to the edge device if the marker that was issued becomes invalid. For example, if the information that the bandwidth broker received from the directory server specifies that a privilege is valid until 5:00 P.M., at 5:00 P.M., the bandwidth broker issues a message to the edge device indicating that the marker is no longer valid. Figure 6.18 depicts the communication flows between the components of a diffserv network.

Simply put, the directory server and policy server (bandwidth broker) together provide a dynamic binding between statically defined resources (such as network addresses, user profiles, and application profiles) and dynamically implemented policies (in other words, allocating available resources to meet business rules).

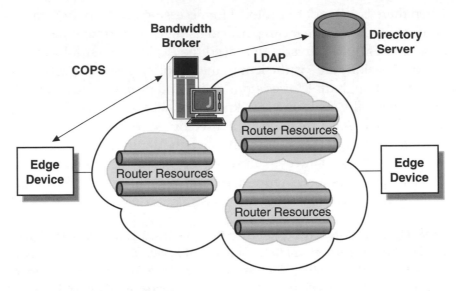

Figure 6.18 Bandwidth broker.

RSVP and Bandwidth Brokers

How does an application make a request to the network for some service level? One approach is to use RSVP in conjunction with the diffserv bandwidth broker.

The RSVP message, with flowspec and filterspec, is constructed and sent from the host to the edge device. The edge device forwards the RSVP message to the bandwidth broker. The bandwidth broker processes the request, and if it is approved, forwards a message to the edge device that sets up the flow packet classification. A message is also sent to the egress router (in the event that the session is traversing ISPs) to add to the aggregate-marked traffic allocation for packet shaping on the outbound link. The RSVP message is also sent across the link to the other ISP ingress router. If the ISP also supports RSVP with a bandwidth broker, the router forwards the frame to the ISP bandwidth broker.

Within the diffserv domain, packets are served solely according to the DSCP.

Other Considerations

Although as emphasized diffserv is almost transparent from the perspective of applications and not difficult to implement in routers, there are

Table 6.5 Comparison: Intserv and Diffserv

ATTRIBUTE	DIFFSERV	INTSERV
Service objective	Multiple service levels, edge to edge	Support real-time and best-effort application traffic flows
Strict delay guarantee	No	Yes
Data path behavior	Traffic control at edge; buffer management and scheduling at each router	State information maintained at each host and router
Classification	DSCP	Packet processed at each router
Signaling	None	Yes
Granularity	Aggregate of flows	Per individual flow

some significant issues. Routers will have to implement more sophisticated queue management and scheduling schemes. In addition, defining QoS in a consistent way is not trivial. Fortunately, vendors are currently at work on developing a predefined QoS template in which case network managers will not have to determine the combination of QoS mechanisms needed to support specific applications. The network device will need to deploy a COPS client or perhaps implement some type of SNMP-based COPS proxy to communicate with the bandwidth broker. Table 6.5 highlights the similarities and differences between Diffserv and Intserv schemes for providing Quality of Service.

Conclusion

The recent Quality of Service initiatives have been focused solely on enabling the Internet, and other networks, to support all types of media: data, voice, and video. The applications must maintain their uniqueness (no one will ever mistake a phone conversation for a file transfer); however, there is much to be gained by utilizing the same physical infrastructure to support all types of media. At what point do the different applications come together so that they can all be transported over the same physical network? The next chapter discusses the issue of convergence; that is, the merging of different applications so that they can all utilize the same physical network.

CHAPTER 7

Technology Convergence

Now that we have defined QoS, how can we structure our networks to best deliver the QoS that will be required to support applications with real-time requirements, such as voice, video, and teleconferencing?

Convergence in this context means a technology or protocol that all communications—voice, data, video, and so on—have in common. The advantage of convergence is that with a converged network, all communications can share facilities, management strategies, and operation staff, resulting in significant cost savings. Another advantage of convergence is that if all applications that are using the network facilities have a common reference point, the applications can be prioritized at that reference point. This capability is important if we want to differentiate the type and quality of service that is being extended to a user.

The telephone network is pervasive. Over the years, it has come to be an integral part of our lives. The telephone network was designed to support voice, and everything is standardized on 64Kbps (DS-0) voice channels. Today, voice can be compressed without sacrificing quality, but redefining the size of the fundamental channel is not trivial, even where SONET/SDH is employed. More significant is the fact that data transmission is becoming increasingly more important and attempting to accommodate bursty data on a fixed-width circuit is inherently inefficient. The

Internet is rapidly rising to the same level of importance as the telephone network. In fact, there is little argument that within a few years, the Internet will surpass the telephone network in the way that it impacts our lives. Unlike the telephone network, the Internet is a data network designed to transmit packets.

Some characteristics inherent in the telephone network optimize the transmission of voice, and some characteristics inherent in the Internet optimize the transmission of bursty data.

Network designers and vendors are starting to pull together the pieces of what will become the new paradigm for a comprehensive network. It will be a packet and cell-based network that is equally adept at handling data, voice, and video. Recent developments in real-time voice compression make voice over a packet feasible. In pulling this network together, it would be folly if the designers and vendors chose to ignore the wealth of information that was learned in designing and building the networks that permeate every aspect of our lives.

Since its inception the telephone industry has relied on the concept of a circuit (real or virtual) to provide traffic management and control. A circuit defines a path through the network. In modern networks, the circuit is a logical concept, such that numerous circuits will exist over the same physical path.

The circuit may have been as simple as a piece of string between two tin cans or as complex as an ATM virtual circuit. Data communications, on the other hand, has not relied on circuits; instead, data communication networks have preferred a packet-switching technique. Conventional packet switching provides resiliency and resource sharing but at the expense of predictable traffic delay and traffic control. In the previous chapter, we discussed enhancements to routing that effectively define different ways of creating virtual circuits for the packet switched network.

Years of experience have shown that where traffic control and management are required, circuits, or a defined and predictable path through the network, are a necessity.

Of course, traffic control and engineering have been vital because the demand for network resources, buffers, and bandwidth has been greater than the supply. If there were an infinite amount of available resources, there would be little need for traffic management. Some pundits believe that emerging technologies will make infinite resources a reality.

There are two types of virtual circuits: permanent and switched. Currently, permanent virtual circuits predominate. Switched virtual circuits, ATM or frame relay, are yet to be deployed in public networks in any sort of large scale, and the likelihood of their deployment in the near future is remote. Permanent virtual circuits involve user intervention. The PVC must be defined and manually configured at every device, when the path changes, or more bandwidth needs to be allocated to a circuit, again requiring manual intervention at every device. The number of PVCs that must be configured is, of course, related to the $O(n^2)$ "order of n-squared" scaling problem, where n is the number of sites that must be interconnected. Obviously, we would prefer switched virtual circuits so that the circuit would be established dynamically, only when needed, and the resource allocation nailed up only for the duration of the circuit. But because switched virtual circuits are difficult to create—they require a routing protocol, an address resolution mechanism, a signaling scheme, and a billing strategy—their deployment has been slow to materialize.

In summary, virtual circuits are necessary. They make it much easier to deal with underlying technologies and to engineer bandwidth and traffic. And switched virtual circuits are more efficient than permanent virtual circuits, though not as pervasive.

Background

In the early 1960s, employees at Bell Labs discovered how to transfer and delineate bits over a four-wire copper trunk at the rate of 1.554Mbps. Since a voice signal requires a 64Kbps stream, the 1.544Mbps could be divided into 193 bit frames with a transmission rate of 8000 frames per second. Each 193-bit frame carries 24 voice streams, each of which is encoded with an 8 bit-per-sample coding, with one bit per frame left over that can be used for overhead functions. This signaling scheme is referred to digital signal level 1 (DS-1). The four-wire (two pairs of UTP wire) carrier transmission physical specification is referred to as T1.

Nyquist discovered that if an analog signal is sampled at a rate equal to two times the frequency of the signal, the analog signal could be constructed from the discrete samples. Voice signals are in the 300–3300Hz range, thus the sampling rate of 8000 samples per second. The 8 bit-per-sample coding permits the voice signal to tolerate multiple analog-digital and digital-analog conversions.

The coding scheme is called *pulse code modulation* (PCM0).

A few years later, the Europeans devised a similar technique that supported 30 voice channels plus a channel for framing and a channel for signaling for a total of $32 \times 64\text{Kbps} = 2.048\text{Mbps}$. (The Europeans took advantage of improvements in the technology that evolved in the several years that passed since the Americans developed DS-1.) This is commonly referred as E-1. We should note that the PCM encoding used with E-1 is different from the one used in DS-1. Figure 7.1 illustrates the difference between DS-1 (or T1) and E1 framing. The European scheme uses A-Law, whereas the North American scheme uses μLaw. The 8-bit sample is different with each technique, and the encodings are not directly interoperable. For international transmissions, a gateway device is required to provide translation between the encoding schemes.

At the time that the T1 carrier system was developed, service providers were interested in carrying only voice. In order to take advantage of the new transmission system, a device to digitize voice was required. The device developed by the telephone company to digitize voice and to multiplex digitized voice channels onto the transport system is called a channel bank. The channel bank was actually a primitive multiplexer that combined 24 digitized voice calls over the four-wire copper trunk. Channel banks at each end of the connection used a fixed byte position within the frame to associate the byte with a call. By the late 1970s, digital voice switching had become popular, and an obvious comparison was made between voice and data switching. Digitized voice is data. It became apparent that a transmission system capable of carrying voice should also be capable of carrying data. PBXs began to appear and supported data ports, and data and voice were multiplexed onto the same transport system. This was the first occurrence of convergence. However, since the

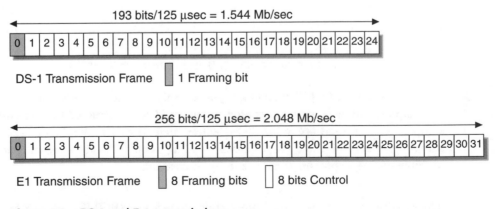

Figure 7.1 DS-1 and E-1 transmissions.

transport system is *time division multiplexed*, it proved to be very ineffi-cient for data, which tends to be bursty and unpredictable.

This technology, which assigns a fixed position within a frame to a partic-ular connection, is referred to as time division multiplexing (TDM). A sig-nificant advantage to TDM is that because the frame position is permanently allocated to a connection, there is no need to further identify the information. All information at a particular position within the frame belongs to a predefined call. TDM is very efficient. The most notable dis-advantage to TDM is that since there is no way to identify information elements, there is no way to reassign the frame position. That is, if the frame position is assigned to particular call, it can't be used to transport other information even if the reserved call has no information to transmit.

Asynchronous TDM—Technology Ahead of Its Time

Troubled by TDM's inability to reallocate frame position when it is not being used by the primary call, Bell Labs developed a TDM modification later in the 1960s. With the new approach, each information element would have an explicit label, and a network connection could be conveyed by an asynchronous series of cells. The frame and each position within the frame would still be synchronous, but ownership of the information at each position would be asynchronous. The tech-nique was referred to asynchronous time division multiplexing (ATDM). Unfortu-nately, implementation of the concept was impossible because of the state of the technology in the 1960s (the multiprocessor and VLSI had yet to be invented). However, the idea of explicitly identifying information elements did not go unno-ticed. Although it was impossible to implement via hardware (that is, within switch-ing devices with low-latency and high-throughput requirements), related forms of element labeling were developed to support longer variable units of data, called packets. Unlike voice, data is not as sensitive to delay and the interarrival rate of the information elements, so the technology available at the time was not a restric-tive factor. SNA, TCP/IP, X.25, and DECnet are some data architectures that imple-mented the concept of packet labeling that the staff at AT&T had envisioned.

The next step in the evolution of digital transmission was to increase the speed of the carrier system. DS-2, which supports a transmission rate of 6.31Mbps, was developed, and later came DS-3, which was designed to operate over coaxial able at a speed of 44.736Mbps. With these digital hier-archies, multiplexing lower-level streams onto higher-level streams is based on bit-interleaving. That is, one bit taken from each of the tributary streams

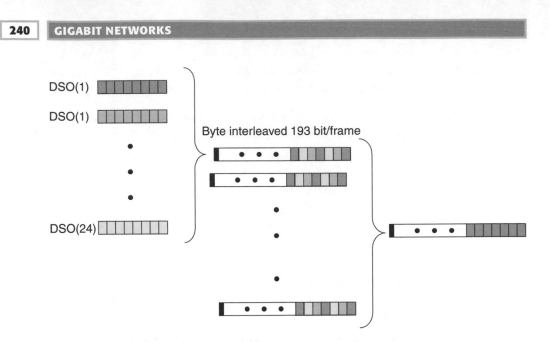

Figure 7.2 PDH multiplexing.

is put into the higher-order stream. At each step, the multiplexer must take into account the fact that the clocks of the tributary streams may be slightly different. This is because the tributaries may be operating on two different *primary reference clocks* (PRCs). Although these PRCs are themselves extremely accurate, there may be a difference between the PRCs.

The system is called *plesiochronous digital hierarchy* (PDH). *Plesio* is a Greek word meaning "almost." A significant problem with the PDH system is that for a lower-order stream to be extracted from a higher-order stream, all the intervening demultiplexing must be performed. So to extract a DS-0 from a DS-3, the DS-3 is demultiplexed into component DS-2 streams and then into component DS-1 streams, and these are demultiplexed into DS-0 streams. Decomposing the primary streams into the lower streams is illustrated in Figure 7.2. The devices that perform these operations are called add/drop multiplexers. A network based on these multiplexes is very difficult to manage and rerouting traffic in the event of a failure is another problem with this approach.

The digital signaling hierarchy is different in the European and North American schemes. This difference further complicates interoperability between the two systems. Tables 7.1 and 7.2 illustrate the fundamental differences between the North American PDH and the European PDH.

During the 1980s, there was a significant shift in the transmission medium preferred by the telecommunications industry. Copper wires

Table 7.1   North American Digital Hierarchy

DIGITAL SIGNAL	SPEED	NUMBER OF VOICE CHANNELS
DS-0	64Kbps	1
DS-1	1.544Mbps	24
DS-3	44.736Mbps	672

Table 7.2   European Digital Hierarchy

DIGITAL SIGNAL	SPEED	NUMBER OF VOICE CHANNELS
DS-0	64Kbps	1
E-1	2.048Mbps	30
E-3	32.768Mbps	480

were being replaced with fiber optic spans on long distance trunks. Because of its favorable physical characteristics, fiber has the ability to carry large amounts of digitized data for long distances. Initially, the fiber cable was terminated at *fiber optic terminal* (FOT), and the fiber was used primarily to transport multiple DS-3 circuits between *central offices* (COs). At the local FOT, the DS-3 channels were multiplexed onto the fiber, and at the remote FOT, the DS-3s were demultiplexed and transmitted on conventional coax cable. The DS-3 could then be delivered to a customer, multiplexed onto another fiber optic span, or perhaps put through an M13 multiplexer, which could extract the component DS-0 or DS-1 channels (see Figure 7.3).

As we mentioned earlier, DS hierarchy (and the E hierarchy) possesses an inherent problem; that is, for a lower-level channel to be removed from a

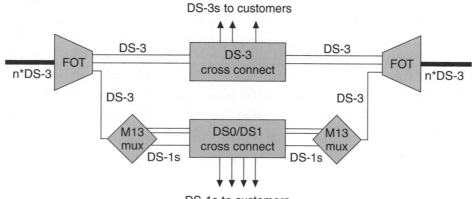

Figure 7.3   Fiber optic multiplexing.

higher-level channel, the higher-level channel has to be demultiplexed and separated into all the component channels. The capacity of the fiber network was very underutilized because the largest circuit available for transport on the fiber was a DS3 circuit. (Although the fiber was being used to simultaneously transport multiple DS3s, the maximum bandwidth that could be provided to any user was DS-3.) Also, these first-generation fiber optic systems in the public telephone network used proprietary architectures, equipment, line codes, multiplexing formats, and maintenance procedures.

SONET

Until the mid-1980s, fiber was used primarily as a replacement for point-to-point copper. In 1985, Bellcore initiated an effort to develop a new framing and digital transmission hierarchy based on an all-digital, fiber optic network. It called the effort Synchronous Optical Network (SONET). This technology was adopted by ANSI, which brought it to the CCITT (which is now called the International Telecommunication Union, Telecommunication Standardization Sector, ITU-T), where it was accepted with minor modifications under the name Synchronous Digital Hierarchy (SDH). Although there are some minor technical differences between SONET and SDH, the fundamental technology is gaining widespread worldwide acceptance—SONET in the United States and Canada and SDH elsewhere.

Compared with the multistep bit multiplexing that is required with both American and European hierarchies, SONET is the essence of simplicity. SONET is based on byte interleaving multiplexing. So any channel, even a DS-0 channel, can be located in any SONET stream, regardless of the size of the SONET pipe, which may be as large as 9.953Gbps. The basic SONET unit of capacity is the *synchronous transport signal level 1* (STS-1) frame, which is 810 bytes and operates at 51.84Mbps. Higher-level signals are integer multiples of STS-1, creating a family of STS-N signals (where N represents the number of STS-1 signals, which are themselves byte interleaved to create the higher levels). STS-1 with a speed of 51.84Mbps was designed as a replacement for DS-3.

ANSI differentiated between the electrical signal framing, which is specified as STS, and the *optical carrier* (OC) specification, which defines the optical characteristics that are required to carry the corresponding electrical frame. (Note that it is possible to transport STS signals over copper, and this method is also sometimes erroneously referred to OC.) The transmission unit within SONET is based on the STS frame. The higher levels of STS are "concatenated" and represented as STS-Nc (*c* is for concatenated), meaning that the payload is to be concatenated and treated as a single channel (for example, used to transport ATM cells). If three STS-1s are multiplexed together to create an STS-3, we don't want the headers from each of the component STS-1s. Rather, we want to create a new frame header (concatenated), thus facilitating interoperability with STM-1. The CCITT designation does not distinguish the electrical signal from the optical signal definition. (This discussion is really for purists; nearly everyone now talks in terms of OC, and usually the c is omitted.) Figure 7.4 contrasts the SONET (ANSI) and SDH (ITU-T) framing hierarchies.

STS-1 with a speed of 51.84Mbps is a fairly efficient replacement for DS-3, which has a speed of 44.736Mbps. (When SONET overhead is factored in, it requires nearly 51.84Mbps to carry 44.736Mbps TDM.) However, STS-1 is a very inefficient replacement for E-3, which has a speed of 32.768Mbps. For this reason, SONET as proposed by ANSI was not endorsed by ITU-T. Rather, ITU-T endorsed SDH with a different framing called *synchronous transport module* (STM). The STM level 1 (STM-1) frame consists of 2,430 bytes, which is equivalent to STS-3. The other difference between SONET and SDH is in how some of the overhead fields are used.

Like everything else in digital telecommunications, the SONET/SDH frame is transmitted at a rate of 8000 frames per second. The different bandwidth supported at the different SONET/SDH hierarchies is a function of the frame size. One frame, regardless of size, is transmitted at a rate of 8000 frames per second (this means that one 64Kbps telephone conversation can be carried in each byte of the payload). The SONET/

Line Rate (Mb/s)	ITU-T Designation	ANSI Designation	Optical Carrier
51.84		STS-1	OC-1
155.52	STM-1	STS-3c	OC-3c
622.08	STM-4c	STS-12c	OC-12c
2,488	STM-16c	STS-48c	OC-48c
9,953	STM-64c	STS-192c	OC-192c

Figure 7.4 SONET/SDH hierarchy.

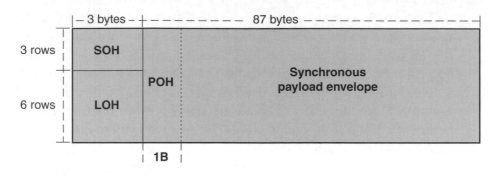

Figure 7.5 STS-1 frame mapping.

SDH frame is represented in a two-dimensional fashion, but of course, bytes are transmitted sequentially from top left to bottom right.

The SONET/SDH frame includes substantial overhead information, allowing simpler multiplexing and substantial *operation, administration, and management* (OAM) capabilities (many argue that SONET/SDH provides too much overhead; it consumes about 3.5 percent of the frame.) The difference between SONET and SDH is in how some of the overhead fields are used. The differences are minor, and many multiplexers can handle both SONET and SDH circuits simultaneously. The overhead information has several layers. *Path overhead* (POH) is carried from end to end; it is added when the component signals are multiplexed together to create the *synchronous payload envelope* (SPE). Figure 7.5 illustrates the format of an STS-1 (51.84 Mbps) SONET frame. For high rates, the payloads are concatenated. For example, an STS-12c frame payload would contain the payloads from 12 STS-1 frames concatenated together. The overhead from each of the 12 STS-1 frames would be incorporated into the header portion of the STS-12c frame. Figure 7.6 illustrates the frame format of higher-level line rates.

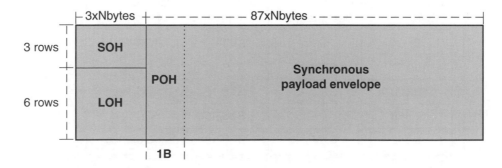

Figure 7.6 STS-Nc frame mapping.

The SONET/SDH *add/drop multiplexers* (ADMs) delineate the line, and the *line overhead* (LOH) facilitates multiplexing and concatenating signals and performance monitoring. The SOH provides a *data communication channel* (DCC), which carries status and OAM information for every network element. The DCC is examined at specified locations that tie into the carriers' management system. The DCC is also used for carrying remote control and test commands to and from remote equipment. Figure 7.7 illustrates the portion of the SONET network that is managed and/or protected by the corresponding portion of SONET Frame header. SOH is responsible for each physical link (or section), LOH is responsible for ensuring the payload is properly transported between the SONET devices (or lines), and the POH provides alarm monitoring and quality control on the end-to-end path, which is the point where the payload is assembled and disassembled.

SONET/SDH Network Configurations

With point-to-point configurations, shown in Figure 7.8, the path and the section are identical. The SPE is not modified end to end. This configuration is generally found where fiber was implemented as a replacement for point-to-point copper.

A point-to-multipoint configuration, shown in Figure 7.9, supports ADMs that are capable of adding and dropping circuits along the way. It avoids the cumbersome task of demultiplexing and remultiplexing that had to be done prior to SONET/SDH. This configuration appeared as carriers that

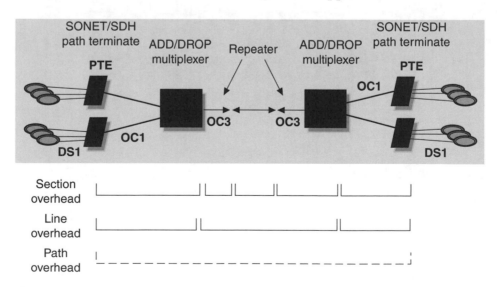

Figure 7.7 SONET/SDH network components.

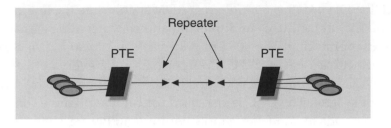

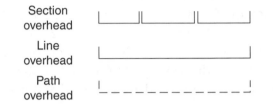

Figure 7.8   Point-to-point configuration.

had point-to-point SONET/SDH networks sought to take advantage of the new capabilities of the emerging SONET/SDH technologies.

ADMs are the building blocks of SONET/SDH ring networks, which are typically deployed by carriers. In order to span large distances, many rings will be interconnected (see Figure 7.10). Multiple ADMs can be put into a dual counter-rotational ring configuration for either bidirectional or

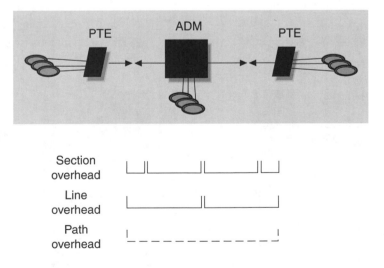

Figure 7.9   Point-to-multipoint configuration.

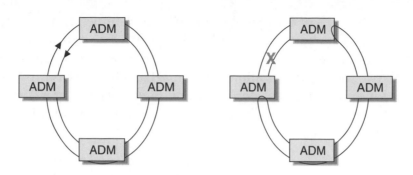

Figure 7.10 Ring configuration.

unidirectional traffic. The main advantage of the ring topology is its resiliency. If there is an outage, the ADMs can have the intelligence to reconfigure around the outage in a very short period of time—typically in under 50 milliseconds. The network will heal itself with little or no noticeable interruption from the perspective of the higher layers.

SONET/SDH has proven to be a very scalable transmission technology capable of efficiently multiplexing, and eventually replacing, PDH circuits.

When the ADM is multiplexing signals together, it does not simply take bytes from PDH circuits and copy them into the payload (SPE) as they arrive. Rather, the PDH signals are first prepackaged into an appropriate virtual container. There are several types of virtual containers each defining how each type of PDH will be carried within the SPE. ATM uses virtual container type VC-4. VC-4 is designed to transport large payloads, and VC-4 payloads are not demultiplexed/multiplexed at ADM. Demultiplexing/multiplexing occurs only at an ATM switch where the entire payload is decomposed into the component ATM cells. Because of this behavior, VC-4 payloads have only a single POH, and it applies to the payload that was assembled at the ATM switch. This is why the concatenation symbol "(c)" is associated with the STS and OC frames that will be transporting ATM cells. Obviously, ATM (container type VC-4) does not rely on the substantial multiplexing capabilities of SONET/SDH.

Asynchronous Transfer Mode (An Argument for ATM Convergence)

In the early 1980s, the CCITT developed *Narrowband Integrated Services Digital Network* (N-ISDN) standards to define a digital transmission and switching architecture to utilize the digital networks that were evolving. N-ISDN defined two access interfaces: *basic rate interface* (BRI), which carries two channels of 64Kbps plus one 16Kbps channel, and *primary rate access* (PRI), which offers access at E1 or T1 speeds. The two key aspects of N-ISDN were universal access and support of data and video in addition to voice. With the standardization of the interfaces to N-ISDN, all N-ISDN compatible devices (such as telephones and personal computers) are able to attach to the network anywhere in the world and to communicate with other attached devices.

By the mid-1980s, ITU recognized that the speeds provided by N-ISDN would be insufficient to support LAN interconnections and the forthcoming multimedia applications, and it began an initiative designed to better utilize the high-speed SONET/SDH digital networks that were being deployed. Broadband-ISDN (B-ISDN), which conceptually is just an extension of N-ISDN, was created to function as a communication network that can provide integrated broadband services such as high-speed-data service, video phone, videoconferencing, and CATV services along with traditional N-ISDN services such as phone and telex. An additional aspect of B-ISDN was the capability to better utilize network resources by allocating only the amount of bandwidth needed by the session.

At the same time, there was another effort within the ITU to develop a brand-new technology that would define a mechanism for the simultaneous transport and switching of various information types. The technology, which attempts to combine the best aspects of both TDM and statistical multiplexing, is called *asynchronous transfer mode* (ATM). ATM is like TDM in that the unit of transfer is fixed in size and called a cell, but since the cell carries a identifier, the timeslot can be reassigned in a fashion that is similar to statistical multiplexing. The technology is asynchronous because the ownership of the cell is not dependent on timeslot or position within a frame. ATM was originally envisioned to operate directly over fiber optic facilities. Built into the technology are capabilities to delineate the cells and mechanisms to provide OAM information between ATM devices in the network.

In 1988, ATM was selected by the B-ISDN (CCITT Study Group XVII) as the switching and multiplexing technique to be used with the SONET/SDH transport.

ATM provides a new dimension to SONET/SDH. ATM provides B-ISDN with a virtual circuit capability and thus enhanced traffic control, as well as sophisticated QoS features. Because of ATM's virtual circuit and Quality of Service capabilities, B-ISDN now offers a highly scalable and reliable network that simultaneously supports many different types of services, such as voice, video, data, image, and graphics, and caters to the specific QoS requirements of the different services. The B-ISDN services are characterized not just by high speed; they may also be described by their utilization of available bandwidth, tolerable cell loss, and amount of tolerable end-to-end delay. However, because the different types of services are encapsulated in cells, they appear the same to the network switches and transmission lines. Although the service characteristics are different, the switching and transport techniques are virtually the same.

Because of ATM's widespread deployment, many believe that SONET/SDH is making ATM the preferred method for building high-speed, multiservice networks.

ATM Characteristics

ATM is a connection-oriented technology that relies on virtual circuits. Both permanent and switched virtual circuits are supported. Because ATM is based on virtual circuits, it supports flexible traffic engineering to accommodate changing traffic patterns. Unlike other technologies, such as Ethernet or frame relay, ATM can be used on the LAN as well as the WAN, so the same technology can be used end to end, eliminating complex time-consuming conversions between technologies. The cell length is 53 bytes, of which 48 bytes are payload, but the payload may not be composed entirely of user information. In addition to user data, the payload may contain overhead information associated with the *ATM adaptation layer* (AAL). ATM provides QoS definitions that result in five different virtual circuit types. It is because of this ability to create virtual circuits with a specific quality of service that ATM can carry traffic for all sorts of applications.

The ATM architecture contains three layers: the physical layer, the ATM layer, and the AAL. The physical layer is typically SONET/SDH, but mechanisms have also been specified to carry ATM cells over various physical networks, including PDH, microwave, and clear channel. The ATM layer provides the switching and QoS functionality to the ATM virtual circuits. The AAL provides a convergence service so that all other service offerings (frame relay, voice, TDM) can be coalesced onto a single platform, the ATM network.

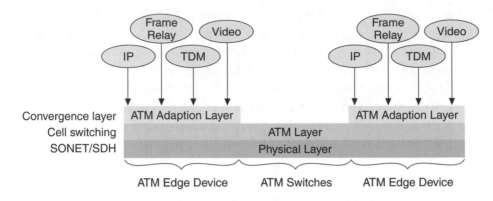

Figure 7.11 ATM architecture.

The AAL enables the ATM converged network. The ATM converged network supports the transporting of different technologies and protocols over an ATM infrastructure. The concept of multiple technologies converging at ATM is illustrated in Figure 7.11 and is in contrast to an IP converged network in which all technologies and protocols are either converted to IP or are encapsulated in an IP datagram. You'll find more on IP convergence later in this chapter in the section entitled *IP—Protocol of the Internet*.

In a typical corporate network, it is not unusual to deploy separate networks and access lines for each service type that must be supported. For example, there will likely be frame relay access lines for data, TDM circuits for voice, and additional TDM access lines for video. There are separate networks, each with different service level requirements and each requiring a different management strategy. Figure 7.12 illustrates the typical corporate network infrastructures. ATM makes it possible to converge the separate networks and to consolidate access to the unified network.

Within the ATM network, a virtual circuit is created for each service and service destination. The service class and bandwidth of each circuit will be consistent with the type of service. For example, the circuit supporting frame relay will be nrt-VBR with SCR appropriate for the circuit's anticipated traffic level, while the virtual circuit supporting the voice network will be CBR with a PCR appropriate for the circuit's anticipated usage.

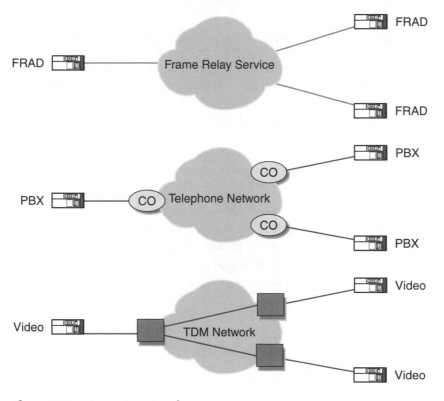

Figure 7.12 Separate networks.

An ATM Converged Network—Here Today

Figure 7.13 shows four ATM switches that are connected via SONET/SDH. Several permanent virtual circuits are configured within the network. There are two virtual circuits between switches A and C. One of the virtual circuits (dotted) is intended to support voice and has been configured with a CBR service category, while the other (dashed) is intended to carry best-effort data traffic and it has been configured with a UBR service category. The switching tables are shown. So if device X has real-time traffic to send to device Y, it creates a cell containing the voice signal (bytes), and within the cell header, the VPI is set to 66 (there will also be a VCI value but for this example it is not important). The cell will be assembled with other cells (either data cells or null cells) to create the SONET/SDH payload, and the SONET/SDH frame will be sent to ATM switch A. At switch A, the payload is disassembled. Switch A will reference its switching table and recognize that the VPI must be changed to 67 and the cell must be delivered to ATM switch B. Since the

Continues

An ATM Converged Network—Here Today *(Continued)*

virtual circuit has been configured as a CBR circuit, this particular cell will receive preferential treatment to ensure that it is forwarded within a very short time. If, subsequently, device X has an IP frame to be sent to device Y, X will segment the IP frame into cells and set the VPI of these IP frame cells to 44, and the cell will be handled in a best-effort fashion.

A critical point is that ATM is providing virtual circuit functionality to the SONET/SDH physical network, enabling traffic engineering and QoS features at the data link layer.

Note that in the diagram, nothing has changed from the perspective of the users. The only difference is that the devices that had connected to service provider networks now connect to an ATM access device. The ATM access device connects to the ATM network. It has performed some special functions to groom the traffic for the ATM network.

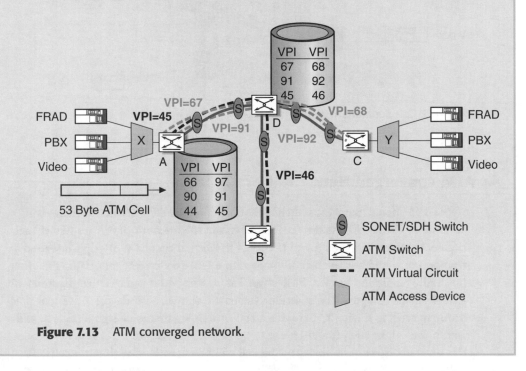

Figure 7.13 ATM converged network.

The Access Device

The convergence of frame relay with ATM is well defined and has been widely deployed. To support the frame relay traffic, the ATM access device runs an *interworking function* (IWF). The Frame Relay Forum (FRF) has specified two interworking implementation agreements that define the interoperability between ATM and frame relay. Frame relay/ATM PVC network interworking (FRF.5) allows two frame relay devices to communicate with each other through the ATM network backbone. Frame relay/ATM PVC service interworking (FRF.8) allows a frame relay device to communicate with an ATM device through a frame relay switch. With the network IWF (FRF.5), the ATM network provides a tunnel for the frame relay traffic (see Figure 7.14). Today most frame relay service providers implement an ATM infrastructure. The service IWF (FRF.8) defines how the frame relay frames are converted into ATM cells. FRF.8 enables a frame relay network to gradually transition to an ATM infrastructure—that is, the transition can occur on a site-by-site basis. Today, many carriers are implementing FRF.8 in their switches. For both FRF.5 and FRF.8, the ATM virtual circuits are nrt-VBR circuits with a SCR equal to the frame relay circuit's CIR.

A new specification of the Frame Relay Forum (FRF.11) defines a voice compression algorithm. The FRF has also defined ways to segment frame relay frames (FRF.12). The biggest problem associated with trying to do real-time traffic (such as voice) over frame relay is the variation in frame sizes; FRF.11 and FRF.12 are addressing these concerns. Also, the Frame Relay Forum is beginning to investigate ways of providing QoS over frame relay.

In order to emulate a point-to-point voice or circuit emulation circuit over the ATM infrastructure, the access device supports a *network interworking function* (N-IWF). The PBX uses either *channel associated signaling* (CAS) or

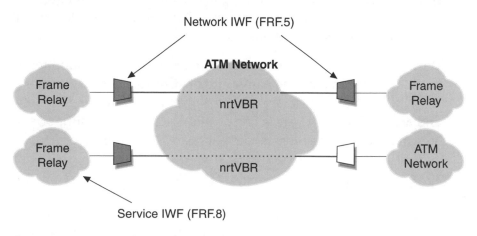

Figure 7.14 Frame relay over ATM.

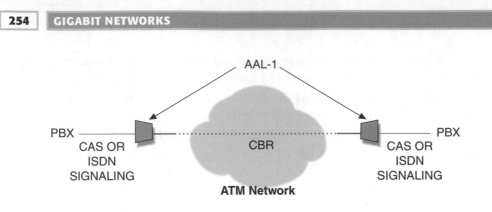

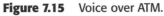

Figure 7.15 Voice over ATM.

ISDN between itself and the ATM' access device. The N-IWF associates the signaled destination telephone number with a CBR virtual circuit (see Figure 7.15).

Ideally, the virtual circuit will be a switched virtual circuit *(SVC); however, SVCs are available only within private networks today. The N-IWF (ATM Forum) specifies a technique whereby the size of the VC can be dynamically increased or decreased depending on the number of phone conversations between two points. So when there is one call between the PBXs, the VC is sized to support 64Kbps. When another call is initiated between the same PBXs, the PBX signals the N-IWF, which in turn signals the ATM network to increase the size of the SVC to support 128Kbps.*

The CBR uses ATM adaptation layer Type 1 (AAL-1) to provide end-to-end clock synchronization. To transport a voice TDM frame over the ATM network, the TDM frame must be converted into ATM cells. Because the ATM cells have 5 bytes of overhead for every 48 bytes of payload, the capacity of the ATM CBR circuit must be about 12 percent greater than the equivalent TDM circuit. (To support the end-to-end clocking, the AAL-1 payload itself contains several overhead bytes.)

Why would a carrier emulate a TDM circuit if the emulation required more bandwidth than the native circuit? Consolidation or convergence—with an ATM infrastructure, the carriers eliminate redundant networks and access devices. There is one physical network that supports several logical networks. The logical networks are defined by the virtual circuits.

IP—Protocol of the Internet (IP Convergence)

Over the past couple of years, telephone companies (and most people) have come to accept the fact that data networks are growing at a much faster rate than voice networks. The Internet is growing exponentially. Service providers, as well as telcos, are installing large IP infrastructures to handle the volume of data traffic. It is a natural progression to start offering voice services over the Internet. Because the Internet is IP based, the convergence of voice and data on IP is a natural occurrence. Another reason it makes sense to converge on IP is that IP is pervasive. Virtually every desktop has an IP device on it. So converging on IP provides the vehicle (IP) to deliver all media types—voice, video, and data—to the desktop.

From the perspective of the OSI Model, ATM is a Layer 2 technology, and IP is obviously a Layer 3 technology. If voice, data, video, and other services converge at Layer 3, is a Layer 2 technology still needed to deliver the IP datagrams? Conversely, if services converge on ATM, a Layer 2 technology, aren't the information elements passing through a Layer 3 technology en route to the ATM? The answer to both questions is yes. So IP convergence means that all services will be represented as IP packets; that is, they are either converted to IP packets or encapsulated in IP packets. And, yes, ATM may well be the underlying transport technology that is used to deliver the IP packets. It's just that all services now have a common representation, the IP packet, so they can all use the same underlying facilities and a single Layer 3 protocol, thus simplifying the management of the facilities and the services.

Another argument for converging services onto IP is that when voice is packetized, compression algorithms are employed so that much less bandwidth is required to support a voice connection. (A 64Kbps voice connection can be compressed to 8–16Kbps with no loss in quality.) Also, with digital transmission, the quality of the signal is independent of distance. This is because noise can be easily removed from a digital signal so that each time the signal is amplified (actually regenerated, not amplified or repeated), it is returned to its original quality. This is in contrast to an analog signal with which the noise is amplified along with the wanted signal. And, of course, there are the regulatory issues, which make transmitting voice over the packet network economically advantageous.

To date, the Federal Communications Commission (FCC) has treated "information services" and "enhanced services" that utilize the facilities of common carriers, such as Internet access and Internet voice services, as separate and distinct from basic telephony and basic telecommunications services. These enhanced voice and data services have not been regulated (and there is no pricing structure/requirement) under the common carrier provisions of the Telecommunications Act of 1996, even though underlying telecommunications and common carrier facilities used to furnish such services may be subject to regulation.

The House of Representatives and the Senate passed the Telecommunications Act of 1996 on February 1, 1996, by overwhelming margins. President Clinton signed the act into law in a ceremony at the Library of Congress on February 8, 1996.

Recognize that packetizing voice does not diminish the requirement for timely delivery of the voice packets. Most ISPs have implemented ATM networks and will use ATM as data link layer, albeit a very sophisticated data link layer because of ATM's significant traffic management capabilities (because it is virtually circuit based) as well as sophisticated QoS functionality that can be used by IP. Ideally, the IP packets that contain voice will be transported on a virtual circuit with a service level that is appropriate for voice—either a CBR or rt-VBR virtual circuit.

If all the elements necessary to simultaneously support data and voice over IP were in place, this is how it would work. What is missing is a standardized mechanism to signal the ATM ingress device of the QoS required on a per-connection basis. For example, "This connection is for voice, so please use, or set up, a CBR virtual circuit to this destination address." Also missing is an address translation mechanism: "I want to connect to this telephone number, which translates to a given IP address, which translates to a given ATM address."

SONET/SDH is a physical layer that provides a transport mechanism for the ATM cells, and ATM enhances SONET/SDH by providing virtual circuit capability. But if services converge onto IP and IP routers are enhanced to provide virtual circuit capabilities, via RSVP or MPLS, then why do we need ATM? Can't we eliminate the significant ATM overhead?

Packets over ATM

Because of ATM's quality of service and virtual circuit capabilities, it is widely employed by ISPs as a data link protocol with SONET/SDH as the physical layer. Virtual circuits are created between the IP routers. Typically, multiple VC paths are created between the routers, and traffic engineering schemes are used to balance the traffic load and to perhaps offer a preferential path to high-priority traffic. The virtual circuit is a Layer 2 concept that provides an efficient transport because all routers are one hop from each other. ATM is attractive to ISPs because its ability to create virtual paths and virtual channels means that multiple customers' traffic can be carried within the same network without security concerns. How-

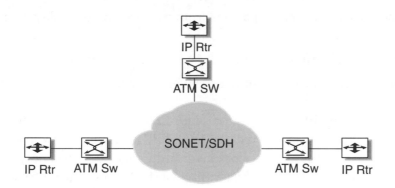

Figure 7.16 IP overlay on ATM model.

ever, because the virtual circuit operates at the data link layer, there is data link layer overhead associated with the virtual circuit, such as the ATM "cell tax." Another downside is that because each router has a virtual circuit to all other routers, (order of number of routers) $O(N^2)$ virtual circuits are required. Also, because each router is logically directly connected to every other router, a very large number of routing updates must be processed, and a very large link state database must be maintained. Figure 7.16 illustrates an IP network over an ATM network. ATM virtual circuits provide the communication paths between the IP routers.

Packets over SONET/SDH

Because IP inherently provides a connectionless service and is not designed to provide any service guarantees, implementers have generally relied on an overlay network in which ATM virtual circuits are used to provide QoS guarantees. Enhancements to IP routing, including MPLS and RSVP, provide a way of building SVCs without relying on ATM or frame relay. In effect, the virtual circuit is constructed at Layer 3 without reliance on a Layer 2 protocol. Therefore, it seems reasonable to transport the IP datagrams directly over SONET, thus eliminating the overhead associated with ATM and frame relay.

SONET/SDH provides a point-to-point network connection between IP routers.

Point-to-point protocol (PPP) is a link layer protocol that provides the following functions:

- Encapsulates and transfers packets from multiple network layers over the same physical link
- Establishes, configures, and monitors the link layer connection
- Determines and configures network layer protocols

The framing used by PPP, as shown in Figure 7.17, is a slightly modified version of *high level data link control* (HDLC). PPP modifies HDLC by adding support for multiple network layer protocols via a protocol identifier field. PPP also includes a *link layer protocol* (LCP) that is used to establish a connection and to negotiate configuration parameters, and *network control protocols* (NCPs) that provide information regarding the configuration and control of the particular network layer protocol that is being used.

The packet data is transported over the SONET network when PPP frames are mapped into the SONET/SDH SPE frame, using only 7 to 10 bytes of transport overhead per frame. There is no ATM header, and obviously, the ATM cell tax is avoided. The IP routers interface directly to the SONET/SDH transport, and the IP traffic natively traverses the high-speed SONET/SDH network. Today, POS is a viable technique that is used by many ISPs. However, POS is used only in a point-to-point fashion. That is, there is no virtual circuit, so there is no provision for bandwidth management. POS provides a simple point-to-point link with no capacity for traffic engineering. The traffic path is determined dynamically by the IP protocol.

This makes POS much easier to set up than IP over ATM. With POS, network administrators assign IP addresses to each interface and define routing mechanisms, such as OSPF or RIP, in a familiar manner. IP over ATM, in contrast, requires not only IP setup, but also ATM virtual circuit (VC) creation and a mapping of the IP routes to the appropriate VCs. Where ATM switched virtual circuits—for example, via ATM Forum LAN Emulation (LANE)—are used, there is no requirement to pre-establish VCs.

Flag	Address	Control	Protocol ID	Information	Padding	FCS	Flag
01111110	11111111	00000011	1 or 2 Bytes	Variable	Variable	2 or 4 Bytes	01111110

Figure 7.17 PPP framing.

Table 7.3 Comparing Capacity

OC LEVEL	DS CAPACITY (MBPS)	ATM CAPACITY (MBPS)	POS CAPACITY (MBPS)
OC1	45	47	52
OC3	135	129	156
OC12	540	563	622
OC48	2160	2254	2488
OC96	8640	9014	9953

However, configuring the ATM network to support LANE services, signaling, and routing to support SVCs is nontrivial.

Although packet over SONET is a viable technology, its purpose is narrow: to send data at high rates. ATM, on the other hand, is intended to integrate multiple services over one switched network and to logically create paths through the network in support of those services. We must pay in overhead for the luxury of allowing users to send data, voice, and video into their network and guaranteeing QoS for priority traffic. The virtual circuit remains a critical component in the solution.

Native IP can't deliver QoS unless it runs over an infrastructure that supports QoS. With IP enhancements such as MPLS and RSVP, QoS can be provided with IP. When (if) MPLS and RSVP are widely deployed, much of the value that is added by ATM will be provided by MPLS/RSVP. Then POS and efficiencies that come with elimination of the cell tax will represent a more viable approach. Table 7.3 shows the size of the user payload for each technology: TDM, ATN, and POS, and for different capacity circuits: OC1, OC3, OC12, OC48, and OC96.

Packets over Glass

An underlying fundamental aspect of QoS is that if the capacity of the network can be increased such that there is no contention, and thus no delay or delay variation, familiar technologies and protocols can be used to deliver voice and video. Guarantees are not required. There is no need to set aside resources. With the emergence of *dense wavelength division multiplexing* (DWDM), which supports multiple simultaneous channels on a single fiber, some pundits believe that future networks will exhibit no contention, and there will be no need for QoS considerations. Networks may well be designed to exhibit no delay and contention; in fact, such networks certainly have been designed in the past. However, this is usually a short-lived situation. In time, the available resource gets consumed.

The basic elements of a fiber optic system traditionally have been the source (laser or light-emitting diode [LED]), the optical fiber over which the signal is transmitted, and the receiver that decodes the light signal back into the electronic domain. In the past, when more bandwidth was required, the approach was to increase the number of light pulses flowing through the fiber by developing faster transmitters and receivers. In order to accommodate the increased pulse rate, new levels of the hierarchy were defined with updated framing schemes such as SDH-3 and SDH-9. With this approach, vendors ignored a fundamental characteristic of optical transmission. Light in the form of photons travels through an optical fiber in a manner that does not require space. Therefore, multiple independent streams of information can be sent on distinct wavelengths, each of which travels through the fiber simultaneously. This is known as *wavelength division multiplexing* (WDM). WDM has now been enhanced so that it is possible to transmit multiple laser colors with less than a nanometer separation between wavelengths in a technique that is referred to as dense wavelength division multiplexing (DWDM), as shown in Figure 7.18. Each wavelength can carry different signals at different speeds, yet all wavelengths can be amplified as a group. Because of this enormous bandwidth potential, some people believe we are on the brink of contention-free networks. Others of a more rational sect believe that the bandwidth promised by DWDM should be used in concert with conventional and emerging IP strategies.

Many people believe that today's IP routers, which are connected with layers of electronic multiplexing (ATM, SONET) equipment, are not capable of taking full advantage of the capacity of DWDM transmission systems. Some envision an optical network in which the networking devices are interconnected via a "link layer" that is based on "dedicated" or "provi-

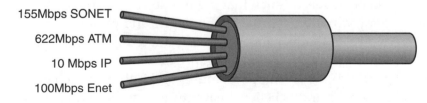

155Mbps SONET
622Mbps ATM
10 Mbps IP
100Mbps Enet

Figure 7.18 Dense wavelength division multiplexing system.

sioned" wavelengths. The electronic layers that come between IP and the DWDM network are eliminated. The optic fibers connect directly to high-performance network routers and the paths between the routers are specified on a wavelength basis. One vision for such a network is an all-optical network in which all the switching is done optically. However, optical packet switching technology is very immature today. Hence, a near-term vision is to use electronic switches to interconnect different DWDM channels where the router controls wavelength access and packet switching. In effect, the optical network delayers the complexity of the existing telecommunications networks and allows the network to be optimized for IP traffic. Connecting the IP routers to optical wavelengths makes it possible to create datagram virtual circuits that function at the network layer. Conceptually, there is a separate wire going from every router to every other router, and this wire is attached directly to the IP layer at each device. These Layer 3 connections provide an efficient path (in other words, Layer 3 overhead), but they do not eliminate the routing update problem associated with the full mesh network.

Provisioning the wavelengths between routers is not trivial. Even with DWDM there will not be enough light paths to permanently allocate wavelength between routers in a full mesh manner. Consequently, there must be some form of optical flow switching protocol to establish light paths between routers in a dynamic fashion. It may be necessary for the application to inform the IP layer of characteristics associated with a particular flow and for the IP layer to then use the optical flow-switching protocol to signal for an appropriate light path to the destination.

Many issues are still to be resolved before IP over DWDM becomes reality. Issues include how to monitor the individual wavelengths and how to detect and isolate faults on a per-wavelength basis.

Conclusion

Assuming that the future of networking will be based on packet switching, such as the Internet, it appears that IP will win the convergence war. However, the winner of the various physical layer convergence schemes remains to be seen, but we can now identify the benefits of the various techniques from pure SONET or ATM to the "packet over" technologies. Figure 7.19 highlights the relationship and benefits of each of the physical layer convergence schemes. Each offers some amount of control and measurability for

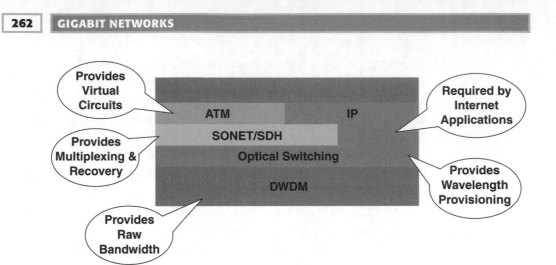

Figure 7.19 Convergence layers.

service levels on a private network but also adds to the complexity or configuration difficulty or creates other management issues.

"There's no such thing as a free lunch" is definitely true in the realm of networking! More frequently, there are rising needs for the corporate network to extend beyond the local level of control into the public domain. In these cases, one needs to assess the viability of virtual private networks (VPNs) to aid in providing a degree of security and manageability for the corporate network design engineer.

CHAPTER 8

VPNs and Firewalls

With remote offices, telecommuters and a mobile workforce, there is an increasing need for extending service levels beyond the intranet. In this chapter, we explore various *virtual private network* (VPN) options and discuss the most appropriate firewall to meet the needs of the VPN and corporate network.

A VPN is a network that traverses some public network but has all (or nearly all) the properties of a private leased-line network. The emergence of VPNs has been fueled by both the pervasiveness of the public data networks and the desire for corporations to provide cost-effective connectivity to a preponderance of users, including remote and mobile users. VPNs provide the flexibility for corporations to communicate with customers, suppliers, and business partners in a secure and cost-effective way while maintaining the control, security, and access rights of corporate information. Because VPNs use the public network to transport corporate data, the primary concern is, of course, security and data integrity. Essentially, a VPN consists of a group of sites that communicate with each other securely over unsecured paths. With VPNs, the communications infrastructure no longer dictates how, or with whom, a company does business.

Types of VPNs

The landscape of virtual private networks has evolved with the maturing and commercialization of the Internet and the businesses' desire to reduce their networking costs. Originally, VPNs were devised to provide remote users with cost-effective access to the private network by eliminating the costly telephone calls and modem banks. VPNs are still used primarily to connect a widely scattered base of individual users, but increasingly, VPNs are being deployed to connect larger sites point-to-point.

Intranet VPN. A corporation with multiple facilities that need to be able to intercommunicate uses an intranet VPN. At each location, a VPN device is implemented. These connections are between trusted users because the connection is between users within the same organization. After the trusted user has been authenticated, the VPN should provide the same access to corporate resources as if the remote users were directly connected. The security policy enforced by the intranet VPN is usually the standard corporate policy.

Extranet VPN. An extranet VPN is similar to the intranet model, except that the remote sites consist of users belonging to different corporations, with one business community partnering with another business community. This connection involves communication between untrusted users. Extranet VPN security requirements are more stringent. What corporate information the external user has access to must be closely controlled and monitored.

Remote access VPN. Remote users (home office or mobile) dial into their local ISP to access the corporate databases. Again, these are trusted users.

From a tactical perspective, VPNs promise significant cost savings because the traditional leased lines between sites are no longer required, and dial-up access for remote users no longer requires a long distance or 800 call. Equipment cost savings are also realized because the number of routers and *remote access servers* (RASs) is reduced substantially. Additionally, management and maintenance of the resources may be outsourced to a service provider if one is providing the access equipment.

From a strategic perspective, the benefits are even more significant. VPNs encourage and facilitate business partnering, resulting in stronger customer and supplier relationships. As a result, business partners can implement new business strategies that were not possible with traditional

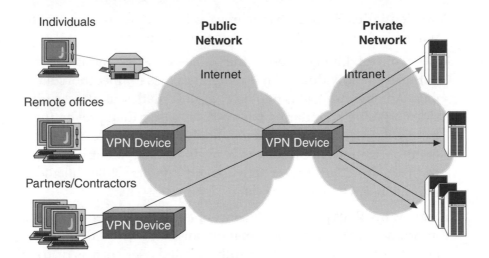

Individuals

Public Network

Private Network

Internet

Intranet

Remote offices

VPN Device

VPN Device

Partners/Contractors

VPN Device

Figure 8.1 VPN overview.

communication infrastructures. Also, VPNs enhance internal corporate communications between employees, which should increase productivity. Figure 8.1 illustrates the many uses for VPNs. Basically, the VPN provides connectivity between users, sites, and corporations across a public packet-switched network (probably, but not necessarily, the Internet).

 **Actually, the VPN exists between the VPN devices. The packet-switched network is an unwitting participant in the VPN. The VPN devices provide the services that are required of a connection across a public network. That is, the VPN devices negotiate the terms of the connection, such as, authenticating, validating, and providing privileges to users, and encrypting and decrypting the packets. From the perspective of the Internet, there is no difference between a VPN packet and a regular user packet. Because the Internet is an unwitting participant, this makes the idea of providing QoS across a VPN an interesting, and currently much talked about, issue.**

VPN Security

Since the public network is being used to transport sensitive information, it is critically important that the VPN does not compromise the security and integrity of the data as it traverses the public network.

Network security is concerned with protecting both physical systems and information resident on them from various types of threats. Security involves four critical functions:

Confidentiality. Ensures that no one reads or copies the information while it is being transmitted across the network.

Access control. Limits access to the private network and its systems to authorized individuals, while denying access to unauthorized individuals. An obvious goal is to protect against malicious attacks from outside corporate boundaries. Often, this is easier than preventing attacks from within. Individual systems should, at least, have some basic form of authorization check, such as requiring a login identity. Minimally, traffic can be controlled at network entry points while still allowing internal users to reach the systems being protected.

Integrity. Involves protecting against unauthorized users' modifying information. For stored information, this can involve determining the extent of access to grant to an authenticated user such as read-only versus read-write access. For transmitted information, this may mean detecting any alteration, accidental or malicious, regardless of whether it is encrypted.

Nonrepudiation. Allows the ability to validate that the sender actually originated the document and that the recipient received the document unmodified. Nonrepudiation of origin protects against any attempt by a message originator to deny sending a message. Nonrepudiation of submission protects against any attempt by the mail system to deny that a message was submitted for delivery. Nonrepudiation of delivery protects against any attempt by a message recipient to deny receiving a message.

Although security measures can be applied at different layers of the *open systems interconnection* (OSI) model—such as the application layer, session layer, network layer and data link layer—VPNs typically implement service at Layer 2 (data link layer) and Layer 3 (network layer). Implementing security services at the lower layers makes many of the security measures transparent to the users.

VPN Requirements

Because a VPN allows remote users to access sensitive corporate data and to transmit sensitive information across a public network, the approach must ensure the privacy and integrity of the data as it traverses a public data network. A VPN solution should minimally provide the following basic requirements:

Authentication. The VPN must verify the user's identity and restrict VPN access to authorized users only. Accounting and audit records should also be kept to monitor who accessed what information when.

Data encryption. Because the data will be transported across a public network, it must be encrypted to render it unreadable as it traverses the network. Adequate data encryption requires proper encryption key management, including generation and refreshment of the keys.

Address management. In order to ensure privacy, the private address space must be concealed from the public domain. To this end, it may be associated with a different public address as the data traverses the VPN.

Because a VPN is essentially a tunnel through a public data network, it is important that the tunneling protocol provide these basic requirements. (A tunnel is synonymous with a virtual circuit, except that whereas a virtual circuit is typically associated with a connection-oriented session, a tunnel is defined by IP and is connectionless. In either case, each packet is routed through the network.) A tunnel is a connectionless virtual circuit.

> **Because a VPN is an extension of a private network over a public network, the public network could be frame relay or ATM. This would make the VPN very secure, give it better QoS, and keep it from being connectionless. Of course, this approach also makes the VPN more expensive.**

Authentication

Authentication is a set of procedures that enables a system to verify a user's identity and thus to control access to the system without ambiguity. One purpose of verification may be to gain access to a system (login) or network. Another may be to ensure a message transmission, such as an e-mail message, is actually from a particular individual. A user's identity may be based on one of the following:

Something the user knows. Knowledge-based systems are based on the user's knowing something; the most common example is a user ID with an associated password. Knowledge-based authentication systems are inexpensive and easy to administer but are the most vulnerable to security threats. For instance, a choosing an obvious password, such as a middle name or user ID spelled backward, or exposing the password by writing it down and storing it next to the computer are security breaches that users commonly make. Single-use passwords are more secure than multiple-use passwords, but they have some of the same problems. Also, there are numerous freeware programs that are designed to automatically generate passwords and attempt to illegally access a system.

Something the user has. Key-based or token-based systems rely on something the user has, such as a smart card. The problem is that the card may be stolen or lost. With smart cards, a token value typically changes dynamically based on the current time. There are also software-based solutions of this type.

Something unique about the user. Biometrics-based authentication relies on something unique about the user such as fingerprints, voiceprints, or retinal patterns. This approach is not currently feasible for use in common networks because of the large amount of processing power required for validation, resulting in unacceptably long delay times in granting access. With the exception of a voiceprint, the processing devices required are expensive or not ready for commercial markets. Typing patterns looked promising, but for users who are not good touch typists, their patterns can be too inconsistent to be useful.

The most common approach is to combine the first two methods of identity verification: what you know with what you have (also known as *two-factor authentication*). Bank ATM cards employ this technique. The user not only needs the card but also must know an authentication number associated with the card to gain access to the bank account.

In a VPN implementation, there are three types of authentication systems that are typically supported: *remote authentication dial-in user service* (RADIUS), *lightweight directory access protocol* (LDAP), or key based. Each of these authentication systems has two responsibilities: validating that users are who they say they are and granting users the appropriate system privileges. The protocols used to validate the identity of the user are *password authentication protocol* (PAP), *challenge handshake authentication protocol* (CHAP), and *Microsoft challenge handshake authentication protocol* (MS-CHAP).

Validating User Identify

PAP is a simple, clear-text authentication scheme. A dial-up gateway, historically referred to as the *network access server* (NAS), requests the user name and password, and PAP returns them in clear text (unencrypted).

Obviously, this authentication scheme is not secure because a third party could capture the user's name and password and use it to get subsequent access to the NAS and all the resources to which it provides access. PAP provides no protection against replay attacks or remote client impersonation once the user's password is compromised.

CHAP is an encrypted authentication scheme that avoids transmission of the clear-text password over the PPP link. The NAS sends a challenge message to the remote client consisting of a session identifier and an arbitrary challenge string. The remote client returns the user name in clear text but uses an MD5 one-way hashing algorithm to generate an encrypted form of the challenge, session ID, and the client's password.

CHAP is an improvement over PAP in that the clear-text password is not sent over the link. Instead, the password is used to create an encrypted hash from the original challenge. The server knows the client's clear-text password and can therefore replicate the operation and compare the result to the password sent in the client's response. CHAP protects against replay attacks by using an arbitrary challenge string for each authentication attempt. CHAP protects against remote client impersonation by unpredictably sending repeated challenges to the remote client throughout the duration of the connection. Figure 8.2 illustrates, a CHAP authentication.

CHAP local name = "client"
CHAP secret = "xyz"

CHAP local name = "server"
CHAP secret = "xyz"

Logon request ──────────────►

◄────────── Challenge (session ID# + arbitrary string)

Client combines the
Challenge with its local
name and encrypts this
using the shared CHAP
secret as the key in
the hash algorithm
producing a hash value.

Hash value ──────────────►

Server performs same
operation as the client and
the hash value.

◄─ ─ ─ ─ ─ ─ ─ ─ ─ ─ ─ ─ ─

If values match, user is authorized.

Figure 8.2   CHAP.

MS-CHAP is an encryption authentication scheme that is similar to CHAP. MS-CHAP provides an additional level of security because it allows the server to store hashed local names instead of clear-text local names. MS-CHAP also provides additional error codes, including a password expired code, and additional encrypted client/server messages.

Granting User Privileges

After the user has been authenticated, policies and access controls can be retrieved from authorization databases. Actually, the authentication protocols are incorporated into the privileges granting schemes (or authentication system).

RADIUS (RFC 2138 and RFC 2139) was specifically designed to support authentication for traditional remote access systems. This type of authentication service provides, at a minimum, a user ID and password checking capability. This information may be solicited via a customized login screen or carried via PPP control packets. Authentication methods typically supported are PAP, CHAP, MS-CHAP, and Unix login. RADIUS also supports optional restriction and challenge features. Examples of a restriction feature may be services the client can use such as Telnet or Rlogin. A challenge mechanism is intended to solicit information from the user that only the user is expected to know. This could be implemented with a personal "smart card." Communication with RADIUS servers assumes encrypted transmissions that involve hashed values generated from a shared secret key are used. The RADIUS solution also allows for proxy communications among RADIUS servers.

RADIUS Walk-Through

RADIUS authentication involves the following steps:

1. A user dials in to one of several RASs,) and PPP negotiation begins.
2. The RAS passes authentication information—username and password—obtained during PPP negotiations to the RADIUS server.
3. If the RADIUS server is able to authenticate the user, it issues an accept response to the RAS, along with profile information required by the RAS to set up the connection (this might include IP address, NetWare network number, maximum connect time, and the like).

4. If the RADIUS server is unable to authenticate the user, it issues a reject response to the RAS, along with a text string indicating the reason.

5. Using this information, the RAS completes PPP negotiation with the user: If the RAS received an accept response, it can now allow the user to begin operating on the network. If the RAS received a reject response, it terminates the user's connection, possibly passing on the reason for termination for display at the user terminal.

LDAP is a general-purpose specification for distributed directory services developed by Netscape. Although it was not developed specifically for authentication purposes, it is one of the more popular uses. An LDAP database consists of entries arranged in a hierarchical manner, implying inheritance for child entries of a parent entry. Each entry has a distinguishing name and one or more information attributes. For example, an entry could have a distinguishing name corresponding to a user ID, and a specific attribute would be the password. A set of users could be associated as a group where common attributes could include such things as allowed connection time period and idle timeout values.

Two VPN tunneling protocols, *point-to-point tunneling protocol* (PPTP) and *Layer 2 tunneling protocol* (L2TP), support authentication using PAP, CHAP, and MS-CHAP protocols that are inherently PPP-based. These password-based protocols were developed primarily in response to the proliferation of traditional, PPP-based, remote access systems.

Encryption

Encryption involves taking plain text and scrambling it to make it unreadable to all but the intended recipient. Encryption is based on two components: an algorithm and a key. The algorithm is typically a mathematical function that manipulates plain text or other intelligible information using a string of digits, called a key, to produce an unintelligible ciphered text. The security of the encryption algorithm is directly related to the length of the key, in which typically 40, 56, or 128 bits are used. Actually, 3-DES supports a 112-bit key, and the emerging *advanced encryption standards* (AESs) will support a 256-bit key. The mathematical algorithms used with modern encryption methods are exceedingly sophisticated algorithms that ensure the only way to break the cipher is to try all the possible keys using a brute force attack. Encryption can be implemented via software or hardware.

There are two primary types of encryption algorithms:

Symmetric encryption. This involves the use of a common shared key. Because the sender enciphers the data with the secret key and the receiver deciphers the data with the same key, the key must be shared. Computationally, symmetric key algorithms are considered more time efficient than the alternative public key algorithms. However, a shared key is problematic with regard to authentication and nonrepudiation; because both users know the key, either of them could encrypt a message and claim that the other sent it.

Asymmetric encryption. This is a public key system that involves two mathematically complementary keys: one called the public key and the other, the private key. If user A wants to encrypt a message to user B, user A will need to know only B's public key. The public keys can be widely available via certificate authorities. User A encrypts the message using B's public key, but in order to decrypt the message B's private key must be used. Only user B knows B's private key. Alternatively, the sender encrypts a message using the private key and the receiver would decrypt the message using the sender's public key. This ensures that the message, in fact, came from the sender. This is referred to as a *digital signature*.

Digital signatures use a special mathematical function called a hash function together with a special private key. First, the electronic message is run through the hash that results in a message digest (the message digest created with MD5 is 128 bits in length). The sender encrypts the message and the message digest with their private key and sends both to the receiver. If the message does not contain sensitive information, the message itself may not be encrypted. In this case, the receiver can be assured that the information came from the sender and that the message has not been altered en route from the sender. However, there is no assurance that the message has not been seen by others. The encrypted message digest is actually the digital signature for the message. After receiving the message, the receiver runs it through the same hash function used by the sender and then decrypts the message using the sender's public key. If the two digests match, the message came from the owner of the sender's private key. Actually, a user that is utilizing a digital signature for authentication will have two sets of keys: one private key will be used for message encryption and the other is for the digital signature. The private key that is used for message encryption will be archived, or *escrowed*, by the certificate authority so that an encrypted message may be decrypted if there is an extenuating circumstance (such as the owner of the private key dies, or forgets the key). The second private key that is used for the digital signature in known only to the owner and to ensure protection it is not archived.

Certificate authorities and the services they provide are part of what is referred to as the *public key infrastructure* (PKI). They provide a notary-like service for public keys by digitally signing them. The certificate authority uses its own private key to sign the certificate that contains a user's public key. If the user knows the public key of the certificate authority, the receiver can verify that the certificate is indeed from the trusted certificate authority.

Address Management

Network address translation (NAT) is the automatic translation of an internal IP addresses to different global addresses. This technique serves several useful purposes. First, it allows an intranet to use a Class A IP address structure, thus facilitating the implementation of a hierarchical addressing scheme. A hierarchical addressing scheme is desirable because it allows efficient route summarization and consequently consumes fewer resources when the IP route forwarding tables are being created. NAT is positioned between the internal network and the Internet. It converts the private addressing scheme to the registered addresses before forwarding the packets to the Internet. The translation is transparent to devices on both sides of the NAT so that standard routing functionality and features are not impacted.

NAT can be done statically or dynamically. In the first case, the assignment of a NAT-IP address to the original source IP address is unambiguous; in the latter case, it is not. In static NAT, a certain fixed original IP is always translated to the same NAT-IP address at all times, and no other IP gets translated to the same NAT-IP address. In dynamic NAT, the NAT-IP address depends on NAT-IP address availability and may be a completely different one for each single connection. When a packet arrives at the boundary, NAT associates the source IP address with another address from the NAT-IP address pool. The NAT pool addresses are considered to be part of the Internet addressing scheme and not part of the private internal addressing scheme. When packets arrive from the Internet, the destination IP address, which is the address from the NAT pool, is substituted with the original source IP address. Thus, participation in NAT is transparent to systems on both sides of NAT. When the session is terminated, the address is returned to the NAT address pool for use.

NAT also provides a mechanism of disguising the internal address from the other Internet users. Another feature is that NAT enables segmentation of subnets because the segmentation is invisible from the perspective of the network devices.

Figure 8.3 demostrates NAT. The packet arrives at the NAT device with a source IP address of 10.12.8.1. NAT modifies the source IP address to 195.10.1.7 so if the packet is compromised as it traverses the public network the actual private address will not be revealed. On the return path, the destination IP address is translated back to 10.12.8.1 and is delivered to the correct user.

Tunneling

The term *tunneling* is a bit misleading. Tunneling was originally used to transport a packet created by one protocol through a network comprising another protocol. It does this by encapsulating the original packet within another packet; for example, to transport an IPX packet over the Internet, the IPX packet could be encapsulated within an IP packet. At the destination, the IP header is removed and the IPX packet is delivered natively to the destination.

VPN tunnels also involve encapsulation of one packet within another; however, before the packet is encapsulated, it is typically authenticated, encrypted, and compressed. The purpose of the VPN tunnel is to transport data across the unsecure network in a secure fashion. In order for the tunnel to function, both ends of the tunnel must be using the same tunneling protocol.

There are two general classes of tunneling: Layer 2 tunneling and Layer 3 tunneling. In Layer 2 tunneling, a Layer 2 protocol—typically PPP—is encapsulated. From a security standpoint, Layer 2 tunneling protocols are

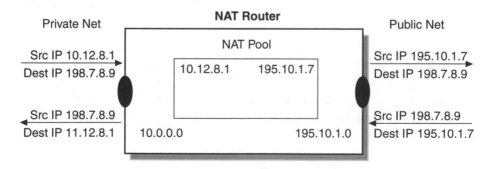

Figure 8.3　NAT.

inadequate. They usually rely on PPP to provide data encryption, authentication, and integrity functions. PPTP and L2TP) are Layer 2 tunneling protocols, each of which encapsulates a PPP frame. In Layer 3 tunneling, a Layer 3 protocol, IP or IPX, is encapsulated. The carrier protocol, or the protocol that is used to encapsulate the native protocol, is usually IP. IP security (IPsec) tunnel mode allows IP payloads to be encrypted and then encapsulated in an IP header.

Layer 2 tunneling is better suited to provide end-to-end encryption while Layer 3 tunneling is better suited to encrypt data within the service provider's network. Because Layer 3 tunneling originates and terminates within the service provider network, it may be argued that this technique is more secure because no external user has access to the tunneling devices. However, vendors implementing Layer 2 tunneling have devised techniques that involve associating random keys for each Layer 2 tunnel created. This method greatly reduces the chance of a security breach.

VPN Service Models

A VPN may implement one of three service models. The service model defines where the end points of the VPN support reside. At both ends of the VPN tunnel are VPN devices running one of the VPN tunneling protocols. These service models are the *enterprise-to-enterprise, service provider-to-enterprise,* and *service provider-to-service provider.*

In the enterprise-to-enterprise service model, the Internet is a transparent transport service. This model represents the VPN solution most likely to be implemented in today's networks. The most commonly used tunneling protocols in this model are PPTP and IPsec. In this model, there are two different scenarios:

VPN tunnel exists between two VPN devices. This scenario may be used for the extended intranet and extranet business applications.

VPN tunnel exists between a client PC and device on a remote VPN. The PC uses VPN client software to function like a VPN device. Unlike in the prior scenario, the end users are not necessarily VPN aware.

Because with this model the VPN tunnel is entirely controlled at the end points, it works with any ISP. In fact, the ISP doesn't even know of the VPN. This approach is shown in Figure 8.4.

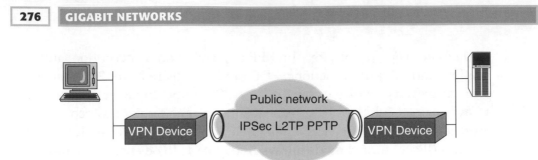

Figure 8.4 Enterprise-to-enterprise VPN service model.

In the service provider-to-enterprise service model, shown in Figure 8.5, the VPN exists between a remote access server owned and maintained by the service provider and a VPN device in the corporate intranet. The VPN tunnel is initiated by the ISP's NAS system when the user connects. The NAS communicates with the remote VPN device to ensure consistent protocol and functionality on both ends of the tunnel. This model is commonly used by remote users. The remote user calls into an ISP, which then creates the tunnel on behalf of the remote user. The tunnel is terminated within the corporation and is managed and controlled by the corporation. The client PC requires no special tunneling software. Of course, not all ISPs offer this service. The L2TP and PPTP tunneling protocols can be used with this model.

In the service provider-to-service provider model, shown in Figure 8.6, the VPN begins and ends within the service provider's environment. The service provider supplies all the equipment and expertise required to implement the VPN. The remote user dials in to a NAS and requests a tunnel to the corporate network. The NAS sets up a tunnel to a router owned by the service provider that connects to the corporate network. This model is the least frequently deployed because the service is not commonly available from ISPs.

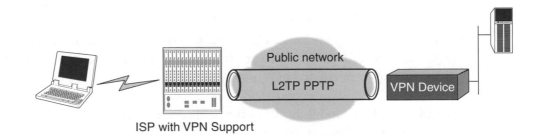

Figure 8.5 Service provider-to-enterprise service model.

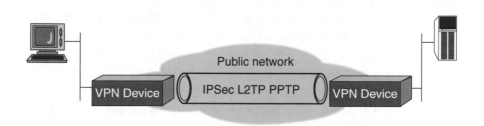

Figure 8.6 Service provider-to-service provider service model.

Tunneling Protocols

The tunneling protocol defines the VPN communication parameters. Before user data is transferred across the VPN, the VPN devices arbitrate the protocol to be used, authentication schemes, encapulation methods, and so forth. Today PPTP is the most common VPN method but IPSec is being widely accepted and deployed now that it has been ratified and deployed. (Note that IPSec is not a *tunneling* model but rather a *security association* model—a semantic distinction that the IPSec Working Group is adamant about.)

PPTP

PPTP, a Layer 2 protocol, was initially designed by a group of companies referred to as the PPTP Forum. The companies included Microsoft Corporation, Ascend Communications, 3Com, ECI Telematics, and US Robotics (now 3Com).

The primary design objective of PPTP was to separate the functions of remote access in a manner that would enable taking advantage of the Internet's infrastructure but at the same time provide secure connectivity between remote users and a corporation's private network. Essentially, a user would be able to dial into an ISP and use a secure tunnel into the private network. PPTP is documented in a draft RFC, "Point-to-Point Tunneling Protocol." This draft was submitted to the IETF in June 1996.

PPP is the most commonly used protocol for dial-up access into the Internet, which PPTP builds upon. Microsoft includes support for PPTP in Windows NT Server and offers free client components for NT and Windows 95/98, making PPTP relatively popular for client-to-LAN tunnel VPNs. Microsoft also plans on releasing LAN-to-LAN tunneling support for Windows NT Server.

Because PPTP is a Layer 2 tunneling protocol, it can transmit protocols other than IP over its tunnels. Current implementations of PPTP encapsulate PPP packets using a *generic routing encapsulation* (GRE) header, which indicates the protocol being carried, such as IPX or NETBEUI. The GRE also contains control information to control access rights and to monitor the session. PPTP relies on authentication mechanisms within PPP; namely, PAP, CHAP, and more recently, Microsoft's version of CHAP called MS-CHAP. Microsoft has also included an encryption method called *Microsoft point-to-point encryption* (MPPE). Although originally designed to provide secure dial-in VPNs, PPTP can also be used in private LAN-to-LAN networking.

PPTP is typically deployed in situations in which a remote PPTP client needs to access the corporate network via an ISP. First, the client connects to a NAS within the ISP using the remote access PPP protocol. PPP mechanisms are used to authenticate the users, negotiate compression, and determine protocol to be transported. After the PPP connection has been established, PPTPs at either end of the connection exchange control packets, which are used to send basic device management and configuration information between the end points. Subsequently, PPTP encapsulates the PPP data packets for transmission over a tunnel. The PPP data packets are encapsulated in IP datagrams. If the user's computer is the termination point of the tunnel—that is, it's running PPTP client software—the encapsulation happens at the user's PC. Otherwise, the tunnel terminates at the ISP's NAS if the user's PC supports only PPP and not PPTP client. If the user's PC supports PPTP client, there is no special ISP requirement.

Although the NAS functions as a server for providing network access, generally, it also functions as a RADIUS client. The NAS accepts the user connection request, gets the user ID and password, and then securely passes this information to the RADIUS server. The RADIUS server returns authentication status and any configuration data required by the NAS to provide service to the end user.

Many shortcomings with PPTP have been identified. PPTP authentication is weak, its encryption support is considered weak and is not extendable to emerging encryption standards, and its compression support is proprietary. Figure 8.7 illustrates the flow of a packet through the PPTP model.

L2TP

The L2TP combines many of the features of PPTP with those of another protocol, *Layer 2 forwarding* (L2F).

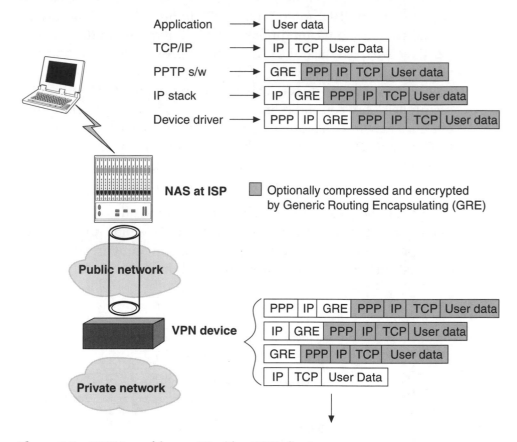

Figure 8.7 PPTP tunnel from a PC with a PPTP client.

L2F is a tunneling protocol that was introduced by Cisco. With its dial-up access, servers frame asynchronous traffic within PPP frames and transmit the PPP frames over WAN links to an L2F Server (a router), which unwraps the packets. Unlike PPTP, L2F is not dependent on IP and GRE, enabling it to work with other various WAN media, such as frame relay, ATM, or X.25. Also, L2F defines connections within a tunnel, allowing the tunnel to be used for more than one connection.

Because L2TP is a Layer 2 protocol, it offers the same flexibility as PPTP for supporting protocols other than IP. Because L2TP uses PPP for dial-up links, it supports PPP authentication mechanisms, PAP and CHAP, as well as RADIUS. Much like PPTP, L2TP defines two different types of messages: control messages, which are used for setting up and maintaining the tunnel, and data messages. Unlike PPTP, the data and control messages are transmitted over the same tunnel.

Although both PPTP and L2TP use PPP to provide the data encapsulation, there are significant differences. PPTP requires an IP network while L2TP requires only that the tunnel media provide point-to-point connectivity. L2TP can be used over IP (UDP), frame relay, ATM, or X.25. While PPTP supports a single tunnel between end points, L2TP supports multiple tunnels between end points, allowing a separate tunnel for different qualities of service. Another significant difference between PPTP and L2TP is that L2TP allows IPsec-based authentication and encryption to be used. However, when IPsec is used, tunnel authentication is provided by IPsec so that additional Layer 2 tunnel authentication is not necessary.

Each L2TP message has an L2TP header that includes a connection identifier, a message type identifier—control or data—and a priority bit to identify a packet that should receive preferential queuing treatment. Figure 8.8 illustrates the flow of a packet through the PPTP model.

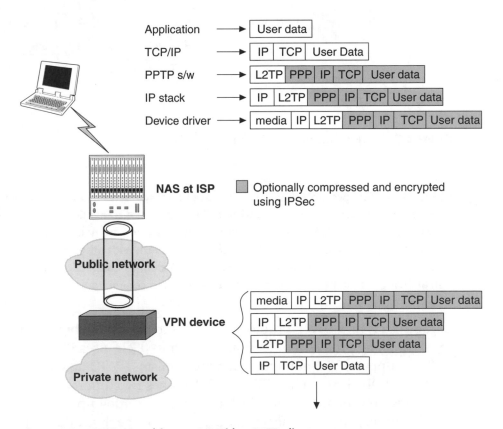

Figure 8.8 P2TP tunnel from a PC with a P2TP client.

IPsec

IPsec is a set of protocols that were originally designed to provide TCP/IP with security in IPv6. IPsec is a Layer 3 protocol, operating only with the IP protocol. The first IPsec authentication and encryption protocols, RFC 1825 to RFC 1829, were published by the IETF in 1995. Because of the slow adoption of IPv6 and the impending need to provide authentication and security in IPv4, IPsec was modified so that it could be incorporated into IPv4. The modification was accomplished with the introduction of a shim or extra fields within the packet header. Actually, IPsec defines two headers within the IP packets to handle authentication and encryption: the IP *authentication header* (AH) for authentication and the *encapsulating security payload* (ESP), which can handle both authentication and encryption. Another important aspect of IPsec is the *security association* (SA).

It is important to note that IPsec operates in two different modes: transport mode and tunnel mode. When it operates in transport mode, it is not really a tunneling protocol because there is no packet encapsulation. The original IP header is not modified or encrypted; it is only authenticated.

In order for two ends of a connection to exchange secured information (that is, authenticated and/or encrypted), both parties must agree on the cryptographic algorithms and the key exchange mechanism and frequency of key changes. These agreements are bundled together in the SA. An SA is a secure channel between the sender and receiver through which information regarding encryption and authentication relative to this connection is exchanged. Because SAs are simplex, a separate SA is required for two-way communication between the end users. Actually, a *security parameter index* (SPI) indicating the SA information is passed within the AH and ESP fields.

The AH provides most of the authentication services for the IP data. The primary component of the AH is the cryptographic checksum that is associated with the packet's content. The AH is inserted into the packet immediately after the IP header.

The ESP is responsible for authenticating and encrypting the packet. (ESP can also be used to provide encryption only.) Because the ESP can support any number of encryption protocols, it is easy to introduce new encryption protocols into IPsec as they are developed.

AH and ESP are applied in different ways for each of the modes specified in IPsec, transport and tunnel modes. If authentication only is required, use AH; if both authentication and encryption or only encryption are needed, use ESP.

In transport mode, only the portion of the packet beyond the IP header, the portion containing the upper-layer protocols, is protected. Transport mode is typically used for end-to-end communication between a client and server or between two workstations. Of course, both end stations must have IPsec client software installed. Typically, ESP is used to encrypt and authenticate the IP payload. AH can be used if the only concern is unauthorized access to the networks. When AH is applied to a transport mode packet, the entire packet is authenticated. When ESP is applied to a transport mode packet, the entire packet is authenticated while the upper layer protocols are encrypted. Transport mode is useful for relatively small networks.

IPsec transport mode is a tunneling protocol in that the original packet is encapsulated in a new outer IP packet. Tunnel mode is more secure than transport mode because the entire user packet may be authenticated and encrypted. Typically, tunnel mode is implemented on a secure router or firewall at the boundary of a private network. When a packet arrives at the boundary device, it is examined to determine if it needs to be processed by IPsec. This determination is usually based on the packet's IP destination address, although other criteria—for example, source IP address or TCP port number—may be considered. The original packet is

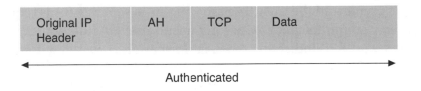

Figure 8.9   Transport mode AH.

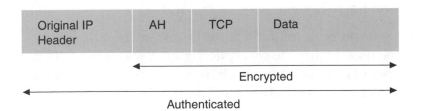

Figure 8.10   Transport mode ESP.

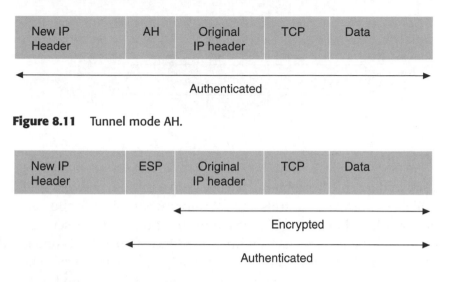

| New IP Header | AH | Original IP header | TCP | Data |

← Authenticated →

Figure 8.11 Tunnel mode AH.

| New IP Header | ESP | Original IP header | TCP | Data |

← Encrypted →

← Authenticated →

Figure 8.12 Tunnel mode ESP.

authenticated and/or encrypted and then encapsulated in a new IP packet header. Because none of the original packet's fields are unprotected, the original packet travels through the tunnel in a secure fashion.

In tunnel mode AH, the entire packet is authenticated, whereas in tunnel mode ESP, the IP header is not encrypted and not authenticated. Figures 8.9 and 8.10 show which portions of the packet are authenticated and/or encrypted with the different transport modes, while Figures 8.11 and 8.12 show which portions of the packet are authenticated and/or encrypted with the different tunnel modes.

Firewalls

As vendors strive to produce devices that provide comprehensive services, the distinction between firewalls and VPNs is becoming increasingly muddled. However, if we reexamine the definition of each, we can better understand the similarities and differences. First, a VPN uses a public network to provide an extension of the private network (see Figure 8.13). It does not delineate the private network but rather extends it. With a VPN, the user is validated before the VPN tunnel is created. After the tunnel is created, the private network is extended between the two remote sites. Access to corporate information is controlled in the same way that it is controlled for the users resident within the private network.

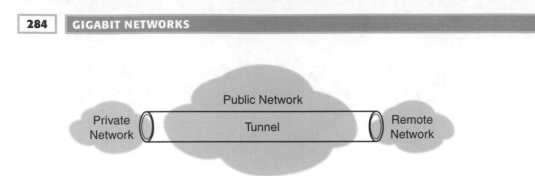

Figure 8.13   VPN tunnel.

A firewall establishes a boundary between a private network and the public network and controls and monitors what traffic is allowed to cross the boundary. No assumption is made about the remote user—it could be anyone on the Internet (see Figure 8.14). Once a business is open to the Internet, implementing system security at the gateway level to keep unwanted users out of the internal network is the first step toward securing the organization. This is the role a firewall plays.

As discussed, VPNs provide a secure method of transporting private information across a public packet network. Because VPNs provide access into the corporate network, it is necessary to control access to critical

What a Firewall Will and Won't Do

While a correctly configured and managed firewall can and does provide a good level of security, many organizations make the mistake of putting them in and then leaving them. The Internet is a rapidly developing environment, which means new security threats are always arising. It is essential to monitor developments and constantly check and upgrade your firewall.

Securing the perimeter is just the start; it is essential to have good internal security too. Depending on the importance and confidentiality of the information, this may warrant tools that combine to provide authentication, encryption, content scanning, and audit.

Access control products that include single sign-on and access control servers should be used to authenticate a claimed identity of a user and prevent unauthorized interactions between a user and an Internet application.

Audit and monitoring products that include antivirus scanners and network scanners should be implemented to monitor all Internet security-related activity and detect security violations. Increasingly, firewalls are becoming multifunction products that integrate across the above categories, providing access control, confidentiality and integrity, and auditing capabilities.

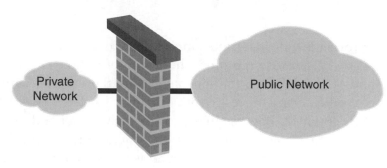

Figure 8.14 Firewall.

resources that reside in the corporate network. This is necessary because the far end of the VPN tunnel may well be a business partner, a mobile worker, or a remote office, and the near end of the tunnel may be positioned at various locations between the local LAN and the ISP.

A virtual private network creates a secure tunnel between two addresses using encrypted data; routing functions ensure that only VPN traffic is sent through the encryption process. VPN servers can act as firewalls, linking a local network to the Internet. They may also work behind firewalls (although this is not recommended). The VPN configuration process automatically sets filters to stop VPN servers from forwarding their IP network addresses to the public network or sending public IP addresses through the VPN system. The firewall essentially acts as a security gate at the network perimeter, monitoring and controlling what traffic is allowed access to the network as well as what traffic is allowed to leave the network.

A firewall is an essential component of a security policy; however, firewalls on their own are not sufficient to ensure reliable transfer and therefore do not provide the same functionality as VPNs. Firewalls cannot monitor or prevent changes to data that may occur as a packet traverses the public network. Also, firewalls provide no protection to internal threats, and they provide no protection against viruses. (Some firewall products can verify a user's identity and establish an encrypted session between the firewall and remote dial-in users, provided the remote client has the appropriate client software installed.)

There are three main types of firewalls: *filtering router, stateful packet filter,* and *application gateway*. Many of today's firewall designs employ a combination of the techniques.

Filtering Router

The filtering router is the oldest and simplest form of a firewall. These devices filter packets based on protocol header information such as IP addresses and TCP or UDP port numbers. Because these devices are first and foremost routers, they process each packet individually. They maintain no state information. Because they process each packet and maintain no state information, implementing complex policies is impractical or impossible. An advantage of a filtering router is that it is transparent to end users. The enforced rules do not require special devices or special applications on the end-user systems.

Filtering routers are not the best firewalls. One of the deficiencies is that filters are based on IP addresses, not authenticated used identification. Other disadvantages of filtering routers include a potentially difficult user interface that may be required to configure filter rules; the interface may in fact require manual manipulation of MIB variables, which is not very user friendly, an inability to handle complex policies, and inadequate logging and alarm functions. Because these devices are primarily routers, they may not scale well when asked to perform the firewall functions. Filtering routers are best used in combination with other firewall technologies to form an adequate firewall topology. For example, a filtering router employed in the internal network could be used to control access to portions of the internal network.

To understand the limitations of a filtering router, consider a case in which we want to allow only mail traffic to go through the router. At first glance, this appears to require simply implementing a filter based on the sendmail well-known port. However, the sendmail well-known port is used only to initiate the mail session. A different dynamically assigned port is used for the mail transfer. Since the filtering router is not smart enough to associate the dynamically assigned port with the original application, the filter blocks packets sent to the new port, and consequently, no mail gets through. But stateful packet filters are smart enough to deal with this situation.

Stateful Packet Filters

Stateful packet filters were designed from the start to be firewalls. Unlike filtering routers, they maintain state information on each connection, and they treat packets as part of a connection. Therefore, it is possible to implement complex policies. Also, stateful packet filters typically provide excellent logging and alarm functions. They are scalable and transparent to users, and they generally have easy-to-use graphical configuration interfaces.

Maintaining state information increases the capabilities of the stateful packet filter. For example, when a client uses the PORT command to request that an FTP server specify the connection to be used, the server-selected port number can be subsequently intercepted and recorded. The client attempting a follow-up connection can then be forced to use the port selected by the server. When the connection is closed, the previously allocated port number is locked out until it is again used by the server.

For connectionless protocols such as UDP and RPC, maintaining state information is more difficult because there is no implied request-and-response relationship. It may be possible to track a pseudo connection state by extracting some context from the packets.

An application that uses dynamically assigned port numbers is another example of a communication scenario that does not involve fixed behavior. In this case, the stateful inspection engine may actually need access to operating system-level control structures to determine valid allocated ports.

Stateful packet filter devices are generally the most expensive type of filtering device.

Application Gateways

An application gateway is run on what is referred to as a bastion host, which is a highly secure system dedicated to support the application gateway software. Bastion hosts typically support no user logins and are configured with minimal functionality and maximum security features installed and enabled. The application gateway serves as a proxy device for hosts on the private network.

Application gateways process, validate, and regenerate each received packet. This means that application gateways can perform more sophisticated functions than other firewalls that have access to only lower-layer information. Application gateways are very effective firewalls that are capable of implementing complex policies. However, application gateways are not transparent to the users. For example, to issue an ftp command, the user on the private network will issue an ftp to some abnormal port number on the ftp application gateway. The ftp application gateway will then query the user for the real ftp command that the user wants to issue, and the ftp application gateway will actually be responsible for

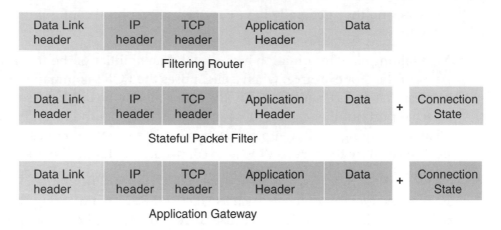

Figure 8.15 What firewalls inspect.

running the command. The application gateway does maintain state information for the connection, and it provides excellent logging and alert capabilities.

Figure 8.15 shows which portions of a packet are examined by each of the different types of firewalls. Note that the filtering firewall does not keep any state information, rather it treats each packet individually.

VPN and Firewall Positioning

VPNs provide encryption and authentication. This ensures that remote users are who they claim to be and protects the integrity of the data as it passes through the VPN tunnel. Firewalls provide authorization, which determines what network resources the user has the right to access. Obviously, to provide true security to private networks connected to the Internet, the functions of both the VPN and the firewall are required. The question is how the VPN and firewall are to be positioned with regard to each other. Should the VPN and firewall functionality reside within the same device?

Companies that want to ensure the privacy of their information while making some information available to Internet-based users or customers should create a *demilitarized zone* (DMZ). The DMZ is delineated by two firewalls: one between the DMZ and the public network and another between the DMZ and the private network. A Web server in the DMZ will store copies of the original Web pages that are located within the corporation's private network. When a change is made to the Web page, the change is relayed to the Web server resident on the DMZ. Mail server and ftp servers are also commonly found on the DMZ. The information within the DMZ should be considered unprotected information. Because servers within the DMZ act as secondary storage of data if they are compromised, there is minimal damage done. The servers within the DMZ should be bastion hosts, making the systems difficult to break into. If a break-in does occur, it will be difficult to extend the break-in to other systems.

The relationship between the firewall and the VPN devices must be carefully planned to ensure optimal performance.

The advantage of terminating the VPN within the private network, shown in Figure 8.16, is that VPN data is protected as it crosses the DMZ network. Although this represents a very secure option, it requires opening "holes" in the firewall so that VPN tunnel traffic can be allowed to pass through. This practice is generally considered to be undesirable because the more complex the firewall rule set becomes, the greater the vulnerability to security attacks.

Terminating the VPN in the DMZ, shown in Figure 8.17, and allowing the unprotected data to flow through the firewall eliminates the need to open

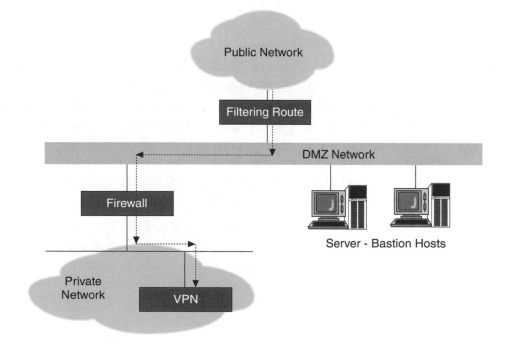

Figure 8.16 VPN terminates on private network.

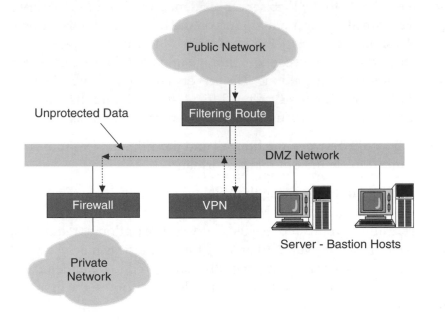

Figure 8.17   VPN terminates in the DMZ.

the firewall. This approach reduces the risk to the protected network. However, the DMZ must be considered an insecure network. The data is exposed and unprotected as it passes from the VPN device to the firewall.

With the VPN device parallel to the firewall, as shown in Figure 8.18, the VPN is terminated in the DMZ, but the unprotected data is delivered directly to the private network. The unprotected data is not exposed to the DMZ. This approach protects the VPN traffic and removes the need to open the firewall to VPN traffic. It also allows the VPN traffic to increase without imposing a performance load on the firewall. In addition, with this configuration, the filtering router can be configured to provide additional security for the VPN device, further increasing security.

Terminating the VPN within the firewall, shown in Figure 8.19, allows the VPN data to be protected across both the public network and the DMZ network. This simplifies configuration and minimizes the number of physical connections. However, with this configuration, we must make sure that the VPN/firewall device can accommodate the traffic load. Another concern is that if the VPN/firewall is compromised, the entire network is compromised.

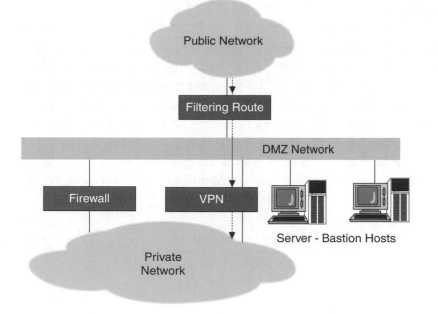

Figure 8.18   VPN in parallel with firewall.

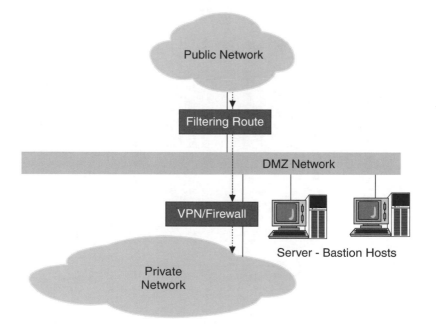

Figure 8.19   VPN and firewall in the same device.

Conclusion

This chapter has given a brief overview of some of the various permutations of VPNs and firewalls. Many configuration options could be deployed, but those covered are the most common and can be quite effective. Selecting an appropriate VPN and firewall combination can offer the network manager a fair degree of control and ability to extend service levels to remote locations. Taking the concept of remote office to the extreme leads one to examine how to extend the network into a home. The next chapter examines the emerging capabilities of cable modems for the home.

CHAPTER 9

Cable Modems

Moving the network to the most remote location—the employee's home—creates its own set of challenges. Although VPNs can offer some measure of control, they are often not available for a singular home connection. Many employees are now seeking to gain high-speed Internet connectivity through their cable TV provider networks. This chapter examines some of the concepts and issues inherent in those networks.

Today, approximately 30 million homes access the Internet Residential access to the Internet continues to grow tremendously despite the frustratingly slow speeds available to users through conventional telephone modem connections, typically 33.6Kbps or less. "Surfing the Net" seems more like "safari-ing the Net" as users click and wait, and wait, and wait. Certainly, low-speed local access is not the only contributor to the response delay, but local access speed is a significant contributor, and it is one aspect of the Internet extravaganza that is under the user's control.

Local telephone companies now offer residential ISDN services that provide connections with speeds up to 128Kbps, and *digital subscriber line* (DSL) technologies with downstream speeds up to 6Mbps are being introduced into some markets. (Note that these approaches allow the user to access the Internet while simultaneously making a phone call.) However, these services are considerably more expensive than the common residential telephone connection.

The telephone line is no longer the only communication medium finding its way into residential homes. Broadband coaxial cable being deployed by cable television companies now passes more than 105 million homes in North America, and more than 75 million of these homes are cable TV subscribers. This near-ubiquitous presence of coaxial cable access provides a powerful platform for providing residential homes and small business with high-speed data access.

The Telecommunications Act of 1982 required AT&T to divest itself of regulated local service. One of the primary concerns of other long distance carriers was that customers had to dial a seven-digit number to access their equipment before dialing their long distance calls. AT&T customers could access AT&T equipment by merely dialing 1 plus the called number. Judge Harold Green ruled that the arrangement was unacceptable and required AT&T to divest itself of the local access. He also mandated that a method be implemented whereby end users could access the carrier of their choice in a manner equal to AT&T access. In essence, AT&T was prohibited from providing "last-mile" connectivity into its wide area, or long distance, telephone network. With the recent purchase of TCI, a cable television company, AT&T seems to have found an alternate, and legal, way to get into the customer premises.

However, before the cable plant that was designed to support cable television could support high-speed data communications for the masses, significant modifications were required. The original cable plant provided one-way communications from the network, or head end, to the subscribers. Of course, support for data communication would require two-way communications. The introduction of a new two-way communication system is technically complex and expensive.

Traditional Cable System

Each TV cable box listens to the all downstream transmissions (that is, transmissions coming "down" from the network, or the "upstream" cable head end). Each transmission, or TV channel, is transmitted at a different frequency.

The cable company uses one of the channels to "program" the cable box that sits on top of a television. Each cable box has an address, typically a MAC (EEPROM) address, and when a household subscribes to, say, HBO, the cable company sends a signal on the control channel with the MAC address of that home's box. The signal instructs the box to begin receiving the HBO's channel frequency. "Black boxes" allow viewers to manually modify the channel frequency window and receive (rather, _steal_) any channel frequency—all channel frequencies are on the cable. The cable company has no way of controlling which channel frequencies go to a particular box. There is also a cable modem Broadcast MAC address so that a single frame can be directed to all cable modems in the domain.

To ensure compatibility with over-the-air broadcast TV signals, cable operators re-create a portion of the _radio frequency_ (RF) spectrum for transmission on the coaxial cable. Traditional cable systems typically operate in the frequency range of 50MHz to 550MHz, divided into 6MHz channels (in Europe, the channels are 8MHz) (see Figure 9.1). Each TV channel is transmitted in a 6MHz (8MHz) channel. Actually, the low end of the spectrum, 5MHz to 50MHz, was designed for traffic from the subscriber to the network; however, with the traditional cable systems, this was not feasible, and this part of the spectrum generally was not used. Logically, video program signals begin around 50MHz, which is the equivalent of channel 2 for over-the-air television signals. So traditional cable systems can support about 60 TV channels. Modern HFC system with 700MHz of downstream bandwidth have the capacity for about 110 TV channels.

The original cable system was based on coaxial cable, end to end. The cable TV head end takes video feeds from various sources and introduces the signal onto the coax cable. Within the coax cable system are amplifiers to amplify (increase) the signal. The amplifiers are placed at regular intervals in the system. There may be as many as 35 amplifiers cascaded between the head end and the subscriber station. Figure 9.2 illustrates the conventional cable system. These amplifiers are designed explicitly to

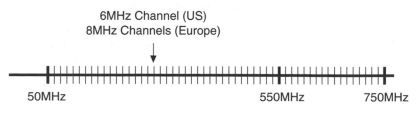

Figure 9.1   Cable frequency spectrum.

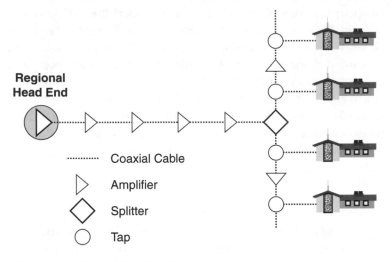

**Regional
Head End**

　Coaxial Cable

▷　Amplifier

◇　Splitter

○　Tap

Figure 9.2　Conventional cable system.

enhance the quality of video to the end user. Because of the large number of amplifiers, the cable system is inherently one way, and communication from the user to the head end is impractical. Certainly, two-way communication is possible with the conventional coaxial system, but because of poor signal-to-noise characteristics, two-way communication was not practical.

Hybrid-Fiber-Coaxial System

Currently, cable operators are in the process of modifying the cable infrastructure by introducing fiber optic cables, replacing the analog signals with digital transmissions, and replacing the amplifiers so that the system becomes a two-way system. The new infrastructure is referred to as a *hybrid-fiber-coaxial* (HFC) system. With HFC, the cable TV head end has a fiber interface instead of the conventional coaxial interface, and with the introduction of fiber, many of the characteristics of a conventional cable network change. Most importantly, the fiber optic amplifiers are capable of regenerating the signal rather than simply amplifying it. Also, baseband filter RF amplifiers replace the conventional echo cancellation amplifiers. These filters allow a certain frequency range to traverse the network in one direction and a different frequency range to traverse the network in the opposite direction. Thus, the new HFC system is a two-way system. Note that upgrading to HFC is a nontrivial task. It is essentially a complete

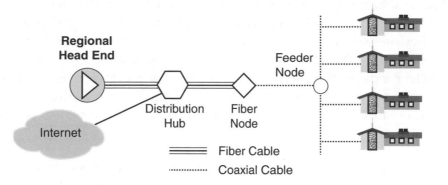

Regional
Head End

Feeder
Node

Internet

Distribution
Hub

Fiber
Node

═══ Fiber Cable

········· Coaxial Cable

Figure 9.3 HFC cable system.

rebuild of a significant portion of the cable system. Fortunately, the last drop, from the fiber node to the neighborhoods and into the homes, does not change; it is still coax-based.

Figure 9.3 illustrates the HFC system. The *regional cable head end* (RCH) typically serves 200,000 to 400,000 homes. It feeds distribution hubs, each of which typically serves 20,000 to 40,000 homes through a metropolitan fiber ring. At the distribution hub, the signals are modulated onto RF carriers and are transported over fiber optic lines to fiber nodes. One to six coaxial cables are attached to each fiber node. In the downstream direction the fiber node splits the analog signal so that the same signal is sent on each coaxial cable. Each coaxial cable serves 500 to 1000 homes. With the introduction of the HFC system and fiber nodes, many of the amplifiers have been eliminated. Generally, fewer than eight amplifiers lie between the distribution hub and the subscriber, so two-way communication is practical.

Cable Modem Data System

Several different schemes have been developed to support the transfer of data over the cable network. Currently, the most widely implemented scheme is the one devised by a consortium of cable companies referred to as the *Multimedia Cable Network System* (MCNS) Partners. In March 1997, it released the *Data over Cable System Interface Specification* (DOCSIS). Our discussion in this section focuses on the MCNS (or DOCSIS) scheme. Later in this chapter, we discuss the IEEE 802.14 scheme.

MCNS describes a system used to transport IP data traffic between a *cable modem termination system* (CMTS) and cable modems that reside in homes and businesses. The CMTS connects to the Internet on one end of a high-speed line and to the cable modem on the other end of the cable network. CMTS resides within the distribution hub. The CMTS converts data from the *wide area network* (WAN), such as POS, into RF signals that are modulated over the HFC plant and then demodulated by the cable modem in the home.

Often the distribution hub is referred to as a *head end*. The CMTS resides in this head end. By definition a head end is point in the cable network that receives satellite and other TV signals and converts them to a form that can be transmitted down a coaxial cable to subscribers. Typically, at the distribution center, local information, such as a local TV channel, is introduced into the cable network. So by definition the distribution hub is a head end. Rather than trying to deal with multiple head ends, we refer to the distribution hub head end as the *head end*. It supports the CMTS.

Just as all video traffic in the cable system is controlled by the head end, all data traffic in the cable system is controlled by the CMTS. All downstream traffic, video, and data, is combined in the distribution hub and sent to subscribers. Because there is only one source of traffic transmitted in the downstream direction, there is no issue regarding contention, and there can be no collisions in the downstream direction. Figure 9.4 illustrates the modern distribution hub.

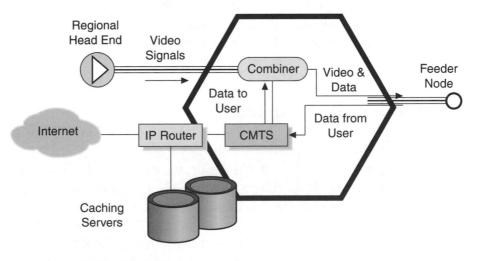

Figure 9.4 Distribution hub.

The head end sends video traffic in the downstream direction encapsulated in 188-byte MPEG II frames. For consistency, data frames in the downstream direction are also encapsulated with MPEG II framing. The MAC frames (data) may begin anywhere within the MPEG packet and may span MPEG packets, or several MAC frames may exist within an MPEG packet.

Cable Modems

The cable modem is a device with two ports; one port attaches to the PC via a standard 10Base-T Ethernet card and UTP wiring, and the other port attaches directly to the coaxial cable. It is also possible to attach a server to the cable modem and have multiple PCs utilize the cable access to the Internet.

Cable providers that offer data services allocate one or more 6MHz channels in the downstream direction, from the head end, and another channel in the upstream direction for traffic from the subscribers. Typically, the downstream data channels are in the 550–750MHz range while the upstream data channel is in the 5–50MHz range. A splitter in the residence separates the TV frequency signals from the data frequency signals (see Figure 9.5). A 6MHz channel can support up to 27Mbps of downstream data throughput from the head end using a 64-point *quadrature amplitude modulation* (QAM) scheme. Actually, QAM encodes 6 bits per Hertz, which results in a downstream data rate of 36Mbps. However, because of framing and forward error correction techniques used by QAM, the user data rate is 27Mbps.

Transmission in the upstream direction is allocated from the low end of the frequency spectrum, 5–45MHz. This frequency range is susceptible to noise generated by all sorts of electromagnetic interference, including poor connections, and other sources of electromagnetic interference commonly found in a home, such as a TV. For this reason, data in the upstream direction is modulated and placed in a 6MHz channel with the *quadrature phase shift key* (QPSK) modulation technique. QPSK is more robust than QAM in terms of its immunity to noise at lower frequencies. Using QPSK, the upstream channel provides from 500Kbps to 10Mbps to subscribers. Obviously, there will be multiple devices transmitting data in the upstream direction, and contention is certainly a concern.

Each time the signal is amplified, the signal-to-noise ratio become less favorable. Because the return path is in a frequency range that is suscepti-

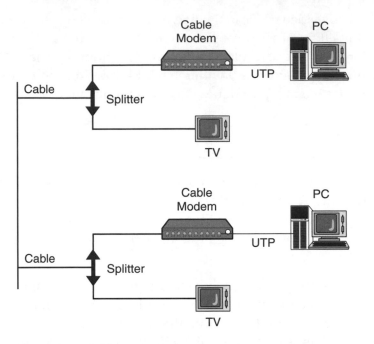

Figure 9.5 Cable system subscriber end.

ble to noise, having a large number of amplifiers results in a signal with poor signal-to-noise characteristics. Another return path concern is funneling, in which return path noise is aggregated, making noise a more important issue in the return path than it is in the forward path. This is why conventional cable systems, which have as many as 35 amplifiers end to end, are not widely used for two-way data communication.

A common misunderstanding is that the maximum cable modem data rate is 10Mbps. Actually, the 10Mbps limitation is imposed by the Ethernet NIC that resides in the PC. The date rate in the downstream direction is 27Mbps.

There are several different approaches to sharing the upstream communication channel among all subscribers. One approach is to subdivide the bandwidth, allocating a portion of the channel, or subchannel, to each subscriber. Consequently, the number of users that can be supported is limited by the number of subchannels. This approach is analogous to *time division multiplexing* (TDM). There is no contention, but because each portion of the bandwidth is permanently assigned to a user even when that user is not using it, the approach is inefficient. Another approach is to have all subscribers share a single channel for upstream transmissions.

This approach requires an arbitration procedure to control which subscriber seizes the channel. However, as the number of users increases, performance will degrade because the subscribers are sharing a fixed amount of capacity.

 Because the cable modem only "sees" traffic from the CMTS, it is not possible to have direct communication between two cable modems. All communication between subscribers must traverse the CMTS. Effectively, the CMTS relays traffic between two subscribers. Data forwarding through the CMTS may be via transparent bridging or IP routing.

Principles of Operation

This section examines the principles of operation as defined by the MCNS, by far the most widely implemented cable modem data system.

Upstream Data Path

Because the upstream path is shared by all subscriber cable modems, there must be some arbitration procedure to allocate use of the path to each user in an equitable fashion. The conventional schemes that are used in other shared media technologies, such as Ethernet and token ring, are ineffective because the distance from the CMTS to the farthest cable modem may be as far as 10 miles, resulting in a very large collision window. The approach that is used to allocate the shared path is a credit-based scheme. The upstream transmission line is logically divided into intervals, or minislots, with each minislot equal to 6.25 μs. Typically, a minislot can accommodate 8 or 16 bytes of data, depending on the modulation technique used. For upstream traffic, the CMTS allocates bandwidth to the cable modems by allocating minislots to a particular cable modem.

Because credits granted to the cable modems reference timeslots, it is critical that all cable modems be synchronized. The CMTS provides a global time reference to each cable modem by transmitting a time synchronization MAC message in the downstream direction. The SYNCH contains a timestamp that identifies the exact time the CMTS transmitted the message. Each cable modem compares the timestamp with the actual time and makes adjustments to the local clock references. Effectively, each local clock is offset by an amount of time equal to the signal propagation delay from the CMTS to the individual cable modem. This process of each cable modem determining its distance, or propagation delay, from the CMTS is called ranging. After all cable modems have completed the ranging function, all cable modems and the CMTS have a consistent systemwide view of time. Because it is critical to the effective operation of the cable modem system, ranging is done on a continual basis.

After synchronization, the cable modem waits for an *upstream channel descriptor* (UCD) message from the CMTS in order to retrieve transmission parameters, such as maximum burst size and modulation type, for the upstream channel. UCD messages, which are addressed to the cable modem MAC broadcast address, are periodically transmitted from the CMTS.

Before the cable modem may actually transmit data it must wait for an upstream *bandwidth allocation map* (MAP) from the CMTS. The MAP allocates minislots to particular cable modem and also identifies unassigned slots, which may be used by any cable modem. Figure 9.6 illustrates the format of the bandwidth allocation map.

The CMTS may set an upper limit on the number of cable modems allowed to share the same upstream channel. If the number of cable modems exceeds this upper limit, the CMTS may allocate another channel and allocate new cable modems to the new channel. The CMTS may also ask a station to switch to another upstream channel.

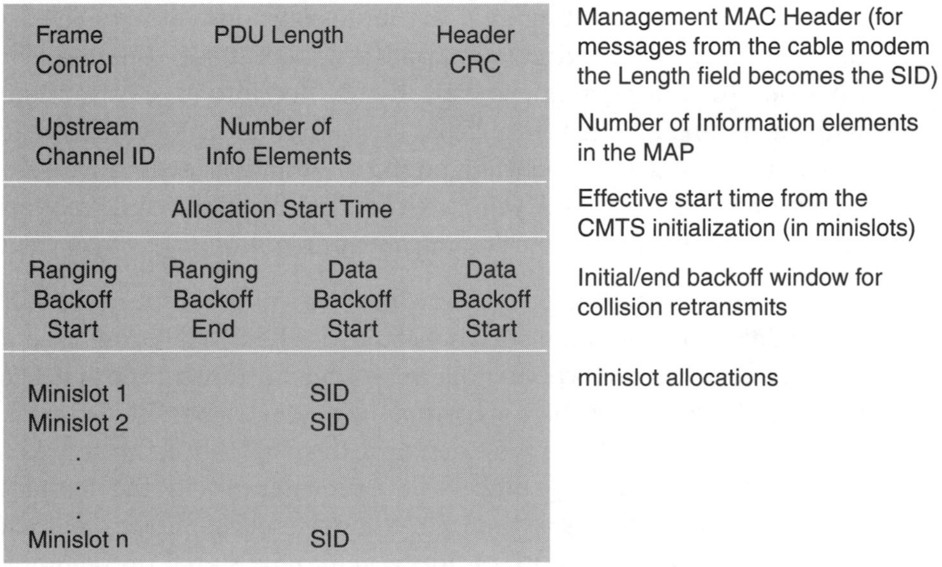

Frame Control	PDU Length		Header CRC	Management MAC Header (for messages from the cable modem the Length field becomes the SID)
Upstream Channel ID	Number of Info Elements			Number of Information elements in the MAP
Allocation Start Time				Effective start time from the CMTS initialization (in minislots)
Ranging Backoff Start	Ranging Backoff End	Data Backoff Start	Data Backoff Start	Initial/end backoff window for collision retransmits
Minislot 1		SID		minislot allocations
Minislot 2		SID		
.				
.				
.				
Minislot n		SID		

Figure 9.6 Bandwidth allocation map.

Example of Time Synchronization

Figure 9.7 illustrates the synchronization of minislots.

Through the "ranging procedure," Station A has determined that the propagation delay to the CBTS is p1, so from A's perspective, logical time τ is equal to real-time t plus p1. From B's perspective, τ1 is equal to real-time t plus p2; and from C's perspective, τ is equal to real-time t plus p3. If A is granted four minislots beginning at τ, A will transmit data during the four shaded minislots. The logical time is offset by the propagation delay, and there is no contention during those minislots. The time interval during which the cable modem is allowed to transmit is limited by the number of grants issued. After the allocated grants have been exhausted, the cable modem must stop transmitting.

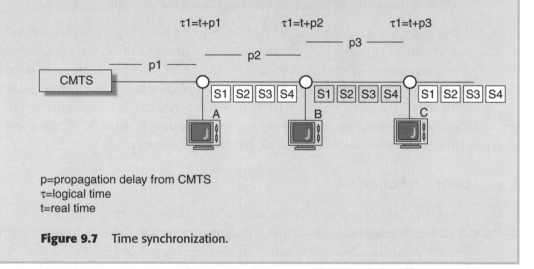

Figure 9.7   Time synchronization.

Registration

After receiving the MAP, the cable modem is ready to register with the CMTS by issuing a request registration message in one of the unassigned minislots. During the registration process, the CMTS assigns a unique *service identifier* (SID) to the cable modem. The SID is returned to the cable modem via a registration response message. The registration response from the CMTS to the cable modem also includes a DES key. Data transmitted between the CMTS and the cable modem will be encrypted with this key. The SID must be included in all subsequent transmissions in the upstream direction.

Next, the cable modem must obtain an IP address to send and receive IP packets. The protocol used for this process is the *dynamic host configuration protocol* (DHCP). DHCP is based on a client/server relationship wherein the cable modem is the client and the server is located somewhere on the network. The cable modem broadcasts a DHCP Discover, which includes its MAC address. The DHCP server responds by broadcasting a DHCP Offer. The cable modem then selects the offer and issues a DHCP request to the specific server. The DHCP server responds with a DHCP reply that includes IP configuration information, IP address, gateway IP address, subnet mask, IP address of the serving TFTP server, and the name of the configuration file to download. The cable modem then downloads the configuration file that contains the cable modem's operating parameters, such as bandwidth limitations and operating frequencies.

All subscribers downstream of one CMTS RF port will be part of one IP subnet. When a PC wishes to communicate with another PC in the same subnet, it will issue an ARP for the destination PC's MAC address. However, since the physical medium does not allow one subscriber to directly communicate with another subscriber, the ARP will be delivered to the router adjacent to the CMTS. The router must be configured to support proxy ARP because it will have to issue an ARP reply on behalf of the destination PC.

Data Exchange

When the cable modem receives a data MAC frame from the PC for upstream transmission, the cable modem encapsulates the data frame with its own MAC header. Upstream data is not encapsulated in MPEG packets. Because the cable modem does not need to generate MPEG packets, the price of cable modems stays down. Figure 9.8 illustrates the format of the upstream data frame.

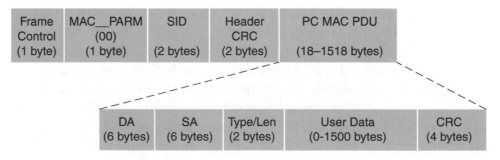

Figure 9.8 Upstream data frame.

The cable modem then determines how many minislots will be required to transmit the frame, which now consists of the MAC frame from the PC plus the CM MAC header that is appended to the PC frame. The cable modem then sends a request MAC header, which is a control frame sent from the cable modem to CMTS requesting the required number of minislots. The SID of the requesting CM is included in the request MAC header frame. The CMTS will grant some number of minislots, which may be contiguous slots (but they need not be), to the cable modem to transmit data. The CMTS grants minislots via a MAC management message that contains a minislot allocation MAP (see Figure 9.9). The MAP will indicate which minislots are to be used for a particular cable modem to transmit data, while other slots will be unassigned. The unassigned slots may be used by any cable modem to issue minislot grant requests or by a new cable modem that is trying to initiate communication with the CMTS. Of, course, there is contention for these unassigned minislots, and consequently, there may be collisions. If a collision does occur, only the CMTS will be aware of it, and the CMTS will initiate a collision resolution scheme.

At the CMTS, the frame is reconstructed and forwarded to the router.

Data frames from the router are delivered to the CMTS. The CMTS encapsulates the data in MPEG II packets, which are converted into RF signals. The RF signals are modulated to the proper downstream frequency and delivered to all cable modems. The cable modem demodulates the signals and reconstructs the data frame. The DA MAC is examined, and if the frame is destined for the cable modem's client PC, the frame is delivered across the UTP cable to the Ethernet NIC.

Collision Resolution

The CMTS controls assignments on the upstream channel through the MAP and determines which minislots are subject to collisions. Typically, collisions will occur only when subscribers submit minislot grant requests. Data packets usually do not collide because they are transmitted in minislots that have been allocated expressly to a particular subscriber by the

Frame Control (1 byte)	MAC__PARM (number of minislolts) (1 byte)	SID (2 bytes)	Header CRC (2 bytes)

Figure 9.9   Minislot request (request MAC header—there is no data portion).

CMTS. However, it is inefficient to require a subscriber that has data to transmit to necessarily wait until the CMTS has granted minislots explicitly for the transmission. This is especially true in a lightly loaded system. In a lightly loaded system, there is minimal chance that multiple subscribers would send data in the same unassigned minislot. So MCNS does allow subscribers to "piggyback" requests for more minislots in data PDUs.

Because subscriber cannot "listen" on the upstream channel, they are unaware of collisions that do occur. The CMTS detects the collision and informs each cable modem that the collision occurred. When informed of a collision, the cable modem randomly selects a number between the backoff start and the backoff end. These values are specified in the MAP message. If the collision occurred during initialization, a random number between ranging backoff start and ranging backoff end is selected, whereas if the collision occurred during a grant request or a data transfer, a random value is selected between the data backoff start and data back-off end. The random number selected is the number of unassigned minis-lots that the cable modem must wait before attempting to resubmit the data element. If the backoff window is sufficiently large, the contending modems will be less likely to collide again.

If the cable modem is involved in another collision, the backoff window is increased by a factor of two, and the contending modems repeat the process. This process may be repeated 16 times, after which the data is discarded. If while transmitting data the cable modem receives a data grant from the CMTS, it must stop the contention resolution process and use the explicit transmit opportunity.

Telephone-Return Path Solutions

Because the demand for consumer cable data services is being driven primarily by the need for faster downstream speeds, telephone-return cable modems are a viable means for cable operators without two-way facilities to enter to residential high-data market. MCNS provides specifications to support data-over-cable systems using a return path via the *public switched telephone network* (PSTN). The telephone-return path scheme is illustrated in Figure 9.10. The system consists of the CMTS, the cable network, a cable modem, the PSTN, and the *telephone remote access concentrator* (TRAC). Typically, the CMTS and the TRAC will be collocated, but this is not a requirement. The data path through the telephone-return system is:

- An IP packet from the Internet, destined for the client PC, is routed to the CMTS.

- The CMTS encodes the IP packet as described previously and transmits it in the downstream path.

- The cable modem recognizes that the frame is destined for its client PC, decodes the frame, and passes via Ethernet to the PC.

- The PC responds to the frame. The response enters the telephone-return capable cable modem.

- The cable modem encapsulates the response IP packet in a *point-to-point protocol* (PPP) frame, and transmits the frame across the PSTN to the TRAC.

- The TRAC decodes the IP packet and forwards it to the router via the CMTS.

In addition to the data path, there are several management paths in the telephone-return system. These include the PPP negotiations between the cable modem and the TRAC, as well as SNMP management messages. It is possible for telephone-return path devices to coexist with regular two-way cable devices in the same system. In this situation, the cable modem will selectively discard downstream MAC management messages that relate to upstream channel acquisition or upstream data traffic.

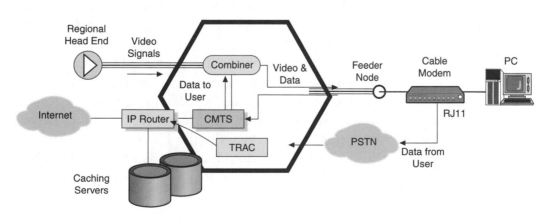

Figure 9.10 Telephone-return path system.

Cable Internet Service Considerations

Cable operators recognize that providing megabits of bandwidth to subscribers does not necessarily correlate to high-speed Internet access or to satisfied customers. Simply stated, a network connection is only as fast as its slowest link, and there are many factors that can contribute to a slow link. Of course, the more links there are in the path, the more likely that a troubled, or slow, link will be encountered. Also, if a Web server has a 56Kbps connection to the Internet, the benefits of a subscriber's megabit connection are lost when that subscriber tries to retrieve information from that Web server.

A solution to the dilemma that is being deployed by many cable operators is to place the information closer to the subscriber or at least provide high-speed access to the information. The simplest approach is to deploy caching servers that store copies of popular Internet content locally. When a subscriber requests a Web page, the safari through the Internet will be avoided; the request is diverted to the caching servers, and the information is retrieved at a very high speed. Another approach that is being supported by several popular ISPs is the construction of a high-speed backbone and cache infrastructure that distributes broadband Internet services through affiliated cable systems.

IEEE 802.14

In 1994 the IEEE 802.14 Working Group was formed to define a *physical layer* (PHY) and a MAC layer for bidirectional data transfer over the HFC Cable network. Whereas DOCSIS utilized variable-length IP packets, IEEE 802.14 specified ATM fixed-length cells as its default solution from the head end to the cable modem. IEEE 802.14 selected ATM because it provides sophisticated quality of service capabilities, and the Working Group felt that the QoS capabilities would expedite the integrated delivery of voice, video, and data over the cable network. The Working Group saw ATM as a long-term solution that would provide the flexibility to deliver more than just Internet access to cable users. The MCNS (DOCSIS) supporters did not agree. They maintained that ATM would add unnecessary complexity and cost to cable modem network. They opted to remain clearly focused on delivering high-speed Internet access.

In fact, the DOCSIS 1.1 specification, April 1999, includes support for fragmentation, dynamic service flows, and service scheduling types, which emulate ATM functions such as CBR and VBR. It now appears that IEEE 802.14 has no significant advantages over DOCSIS.

While 802.14 was haggling over technical details, the DOCSIS supporters were busy bringing interoperable products to market. IEEE 802.14 is still in the development stage. Today, dozens of companies are building DOC-SIS products, but no company has stepped forward to build an 802.14-compliant product. It appears in all likelihood that 802.14 will ultimately be little more than an academic exercise.

Conclusion

Clearly, these cable modem schemes are still evolving and lack the corporate control mechanisms needed to provide any service-level extension to home users. Standards must evolve to make two-way interactive traffic more viable and interoperable with existing network infrastructures.

CHAPTER 10

Digital Subscriber Line

S ince the inception of the data communications industry, the *public switched telephone network* (PSTN) has been an unwitting participant. After all, the PSTN copper lines go everywhere. Since the early day of the ARPANET, lines have been provisioned from the PSTN and used to transport data from site to site. In fact, most data network protocols were devised explicitly to enable the telco copper-based facilities, which of course were installed to support voice, to effectively transport data. Even today, all the voice traffic and most of the Internet traffic is traveling over the installed copper telco lines. Increasing demand for new telephone services and direct connection from the residence into the Internet have impacted the existing copper supply. In many homes, access to the Internet has become a virtual necessity. Not long ago, the typical home computer user would access the Internet only occasionally. It was a minor inconvenience for the home user to seize the household's telephone line and to access the Internet via an analog modem. The phone line, which is an *unshielded twisted pair* (UTP) copper line, runs from the home to a telco's central office switch. This connection is the local loop, sometimes referred to as the last mile. Unfortunately, analog modems cannot support voice communication and data transfer simultaneously.

No longer is it only occasionally that a home user wants to access the Internet. In many homes, access to the Internet is considered no more a privilege than watching TV or listening to the stereo. For many, accessing the Internet is becoming part of a daily routine. To meet this new way of life, second telephone lines are increasingly being installed in private residences.

As noted in the last chapter, cable modems provide alternative access to the Internet, but cable modem capability is not nearly as pervasive as telephone lines. Also, cable modems do not provide a dedicated path because the medium is shared, preventing broad acceptance.

From the business perspective, demand for Internet connectivity is being fueled by such critical Internet applications as e-mail, e-commerce, telecommuting, and remote office connectivity. The Federal Communications Commission (FCC) estimates the number of U.S. telephone lines serving business customers to be about 50 million. This number is growing rapidly as more and more businesses become connected to the Internet. The supply and capacity of copper is becoming strained. Lately, small businesses have become increasingly dependent on sophisticated voice and data products and services. Typically, bandwidth to support these services is purchased on a line-by-line basis. A small business may have five analog phone lines and an additional line for Internet access.

For larger companies, integrated voice and data services are delivered via digital T1 (1.544Mbps) or E1 (2Mbps) service. Increasing demand for T1/E1 access lines coupled with the dwindling supply of copper loops and more competition in the local loop is driving the market for increased bandwidth over conventional copper wires.

Although this chapter focuses on the technical aspects of last-mile connectivity (that is, connectivity from the residence or home), there are also significant business implications. The Telecommunications Reform Act of 1996 ended local service monopolies and allowed competition among local phone companies, long distance carriers, and *Internet service providers* (ISPs). The *local exchange carriers* (LECs) need a broadband service for the local loop to combat cable companies' plans to offer cable modem and telephony services and to prevent *interexchange carriers* (IXCs) from gaining access to the local carriers' former monopoly.

Enhancing Internet Access

Most private residence and small business access to the Internet is over traditional telephone lines using an analog modem. The digital signal from the computer is converted into an analog signal for transmission on the telephone line. At the central office, a codec reconverts the analog signal to a digital signal for transmission through the telephone network. In the opposite direction, the codec converts the digital signal to analog for transmission on the local loop to the modem, which again reconverts the signal to digital before delivering it to the computer. Because the modem/codec operates in the same bandwidth, 0–4KHz, as voice communication, the data capacity is limited to 33.6Kbps or less. This analog transmission represents only a small portion of the amount of available bandwidth on the copper local loop.

56k Modem Support

Current V.90 modems support up to 56Kbps, which is actually asymmetric. That is, the communication from the home modem is limited to 33.6Kbps, but the transmission from the central office may be up to 56Kbps.

Network requirements to achieve maximum throughput from a 56Kbps modem, namely the end-to-end path, must be mostly digital (shown in Figure 10.1). The 56k DSU at the subscriber end of the circuit has a digital local loop and the 56k DSU. 56Kbps modems operate using *pulse amplitude modulation* (PAM) and not *quadrature amplitude modulation* (QAM). QAM operates by modulating a carrier wave signal in both amplitude and phase with each unique combination of amplitude and phase representing a symbol. The DSU encapsulates the data traffic into a PAM-encoded digital stream. PAM is the technique used to digitally represent an analog signal; however, the 8-bit values being sent from the 56k DSU no longer represent samples of analog signals—they are values used as symbols. The codec turns the PAM-encoded digital stream back into an analog signal and transmits it over the analog local loop. The 56k modem has a PAM decoder. The PAM decoder does the reverse of the PAM-encoding process. It converts the PAM stream back to digital and then extracts the 7 bits of data. A significant limitation of the PAM decoder is that the signal may only be converted to analog once, at the CO adjacent to the 56k modem.

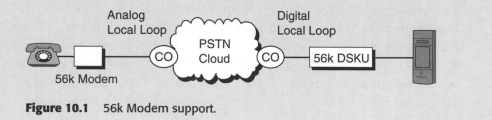

Figure 10.1   56k Modem support.

The first attempt to better utilize the bandwidth available on the local loop, called *integrated digital services network* (ISDN), was proposed in the mid-1980s. ISDN was designed to provide an end-to-end digital communication path. The standard defines a general digital telephone network specification and has been in existence since the mid-1980s. The ISDN standard is governed by ITU-T.

The basic assumption of ISDN was that the telco switches and connections, called trunks, between the digital switches are digital, typically T1/E1 or T3/E3. These digital switches and trunks support data and voice communication simultaneously. The only component of the network that was not digital is the local loop from the central office to the customer premise. ISDN is a standard for digitizing the local loop and thereby extending the digital services—that is, integrated voice and data—of the network to the customer premises.

There are two basic types of ISDN access: *basic rate interface* (BRI) and *primary rate interface* (PRI). BRI consists of two 64Kbps "B" channels and one 16Kbps "D" channel. This basic service is intended to meet the needs of most individual or residential users. To access BRI, service there must be an ISDN *terminal adapter* (TA) (sometimes called, incorrectly, an ISDN modem) at the customer site, and the switch at the central office must be ISDN capable. Typically, the ISDN TA contains a codec so that one of the B channels can be used to support voice. The codec converts the analog signal generated by the telephone into a digital signal that can be carried over the B channel. In this way, voice and data are carried simultaneously over individual B channels. It is also possible to combine the two B channels into a single 128Kbps channel to support data or video services.

The D channel is a control channel used to provide out-of-band signaling. The ISDN local loop uses the standard local loop UTP, but some reengineering may be required. The local loop must be "unloaded," meaning that load coils and bridge taps must be removed. Inductive load coils are used to extend the distance and limit the bandwidth to a 4KHz passband for standard telephone service. Bridge taps are created when wire pairs are reassigned and the existing copper wire is simply tapped with a branch instead of rerouted to a new location. Eliminating the coils and bridge taps is difficult and costly. The local loop distance is also reduced to 18,000 feet as opposed to the 25,000 feet usually associated with the local loop. Another concern is that ISDN TAs are typically powered locally, so if the site loses power, phone service is also unavailable.

Analog versus Digital Signaling

With analog signaling the carrier wave (see Figure 10.2 A) continuously conveys information. The information is represented by a modification in either the amplitude (see Figure 10.2 B) or the frequency. As the wave travels along the medium, spurious noise may be introduced, increasing the amplitude of a portion of the wave. Since the wave is continuous and all variation conveys information, there is no way for the receiver to determine which aspect of the wave is noise and which is valid information.

Digital signaling also involves sending a carrier, but it does not use the continuously varying properties of the carrier to convey information. Rather discrete values of the wave are used to represent either a 0 or a 1 (see Figure 10.2 C). The carrier is modified to best produce a signal pulse that can be clearly distinguished as one of only these two basic binary states.

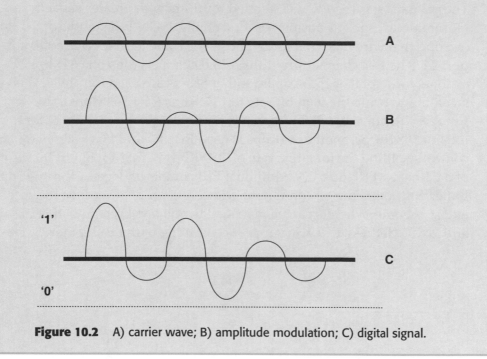

Figure 10.2   A) carrier wave; B) amplitude modulation; C) digital signal.

Basic rate ISDN is transmitted to and from a subscriber's premise via two wire pair UTP cable using a 2B1Q signal at a bit rate of 160Kbps—two 64Kbps B channels, one 16Kbps D channel, and 16Kbps of framing and synchronizing bits. A 2B1Q coding with four-level PAM is the standard used in North America. With 2B1Q, two bits are combined to form a single quaternary line state—2B1Q combines two bits at a time to represent one of four amplitude levels on the line. The signaling, therefore, is 80KB. It operates with a maximum frequency of 40KHz. 2B1Q coding is defined in ANSI T1.601 and ETR 080, Annex A. It can operate at distances up to about 18,000 feet (5.5KM). Echo cancellation techniques allow full-duplex operation on the line. 2B1Q transmission can be simply described as an amplitude modulation scheme for DC pulses, as indicated in Figure 10.3.

In Europe and elsewhere in the world, basic rate ISDN uses a coding scheme called 4B3T. It relies on return-to-zero states on the line. 4B3T combines 4 bits to represent one "ternary" line signal state. In 4B3T coding, there are three line states: a positive pulse (+), a negative pulse (–), and a zero-state (no pulse, –0). 4B3T transmits a data rate of 160Kbps at a signaling rate of 120Kbaud.

The primary service, PRI, is intended for users with greater capacity requirements, such as businesses. Essentially, ISDN PRI standardizes existing two wire pair UTP local loops—the same local loop used to support T1. The PRI channel structure is 23 B channels plus one 64Kbps D channel for a total of 1536Kbps; another 8Kbps are used for physical layer signaling to bring the total bit rate to 1544Kbps (or 1.544Mbps). (In Europe, PRI consists of 30 B channels plus one 64Kbps D channel for a total of 1984Kbps; another 64Kbps is used for physical layer signaling and control, yielding the total line rate of 2048Kbps [2.048Mbps].) In the case of a T1-based PRI, up to 19 additional PRI circuits between the same customer endpoints can be configured with 24 B channels because the second and subsequent circuits can be managed by the one D channel that has already be defined. PRI also support combining of the B channels to cre-

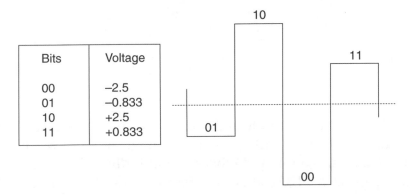

Bits	Voltage
00	–2.5
01	–0.833
10	+2.5
11	+0.833

Figure 10.3 2B1Q line coding.

ate either 384Kbps (6 B channels, denoted H0),1.536Mbps (24 B channels, denoted H11), or 1.920Mbps (30 B channels, denoted H12).

Digital Subscriber Line

As was demonstrated by ISDN, bandwidth on the local loop is not limited by the physical constraints of the local loop. Bandwidth on the analog local loop is limited, primarily by constraints at the central office. Filters in the central office codec limit the local loop to voice grade bandwidth of 4KHz. Specifically, the codec converts a voice-grade analog signal to μlaw or A-law encoded digital samples for transmission on the digital telco network. And, in the opposite direction, it converts the digital signal to analog signal between 0 and 4KHz. So the analog transmission between the residence or business and the phone company is a bandwidth bottleneck. Remove the filters and the local loop copper lines can pass frequencies into MHz range, albeit with substantial attenuation. Without the 4KHz barrier, attenuation—which increases with line length and frequency—dominates the constraints on the data rate over the local loop. Another factor impacting attenuation is the quality of the copper line itself. Figure 10.4 illustrates practical limits on data rate *in one direction* compared with the line length (24-gauge copper twisted pair). *Digital subscriber line* (DSL) is a descendant of ISDN. It is a technology that provides cost-effective high-bandwidth access to the Internet, or other central location, to homes and small businesses over existing, ordinary copper telephone lines.

Some variations of DSL simultaneously allow the phone line to be used for voice and data communication. The variations of DSL that support voice do so unlike ISDN, which integrates voice and data communications on the same network. DSL transmits voice and data on logically separate networks; that is, a different frequency spectrum is used. Effectively, the voice remains analog, while the data is digital. This is an important advantage because it provides the homes user with a continuously active data connection while the telephone service operates in the usual way.

Actually, DSL is an umbrella term that refers to the transmission of a digital signal over an unloaded local loop, while *x*DSL refers to the family of digital subscriber line technologies. There are about 10 *x*DSL technologies, each of which is a variation on one of three DSL categories: symmetrical DSL, asymmetrical DSL, or high-speed DSL. DSL offers a range of speeds

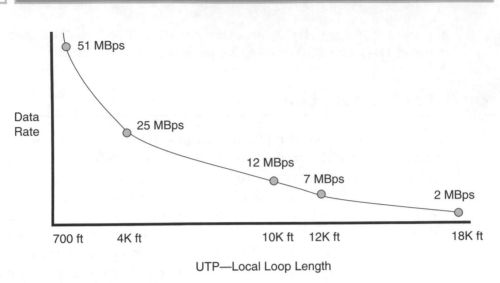

Figure 10.4 Potential DSL capacity on an unloaded local loop.

from 32Kbps to 50Mbps. Because DSL uses the existing local loop wire pair, the term DSL signifies a modem or, more explicitly, a modem pair and not the line at all. That is, a pair of DSL capable modems applied to a local loop creates a digital subscriber line. Figure 10.5 illustrates a typical residential DSL implementation.

Some carriers are implementing digital fiber optics from a remote line controller to the central office and placing the DSLAM at the remote line controller. The result is that the local loop is much shorter. This configuration is illustrated in Figure 10.6. Some cable operators are also offering DSL service to residences over their coaxial cable.

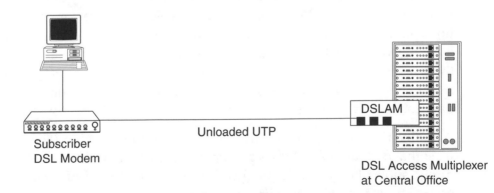

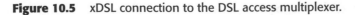

Figure 10.5 xDSL connection to the DSL access multiplexer.

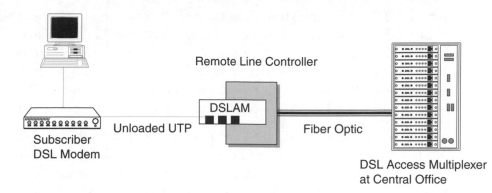

Figure 10.6 Shortening the effective local loop.

Symmetrical DSL Technologies

The main characteristic of symmetrical DSL technologies is that an equal amount of bandwidth is available in both directions. Symmetrical DSL use a 2B1Q modulation scheme, and symmetrical technologies do not support an analog voice channel. We will look at three symmetrical DSL technologies: HDSL, SDSL, and HDSL2.

High Bit-Rate Digital Subscriber Line

The first application of *x*DSL was designed to make T1 service (bidirectional, high-quality 1.544Mbps service) more cost-effective and deliverable in a more timely manner.

T1 transmission was originally based on a modulation technique called *alternate mark inversion* (AMI). A digital 1 (mark) is transmitted as a three-volt pulse whose shape is rather strictly defined, and a digital 0 is sent as no pulse. Each mark is of opposite polarity from the previous mark. Because of AMI modulation, T1 circuits required conditioned unloaded loops. The wire pair spans between repeaters needed to be continuous pieces of single-gauge copper, and repeaters were required every 3000 to 6000 feet. Because AMI requires a sufficient density of 1's, or the receiver loses its synchronization, *Bipolar 8-zero Substitution* (B8ZS) was introduced. B8ZS is a technique that replaces a string of eight zeros with a special pattern that would otherwise signal an error because it has two successive pulses of the same polarity.

Originally, telcos provisioned T1 circuits for transmissions between offices in the core switching network. (Again, T1 circuits required two pairs of UTP.) Over time, the telcos tariffed T1 services and offered them for private networks, primarily connecting PBXs and T1 multiplexers across wide area networks. However, T1 was not very suitable for connecting to individual residences or small businesses. AMI is so demanding of bandwidth and repeater requirements that deployment of T1 to these locations proved to be a costly and time-consuming proposition.

In 1990, Bellcore proposed HDSL, an extension of basic rate ISDN. HDSL uses the 2B1Q line code standard used by ISDN. HDSL is capable of transmitting 1.5Mbps over the two local loops. Each loop transmits and receives half the payload. Full-duplex operation is achieved through adaptive filtering and echo cancellation to separate the transmit signal from the receive signal. At the far end, the two payloads are recombined to deliver the full T1 payload. Nonlinear equalizers are used to equalize the desired 2B1Q signal without increasing the noise. As a result, normal impairments in the unloaded loop could now be tolerated; that is, the line no longer needs to be conditioned. HDSL is capable of transmitting signals over the full carrier serving area, 12,000 feet, without repeaters. Also, because HDSL operates using DS-1 framing techniques, it interoperates with AMI-based T1 implementations. HDSL is a stable technology and is now the dominant choice among carriers for delivery of T1 (and E1) service. Currently, 70 percent of the T1 circuits being deployed in the United States is based on HDSL technology. If you buy T1 from the telco today, you are likely getting HDSL behind the scenes; there is no difference between traditional T1 and HDSL-based T1 in your premise equipment.

Single Line Digital Subscriber Line

Carriers do not provide fractional HDSL; if the user requires only 10 DS-0 channels, the carrier delivers a full HDSL. *Single line digital subscriber line* (SDSL) is basically half HDSL. As stated above, HDSL operates on two-pair UTP, and each pair transmits half the T1 signal. SDSL uses only a single UTP and delivers the bit rate equivalent of one half a T1 (768Kbps), usually enough bandwidth for most home users. SDSL has an important advantage over HDSL in that it is more suitable for individual subscribers who are usually equipped with a single telephone line. SDSL is a symmetric service, with equal bandwidth in both directions and operates up to only 10,000 feet.

SDSL has not been widely deployed by providers.

High Bit-Rate Digital Subscriber Line 2

Today, many large businesses get their telephony and Internet connectivity through T1 trunks and private lines. Because of increasing demand for multimedia applications, such as videoconferencing, many smaller companies are looking to increase bandwidth on the local loop to support symmetric services. Because of this increased demand for symmetric services and a greater need for high-speed access on the local loop, as well as a shortage of available copper pairs required of T1 and HDSL, providers are looking for enhanced DSL technologies that provide T1/E1 provisioning on a single-pair UTP local loop. High bit-rate digital subscriber line 2 (HDSL2) has emerged as a new standard that addresses these requirements. (The final standard from the ANSI T1E1.4 Working Group is due in the first quarter of 2000.) It is designed to transmit T1 rates (1.544Mbps) at full carrier service area reach, which means it can travel up to 12,000 feet on 24 AWG.

Traditional T1 delivery, via DSL, utilizes HDSL, which uses two pairs of UTP. HDSL2 offers the same performance and the same spectral compatibility but with a single UTP pair. Supporting T1 on a single pair is possible because of a new line-coding scheme called *overlapped pulse amplitude transmission with interlocking spectra* (OPTIS). The OPTIS proposal is based on 8-PAM (Pulse Amplitude Modulation) line code, which is an extension of 2B1Q line code, with the addition of a sophisticated trellis-coded modulation. OPTIS goes beyond other DSL line codes like 2B1Q, CAP, or DMT, and uses advanced concepts in spectral shaping and error-correction codes to achieve performance near the theoretical limit of UTP.

As with HDSL, HDSL2 will use DS-1 framing techniques and it will interoperate with other T1 implementations.

We should note the end users will not be the consumers of HDSL/HDSL2. An end user will order a T1. The telco will deliver the T1 service on a standard two pair using AMI/B8ZS, two pair using HDSL, or a single pair using HDSL2. The termination of the telco wire is a smartjack and the interface to the customer is an RJ-45 connector. The customer does not have a choice regarding standard or HDSL-base deployment. However, because the new HDSL technologies provide a more favorable cost point for the telco, users may benefit from a pricing perspective.

Asymmetrical DSL Technologies

Asymmetrical DSL technologies provide an unequal amount of bandwidth in each direction. The asymmetrical DSL technologies are targeted at residential users because traffic patterns of residential users are typically asymmetrical—little traffic upstream to the server and much more traffic downstream from the server. Because the asymmetric nature of Asymmetrical DSL high data rates are attainable. This is because *crosstalk* is minimized. Crosstalk is the unwanted transfer of energy from one UTP to an adjacent UTP. It limits the amount of signal manipulation that can be performed on the copper line, consequently limiting the amount of data throughput that can be achieved on the line. However, if data is traversing the line in only one direction, the effects of crosstalk are negligible, thus the high data rates achievable with Asymmetrical DSL.

Asymmetrical DSL technologies typically use discrete multitone (DMT) or carrierless amplitude/phase modulation (CAP) line coding. Asymmetrical DSL technologies do provide support for an analog voice channel. We will look at three asymmetrical DSL technologies: ADSL, RADSL, and G.lite.

Asymmetric DSL

Asymmetric DSL (ADSL) is the variation of DSL that provides significantly more bandwidth than HDSL and will likely become most widely implemented for home users (note: *asymmetric* DSL is one variation of the *asymmetrical* DSL technologies). ADSL is termed asymmetric because most of the available bandwidth is reserved for sending data in the downstream direction from the network to the user. Only a small amount of bandwidth is used for upstream traffic from the user to the network. This is desirable for home users because typical Internet usage involves a majority of data being sent to the user (Web pages, graphics, multimedia) with minimal upload capacity required (keystrokes and mouse clicks). With ADSL, from 1.5Mbps to 9Mbps of data can be sent downstream and from 64Kbps to 640Kbps upstream. The available bandwidth is predicated on the attenuation characteristics of the local loop. Maximum bandwidth of 640Kbps upstream and 9Mbps downstream is achievable at distances up to 9000 feet, while 64Kbps upstream and 1.5Mbps is obtainable at the far reach of the local loop spectrum—18,000 feet.

The high downstream bandwidth means that the telephone line will be able to bring motion video and audio from the Internet to a household's PC or hooked-in TV set. And customers won't be competing for bandwidth with neighbors, as is the case with cable modems. Additionally, a small portion of the downstream bandwidth can be devoted to voice-enabling voice conversations without requiring a separate telephone line. A typical ADSL configuration is illustrated in Figure 10.7.

In addition to the ADSL modem, ADSL makes use of a signal splitter that allows a standard telephone to have access to the local loop. The provider side of the connection also has a splitter to remove the phone signal before the provider's ADSL equipment processes the signal. The voice signal is passed to the central office codec while the DSL signal terminates at the DSLAM. Another advantage to this approach is that the telephone line remains active even if the ADSL modem fails.

The ADSL modem attains its high data rates by using various advanced signal processing techniques and sophisticated digital line coding schemes. Also, ADSL employs Reed-Solomon forward error correction. Currently, two contending line encoding schemes are being implemented in ADSL products.

Discrete multi-tone (DMT) line coding, specified in ANSI (T1.413), uses *frequency division multiplexing* (FDM). FDM divides the local loop available bandwidth, about 1MHz, into 256 smaller channels, or narrowband carriers, of 4KHz each. The low-end subchannel is used for voice, 32 subchannels are for upstream traffic, and the remainder is used for downstream traffic (see Figure 10.8).

DMT uses the many narrowband carriers, all transmitting at once in parallel, with each carrying a small fraction of the total information. The dis-

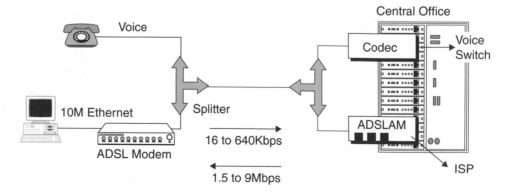

Figure 10.7 ADSL configuration.

crete bands are modulated independently with a carrier frequency that corresponds to the center frequency of the subchannel.

DMT tailors its signal to the channel, analyzing the line quality at initialization. It then varies the bit density on each of these channels to overcome noise and interference that may be present in sections of the frequency spectrum. At the receiving end, the signal is re-created from the individual components.

Carrierless amplitude and phase modulation (CAP) is a proprietary standard (AT&T and Globespan) that is widely implemented. Currently, there are more ADSL devices using CAP than DMT, but the tide is turning. CAP relies on a single carrier, and each symbol transmitted takes the whole channel bandwidth; hence, CAP may have problems sustaining high data rates on noisy transmission lines. CAP uses techniques similar to QAM used in V.34 (28.8Kbps) modems. CAP relies on echo cancellation to separate the upstream path from the downstream path (see Figure 10.9). Echo cancellation uses sophisticated signal processing (analog, digital, or both) to separate the strong transmitted signal from the weaker received signal, passing only the received signal to the demodulator. In the conversational model, this is analogous to a person who can effectively talk and listen at the same time. As with DMT, CAP isolates a voice channel at the low end of the spectrum.

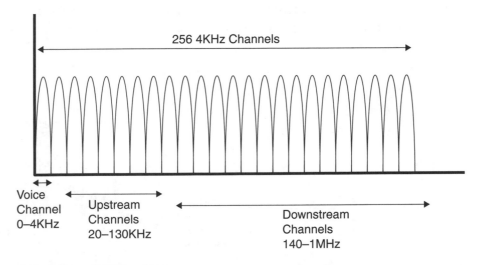

Figure 10.8   DMT for ADSL.

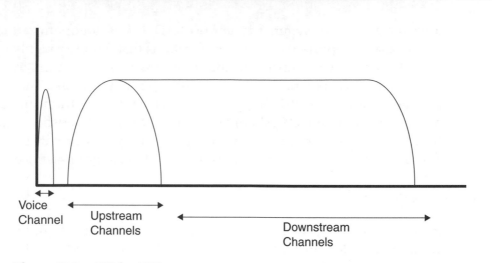

Voice
Channel

Upstream
Channels

Downstream
Channels

Figure 10.9 CAP for ADSL.

Some products support both, and there are advantages and disadvantages to each. CAP is currently more widely implemented, but it is not standardized. CAP is less expensive to implement, but some argue that DMT is better on noisy lines because of its ability to maximize throughput on good channels and minimize throughput on channels with interference. On the other side of the argument are those who believe that CAP introduces less latency than the DMT approach. Be aware that the two approaches do not interoperate—the technology implemented on the ADSL modem must be consistent with the technology implemented at the DSLAM.

Another important aspect of ADSL involves the interface from the PC to the ADSL modem and the transport mode of data on the local loop. The ADSL specifications mention two interface possibilities: Ethernet and ISDN. Certainly, the 10Mbps Ethernet interface is more popular and probably will be deployed much more frequently. The PC Ethernet card connects directly to the ADSL modem.

With so many applications for ADSL and HDSL, how does one choose between the two?

The choice should depend on the characteristics of the applications. When downstream bandwidth, from the network to the user, is the priority, ADSL is indicated. This is the case for the majority of consumer applications. This approach will address the needs of most homes as well as small businesses.

However, given the asymmetric nature of ADSL, it is not optimized to support many important business applications that require roughly equal amounts of bandwidth upstream and downstream, such as LAN interconnection, videoconferencing, and many legacy applications. These applications are symmetric, supporting equal amounts of traffic upstream and downstream, so HDSL should be used. HDSL characteristics generally address the needs of a corporation, particularly in corporate business campuses where T1 is prevalent for high-quality symmetric service.

Rate Adaptive DSL

As mentioned above, when ADSL is initially provisioned, the service provider must determine the line quality and distance, and based on these parameters, the ADSL modem is programmed to operate at a single programmed rate. In areas where there is a large variance in local loop length, wire gauge, and the condition of the line, it becomes difficult to determine how the ADSL modem should be configured; that is, what speeds should be provisioned over the line. If the line quality changes, the ADSL modem must be reprogrammed to accommodate the new quality. *Rate adaptive DSL* (RADSL) allows the individual modem pairs to automatically and dynamically determine the line quality and to match their transmission speeds based on line quality. The primary difference between ADSL and RADSL is that RADSL can work at different speeds. Although remote customers may not get the fastest RADSL speeds because of the distance of the copper wire needed, they'll get the best possible rate given the circumstances.

There currently are no RADSL standards, although several proprietary implementations are available.

User-Installed DSL: G.lite or Splitterless DSL

ADSL, although available, is not *widely* available. One of the reasons for the slow deployment is that a splitter must be installed at the residence by a service technician. This is commonly referred to as a *truck roll*.

The term is derived from the scene of a technician arriving at a home to configure or troubleshoot a line or to install the splitter. The significance of the term is that it implies a real cost to the service provider.

The splitter is designed to separate the voice band from the data bands. *User-installed DSL* (UDL), commonly called *G.lite* or *splitterless* DSL, is a modified version of ADSL. The technology delivers data transmission speeds of up to 1.5Mbps downstream and up to 512Kbps upstream. The significance of G.lite, which is DMT based, is that it has been designed for easy, low-cost deployment and removes the need for a voice-data splitter at every user site. DMT signal modulation for G.lite is illustrated in Figure 10.10. The elimination of the voice-data splitter removes a major deployment bottleneck, the telephone company truckroll, thereby helping to speed the deployment of DSL. G.lite allows for simpler and more economical deployment of ADSL in applications where the speed of full-rate ADSL is not needed.

The G.lite (UDSL) standard, G.992.2, was approved by the ITU in June 1999.

With G.lite, the telephone and ADSL service are carried on a common in-house wire in much the same way that an additional phone set is added in a household. The challenge for G.lite is sharing the voice and ADSL signals on the same in-house wiring. The function of the splitter is to separate the voice and data signal and then send each signal on a separate wire. The problem with using the same wire is that noise generated by the telephone in the same frequency range as the ADSL signal can be disruptive to the ADSL signal. Additionally, impedance of a telephone when it is off-hook may be so low that it shunts the ADSL signal. G.lite operates on a lower available bandwidth of the greater noise impairments because the signal is carried on all of the house wiring. G.lite supports downstream speeds up to 1.5Mbps and upstream speeds to 512Kbps. However,

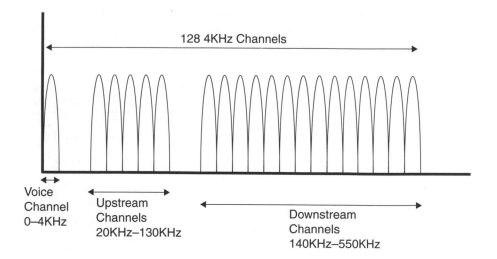

Figure 10.10 DMT for G.lite.

because of the lower frequencies, G.lite can be deployed over longer local loops of up to 25,000 feet.

Although G.lite does not require a splitter, it does require a microfilter, or low-pass filter, between the wall jack and the telephone. The microfilter allows only the low-bandwidth voice traffic to enter and leave the telephone. The filter is inexpensive and can be easily installed by the customer. The filter, which may be thought of as a distributed splitter, effectively accomplishes the same thing for G.lite as the splitter did for ADSL. It eliminates disruptive noise and raises the impedance at DSL frequencies to prevent the shunting of the ADSL signal.

Within the PC, a G.lite modem is required. The intent is that G.lite modems all be as easy to install as conventional modems—you install the modem and connect it to the phone line. Note, the splitter is still required at the central office. A G.lite implementation is illustrated in Figure 10.11.

Very High Bit-Rate DSL

Very high bit-rate DSL (VDSL) is a modification of ADSL. It provides asymmetric data rates higher than ADSL but over very short reaches of UTP. VDSL uses signaling similar to ADSL but it will operate at frequency bands above ADSL. The range depends on the actual copper line length. The basic idea is to take advantage of the *optical network units* (ONUs) being installed by the telcos. An ONU is a combination of *fiber to the neighborhood* (FTTN), resulting in very short copper line lengths to the residence. The maximum downstream rate under consideration is between 51 and 55Mbps over lines up to 1000 feet. Downstream speeds as low as

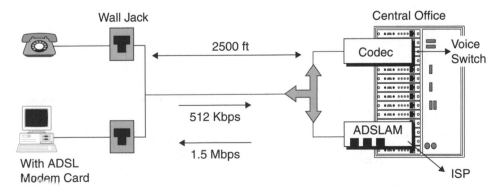

Figure 10.11   Splitterless ADSL configuration.

13Mbps over length greater than 4000 feet are also under consideration. Upstream rates will be from 1.6 to 2.3Mbps. There is currently no standard for VDSL.

DSL Summary

Table 10.1 outlines the various DSL technologies, their bandwidths, effective ranges, and suitable applications.

Table 10.1 DSL Technology Overview

TECHNOLOGY	DOWNSTREAM BANDWIDTH	UPSTREAM BANDWIDTH	MODULATION SCHEME	MAXIMUM RANGE	VOICE SUPPORT	APPLICATION
HDSL	1.544Mbps (2pairUTP)*	1.544Mbps (2pairUTP)*	2B1Q	12,000 ft	No	T1/E1 service, LAN or WAN server access
SDSL	768Kbps (2 pair UTP)	768Kbps (2 pair UTP)	2B1Q	10,000 ft	No	T1/E1 service, LAN or WAN server access
HDSL2	1.544Mbps	1.544Mbps	OPTIS	12,000 ft	No	T1/E1 service, LAN or WAN server access
ADSL	16 to 640Kbps	1.544 to 9Mbps	CAP/DMT	18,000 ft	Yes	Web access, Video on demand
RADSL	272Kbps to 1.088Mbps Adaptive	640Kbps to 2.2Mbps Adaptive	CAP/DMT	Adaptive	Yes	Web access, Video on demand
G.lite	1.544Mbps	512Kbps	DMT	25,000	Yes	Splitterless Web access, Video on demand
VDSL	1.6 to 2.3Mbps	52Mbps	DMT	1000m	Yes	HDTV

*2.048 Mbps (3 pair UTP) in Europe

Conclusion

As the different flavors of DSL become available, the last-mile bottleneck to providing high-bandwidth, quality-of-service-sensitive applications to the home is lifted. Access to the Internet becomes a different experience, as volumes of information or video programming goes screaming into homes. DSL offers other opportunities in corporate environments. At remote sites, DSL could provide cost-effective, high-speed service to a wide area frame relay or ATM network. In the campus, a DSLAM could be linked to the LAN and PBX to provide voice and data services over existing phone lines.

DSL is another of the important standards and schemes of next-generation networking that have been discussed.

Glossary

100Base-FX. A physical layer specification. A variation of 100Base-TX, it operates on two pairs of optic fiber. A major difference between the two specifications is that unlike 100Base-TX, 100Base-FX does not support autonegotiation.

100Base-T2. A physical layer specification that operates over two pairs of Category 3 UTP. Equalization and noise cancellation techniques are employed with sophisticated, multilevel coding to achieve 100Mbps over two pairs of Cat 3. There are currently no implementations of 100Base-T2.

100Base-T4. A physical layer specification designed to operate with Category 3 UTP. Because a special-purpose, integrated silicon must be developed, deployment is slower with 100Base-T4 than with 100Base-TX, and 100Base-T4 has not been widely implemented.

100Base-Tx. A physical layer specification that is by far the most common 100Base-T PHY and merges the FDDI PHY with the CSMA/CD MAC. 100 Base-TX is similar to 10Base-T in that it operates over two pairs of Category 5 UTP.

1000Base-T. A physical layer specification (IEEE 802.3ab) which operates over Category 5 UTP.

802.14. IEEE standard for defining a physical layer (PHY) and a MAC layer for bidirectional data transfer over the HFC cable network.

802.1D. IEEE standard for media access control bridges.

802.1p. IEEE standard that extends 802.1D. The 802.1p standard adds the ability for bridges to dynamically and proactively modify the filtering database so that multicast traffic is forwarded only onto ports that have a station either directly attached or further downstream that needs to receive the multicast frame. 802.1p also provides a frame prioritization scheme to support the expedited transmission of time-critical information in LAN environments.

802.1Q. IEEE standard extends 802.1p for virtual bridged local area networks. For example, 802.1Q extends the priority handling aspects of 802.1p to make use of the ability of the vLAN frame format to carry user priority information end to end across any set of underlying MAC services.

802.3ab Working Group. The IEEE standards group that is responsible for physical layer specification 1000Base-T.

add-drop multiplexor (ADM). A device that merges lower-speed electrical and optical signals into a high-speed optical channel and vice versa; commonly deployed with SONET. The benefit of an ADM is that the high-speed data channel does not have to be fully demultiplexed to get to individual channels. (For example, to get to an individual DS1 from a DS3, the DS3 has to first be demultiplexed to a DS2, and then the DS2 is demultiplexed to a DS1.

Address Resolution Protocol (ARP). A TCP/IP protocol used to find a node's physical address from a known IP address.

admission control policy. Part of end-to-end QoS, it determines if the network resources requested by the user are available.

Advanced Encryption Standard (AES). An emerging secret key encryption standard from the National Institute for Standards and Technology (NIST) that will support 128, 192, and 256-bit key length.

Aggregate Route-Based IP Switching (ARIS). An IBM approach to Layer 3 switching. Based on multipoint-to-point trees rooted at the edge of the network, ARIS uses route aggregation to reduce the number of paths and state information that the core switches must support. ARIS also provides a means of mapping network-layer routing information to link-layer switched paths, enabling traffic to traverse a network at media speeds.

American National Standards Institute (ANSI). Coordinates the development of information technology standards; the U.S. equivalent to ISO and IEC.

application gateway. A type of firewall that processes, validates, and regenerates each received packet so it can perform more sophisticated functions than other firewalls that have access to only lower-layer information. It runs on a bastion host, a highly secure system that is dedicated to support the application gateway software. Also known as *proxy server*.

application-specific integrated circuit (ASIC). A custom-designed chip for a specific application.

asymmetric encryption. A public key cryptography system that uses two mathematically complementary keys: a public key and a private key based on the prime factors of very large numbers. The benefit of this approach is that either key can encrypt the message and the other key will decrypt it. In addition, knowledge of one key does not help an attacker learn the other key.

asymmetric flow control. A switch can control the flow of network traffic from the attached device, but the attached device cannot control the flow of traffic from the switch. The intent is to stop traffic at the source so that additional buffering in intermediate switches is not needed.

asynchronous time division multiplexing (ATDM). A 1960s time division multiplexing (TDM) modification in which each information element would have an explicit label. With this approach a network connection could be conveyed by an asynchronous series of cells. The frame and each position within the frame would still be synchronous; however, ownership of the information at each position would be asynchronous. Unfortunately, implementation of the concept was impossible because of the state of the technology in the 1960s (things like the multiprocessor, and VLSI had yet to be invented).

asynchronous transfer mode (ATM). Transfer of data in cells or packets of a fixed size. ATM allows transport of data, audio, and video over the same network and ensures that no single type of data takes all the bandwidth.

ATM access device. Connects to the ATM network and performs special functions to groom the traffic for the ATM network.

ATM Adaptation Layer (AAL). Service-dependent sublayer of the data link layer. Provides a convergence service so that all other service offerings (frame relay, voice, TDM) can be coalesced onto a single platform—the ATM network. AALs differ on use of source-destination timing, use of CBR or VBR, and use for connection-oriented or connectionless mode data transfer. AALs recommended by the ITU-T include AAL1, AAL2, AAL3/4, and AAL5.

ATM Forum. An organization that promotes ATM networking technology and helps to set standards like the user-network interface (UNI).

attachment unit interface (AUI). Part of IEEE's Ethernet standard. An AUI transceiver cable provides a path between the media access unit (MAU) and a node's Ethernet interface.

authentication. In VPN security, a minimum requirement. The VPN must verify the user's identity and restrict VPN access to authorized users only. Accounting and audit records should also be kept to monitor access to information.

authorization databases. Part of providing VPN security and granting user privileges. After the user has been authenticated, policies and access controls can be retrieved from authorization databases.

autonegotiation. The capability of a switch port to determine the speed of the attached device automatically with no user intervention. It may also involve determining the full-duplex capability of the attached device. Autonegotiation is specified only for 100Base-T PHYs.

available bit rate (ABR). An ATM service level that adjusts bandwidth according to the level of congestion in the network.

backoff algorithm. An Algorithm that defines how an end station behaves after detecting that a frame that it sent was involved in a collision.

backplane. An interconnecting device with sockets that cards/boards plug into.

bandwidth. Transmission capacity of an electronic line (like a network or computer bus).

bandwidth broker. Diffserv policy server. Configures with organizational policies to monitor available bandwidth and other network resources, interprets service-level requests from clients, and keeps track of the current allocation of marked traffic. The bandwidth broker can also proactively reconfigure the router with regard to DSCP-marking a flow and can communicate with bandwidth brokers in other diffserv domains (like another ISP) to ensure viability of end-to-end traffic agreements.

Base. The part of an Ethernet CSMA/CD designation that refers to baseband transmission mode.

baseband transmission mode. Use of the entire medium for a discrete signal transmission. Contrast with broadband "broad" signaling wherein the medium transmits multiple signals simultaneously, each at a different frequency.

basic rate interface (BRI). One of two N-ISDN defined access interfaces. Basic rate interface carries two 64Kbps channels plus one 16Kbps channel.

bit rate. The transmission speed of binary coded data.

blocking switch. If backplane throughput (or transfer capacity) is not at least as large as the sum of the theoretical maximum speed of all the ports, the switch is considered a blocking switch.

Border Gateway Protocol (BGP). An IETF routing protocol used to span autonomous systems on the Internet.

bridge. A device that connects two LAN segments (like Ethernet or token ring). Bridges work at the data link layer (Layer 2) and are protocol independent.

bridge ID. The root bridge priority plus the MAC of the sending bridge.

Bridge Protocol Data Unit (BPDU). Initially, each bridge believes that it is the root bridge and issues a BPDU configuration message indicating its own root bridge priority, hello time, forward delay time, and max age time. In Ethernet v2 BPDU messages were called hello messages; the terms BPDU and hello message are often used interchangeably.

broadband. High-speed transmission.

broadband signaling. Signaling in which the medium transmits multiple signals simultaneously, with each at a different frequency.

buffered distributor. A Gigabit repeater.

buffer management. An important part of providing quality of service, flow control, discard schemes, and congestion control. Typically the buffer space is physically, or logically, allocated to queues. These queues serve to separate the physical locations within memory of the data from the logical view of the data's position or relative importance.

buffer separation. A fixed portion of buffer space allocated to each of the output queues. With switches that support traffic prioritization, more than one queue is associated with each output port. Each queue supports traffic of a different priority. This scheme is easy to implement, but because of the lack of sharing, it may result in unnecessary congestion and data discard. If there is too much traffic of a particular priority destined for an output port, this queue may overflow, resulting in data discard, even if there is unused buffer space allocated to a different queue.

cable modem. A modem used to connect a computer to a cable Internet service. Cable modems link to the computer via Ethernet.

canonical format identifier (CFI). A single-bit flag value. CFI, when set, indicates that an RIF field is present and that MAC data carried by the frame is in canonical format. When it is unset, there is no RIF, and the carried data is in non-canonical format—that is, Ethernet format.

capture effect. Occurs when two stations both have a large amount of data to send. The first station that wins the contention (draws the low backoff number) will transmit, until eventually the loser completes its backoff algorithm.

Carrier Sense Multiple Access with Collision Detection (CSMA/CD). A low-level network protocol used for traffic arbitration on Ethernet. Collision detection during transmission reduces the amount of bandwidth wasted on collisions.

Category 3 UTP. A cable standard for voice-grade network cabling capable of transmitting data at up to 16Mbps.

Category 5 UTP. A cable standard for cable capable of transmitting data at up to 100Mbps

cell delay variation (CDV). Variation in the cell arrival rate.

cell loss ratio (CLR). Ration of cells that are not delivered to the destination.

cell transfer delay (CTD). Delay associated with cell transfer.

central office (CO). A telephone company switching facility that covers a small geographic area.

Challenge Handshake Authentication Protocol (CHAP). An encrypted authentication scheme that avoids transmission of the clear-text password over the PPP link. The NAS sends a challenge message to the remote client consisting of a session identifier and an arbitrary challenge string. The remote client returns the user name in clear text but uses an MD5 one-way hashing algorithm to generate an encrypted form of the challenge, session ID, and the client's password.

channel associated signaling (CAS). Signaling bits transmitted in-band, along with the digitized voice itself.

channel bank. A device developed by the telephone company to digitize voice and to multiplex digitized voice channels onto the transport system.

channel capacity. The maximum rate at which data can be transmitted over a circuit.

class-based queuing (CBQ). An enhancement to priority queuing. CBQ attempts to provide fairness by allocating portions of link bandwidth to specific types of traffic. Instead of providing absolute service to the high-priority queue, it deploys a more equitable scheme.

classifier. Component of the edge device that examines fields within the packet to determine which PHB bits get set. Fields examined are determined by the policies configured on the edge device.

class of service (CoS). Class of service is generally used to describe packet switched networks, such as the Internet, while quality of service is generally used to describe connection-oriented networks, such as PSTN and ATM. With class of service, the quality parameters are specified within the router/switch.

Class I repeater. In 100Base Ethernet, the class of repeater that allows more generous delays. It allows conversion between coding schemes, so all media types can be connected to the repeater.

Class II repeater. In 100Base Ethernet, the class of repeater that was defined with more stringent timing specifications, thereby allowing optimization for one specific coding scheme.

clumping. In guaranteed load-service, the traffic rate skews because of queuing-delay variations and subsequently delivers in a manner that exceeds peak traffic rate.

coaxial cable, coax (CX). Coaxial cable. High-capacity cable used in video and communications transport.

collision (COL). The transmission of two interfaces on the same physical network at the same time such that the packets interfere with each other. Collision causes data loss, so interfaces must retransmit the data.

collision domain. The collection of devices that "hear" a collision. Typically delineated by bridge or switch.

common buffer. Buffer space allocation method. Common Buffer with push-out schemes offer the most sophisticated buffering approach. With this scheme, all queues share the common buffer pool. However, if there are no buffers available when high-priority traffic arrives, lower-priority data is discarded, and the buffers are made available to the higher-priority data. This scheme is very efficient, but it is the most complex and difficult to manage.

common open policy server (COPS). A client/server protocol for propagating network policy information to edge devices. COPs uses TCP as the transport.

Community Antenna Television (CATV). The original name for cable TV.

conditioned launch. In fiber, conditioning of the laser light source to address differential mode delay. The conditioned launch is usually implemented either internally to the transceiver or externally via a patch cord and is designed to introduce an offset to the laser launch that directs the laser beam away from the center of the multimode fiber. However, even with conditioned launch, gigabit transmission over multimode fiber is subject to the length limitation.

Connection Admission Control (CAC). Actions performed by the network to enforce network admission policies.

constant bit rate (CBR). One of five service categories of the ATM layer. CBR allows a user to define a specific cell delay or cell delay variation (CDV) and to reserve a specific, fixed bandwidth on the network.

convergence. The merging of different applications so that they can all utilize the same physical network.

crossbar switches. A switching device that provides for a fixed number of inputs and outputs. Crossbar switches are nonblocking switches with a fully inter-connected structure. Each input port is effectively connected to each output port. The effective capacity of the switch fabric increases as line cards are added and more of the fabric becomes active. The density of the backplane—that is, the number of crosspoints required—is the square of the number of slots in the switch.

cut-through bridge. When frames arrive on a port of a cut-through bridge, the frame is buffered only long enough so that the bridge can perform filtering and forwarding. The prime advantage of the approach is that the delay associated with the store-and-forwarded device is reduced significantly.

cut-through Layer 3 switching. Schemes that map Layer 3 paths into Layer 2 cir-cuits, eliminating the header processing and performing the next-hop deter-mination in hardware.

cyclic redundancy check (CRC). An error-checking technique used for ensuring the accuracy of transmitted digital data.

data communications channel (DCC). Provided by section overhead (SOH), car-ries status and OAM information for every network element. The DCC is examined at specified locations that tie into the carriers' management system. The DCC is also used for carrying remote control and test commands to and from remote equipment.

Data over Cable System Interface Specification (DOCSIS). A set of standards for transferring data over the cable TV system.

data terminal equipment (DTE). A communications device (typically a terminal or computer) that is the source or destination of signals on a network.

DECnet. Digital's proprietary group of communications products and protocols that adhere to Digital's Network Architecture (DNA).

delay. The amount of time it takes to send information between two systems.

demilitarized zone (DMZ). A portion of a Corporate network between the private Corporate network and the public network. Typically the Web Server, Mail Servers, and other devices that are generally available to the public network reside there.

dense wavelength division multiplexing (DWDM). A technology that supports multiple simultaneous channels on a single fiber.

Distributed Management Task Force (DMTF). An industry consortium that develops standards that aim to reduce the cost and complexity of network/PC management. Efforts include the Desktop Management Interface (DMI), the Common Information Model (CIM), and Directory Enabled Networks (DEN).

destination address. Part of the packet header that identifies the packet's recipient.

destination service access point (DSAP). Part of an LLC 2-byte address used to identify the network protocol entities that use the link layer service.

differential Manchester encoding. Digital coding scheme used by IEEE 802.5 and token ring networks. A mid-bit-time transition is used for clocking, and a transition at the beginning of each bit time denotes a zero.

differential mode delay (DMD). A condition identified by the IETF 802.3z Task Force in which a jitter is created that limits the reach of Gigabit Ethernet. DMD can occur in any high-speed technology using a laser source for transmission over multimode (MM) fiber.

differentiated services codepoint (DSCP). Diffserv type of service (ToS) field.

Differentiated Services (diffserv) Working Group. An IETF group developing a standard to provide differentiated classes of service for Internet traffic, support for various types of applications, and specific business requirements. The differentiated services approach to providing quality of service in networks uses a small, well-defined set of building blocks for creating a variety of services.

digital signal level 1 (DS-1). Bit format for transmission on a T1 (1.544Mbps) data communications link.

digital signal level 3 (DS-3). Bit format for transmission on a T3 (44.736Mbps) data communications link.

digital signal processing (DSP). A category of encoding techniques used to analyze signals from various sources. Signals are converted into digital data and analyzed using algorithms like Fast Fourier Transform. When a signal has been reduced to numbers, its components can be isolated, analyzed, and rearranged more easily than if it were in analog form.

digital signature. An unforgeable electronic signature based on text encrypted and sent with a text message. The recipient decrypts the signature, and if the information matches, the message is authenticated and verified as intact from the sender.

digital subscriber line (DSL). Public network technology that delivers high bandwidth over conventional copper wiring at limited distances. There are four types of DSL: ADSL, HDSL, SDSL, and VDSL. All use modem pairs, with one at a central office and the other at the customer site. Because most DSL technologies do not use the entire bandwidth of the twisted pair, a voice channel is left open.

Dijkstra algorithm. An algorithm used to find the shortest path from a single-source vertex to all other vertices in a weighted, directed graph. In multicast extensions to open shortest path first (MOSPF), the router runs the Dijkstra algorithm to build a source-rooted delivery tree dynamically to every group member.

directory-enabled network (DEN). A DMTF scheme for management of a network from a central repository of information about users, applications, and network resources.

discovery message. One of four categories of label distribution protocol (LDP) messages used to announce and maintain the presence of a label switching router (LSR) in a network.

Distance Vector Multicast Routing Protocol (DVMRP). Internetwork gateway protocol that implements a typical dense mode IP multicast scheme. DVMRP uses internet group management protocol (IGMP) to exchange routing datagrams with its neighbors.

distributed shared memory switch. A routing switch design in which each line card is effectively a miniature switch and all switch functions are performed on the line card. Data transfer between line cards is via a backplane bus.

Domain Name System (DNS). Name resolution software that lets users locate computers on a Unix or TCP/IP (Internet) network by domain (host) name.

downstream label allocation. The downstream label switching router. The one that will to receive traffic from its upstream neighbor, it binds labels to the IP-destination address and FEC and informs the upstream LSR of the bindings.

dynamic adaptive algorithms. Routers support dynamic adaptive algorithms, which provide the capability for a network to recover from link and node failures.

Dynamic Host Configuration Protocol (DHCP). Provides a mechanism for allocating IP addresses dynamically, allowing addresses to be reused when hosts no longer need them.

edge devices. A network device used to convert LAN frames (like Ethernet, token ring, and FDDI) to ATM cells and vice versa. Usually a switching device with one ATM port and multiple LAN ports.

encryption. Encoding of data for security purposes.

encryption algorithm. A formula used to encode data. The algorithms use a string of bits (a key) to perform the calculations. The larger the key (more bits), the more difficult it is to break the code.

Establish message. An ARIS control message containing a hop-count set to 0 if the Egress is the switched-path endpoint. Otherwise, the hop-count is set to 1.

Ethernet. A baseband LAN specification developed jointly by Xerox, Intel, and Digital Equipment Corporation. Ethernet networks run over a variety of cable types at 10Mbps and use CSMA/CD. See also IEEE 802.3 standards.

Ethertype. A field within the ethernet frame that identifies the upper layer protocol that is to receive the frame.

Extended Interior Gateway Protocol (EIGRP). A proprietary distance vector routing protocol from Cisco Systems.

extranet. A network that connects two business partners using the public Internet as its transmission system.

extranet VPN. Similar to intranet VPN, but the remote sites serve users from different corporations to allow one business community to partner with another business community. This connection involves communication between untrusted users. Extranet VPN security requirements are more stringent, and types of corporate information accessible to external users must be closely controlled and monitored.

Fast Ethernet. Based on an extension to the IEEE 802.3 specification, any of the 100Mbps Ethernet specifications. Speed increase is 10 times the 10BaseT Ethernet specification, yet it preserves qualities like frame format, MAC mechanisms, and MTU. These similarities allow the use of existing 10BaseT applications and network management tools on Fast Ethernet networks.

Federal Communications Commission (FCC). The U.S. government agency that regulates interstate and international communications, including wire, cable, radio, TV, and satellite.

fiber. A thin glass wire designed for light transmission, capable of transmitting trillions of bits per second. Two primary types of fiber are multimode and single mode.

Fiber Distributed Data Interface (FDDI). A LAN standard that specifies a 100Mbps token-passing network using fiber optic cable, with transmission distances of up to 2km. FDDI uses a dual-ring architecture to provide redundancy.

Fibre Channel. A high-speed transmission technology that can be used as a back-end storage network, a front-end communications network, or both at the same time.

File Transfer Protocol (FTP). A client/server protocol that allows a user on one computer to transfer files to and from another computer over a TCP/IP network. Also refers to the application used to transfer files.

firewall. Used to make a network secure. A firewall can be implemented in a single router that filters out unwanted packets, or it may use various technologies in routers and hosts.

flag. A code in the transmitted message that indicates that the following characters are part of a control code and not data.

flow control. Used for transmission management, ensures a transmitting entity (for example, a modem) and does not overwhelm a receiving entity with data. When the buffers on the receiving device are full, a message is sent to the sending device to suspend the transmission until the data in the buffers has been processed.

flowspec. In IPv6, the traffic parameters of a stream of IP packets between two applications.

forwarding delay time. The amount of time an interface spends listening for topology change information after that interface is activated for bridging and before forwarding actually begins.

forwarding information base (FIB). An extended routing table.

frame bursting. A technique that allows a transmitting device to keep control of the gigabit ethernet so that the transmitting station can transmit multiple frames before relinquishing control of the media. The net effect is an increase in the efficiency of the gigabit channel.

frame check sequence (FCS). Extra characters that are added to a frame for error-control purposes. Used in HDLC, frame relay, and other data link layer protocols.

frame relay. A switched data link layer protocol that handles multiple virtual circuits using HDLC encapsulation between connected devices. Frame relay is more efficient than X.25, the protocol it replaces.

Frame Relay Forum (FRF). An association of corporate members made up of vendors, carriers, users, and consultants who are committed to the implementation of frame relay in accordance with national and international standards.

frames. Variable-length data units, usually associated with the data link (for example, frame relay or X.25) or MAC (for example, Ethernet) layer.

full duplex. Describes the capability for simultaneous data transmission between a sending station and a receiving station.

GARP Multicast Registration Protocol (GMRP). Part of the 802.1p standard, developed by the 802.1 Working Group of IEEE. GMRP uses generic attribute registration protocol (GARP) to register and propagate multicast membership information in a switching domain.

GARP vLAN Registration Protocol (GVRP). Part of 802.1Q; by making aspects of VLAN configuration dynamic, it simplifies configuration management in large networks.

General Switch Management Protocol (GSMP). IEEE protocol that provides an interface to allow a router to control a label switch. The GSMP interface provides the commands necessary for switch configuration control and reporting, port management, connection control, QoS and traffic engineering control, and reporting of statistics and asynchronous events.

Generic Attribute Registration Protocol (GARP). Part of the 802.1p standard, a Layer 2 transport mechanism that allows switches and end systems to disseminate useful information throughout the switching domain.

generic routing encapsulation (GRE). A tunneling protocol developed by Cisco that can encapsulate a wide variety of protocol packet types inside IP tunnels. It thereby creates a virtual point-to-point link to Cisco routers at remote points over an IP internetwork.

Gigabit Ethernet interface converter (GBIC). Modular technology interface that allows a Gigabit Ethernet port to support short-wave and long-wave lasers as well as copper physical interfaces.

Gigabit Media-Independent Interface (GMII). A synchronous digital interface between Gigabit Ethernet physical layer components and the MAC layer that carries unencoded data over separate transmit and receive paths.

guaranteed load service. A category of real-time traffic intended for applications that require bandwidth guarantees and have stringent bounds on the delay and delay variation that they can tolerate.

half duplex. Transmission of data in just one direction at a time; contrast with *full duplex*.

hash function. An algorithm that turns text into a fixed string of digits for security or data management purposes.

head of line blocking (HOLB). A consequence of input buffering, used in many crossbar switches. With HOLB, data elements at the front of the input port queue (head of the line) that are destined for a busy output port will block traffic destined for a nonactive output port. Eventually, data is discarded as the input buffers fill. Head-of-line blocking introduces delay and delay variation and creates artificial and unnecessary congestion on the network.

HELLO message. A bridge protocol data unit (BPDU) message.

High-Level Data Link Control (HDLC). A generic data link control protocol defined by ISO for use on both point-to-point and multipoint data links that supports full-duplex, transparent-mode operation.

host membership leave message. Part of Internet group multicast protocol (IGMP), a message that informs the router that the host is no longer a member of the multicast joining and tells it to forward the multicast onto the LAN.

hot-swappable. The ability to connect or disconnect peripherals or other components without interrupting system operation.

hub. A device used to connect several other devices.

hybrid fiber coaxial (HFC) system. Currently, cable operators are in the process of modifying the cable infrastructure by introducing fiber optic cables, replacing the analog signals with digital transmissions, and replacing the amplifiers so that the system becomes a two-way system. The new infrastructure is referred to as HFC.

independent vLAN learning (IVL). Uses a separate forwarding database for each vLAN.

integrated services architecture. Provides a set of extensions to the best-effort, traffic-delivery model currently used on the Internet. The approach provides special handling for certain types of traffic and a mechanism for applications to identify traffic and delegate the traffic to the appropriate service level.

integrated services digital network (ISDN). A communication protocol from the telephone companies that permits telephone networks to carry data, voice, and other source traffic.

Integrated Services (intserv) Working Group. An IETF working group whose mission is to expand the Internet service model to best use packet-switching protocols to support integrated services: the transport of audio, video, real-time, and classical data traffic within a single network infrastructure. The group will specify an enhanced service model and then define and standardize interfaces and requirements necessary to implement it.

integrated switch router (ISR). A router that supports the ARIS protocol.

interframe gap (IFG). A 9.6 microsecond quiet time that allows the clock recovery circuitry within repeaters and DTEs to recover and relock to the known good local clock.

International Telecommunication Union, Telecommunication Standardization Sector (ITU-T). Studies technical, operating, and tariff questions and adopts recommendations on them in order to standardize telecommunications on a worldwide basis.

Internet. An immense global collection of networks interconnected by routers and other devices. The Internet evolved as a scientific and research tool in part from ARPANET and was at one time called the DARPA Internet.

Internet Control Message Protocol (ICMP). A component of IP that supports control functions.

Internet Engineering Task Force (IETF). A large open international community of network designers, operators, vendors, and researchers concerned with the evolution of the Internet architecture and the smooth operation of the Internet. Through the efforts of working groups, the IETF endeavors to standardize protocols and their usage in the Internet.

Internet Group Management Protocol (IGMP). A protocol used by IP hosts to report their multicast group memberships to an adjacent multicast router.

Internet Protocol (IP). A network layer protocol in the TCP/IP stack that offers a connectionless internetwork service. IP provides features for addressing, type-of-service specification, fragmentation and reassembly, and security.

Internet service provider (ISP). A company providing Internet access to other companies and individuals.

internetwork packet exchange (IPX). A NetWare network layer (Layer 3) protocol similar to IP that is used for transferring data from servers to workstations.

intranet. A corporate network that uses the same communications protocols and hypertext links as the Web to serve employees of the organization.

intranet VPN. Used in corporations with multiple facilities that must intercommunicate. At each location, a VPN device is implemented. These connections are between trusted users because the connection is between users within the same organization. After the trusted user has been authenticated, the VPN should provide the same access to corporate resources as if the remote users were directly connected. The security policy enforced by the intranet VPN is usually the standard corporate policy.

IP address. The address of a computer attached to a TCP/IP network; it is written as four sets of numbers separated by periods.

IP Authentication Header (AH). IPsec-defined header within the IP packets to handle authentication.

IP Class D address. Used for IP multicasting, bits 31, 30, 29, and 28 contain 1, 1, 1, and 0, respectively, and identify the address as a multicast. Bits 27 through 0 identify the specific multicast group.

IP encapsulation security payload (ESP). An IPsec protocol that provides confidentiality and integrity by encrypting data and placing it in the data portion of the payload.

IPsec. An IETF framework of standards that provides security for transmission of sensitive information over unprotected networks such as the Internet. IPsec acts at the network layer, protecting and authenticating IP packets between participating IPsec devices like routers.

Ipsilon Flow Management Protocol (IFMP). A proprietary protocol used in IP switches for flow redirection.

Label Distribution Protocol (LDP). An MPLS protocol that describes the set of procedures and messages for label switched routers (LSRs) to establish label switched paths (LSPs) through a network by mapping network-layer routing information directly to data-link layer switched paths.

label edge router (LER). A device that sits at the edge of a multiprotocol label switching (MPLS) domain; it uses routing information to assign labels to datagrams and then forwards them into the MPLS domain.

label information base (LIB). The database of information in multiprotocol label switching that contains label bindings.

label stacking. In MPLS, an ordered set of labels.

label switching router (LSR). A MPLS device that can forward datagrams based on a label. An LSR may be a modified ATM switch that forwards datagrams based on a label in the VPI/VCI field.

label switch path (LSP). The path through a network that a datagram follows, based on its MPLS labels.

LAN emulation (LANE). A technology that allows an ATM network to function as a LAN backbone. Multicast and broadcast support, address mapping (MAC-to-ATM), SVC management, and a usable packet format are required for LANE.

latency. Delay time from when a device requests access to a network to the time it is granted permission to transmit. Also, the delay from when a device receives a frame to the time it is forwarded from the destination port.

Layer 2. Part of the OSI seven-layer model of network architecture. Layer 2 is the data link layer or MAC layer and contains the address inspected by a bridge or switch.

Layer 2 tunneling. One of two general classes of tunneling—(Layer 2 tunneling and Layer 3 tunneling). In Layer 2 tunneling, a Layer 2 protocol, typically PPP (point-to-point protocol), is encapsulated. From a security standpoint, Layer 2 tunneling protocols are inadequate.

Layer 2 Tunneling Protocol (L2TP). An IETF protocol that combines elements of Microsoft's point-to-point tunneling protocol and Cisco's Layer 2 forwarding (L2F) technology; used for creating virtual private networks (VPNs). It supports IPsec encryption, and non-IP protocols like AppleTalk and IPX.

Layer 3. Part of the OSI seven-layer model of network architecture. Layer 3 is the network layer and determines routing of data packets from sender to receiver via the data link layer. IP is a network layer protocol.

Layer 3 switches. Layer 3 devices, like switches, maintain no per-flow state information, so that in the event of an outage, the packets are forwarded around the outage as soon as the routing table has been updated.

Layer 3 tunneling. One of two general classes of tunneling (Layer 2 tunneling and Layer 3 tunneling). In Layer 3 tunneling, a Layer 3 protocol, typically IP or IPX, is encapsulated. The carrier protocol, or the protocol that is used to encapsulate the native protocol, is usually IP.

light emitting diode (LED). A semiconductor device that converts electricity into light. A laser or LED is often the source of a fiber optic system.

Lightweight Directory Access Protocol (LDAP). A protocol used to access a directory listing in management and browser applications. LDAP is a simplified version of the DAP protocol, used to access X.500 directories.

line. SONET layer that transports frames from one end of a line to the other. Synchronization and multiplexing of data onto SONET frames occur at the line layer.

line overhead (LOH). In SONET, functions that facilitate multiplexing and concatenating signals and performance monitoring.

link. A communications path between two devices or nodes in a network.

link code word (LCW). In autonegotiation, a 16-bit code formed by the fast-link pulse as part of a link integrity test. By assembling and interpreting the LCW, the stations at either end of the link arbitrate the speed (10/100) at which to operate, as well as negotiate half-duplex (CSMA/CD) or full-duplex and flow-control capabilities.

link integrity test. A key characteristic of 10Base-T required for autonegotiation. If there is no frame to send, a link integrity test signal is transmitted. The link integrity test is used to monitor the receive data path for activity as a means of checking that the link is working correctly.

listening period. In spanning tree operation, one of two components of the port waiting period. The listening period ensures that the spanning tree configuration has stabilized.

local area network (LAN). A data communications system made up of interconnected computer equipment in a limited geographical area. A LAN is typically composed of servers, workstations, a network operating system, and a communications link.

Logical Link Control (LLC). The higher of two data link layer sublayers defined by the IEEE. It handles error control, flow control, framing, and MAC-sublayer addressing.

loss ratio or reliability. The average error rate, or the ratio of packets that arrive and are usable at the destination to the packets that either don't arrive or are unusable at the destination. An example of an unusable packet is one that arrives too late to be of any value to the recipient application.

management information base (MIB). An SNMP structure that describes a device being monitored.

Manchester encoding. A self-clocking data encoding method that divides the time required to define the bit into two cycles. The first cycle is the data value (0 or 1), and the second cycle provides the timing by shifting to the opposite state.

media access control (MAC). Lower of the two sublayers of the data link layer. The MAC sublayer handles access to shared media.

media attachment unit (MAU). Provides the interface between the AUI port of a station and the common medium of the Ethernet. The MAU performs physical layer functions like conversion of digital data from the Ethernet interface and collision detection.

medium-dependent interface (MDI). Refers to the type of connector and signaling with regard to the particular connector pin-out. For 100Base-TX, an RJ45 connector is specified for Category 5 UTP straight through (MDI) or crossed over (MDI-X) for connection to a switch. Several MDIs are also specified in 100Base-FX.

medium-independent interface (MII). Separates the MAC layer from the physical layer. The MII decouples the MAC from the particulars of the underlying PHY and so permits the MAC to operate unchanged with a variety of PHYs.

Message Digest 5 (MD5). A one-way hash function (function that takes a variable-length message and produces a fixed-length hash) defined in RF 1321.

Microsoft Challenge Handshake Authentication Protocol (MS-CHAP). An encryption authentication scheme similar to CHAP. MS-CHAP provides an additional level of security because it allows the server to store hashed local names instead of clear-text local names. MS-CHAP also provides additional error codes, including a password expired code, and additional encrypted client/server messages.

Microsoft Point-to-Point Encryption (MPPE). An encryption protocol that can be used with PPTP to provide an encrypted connection.

modal bandwidth. Bandwidth for multimode fiber. It varies with the modal field (or core diameter) of the fiber. Modal bandwidth is specified in units of MHz/km and refers to the total number of light pulses transmitted over some prescribed length of fiber that is still discernible at the far end.

multicast. A technique where individual packets are delivered to multiple recipients.

multicast backbone (MBONE). A collection of Internet sites that support the IP multicast protocol (one-to-many) and enable live audio and videoconferencing.

Multicast Open Shortest Path First (MOSPF). An intradomain multicast routing protocol used in OSPF networks.

multicast vLANs. Category of multicast groups operating in a LAN environment.

Multimedia Cable Network System (MCNS) partners. A consortium of cable companies that developed a scheme to support the transfer of data over the cable network called Data over Cable System Interface Specification (DOCSIS).

multimode fiber (MMF). Optical fiber that supports propagation of multiple frequencies of light.

multiplexor. A device that merges several low-speed transmissions into one high-speed transmission and vice versa.

Multipoint-to-Point Tunneling (MPT). A method used in IP Navigator to address the order of n-squared virtual circuit scaling problem (where n is the number of sites that must be interconnected) for IP service providers. MPT allows each trunk line in the network to carry only a single virtual circuit for each switch.

Multiprotocol Label Switching (MPLS). A protocol that defines a mechanism to enable IP devices to forward packets at Layer 2 by replacing the standard Layer-3 destination-based, hop-by-hop-forwarding paradigm with a Layer-2 label swapping technique. The technique has the benefit of simplifying packet forwarding; the routing table does not have to be examined at every hop, enabling easier scaling to gigabit and terabit network links.

Multiprotocol over ATM (MPOA). A standard from the ATM Forum that allows devices in different Emulated LANs (LANEs) to communicate directly over an ATM virtual circuit.

multistage (Banyan) switches. Space-division switches with a separate physical path between each input port and each output port.

Net BIOS extended user interface (NETBEUI). A network transport protocol used by all of Microsoft's network systems and IBM's LAN server-based systems.

network access server (NAS). A device that authenticates and validates a remote user and is responsible for establishing the connection between the remote user and the private network.

network address translation (NAT). Provides an IP address translation service. It educes the need for globally unique IP addresses. NAT allows an organization with addresses that are not globally unique to connect to the Internet by translating them into globally routable address space.

network basic input/output system (NetBIOS). An application programming interface used by applications on an IBM LAN to request services from lower-level network processes, like session establishment and termination and information transfer.

network control protocols (NCPs). Protocols used to establish and configure different network layer protocols.

network interworking function (N-IWF). In frame relay over ATM, associates the signaled destination telephone number with a constant-bit-rate virtual circuit.

nonblocking. The ability of a signal to reach its destination without delay or interference. In a nonblocking switch, all ports are able to run at full wire speed without any loss of packets or cells.

open shortest path first (OSPF). A link-state, hierarchical interior gateway protocol routing algorithm proposed as a successor to routing information protocol by the Internet community. OSPF features include least-cost routing, multipath routing, and load balancing.

Open Systems Interconnection Reference Model (OSI-RM). A network architectural model developed by ISO and ITU-T. The model consists of seven layers: physical, data link, network, transport, session, presentation, and application. The layers specify particular network functions like addressing, flow control, error control, encapsulation, and reliable message transfer. The lower two layers are implemented in hardware and software, while the upper five layers are usually implemented in software.

Operation, Administration, and Management (OAM). An ATM Forum specification for cells used to monitor virtual circuits. OAM cells provide a virtual circuit-level loopback; a router responds to the cells and signifies that the circuit is up, and the router is operational.

Optical Carrier level (OC). A series of physical protocols for SONET optical signal transmissions.

organizationally unique identifier (OUI). A 24-bit globally unique number assigned by the IEEE in a block of 48-bit LAN addresses.

packet-by-packet Layer 3 switches. High-performance routing devices. See *routing switch*.

packet filter. Provides a means to discard unwanted network traffic according to originating address, a range of addresses, or traffic type. Packet filtering is commonly performed in a router.

Packet over SONET. A WAN transport technology that carries IP packets directly over SONET transmission without a data link facility like ATM.

packet scheduler. Determines queue-servicing order—when to deliver a packet from a particular queue onto the output link.

partial buffer sharing. Buffers are allocated on a port basis rather than a queue basis. If a high-priority queue becomes filled, it can utilize buffers allocated to a lower-priority queue. Some implementations of this buffering scheme allow management to adjust thresholds to compensate for system loads.

Password Authentication Protocol (PAP). An authentication protocol for PPP peer authentication. When a remote router tries to connect to the local router, it must send an authentication request. PAP doesn't prevent unauthorized access; it just identifies the remote end, after which the router or access server determines if the user is allowed access.

path overhead (POH). An overhead field in SONET/SDH that is carried from end to –end. It is added when the component signals are multiplexed together to create the synchronous payload envelope (SPE).

per-hop behavior (PHB). The name given to routers that implement the diffserv protocol. Each router treats the packet according to the information in its DSCP field.

permanent virtual circuit (PVC). Saves time associated with establishing and tearing down circuits. PVCs are configured manually and require manual intervention at each switch that the virtual circuit traverses.

physical layer (PHY). The lowest layer in the OSI seven-layer model. It is concerned with electrical and mechanical connections to the network. The physical layer is used by the data link layer.

physical medium attachment (PMA). In the Gigabit Ethernet physical layer, a sublayer that performs 10-bit serialize/deserialize functions (referred to as SERDES). The PMA receives 10-bit encoded data at 125MHz from the PCS and delivers a serialized data stream to the PMD sublayer. The PMA also receives serialized data from the PMD sublayer and delivers deserialized 10-bit data to the PCS sublayer.

physical medium-dependent (PMD) sublayer. In the Gigabit Ethernet physical layer, along with the *medium dependent interface* (MDI), provides the media transceivers and connectors for the various media.

physical signaling sublayer (PLS). For media access management purposes, reports the state of attached media.

plain old telephone service (POTS). The traditional voice service provided by phone companies.

playback buffer. To compensate for any delays introduced by the network, the buffering of data before it is replayed. It introduces some additional delays but minimizes delay variations.

plesiosynchronous digital hierarchy (PDH). A voice transmission system that uses digital hierarchies for multiplexing lower-level streams onto higher-level streams based on bit-interleaving.

Point-to-Point Protocol (PPP). A protocol that provides router-to-router and host-to-network connections over synchronous and asynchronous circuits.

Point-to-Point Tunneling Protocol (PPTP). A Microsoft extension of PPP. It is a tunneling protocol for connecting Windows NT clients and servers over remote access services (RASs) and can be used to create a virtual private network between computers running NT.

policing. In diffserv, a component that validates traffic submitted to the connection-oriented network as in compliance with the service agreement.

port cost. In spanning tree protocol (STP), the configuration of each bridge with information about costs associated with using the port.

predictive QoS. A consequence of overprovisioning the network. The underlying premise with overprovisioning is that if there is no congestion, there is no need for concern with quality of service; rather, monitor the network and increase the capacity as the demand increases.

premium service. In diffserv, a peak-limited, extremely low-delay service, resembling a leased line.

primary rate interface (PRI). One of two types of ISDN service, along with basic rate interface (BRI). PRI is intended for users with greater capacity requirements, like businesses.

primary reference clock (PRC). The top of the hierarchy of interconnected clocks that provide timing and synchronization information to the equipment elements of a digital transmission system or network.

priority queuing. The emptying of the highest-priority queue before other queues are serviced.

propagation delay. The time required to transmit a signal. Propagation delay depends on distance and two-thirds the speed of light (the speed at which signals go through a wire or fiber travel).

public key infrastructure (PKI). The policies and procedures for establishing a secure method for exchange of information.

public switched telephone network (PSTN). The worldwide voice telephone network.

pulse code modulation (PCM). An 8-bit-per sample coding scheme that permits a voice signal to tolerate multiple analog-digital and digital-analog conversions.

push-out schemes. A buffering scheme where all queues share the common buffer pool. However, if there are no buffers available when high-priority traffic arrives, lower-priority data is discarded, and the buffers are made available to the higher-priority data.

quality of service path first (QOSPF). A protocol that adds QoS extensions to OSPF.

quadrature amplitude modulation (QAM). A method for encoding digital data in an analog signal. Each combination of phase and amplitude represents one of sixteen 4-bit patterns. The technique generates four bits out of one baud, so that a 600 baud line could transfer 2,400 bits per second.

quadrature phase shift key (QPSK). A digital frequency modulation technique used for sending data over coaxial cable networks.

quality of service (QoS). A measure of the overall level of service delivered to the customer. QoS performance criteria include high availability, error performance, response time and throughput, connection set-up time, and speed of fault detection and correction.

queuing delay. The amount of time a packet is in a queue.

random early detection (RED). A congestion-avoidance algorithm built on the base-level TCP behavior of automatically slowing transmissions upon detection of packet loss. RED monitors the queue on a router, and when the congestion reaches specified threshold, it randomly discards packets. Packet discard signals originating applications to slow their transmissions before congestion becomes severe.

real time. Describes an application that requires a program to respond within a small upper-limit of response time. Often requires special operating systems and speed-tuned hardware.

real-time variable bit rate (rt-VBR). Part of the ATM variable bit rate (VBR) QoS class that guarantees bandwidth for certain types of traffic. Real-time variable bit is used to support interactive multimedia that can tolerate only minimal delays.

reduced instruction set computer (RISC). A processor designed to rapidly execute a sequence of simple instructions (as opposed to a large variety of complex instructions).

regional cable head end (RCH). Part of an HFC system, serving 200,000 to 400,000 homes. An RCH feeds a distribution hub that serves 20,000 to 40,000 homes, typically through a metropolitan fiber ring.

remote access VPN. Remote trusted users (home office or mobile) use remote access VPNs to dial into their local ISP to access the corporate databases.

Remote Authentication Dial-In User Service (RADIUS). A database used to authenticate modem and ISDN connections and to track connection time.

repeater. A device that regenerates and propagates electrical signals between two network segments.

reshaping. In guaranteed service, an attempt by the router to restore the flow's traffic rate.

Resource Reservation Setup Protocol (RSVP). A protocol that supports the reservation of resources across an IP network.

reverse-path forwarding tree. In a reverse-path forwarding tree, traffic flows from the leaves of the tree toward the root, unlike a multicast delivery tree where the traffic flows from the root to the leaves.

root bridge. Exchanges topology information with designated bridges in a spanning-tree implementation to notify all other bridges of required topology changes in order to prevent loops and defend against link failure.

root path cost. Part of BDPU information, the cost of the least expensive path from a given bridge to the root bridge.

Routing Information Field (RIF). A field in the IEEE 802.5 header used by a source-route bridge to determine transit path packets on a token ring network segment. A RIF is contains ring and bridge numbers and other information.

Routing Information Protocol (RIP). An interior gateway protocol for Unix BSD systems. RIP uses hop count as a routing metric.

routing switch. High-performance routing device that forwards traffic based on Layer 3 information at very high speeds.

RSVP admission policy (RAP) Working Group. IETF group working to establish a scalable policy control model for RSVP. The working group will specify a protocol for use among RSVP-capable network nodes and policy servers.

scalability. The capacity a system has for expansion.

section overhead (SOH). In SONET/SDH, provides a data communication channel (DCC) that carries status and OAM information for every network element.

Security Association (SA). A simplex "connection" that affords security services to the traffic carried by it. A security association is uniquely identified by a security parameter index (SPI), an IP destination address, and a security protocol (AH or ESP) identifier.

Security Parameter Index (SPI). The 32-bit value used to distinguish among different SAs terminating at the same destination and using the same IPsec protocol.

Segmentation and Reassembly (SAR). Segmentation of the frame into cells and subsequent reassembly of the cells into a frame.

service class. In ATM, QoS there are five service classes: constant bit rate (CBR), real-time variable bit rate (rtVBR), non-real-time VBR (Nrt-VBR), available bit rate (ABV), and unspecified bit rate (UBR).

service identifier (SID). A cable modem registration number assigned by the cable modem termination system (CMTS).

service level agreement (SLA). A contract between the service provider and customer that describes the behavior characteristics that traffic receives end to end.

session messages. A category of LDP message used to establish, maintain, and terminate sessions between LSR peers.

shared delivery tree. In multicasting, the delivery tree type that has a single tree between all sources and receivers of a given multicast group. Because flooding every packet is inefficient, both dense and sparse-mode multicast routing protocols rely on two types of delivery trees. The other type is the source-rooted tree.

shared explicit (SE). RSVP filter reservation style. The filterspec specifies a unique sender, and only packets from the explicit sender are merged on the RESV path. It uses explicit sender selection and shared reservations.

shared memory switches. A routing switch architecture that uses a pool of high-speed RAM to store incoming data. It is simple to implement but can scale only to a certain point before the memory storage operations introduce delay.

shared vLAN learning (SVL). Uses a single forwarding database with shared learning. Because the forwarding database is shared, the MAC will be associated with only a single port, and this may create end station-to-server communication problems.

signal quality error (SQE). In frame transmit, notifies the MAC that the collision circuitry is operational and that the AUI cable is functioning properly.

Simple Network Management Protocol (SNMP). A network management protocol used almost exclusively in TCP/IP networks that provides a means to monitor and control network devices, and to manage configurations, statistics collection, performance, and security.

singlemode fiber (SMF). An optical fiber with a core diameter of less than 10 microns.

slot time. In collision handling, the time it takes before a station "knows" it has seized control of the medium and no longer needs to concern itself with a collision smart card.

source address. The address of a network device that is sending data.

source service access point (SSAP). Service access point of the network node designated in the source field of a packet.

Spanning Tree Protocol (STP). A bridge protocol that uses a spanning-tree algorithm to allow a learning bridge to work dynamically around loops in a network topology by creating a spanning tree.

stateful packet filter. Designed from the start to serve as a firewall. Unlike filtering routers, stateful packet filters maintain state information on each connection and treat packets as part of a connection. Stateful packet filters typically provide excellent logging and alarm functions. They are scalable and transparent to users, and they generally have easy-to-use graphical configuration interfaces.

store-and-forward. A switching device that stores a complete incoming data packet before it is sent out. It is used when incoming and outgoing speeds differ.

Subnetwork Access Protocol (SNAP). A protocol developed to extend the protocol identification field because IEEE 802.2 provided only one byte to identify upper-layer protocols.

switched virtual circuit (SVC). A network connection established at the time the transmission is required. SVC is typically implemented in connection-oriented systems like the analog telephone network and ATM networks.

switching router. A device that forwards packets based on the Layer 3 information contained within the packet, like a conventional router. However, the forwarding is done in hardware via application specific integrated circuits (ASICs) with throughput and latency characteristics that greatly exceed the performance characteristics of conventional Layer 3 routers.

symmetric encryption. A secret key cryptography system that uses a single key for both encryption and decryption.

synchronous transport module (STM). SDH format that specifies the frame structure for the 155.52Mbps lines used to carry ATM cells.

Synchronous Optical Network/Synchronous Digital Hierarchy (SONET/SDH). Provides a point-to-point network connection between IP routers.

synchronous transport signal level 1 (STS-1). A basic building block signal of SONET that operates at 51.84Mbps.

T1. A digital WAN carrier facility that transmits DS-1-formatted data at 1.544Mbps through the switched telephone network.

tag control information (TIF). Part of IEEE 802.1Q frame header, 2 bytes in length. The "priority" is a 3-bit field that indicates the priority level (0 through 7) of the frame, with 0 representing the lowest priority level.

Tag Distribution Protocol (TDP). Relies on a connection-oriented protocol, typically TCP, to distribute, request, and release tag bindings between TSRs.

tag switch router (TSR). A router that supports TAG Switching.

Telnet. A terminal emulation protocol used on the Internet and TCP/IP-based networks.

tiered service. Allows traffic to be categorized with different levels of precedence. The precedence information will be conveyed to the router from a policy server. The tiered service will provide the most flexibility. It is a "better than best effort" delivery mechanism.

time division multiplexing (TDM). A technology that transmits multiple signals simultaneously over a single transmission path.

time to live (TTL). Field in an IP header that tells length of time a packet is considered valid.

traffic prioritization. The concept of providing preferential forwarding to a packet.

transfer variations. In switch backplane, jitter that occurs with variable frame sizes as frames traverse the switch.

Transmission Control Protocol (TCP). Part of the TCP/IP frame stack, a connection-oriented transport layer protocol capable of providing reliable full-duplex data transmission.

Transmission Control Protocol/Internet Protocol (TCP/IP). The suite of protocols developed by the U.S. Department of Defense during the 1970s for construction of worldwide internetworks.

transmit specification (Tspec). In an RSVP Path message, a subdivision of flowspec, specifying the transmission characteristics of the sending application.

transport overhead (TOH). In SONET/SDH, the sum of LOH and SOH.

type of service (ToS). A field within an IP header that can be used by the device originating the packet, or by an intermediate networking device, to signal a request for a specific QoS level.

type of service (ToS) field. Differentiated services codepoint (DSCP) field.

unicast. Transmission from one station to another, as in from client to server or server to server.

unshielded twisted pair (UTP). Normal U.S. telephone wire often used for computer-to-computer communications using a version of Ethernet or localtalk. It is far less expensive than standard Ethernet cable.

unspecified bit rate (UBR). An asynchronous transfer mode (ATM) level of service that does not guarantee available bandwidth.

upstream bandwidth allocation map (MAP). Before a cable modem can transmit data it must wait for a MAP from the CMTS. The MAP allocates minislots to particular cable modem, and also identifies unassigned slots, which may be used by any cable modem.

upstream channel descriptor (UCD). In cable modems, a message from the CMTS that allows it to retrieve transmission parameters, such as maximum burst size and modulation type, for the upstream channel.

upstream label allocation. In MPLS architecture, the upstream neighbor informs the downstream TSR of label bindings. Consensus is that upstream label allocation is less desirable than the downstream methods.

user priority regeneration table. In port priority, a switch may modify the priority of a received frame according to a manually configured user priority regeneration table.

user-to-network interface (UNI). In ATM and frame relay, the interface between the end user and the network.

virtual circuit (VC). A logical connection between two network nodes that acts like a direct physical connection even though it may be packet based. The term is frequently used to describe connections between two hosts in a packet-switching network.

virtual LAN (vLAN). A networking architecture that allows end systems on topologically disconnected subnetworks to seem to be connected on the same LAN. The term is used mainly in reference to ATM networking; in function, it is similar to bridging.

virtual private network (VPN). A private data network that uses the public switched telephone network but maintains privacy through the use of a tunneling protocol and security procedures.

Virtual Redundancy Router Protocol (VRRP). A protocol that allows several routers on a multiaccess link to utilize the same virtual IP address.

vLAN identifier (VID). A numeric value that identifies a virtual LAN.

VPN security. Confidentiality, access control, integrity, nonrepudiation, authentication, data encryption, and address management.

wavelength division multiplexing (WDM). A mechanism that allows multiple signals to be encoded into multiple wavelengths.

weighted fair queuing. With random early discard (RED), a technique that attempts to intelligently manage buffer space by influencing the type of traffic (priority) that is allowed into the network.

wide area network (WAN). A data communications system made up of interconnected computer equipment in a wide geographic area, such as state or country. See also *LAN*.

wildcard multicast receiver (WCMR). In MOSPF, a router to which all multicast traffic in the area is forwarded.

wire speed routers. Capable of transmitting frames onto a link at a rate that would saturate the link.

point-to-point protocol (PPP),
257–258, 307
point-to-point tunneling protocol
(PPTP), 271, 277–278
PPP. *See* point-to-point protocol
PPTP. *See* point-to-point tunneling
protocol
previous hop (Phop), 206
PRC. *See* primary reference clock
PRI. *See* primary rate interface
primary rate interface (PRI), 314
primary reference clock (PRC), 240
private-network-to-network
interface (PNNI), 189–190
propagation delay, 140
protocol identifier (PID), 19
protocol independent routing
(PIM), 173–174
dense mode (PIM-DM), 174–175
sparse mode, 175
PSINet, 7
PSTN. *See* public switched telephone
network
public key infrastructure, 273
public switched telephone network
(PSTN), 182–183, 306, 311
pulse amplitude modification, 69
pulse code modulation (PCM0), 237

Q
QAM. *See* quadrature amplitude
modulation
QoS. *See* Quality of Service. *See also*
Class of Service
QPSK. *See* quadrature phase shift key
Quality of Service (Q0S), 177–179, 186
access to the Internet, 195–196
requirements, 179–180
vs. CoS, 187
quadrature amplitude modulation
(QAM), 299
quadrature phase shift key
(QPSK), 299
quality
class-based, 181–182
flow-based, 181

parameters of, 179
predictive, 180–181

R
RADIUS authentication, 270–271
RADSL. *See* rate adaptive DSL
random early discard (RED), 204
rate adaptive DSL (RADSL), 326
RCH. *See* regional cable head end
RED. *See* random early discard
regional cable head end (RCH), 297
remote fault, 45
repeater, 28–29
Request for Comments (RFC), 8
Request for Proposal, (RFP), 3
reservations, 211–213
resource reservation setup protocol
(RSVP), 204–205
and signaling, 213
in intranet, 214
operation, 205–206
PATH message, 206
RESV messages, 208–210
scalability, 213
service, quality requirements of, 209
support of, 213
RESV message format, 208
reverse path multicast, 171
RFC. *See* Request for Comments
RFP. *See* Request for Proposal
RIP. *See* routing information protocol
RISC processors, 152
root bridge, 33
root servers, 5
router switch, 107
routers, 103–104
changes in traffic patterns, 105–106
enhanced functionality in, 153–154
layer 2 issues, 104–107
routing information protocol
(RIP), 170
routing switch, 138
advantages, 141–142
architectures, 143
switch backplane, 144–149
techniques, 142–143